TRIUMPH OF THE OPTIMISTS

TRIUMPH OF THE OPTIMISTS

101 Years of Global Investment Returns

Elroy Dimson

Paul Marsh

Mike Staunton

Princeton University Press

Princeton, New Jersey and Oxford

Princeton University Press

Published by Princeton University Press, 41 William Street, Princeton, New Jersey 08540, USA
In the United Kingdom: Princeton University Press, Chichester, West Sussex, UK

This book is available at special quantity discounts for promotional or educational use. For more information, please write to Princeton University Press, 1445 Lower Ferry Road, Ewing, NJ 08618, USA.

For permission to use material from this publication, contact the publisher at:

Permissions, Princeton University Press, 41 William Street, Princeton, NJ 08540, USA.
Fax: United States (609) 258-6305
Web: http://www.pupress.princeton.edu

Authors: Dimson, Elroy; Marsh, Paul R; Staunton, Michael
Title: Triumph of the Optimists: 101 Years of Global Investment Returns
Edition: 1st ed.
Published: Princeton, NJ: Princeton University Press
Description: p. cm.
ISBN: 0-691-09194-3
Notes: Includes 95 tables, 131 full-color charts, bibliographical references, and index
Library of Congress Control Number: 20010958146.

To Helen, Steff, and our parents

Contents

Preface

Triumph of the Optimists analyzes the financial record of stock market investors around the world. We present the performance of equity, bond, and treasury bill investments over the very long term. Our study reveals that the risk-takers who optimistically invested in equities were the group who triumphed over the long term.

There were also optimists who invested in us—London Business School and stockbrokers Hoare Govett, now a part of ABN AMRO. In the late 1970s, we started research at London Business School on the UK equity and small-firm premia. Two studies, publicized in 1984, made our work more visible. First, our back-history for the FTSE 100 Share Index (Dimson and Marsh, 1984) confirmed the performance gap between large and small UK companies. Second, our market-capitalization decile indexes for UK equities provided evidence on the consistency of the small-firm effect (Dimson and Marsh, 1986). These articles led us to design what was to become the Hoare Govett Smaller Companies (HGSC) Index. The HGSC is unique among commercial stock market indexes in having a consistent total return history spanning nearly half a century. We have now produced this authoritative measure of UK small-cap performance continuously for fifteen years. The work on the FTSE and HGSC Indexes was the bedrock that underpinned our study of UK, and then global, financial market returns.

We received invaluable support while researching and writing this book from both ABN AMRO and London Business School. Preliminary versions of the book were privately distributed with the titles *The Millennium Book* (published in 2000) and *Millennium Book II* (2001), and we presented our findings to investment professionals and academics at a number of conferences and professional meetings. Venues included Austria, Australia, Belgium, China, Denmark, England, France, Germany, Ireland, Israel, Italy, The Netherlands, Scotland, Spain, and the United States, with multiple presentations in many cities. The responses we received provided an expanding research agenda, enlarging the book's coverage of assets, countries and analysis. We benefited greatly from the dialogues we had with colleagues around the world.

Acknowledgments

We are pleased to acknowledge our substantial debt to Mark Brown, formerly of ABN AMRO, and to Chris Johns and Kevin Darlington of ABN AMRO. Without their encouragement, this book would not have seen the light of day. We also received generous help and guidance from many colleagues. We would particularly like to mention the suggestions and encouragement we received from John Bachmann, Dale Berman, Peter Bernstein, Dick Brealey, Roger Brown, Ian Cooper, Ken French, Will Goetzmann, Marty Gruber, Harry Markowitz, Narayan Naik, Harold Rose, Stephen Schaefer, Bill Sharpe, Jeremy Siegel, and Jack Treynor. Our confidence was raised by being awarded the Inquire UK and Inquire Europe medal for research innovation, and by being awarded first prize by the Institute for Quantitative Research in Finance ("Q Group") in its Roger Murray Prize Competition; we appreciate the esteem with which the prize committees regarded this research.

In chapters 18–33 within Part Two, we express our appreciation to colleagues who assisted us with data on individual countries. We especially wish to thank those who made available proprietary, and sometimes provisional, estimates of long-term index returns. Without their contributions, our study would not have been so ambitious. They include Philip Brown and John Bowers (Australia), Jan Annaert and Frans Buelens (Belgium), Pat O'Brien and Lorne Switzer (Canada), Claus Parum and Allan Timmermann (Denmark), Georges Gallais-Hamonno (France), George Bittlingmayer and Richard Stehle (Germany), Shane Wheelan (Ireland), Fabio Panetta (Italy), Kenji Wada (Japan), Roger Otten and Frans van Schaik (The Netherlands), Colin Firer (South Africa), Santiago Valbuena (Spain), Per Frennberg and Bjorn Hansson (Sweden), Daniel Wydler (Switzerland), Stefan Nagel and David Stolin (United Kingdom), and Ken French and Jack Wilson (United States). Of these, Jan Annaert, Frans Buelens, Lorne Switzer, Claus Parum, and Colin Firer undertook special-purpose data collection and index construction, expressly to rectify gaps in our series. We are doubly indebted to them.

As described in Part Two, we went back to original sources for compiling the UK, Irish, and South African series. We are grateful to the staff at the Guildhall Library and at the British Library for their assistance in accessing historical documents; staff of the London Business School Share Price Database (LSPD); and London Business School doctoral students who worked with Stefan Nagel on compiling the UK accounting data used in chapter 10. We thank Bryan Taylor of Global Financial Data for providing exchange rates and supplementary index data, as described in Part Two. We also thank Anna-Maria Velioti for her careful reading of the text. As we developed the text for publication, we received wise and patient counsel from Andrew Lansdown and Polly Trotman of ABN AMRO, Richard Baggaley and Tim Sullivan of Princeton University Press, and from their respective colleagues.

Finally, the closing stages of writing and producing this volume tested the endurance of most of our friends and families, and particularly Helen and Steff. Their names, too, should really be on the spine of this book.

Elroy Dimson
Paul Marsh
Mike Staunton

London Business School

October 2001

PART ONE:

101 years of global investment returns

Chapter 1 Introduction and overview

The year 2001 was scarred by terrorism, and financial markets were beset by turmoil. As we look to the future, investors have more cause than ever to ask: Where are the markets heading? What returns can be expected from equities, bonds, and bills around the world? What are the long-term risks of stock and bond market investment? What are the likely long-term rewards?

Corporations also need answers to these questions to understand what returns their stockholders and bondholders require, and to ensure they raise and use capital to best effect. Similarly, these are crucial issues for governments, since market returns provide the yardsticks for judging the worth of public sector projects, and for raising and managing government debt. Regulators, too, need to know the cost of capital to set appropriate rates of return for regulated industries.

It is hard to form a judgment about future prospects, or about required or allowable rates of return, without making comparisons with the past. Recent market returns are widely publicized. But it has hitherto been difficult to get a reliable impression of what investors have achieved over the long-term. Accurate historical records are available for the United States. However, the US economy has been remarkably successful. It would be dangerous for investors to extrapolate into the future from the US experience. We need to also look outside of the United States.

We also need to look long-term. Brief snippets of stock market history are not very helpful, unless our principal focus is on short-term volatility. For example, if we were interested in the volatility that can be anticipated over the next five years, the variability of the last 60 one-month returns or 260 one-week returns might be informative. But if we wish to say something about the expected return over the next five years, we cannot extract much information from the last five years. Further, the annual rate of return estimated from the last 60 months or 260 weeks is the same as the annual rate of return estimated over a single five-year interval. To estimate the expected return, we need a long run of data. We cannot improve estimates of the expected return by subdividing an interval into many short subperiods. While there are also benefits to looking at risk over the long haul, the need for long-term data is especially great when we are interested in expected returns.

To answer the key central questions about markets and investment prospects, we therefore need evidence that spans time and spans the world. The purpose of this book is to provide this evidence, and to point readers toward analysis that can help answer their questions.

1.1 Need for an international perspective

This book provides a comprehensive record of past investment returns around the world. It aims to help readers understand the historical record so that they can make informed judgments about the future. It does this by documenting the returns from equities, bonds, and bills, as well as inflation rates and currency movements, in four continents and sixteen countries, over the whole of the 101-year period from 1900–2000. We also have century-long evidence on the small-firm and value/growth phenomena. We have put significant effort into compiling complete financial market histories, so that we can present consistent and comparable records for different countries. But *Triumph of the Optimists* is about much more than just data, since it has description and analysis at its core.

There is an obvious need for a reliable and truly international dataset for the investment industry as it continues relentlessly toward full market globalization. One of the many changes taking place in the investment business is the increasing demand for locally sourced research placed in a global context. Another innovation is the growing number of truly global mandates being given to fund managers. Globalization may be a cliché, but for portfolio managers it is fast becoming a reality. Access to a properly constituted and rigorously maintained international database is a sine qua non for the start of any investment process.

The period since spring 2000 has come as a shock to those who had become used to the bull market conditions of previous years. The bursting of the technology bubble, the rapid decline in economic growth rates, especially in the United States, and the advent of international terrorism raised questions about what we can expect for the future. We assert in this book that the single most important variable for making investment decisions is the equity risk premium, and we argue that high long-term returns on equities, relative to bonds, are unlikely to persist. Even after the setbacks of 2000–01, it is necessary to justify the relatively high rating of today's stock markets in terms of a historically low forward-looking equity risk premium. For the investment strategist this raises the most fundamental question of all: Do investors realize that returns are likely to revert to more normal levels, or do current valuations embody exaggerated expectations based on an imperfect understanding of history?

Good data is the key to understanding history. With this as our guiding principle, assembling the data for this book was a major task. For the United Kingdom, ABN AMRO supported us in compiling an authoritative record of UK equity market performance over the last 101 years. We did this because we were not satisfied with the data that previously existed, and there was anyway no comprehensive record of equity returns extending back to 1900. To construct our UK indexes, we devoted intensive efforts to financial archaeology. This involved transcribing original source data from dusty newspaper archives and ancient reference books into our database. A resulting benefit is that we have not simply assembled an index, but we also have the underlying stock-by-stock data, so we can now study the performance of segments of the market, such as industry sectors and market-capitalization bands. We also compiled a series of UK government bond indexes especially for this study.

For the other fifteen countries covered in this book, we have linked together the best quality indexes and returns data available from previous studies and other sources, a number of which are previously unpublished, and some of which are still work in progress. In addition to the United Kingdom, we cover two North American markets, the United States and Canada; ten other European markets, namely, Belgium, Denmark, France, Germany, Ireland, Italy, The Netherlands, Spain, Sweden and Switzerland; two Asia-Pacific markets, Australia and Japan; and one African market, namely, South Africa. Taken together, these sixteen countries make up over 88 percent of today's world market capitalization, and were also dominant at the start of the twentieth century. We estimate that in 1900 these countries represented at least as high a proportion of the world equity market as they do today.

In each country we cover the same asset classes: equities, bonds, bills, inflation, and the local currency. We are therefore able to make comparisons between the investment performance of different asset classes, in different economic and political environments while focusing on whichever time period is of interest. We also have annual gross domestic product (GDP) data for all sixteen countries over the entire period.

Unlike most previous long-term studies of global markets, our investment returns all include reinvested income as well as capital gains. Our new indexes are more representative than those used in any previous study, and cover a longer time span for a larger number of countries. Furthermore, the common start date of 1900 facilitates cross-country comparisons. We can now set the US data alongside comparable length series for the same asset classes for fifteen other countries, and make international comparisons that help set the US experience in perspective.

Measuring what has happened in the past is only the starting point for assessing the future. Interpretation of the data and being able to apply it to a modern-day canvas are as important. Throughout this book, therefore, our emphasis is not simply on describing the past, but also on interpreting what has happened, with an eye to what it tells us about the future.

1.2 The historical record

Our story opens in the following chapter, not at the beginning but at the end of our 101-year period. We look in chapter 2 at world markets as they stand today—their overall size and significance and the split between markets and countries. Global league tables set in perspective the importance of the sixteen countries covered in this study. We look back to the beginning of our period to review what stock markets looked like 101 years ago, at the start of the twentieth century, and at how, and why, they had evolved since their origins several centuries before.

Using the detailed stock-by-stock data that we have assembled for the United Kingdom, together with comparable data for the United States, we provide some snapshots of how the corporate landscape has changed over the twentieth century. In particular, our analysis of industrial composition reveals some major contrasts—and some surprising similarities—between the structure of the US and UK equity markets today and 101 years ago. We also show how stock exchange concentration has increased in recent years, while showing that markets have several times in the past been even more concentrated than today.

In chapter 3, we begin by considering the guiding principles that underpin measures of long-term investment performance. Even with good index construction, an index is only as reliable as the underlying data and sample, so we also discuss the coverage of indexes, both across securities and over time. We highlight the dangers of survivorship and success bias. Taking the United Kingdom as an example, we show how these biases have in the past exaggerated the historical attractiveness of investing in common stocks.

Turning to the international evidence, when making comparisons across markets there has been a reliance on index series for countries that have not experienced a material break in trading. Even more marked, however, is the impact of initiating an index series after unrest, or wars, and their aftermath have been resolved. We show that this "easy data bias," the tendency by researchers and index compilers to limit their research and indexes to easily obtained data, has provided investors with a misleadingly favorable impression of long-term equity performance.

The remainder of the book is therefore devoted to a detailed examination of stocks, bonds, bills, inflation, and currencies over the period since 1900. Chapter 4 provides an overview of international capital market history, focusing on our 101-year study of the United States, the United Kingdom and fourteen other markets. We quantify the impact of inflation on the total return from US and UK equities, and then examine real and nominal stock market performance across our full sample of international capital markets. We show the extent to which rates of return on equities have been higher than the return on government bills and bonds, though this is by a smaller margin than many investors have perceived.

We report on the volatility of equity and bond returns, and show the extent to which diversification across stocks reduces the risk of a domestic equity portfolio. We examine how risk varies across asset classes and countries. We find that while equities were riskier than bonds, which in turn were riskier than bills, these risks were rewarded. Equities performed better than bonds in every single country, while bonds beat bills almost everywhere.

The next two chapters deal with the returns from investing in short-term deposits (treasury bills) and long-term bonds. Chapter 5 describes the historical record on interest rates and inflation. Chapter 6 presents the evidence on bond returns and bond maturity premia—the reward from investing in long- rather than short-term bonds. We compare bond maturity premia across different time periods and national markets. We also analyze inflation-indexed government bonds and corporate bonds for countries that present a sufficiently long history for these assets. In chapters 5 and 6, we see the twentieth century through the lens of the financial markets. The financial data reveals the turbulence of the past—inflation and hyperinflation, extreme periods when even bond and bill investors lost everything, deflation, and the Great Depression, as well as two world wars and their legacies.

For the international investor, currency movements matter since investment returns need to be converted from local currencies into the investor's reference currency. Exchange rate changes thus impact performance, and are critical for measuring and comparing the returns from different countries. In chapter 7, we report on the exchange rate fluctuations that were experienced by our sixteen countries over the course of the 101 years from 1900–2000.

Chapter 7 also examines the extent to which purchasing power parity has held over the long run. Purchasing power parity implies that goods and services will have a similar price experience in different countries, but this is a poor description of year-to-year foreign exchange fluctuations. Over the long run, however, we find that changing relative price levels do tend to be reflected in changes in exchange rates, and that real exchange rates are relatively stable. This means that when we compute the common-currency returns on equities and bonds across our sixteen countries, and compare these with the earlier rankings from chapter 4 based on the real, inflation-adjusted returns within each country, we find a very similar picture.

Chapter 8 focuses on international investment, addressing the question of how investors from around the world, including the United States, would have fared from foreign investment. In doing this, we recognize that international investors are concerned not just with the returns from investing abroad, but also the risks. We examine the impact of exchange risk, and the risk reduction benefits from international diversification.

We create benchmarks for assessing the risk and return from international diversification by constructing a sixteen-country, twentieth century world index for both equities and bonds. We find that investors in most countries would have been better off investing worldwide rather than restricting their portfolios to domestic securities. International diversification reduces risk because different countries' markets and currencies are less than perfectly correlated. We report the pairwise correlations between national market indexes, and find that correlations based on recent periods are higher than when based on long-term history. The potential gains from international diversification are thus lower than they once were.

Nevertheless, there are discernable and worthwhile gains from diversifying internationally. Despite this, investors in most countries still hold portfolios that are heavily weighted toward domestic assets. We document this "home bias" puzzle, and discuss the costs and impediments to international investment that existed at various stages during the twentieth century, some of which remain in place today.

1.3 Inside the markets

For some markets, we have access to the underlying security-level data that underpins the index series. Using this data, we can look in depth at stock market attributes within a national market. This is the focus of the next three chapters.

In chapter 9 we return to the equity markets to focus on two particular aspects of investment in stocks, namely, the effects of size and seasonality. Over the last twenty years, the small-firm premium, or the tendency for smaller companies to outperform larger ones, has become the best-documented stock market anomaly around the world. In this chapter, we review the international evidence, starting with the well-known record of smaller companies in the United States. We then draw comparisons with corresponding research for the United Kingdom, and extend to reviewing the relative performance of small companies around the world. A frustrating feature of the size effect is that soon after its discovery the size premium went into reverse, with smaller companies subsequently underperforming their larger counterparts. We show that this reversal was a worldwide phenomenon.

Chapter 9 also touches on stock market seasonality, briefly reviewing the calendar-related anomalies that have been noted in the world's stock markets. While a fuller analysis is beyond the scope of this book, we single out the January effect for closer attention. There are two reasons for this. First, of all the calendar anomalies, the January effect is the best known and most important. Second, it is closely intertwined with the size effect since in the United States, the entire historical outperformance of smaller stocks is attributable to their returns in January. Intriguingly, however, when we seek to replicate the US findings for the United Kingdom, we find no evidence of a size-based seasonal in January, or any other month.

In chapter 10 we turn to another aspect of equity investment: the performance of value and growth stocks. We confirm the superior long-term performance in the United States of value stocks, namely, those with a high dividend yield and/or a high ratio of book to market value of equity. Value stocks have performed markedly better than their growth-stock counterparts, that is, shares that sell at a low yield and/or a low book-to-market ratio.

The US evidence covers three-quarters of a century but the United States is hitherto the only country for which there is long-run data. We present new value and growth indexes for the United Kingdom, based on a comprehensive sample of companies and data that spans a century. The United Kingdom provides further support for the superior results, over the long haul, from following a value strategy. International evidence for other countries covers a shorter period but supports the claim that value investing has tended to provide higher returns in almost all countries that we consider in this book.

The above discussion highlights the importance of dividends, and these are discussed in chapter 11. This chapter shows the crucial contribution that dividends make to long-term stock market performance. We look at dividend growth over the last century in the United States, the United Kingdom and around the world, and draw comparisons with growth rates in national GDP. Real dividends have grown more slowly than per capita GDP in all countries, a fact that puts in context the debate about the likelihood of dividend growth outstripping GDP. We quantify the recent decline in dividend payments in the United States and the United Kingdom, and emphasize the need to consider the total payout as well as cash dividend payments.

1.4 The equity premium

Investment in equities over the twentieth century has proved rewarding, but has been accompanied by correspondingly greater risks. In chapter 12, we examine the historical rewards that investors have enjoyed for bearing this risk. We do this by comparing the return on equities with the return from risk free investments. When measured over a sufficiently long period, the difference between these two returns is called the equity risk premium.

In chapter 12, we provide evidence on the long-run magnitude of the equity risk premium, estimated relative to both bills and bonds. Our risk premia are lower than those that have been reported in previous studies of US and UK stock market performance. The differences arise from previous biases in index construction (for the United Kingdom), and (for both countries) from the use of a rather longer time frame, extending back to 1900.

The equity risk premium is a very important economic variable. An estimate of the premium is central to projecting future investment returns, calculating the cost of equity capital, valuing companies and stocks, appraising capital investment projects, and determining fair rates of return. All these applications need an estimate of the prospective risk premium, whereas the only premium we can measure is the historical premium. The prospective risk premium forms the subject of chapter 13.

Many people argue that the historical risk premium, if measured over a long enough time span, gives an unbiased estimate of the prospective premium. We review evidence that suggests that academic experts typically subscribe to this view, and that their own forecasts are heavily influenced by the historical record. The research conducted for this book, however, leads us to question whether the historical risk premium really does provides a reasonable estimate of the prospective premium. Our belief is that historical equity returns have almost certainly exceeded investors' *ex ante* risk premium requirements, and also that the required risk premium has itself fallen over time. We use evidence from historical dividend growth to back up these assertions, and to suggest an alternative, rather lower, estimate of the future risk premium.

The final two chapters in Part One of this book use our new international database to look toward the future. Chapter 14 explores the implications of our findings for investors. We examine the evidence that supports the thesis that stocks are a (relatively) safe investment over the long run. In the United States and the United Kingdom stocks have historically equalled or beaten risk free investment over holding periods of approximately twenty years or longer. We discover that this is not the usual pattern. For equity investors to have beaten bond investors, it would often have been necessary to have an investment horizon of forty years or more.

We discuss some of the investment implications of our findings. We emphasize how we should alter our judgments in the light of a reduced estimate for the future equity risk premium. There are strong inferences that can be drawn about the role for active management, the case for index funds, levels of management fees, tax management, asset allocation, international diversification, and strategies for exploiting anomalies and regularities. Chapter 14 summarizes the implications of our research for investors and investment institutions.

In chapter 15 we extend this discussion to the cost of capital and the impact of an attenuated equity premium on real investment decisions. We express a concern that companies may themselves be seeking too high a rate of return, and if so, that they run the risk of under-investing. We again explore a range of implications, with an accent on the valuation of shares and companies, and on corporate financing decisions. We conclude Part One of the book with chapter 16, which provides a summary of *Triumph of the Optimists*, and a review of conclusions based on our international dataset and on the analysis presented in this book.

1.5   Sixteen countries, one world

Part Two of the book commences with chapter 17, which provides an overview of the following sixteen chapters, each of which describes the individual database for a particular country, and presents a 101-year study of risk and return in that national market. We explain the common features of each country study, and how our results are presented. Readers who are interested in a particular country are urged to read this chapter first.

Chapters 18–33 provide highlights of the research results for each individual market, listed in successive chapters in alphabetical order. We explain our data sources and the specifics of the research methodology for the country in question. In each chapter we include a record of nominal and real (inflation adjusted) returns and of risk premia, estimated over a variety of recent and long-term intervals, and presented in both tabular and graphical formats.

Finally, in chapter 34, we bring together our results for individual countries by assembling a world index. This presents the performance of a sixteen-country portfolio, weighted by market capitalization (or, in the early decades, by relative GDP). As with the individual countries, we record returns and equity premia over various intervals. This index series is to date the most accurate estimate of the long-run total return, including reinvested dividends, from investing in stocks and bonds around the world.

A feature of our research is that we make extensive use of long-term rate-of-return studies undertaken by scholars in a variety of countries. These individuals are identified in the relevant chapters, and their contributions are listed among the references at the end of the book. The research effort that underpins our database therefore embodies many months and years spent by our contributors (and by us) in library vaults and archives. The reason for these efforts is the importance each researcher attaches to the markets we cover in this book. In the next chapter, we describe global financial markets, and put our sixteen countries in perspective on the world stage.

Chapter 2 World markets: today and yesterday

This book is about the long-run performance of equities, bonds, bills, inflation, and exchange rates around the world over the 101-years from 1900–2000.

Our story begins at the end of our 101-year period by looking at world markets as they stand today. In sections 2.1 and 2.2, we examine the world's stock and bond markets in terms of their size and significance and the split between markets and countries. This helps set in perspective the importance of the markets and the sixteen countries covered in this study.

In section 2.3, we review why these huge markets exist and what functions they perform. Then in section 2.4, our story moves back to the start of our period and we review what stock and bond markets looked like at the end of 1899. Stock and bond markets, of course, existed long before 1899, and so we also delve back into history to examine briefly their origins. Section 2.5 looks more closely at the US and UK stock markets at the end of 1899, and compares their relative size and importance then with the position at the end of 2000.

Continuing on this comparative theme, section 2.6 provides some interesting snapshots of how the corporate landscape has changed over time by looking at the industrial composition of the US and UK stock markets, and how this has evolved since 1900. Similarly, section 2.7 provides international comparisons of stock market concentration, showing how this has changed over the last 101 years in the US and UK markets. This sheds light on an issue of current concern in many countries, namely, whether markets have become unusually or overly concentrated in a relatively small number of stocks. Section 2.8 provides a summary.

2.1 The world's stock markets today

Today, there are stock markets in at least 111 different countries around the world. At the start of 2000, the combined value of the shares traded on these markets exceeded $36 trillion (i.e., $36,000,000 million, or if you really like zeros, $36,000,000,000,000).

Table 2-1 lists the world's major stock markets by country. Many countries have more than one stock exchange. For example, the United States has not only the New York Stock Exchange (NYSE), but also Nasdaq, the American Stock Exchange (Amex), and several smaller exchanges. In Table 2-1, for simplicity, we have aggregated all exchanges within each country to show just a single countrywide figure. The table lists the world's top twenty countries by aggregate equity market capitalization, as well as three other countries that are included here because they form part of the sixteen countries covered in this book. For each country, Table 2-1 shows the total value of the equity market in billions of dollars, the percentage of the total world market which this represents, and the country's ranking by market size. The next two columns show the country's GDP in billions of US dollars, and the proportion of the total GDP that this represents. The final row of the table shows the world total, while the penultimate four rows show the aggregated figures for all the remaining countries that have stock markets, sub-totalled by geographical region.

Table 2-1: Capitalization of world stock markets at start-2000

Country/region	Market capitalization $ billion	Percent of world	Rank in world	GDP in 1999 $bn	Percent of GDP	Covered in this book
United States	16,635	46.1	1	9,152	35.6	✓
Japan	4,547	12.6	2	4,347	16.9	✓
United Kingdom	2,933	8.1	3	1,442	5.6	✓
France	1,475	4.1	4	1,432	5.6	✓
Germany	1,432	4.0	5	2,112	8.2	✓
Canada	801	2.2	6	635	2.5	✓
Italy	728	2.0	7	1,171	4.6	✓
The Netherlands	695	1.9	8	394	1.5	✓
Switzerland	693	1.9	9	259	1.0	✓
Hong Kong	609	1.7	10	159	0.6	
Australia	478	1.3	11	404	1.6	✓
Spain	432	1.2	12	596	2.3	✓
Taiwan	376	1.0	13	288	1.1	
Sweden	373	1.0	14	239	0.9	✓
Finland	349	1.0	15	130	0.5	
China	331	0.9	16	990	3.9	
South Korea	309	0.9	17	407	1.6	
South Africa	262	0.7	18	131	0.5	✓
Brazil	228	0.6	19	752	2.9	
Greece	204	0.6	20	125	0.5	
Belgium	185	0.5	22	248	1.0	✓
Denmark	105	0.3	27	174	0.7	✓
Ireland	65	0.2	32	93	0.4	✓
World subtotal	**34,248**	**94.9**		**25,680**	**100**	✓
Other Asia-Pacific	1,065	3.0	21*	na	na	
Other Europe	365	1.0	31*	na	na	
Other South/Central America	359	1.0	24*	na	na	
Other Africa	62	0.2	41*	na	na	
World total	**36,099**	**100**	**1-111**	na	na	

Source: Global Financial Data (market capitalizations); World Bank (GDPs). *Indicates highest ranked country in this residual/regional grouping

Clearly, the United States dominates the world, with the shares traded on the combined US exchanges capitalized at $16.6 trillion or nearly half (46 percent) of the world's total. Japan is in second place, but accounts for only just over a quarter of the US total. While it seems hard to believe today, there was a two-year period in the late 1980s when the Japanese equity market overtook the United States. At the end of 1988, Japanese equities accounted for 40 percent of the world total, compared with 29 percent for the United States. Even adjusting for the 20 percent or so cross-holdings in Japan at that time, the capitalization of the Japanese market was still appreciably larger than that of the US market. Since then, although other world equity markets have performed strongly, the Japanese market has fallen by 41 percent in US dollar terms in one of the most prolonged bear markets in history.

Table 2-1 shows that the United Kingdom was the world's third largest equity market at start-2000, accounting for 8 percent of the world's total. Since then, and if cross-holdings are excluded, the United Kingdom has overtaken Japan. Morgan Stanley Capital International (MSCI) data for May 2001 based on "free flotation" market capitalizations shows the UK market at 10.4 percent of the world total, versus 9.4 percent for Japan. Table 2-1 shows that France and Germany take fourth and fifth place, respectively, with roughly half the market capitalization of the United Kingdom (but rather less on a free flotation basis).

Table 2-1 reveals that there is a strong correlation between each country's economic weight as measured by its GDP, and its stock market weighting as a percentage of the world total. The relationship is by no means perfect, however, and some countries punch above their weight in the world equity market, while others punch below. Countries with larger equity markets than might be expected from their GDP tend to be those where few businesses are in state hands, most firms are publicly held, and where the country has a highly developed financial services industry. The United States, the United Kingdom, and Switzerland are examples of this. Other countries with relatively large equity markets are those serving as regional centers, e.g., Hong Kong (which we treat as a separate country) serving the rest of China, and Greece serving southeast Europe. The countries with smaller equity markets than might be expected are those where much business activity remains in state hands, such as China, or where a smaller proportion of privately held businesses have stock market quotations, as in Italy or Germany.

This relationship between GDP and equity market capitalization is not simply of passing interest. In chapter 3, we discuss the construction of a worldwide equity index for the entire twentieth century and beyond, based on our sixteen countries. Each country in this index is weighted by GDP throughout the earlier part of the last century, until reliable market capitalization data became available. It is therefore important to have established a strong correlation between the two variables, but equally important to have noted the caveats.

Figure 2-1 summarizes the market capitalization data in Table 2-1, grouping it by geographic region. Because of the huge US equity markets, North America is obviously the dominant continent, followed by Europe and then Asia. There is a clear north-south divide, with equity markets in Central and Southern America, Africa, and Australasia making up only a very small proportion of the world's total.

The final column of Table 2-1 indicates which countries we have included in our research. Our criterion for inclusion is straightforward; we have incorporated all countries for which we can obtain data on equities, bonds, bills, inflation, and the exchange rate over the period from end-1899 to end-2000, that is, for a total of 101 years. To date, there are sixteen countries that meet this test, and in future years, we hope to add to this number. As Table 2-1 shows, the sixteen countries include the two main North American markets; the United Kingdom, together with all of the major European markets; two Asia-Pacific markets, namely, Japan and Australia; plus South Africa. Together, these countries account for over 88 percent of the value of today's world equity market.

Figure 2-1: World markets: geographical groupings

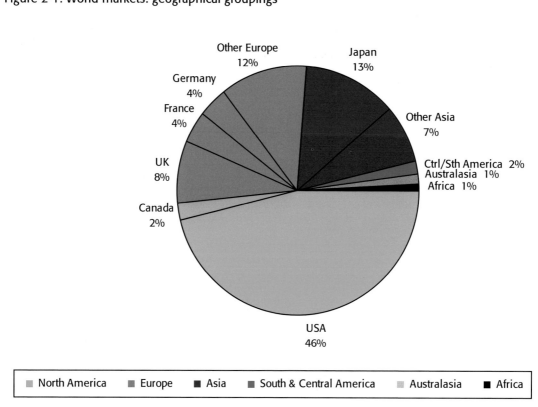

2.2 The world's bond markets today

Bonds are the most important asset class rivaling equities. At the start of 2000, the size of the world bond market was $31 trillion, just below the $36 trillion value of world equities. Most developed countries have active bond markets, trading government and corporate bonds, and their size and trading volume can exceed that in equities. The bond markets facilitate long-term borrowing and lending. Most countries also have active money markets for short-term lending and borrowing, trading in securities such as treasury bills, certificates of deposit, and commercial paper.

Table 2-2 provides summary data on the world's major bond markets taken from a recent survey by Merrill Lynch (2000). It lists the top twenty countries ranked by the value of bonds outstanding, plus South Africa and Ireland, which are included because they form part of the sixteen-country coverage of this book. Table 2-2 shows the value of each country's bond market, its percentage of the world total, its ranking, its value as a percentage of the country's GDP, and the percentage of its market comprising domestic government bonds. The final row shows the world total, while the penultimate three rows show the aggregate figures for the other countries covered by the survey, sub-totalled by geographical region.

Table 2-2: Value of world bond markets at start-2000

Country/region	Total outstanding $ billion	% of world	Rank in world	Bond value as % GDP	% bonds which are Government	Covered in this book
United States	14,595	47.0	1	159	53	✓
Japan	5,669	18.3	2	130	72	✓
Germany	3,131	10.1	3	148	25	✓
Italy	1,374	4.4	4	117	68	✓
France	1,227	4.0	5	86	58	✓
United Kingdom	939	3.0	6	65	50	✓
Canada	539	1.7	7	85	73	✓
The Netherlands	458	1.5	8	116	38	✓
Belgium	324	1.0	9	131	60	✓
Spain	304	1.0	10	51	73	✓
Switzerland	269	0.9	11	104	18	✓
Denmark	264	0.9	12	152	31	✓
South Korea	227	0.7	13	56	52	
Brazil	209	0.7	14	28	na	
Australia	198	0.6	15	49	42	✓
Sweden	188	0.6	16	79	50	✓
Austria	149	0.5	17	72	54	
India	136	0.4	18	30	70	
Greece	88	0.3	19	70	78	
China	73	0.2	20	7	67	
South Africa	72	0.2	21	55	65	✓
Ireland	32	0.1	31	34	74	✓
Other Asia-Pacific	310	1.0	22*	29	46	
Other Europe	235	0.8	24*	28	70	
Other South/Central America	44	0.1	30*	6	na	
World total (40 countries)	**31,054**	**100**	**1-40**	**109**	**55**	✓

Source: World Bank and Merrill Lynch (2000). We have reallocated Merrill Lynch's Eurozone Eurobond total to the individual member countries based on the previous year's (pre-euro) split.   * Indicates highest ranked country in this residual/regional grouping.

Table 2-2 shows that the $14.6 trillion US bond market is the world's largest, representing 47 percent of the global total. Japan and Germany are in second and third places, with 18.3 and 10.1 percent of the world's total, respectively, followed by Italy, France, and the United Kingdom. The sixteen countries covered in this book account for over 95 percent of the world bond market. Geographically, North America makes up 48.7 percent of the world market; Europe, 28.9 percent; Asia, 20.6 percent; with Latin America, Australasia, and Africa accounting for the balance of 1.8 percent. Bonds denominated in the world's three largest currencies, the US dollar, Euro, and Japanese yen, account for 88 percent of the world bond market.

Governments, including central, local and state governments, municipalities, government agencies, and inter-governmental organizations, have always been important bond issuers. During the 1990s, however, government debt declined in relative importance. Merrill Lynch

(2000) report that in 1990, domestic government bonds made up 62 percent of the world market, but by start-2000, the figure was 55 percent (see Table 2-2). Of the balance, 26.4 percent is domestic corporate bonds; 15.1 percent, Eurobonds; and 3.6 percent, foreign bonds. Foreign bonds are issued on domestic markets by non-resident entities, while Eurobonds are issued internationally, not on specific national markets. Foreign bonds and Eurobonds, like domestic bonds, are issued mostly by governments and corporates. Assuming the same split between issuers as for domestic bonds, this suggests that two thirds of all outstanding bonds were issued by governments, and one third by corporates.

Many countries have larger bond markets than equity markets. For the sixteen countries covered in this book, the left-hand (red) bars in Figure 2-2 show the size of each country's bond market expressed as a percentage of its equity market value. The United States, with its vast markets in both equities and bonds, is closest to parity, with bond markets that are 88 percent the size of its equity markets. Five countries have larger bond than equity markets, including the large bond markets in Japan, Germany, and Italy. In contrast, South Africa, the United Kingdom, Switzerland, Australia, and Sweden have equity markets between 2 and 3½ times the size of their bond markets. The United Kingdom is especially noteworthy since its bond market is the world's fifth largest, yet it is less than a third the size of its equity market. Figure 2-2 shows that the world bond market is just slightly smaller than (86 percent of the value of) the world equity market. The two values may be even closer since our world equity value is based on 111 countries, while the Merrill Lynch bond survey covers 40 countries.

Figure 2-2: Size of world bond markets relative to equity markets and GDP at start-2000

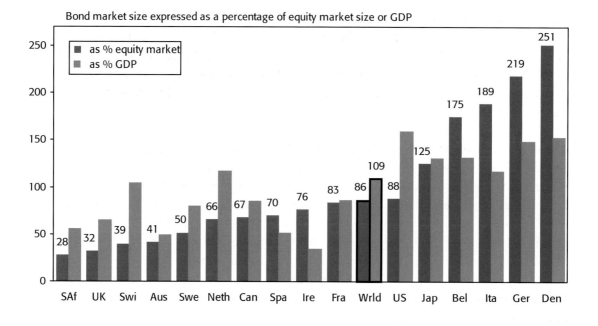

Interestingly, not only are the world bond and equity markets roughly the same size, but at start-2000, they were both approximately the same size as world GDP. Merrill Lynch (2000) estimates that the world bond market has risen from 60 percent of world GDP in 1990 to 98 percent at start-2000. The right-hand bars in Figure 2-2 show the value of each country's bond market as a percentage of its GDP. The figure of 109 percent shown for the world is based on the aggregate GDP for the 40 countries covered in the Merrill Lynch survey, whereas the 98 percent figure cited above is based on total world GDP. Within countries, there is clearly considerable variation in the sizes of bond markets relative to national GDP, ranging from just 34 percent for Ireland to 159 percent for the United States.

Many factors contribute to these differences in bond market sizes. Since governments are key issuers, differences in macroeconomic policy, government borrowing, and budget deficits strongly influence bond market size. Countries with larger public sectors and more nationalized industries have more government debt, while those with large privatization programs often use the proceeds to retire debt. For the corporate sector, companies operating in countries with so-called bank-based financial systems (e.g., Germany, Japan, and Italy) have tended to place more emphasis on debt than equity financing, which has fostered larger corporate bond markets. Another factor is the balance between the usage of short-term debt versus bonds. For example, the Japanese bond market would be even larger were it not for the government's heavy reliance on short-term borrowing to finance its budget deficit. Conversely, the size of the US bond market increased greatly during the 1990s with the dramatic shift away from bank lending toward the capital markets as the primary source of funding. At start-2000, bank loans accounted for just 10 percent of financial assets in the United States, versus 40 percent in Japan and 50 percent in the Eurozone, the group of eleven countries that have adopted the euro as their single, common currency.

Our focus in this book with respect to bonds is on the long-term returns, mostly from government bonds, in each of our sixteen countries over the period 1900–2000. While we look at cross-border investment, and at the returns from a diversified world bond portfolio, much of our analysis is comparative national. While this seems the natural approach over the twentieth century, viewing bond markets on a strictly national basis seems somewhat less appropriate in the twenty-first century.

There are at least three reasons for this. First, cross-border investment has increased dramatically, as has cross-border issuance. Second, the Eurobond market—a truly international market—continues to grow rapidly. Furthermore, its methods and techniques have increasingly been copied in the domestic markets, blurring the distinction between Eurobonds and domestic bonds. Finally, and most important, the introduction of the euro at the end of 1998 immediately brought together eleven Eurobond markets into one, improving liquidity and removing currency risk. In 1999, net new issuance of euro-denominated securities exceeded that in US dollars. The advent of the euro seems certain to lead to almost total integration of the member countries' bond markets, so that in future we need to think in terms of the Eurozone—which more countries anyway seem destined to join—rather than the individual countries' bond markets.

2.3 Why stock and bond markets matter

It is worth reflecting on why such large and liquid stock and bond markets exist. Given their pervasiveness, they have clearly not arisen by accident, but rather because they fulfil a vital economic purpose. In fact, they perform two closely interlinked functions, namely, a primary and a secondary market role. The primary market is where companies raise new money through the sale of equities, bonds, or other securities. The secondary market is the "second hand" market where investors trade in securities that have already been issued, often long ago. The health of the primary market depends on the existence of a liquid and efficient secondary market. The latter is where most trading activity and volume takes place.

The fund-raising, or primary market function arose because the emergence of larger corporations led to a need for large sums of money for business investment—typically more than a single investor, family, or partnership could afford. The obvious solution was to tap a wider pool of investors, but this needed an organized exchange where companies could access potential investors. It also required corporate structures that allowed the dispersal of ownership (and hence the separation of ownership and control) and transferable securities, which could be traded on the exchange. To function efficiently, exchanges also require specialized intermediaries, such as market makers and brokers, who buy and sell securities, as either principal or agent, under a common set of rules and regulations.

The importance of the secondary market or trading function is that it provides an efficient savings and investment forum that allows the uncoupling of companies' and investors' time horizons. For example, General Electric Corporation or Vodafone may need money to invest in ten- or twenty-year risky projects. But meanwhile, investors with shorter horizons can still invest in their shares, safe in the knowledge that they can sell them in the market whenever they wish. Similarly, stock markets allow companies and investors to uncouple their risk preferences. Thus, if Vodafone's business or projects imply a higher level of risk than an investor is comfortable with, investor can reduce their risk through the capital markets by putting only a proportion of their money in Vodafone, and the balance in safer bills or bonds.

The world's stock markets perform many other functions that arise either as an integral part, or as by-product, of their fund raising and savings roles. First, they allow investors to diversify their portfolios across many securities, both domestically and internationally, thus greatly reducing risk and thereby lowering the cost of capital. They also serve as focal points for regulation and information transmission. Regulation is important to minimize fraud, counterparty risk, and ensure fair play, thereby enhancing market liquidity and lowering the cost of capital. Information generation and transmission—about companies, industries, and economies—is also a key ingredient and indeed by-product of an efficiently operating stock market. The other important by-product is prices. Through their price formation activities, stock exchanges provide an important "free" valuation service for companies and investors, and serve as a barometer and leading indicator of economic activity.

Bond markets perform a similar function to stock markets, but they widen the set of choices so that issuers can raise debt capital of differing types and maturities, in addition to equity.

Just as with equities, the secondary market in bonds then allows investors to uncouple their investment horizons from the maturity of the bonds. As we have seen, bond markets are accessed not just by corporations but, even more importantly, by governments and international bodies. Finally, the money markets and the bill markets cater for the shorter-term requirements of companies, financial institutions, governments, other organizations, and investors, allowing them to borrow and lend money as and when required.

This book covers all three types of market: equity, bond, and bill. We take the perspective of an investor who wishes to know what returns have been achieved in these markets in different countries, what risks this has involved, and what this tells us about the future.

2.4   The world's markets yesterday

This book focuses on investment returns since the start of the twentieth century. Although stock markets in 1900 were rather different from today's, they were by no means a new phenomenon. The Amsterdam exchange had already been in existence for nearly 300 years; the London Stock Exchange had been operating for over 200 years; and five other markets, including the New York Stock Exchange (NYSE), had been in existence for 100 years or more.

Michie (1992) points out that some forms of stock trading occurred in Roman times. Organized trading, however, did not take place until transferable securities appeared in the seventeenth century. These were mostly either government debt, frequently issued to fund wars, or the stocks of large joint stock companies, often issued to pioneer long-distance trade between Europe and India. The Amsterdam market dates back to 1611, and Frankfurt to 1685, with the latter tracing its origins back a further 400 years to the medieval Frankfurt fairs. Amsterdam was the world's main center of stock trading in the seventeenth and eighteenth centuries, but while it was the oldest exchange, it lacked official organization until 1787. This allows Paris, set up in 1724, to claim to be the oldest formal exchange. Organized dealing in London dates from 1698, much of it taking place in coffee houses, but it was not until 1801 that the London Stock Exchange obtained its constitution and its own building.

The New York Stock Exchange (NYSE) traces its origins to 1792, when 24 brokers signed an agreement on trading methods (White, 1992). This followed in the wake of speculative excesses and market manipulation in the trading of bank stocks. In 1817, a formal constitution was adopted, creating the New York Stock and Exchange Board, later renamed the NYSE in 1869. In 1853, the first disclosure requirements were introduced. Companies that could not comply were traded in the out-of-doors market, the Curb.

At the start of the nineteenth century, the principal stocks traded on the major stock exchanges were banks, and subsequently insurance companies. In the early years of the century, transportation stocks came to prominence: at first docks, canals, and bridges, and then, from the 1830s on, railroads. Later, mining and manufacturing stocks emerged in larger numbers, although, as we will see in the next section, railroads still dominated the world's stock markets in 1900.

During the Industrial Revolution, many regional and city—as opposed to national—stock exchanges sprung up throughout western Europe and the United States. Before there were efficient communications and transport, it was natural for investors to be located close to the firms in which they invested. This lowered their risk by giving them better access to information so they could monitor their investments. By 1900, the United States and the United Kingdom each had 20–30 regional exchanges serving local needs. They included Manchester and Liverpool in the 1830s to serve the canal and railway boom; Oldham in 1875 for its cotton mills; San Francisco in the 1850s for the mining industry; Chicago in 1882 for meatpacking; and Los Angeles in 1900 for the southern Californian petroleum industry (see Odell, 1992).

By the start-date of our study in 1900, the tide had turned firmly in favor of national exchanges, and while regional exchanges survive today, they are generally far less important. The dominance of national exchanges was made possible by better communications, but was also stimulated by the growing capital needs of large, less locally based projects, including international ventures, often by foreign firms. The larger, centralized markets provided access to a much wider pool of investors, and generated greater liquidity and better diversification opportunities both domestically and internationally.

Table 2-3, taken from Goetzmann and Jorion (1999), shows the founding dates of national stock markets. Rather surprisingly, it shows that by our 1900 start-date, exchanges already existed in at least thirty-three of today's nations. Many of these were not independent states

Table 2-3: Founding dates of the world's stock markets

The Netherlands	1611	Argentina	1872	Indonesia	1912
Germany	1685	New Zealand	1872	Korea	1921
United Kingdom	1698	Brazil	1877	Slovenia	1924
France	1724	India	1877	Uruguay	1926
Austria	1771	**Japan**	1878	Philippines	1927
United States	1792	Norway	1881	Columbia	1929
Ireland	1799	**South Africa**	1887	Luxembourg	1929
Belgium	1801	Egypt	1890	Malaysia	1929
Denmark	1808	Hong Kong	1890	Romania	1929
Italy	1808	Chile	1892	Israel	1934
Russia	1810	Greece	1892	Pakistan	1947
Switzerland	1850	Venezuela	1893	Lebanon	1948
Spain	1860	Mexico	1894	Taiwan	1953
Canada	1861	Yugoslavia	1894	Kenya	1954
Hungary	1864	Sri Lanka	1900	Nigeria	1960
Turkey	1866	**Sweden**	1901	Kuwait	1962
Australia	1871	Portugal	1901	Thailand	1975
Czech Republic	1871	Singapore	1911		
Poland	1871	Finland	1912		

Source: Goetzmann and Jorion (1999), based on the founding dates of exchanges now within the borders of the identified countries with some additions/modifications by the authors. Bold face type indicates countries covered in this book.

in 1900. The Czech Republic, Austria, Hungary, and Slovenia were all part of Austria-Hungary; Poland was part of the Russian Empire; and Ireland, part of the United Kingdom. The markets in Ljubljana, Prague, Budapest, and Warsaw were thus just modest regional exchanges. Table 2-3 shows that, mostly, the exchanges founded during the nineteenth century were set up either in Europe, or by Europeans abroad. Of the non-European exchanges that pre-date 1900, Canada, South Africa, Hong Kong, Australia, New Zealand, India, and Sri Lanka were all part of the British Empire, while Egypt was effectively a British protectorate. The exceptions to the European/colonial rule are the United States, Japan, Turkey, and the five Latin American markets, Mexico, Brazil, Argentina, Chile, and Venezuela.

The important issue that Table 2-3 raises is the extent to which the sixteen countries covered in this book and shown in bold typeface were representative of the world's stock markets at the start of our research period in 1900. The left-hand pie chart of Figure 2-3 reminds us of their importance today, showing that they cover 88 percent of world stock market value. Of the balance not represented, roughly half (i.e., 6 percent) came from markets which existed in 1900, while the rest came from exchanges set up after 1900, and which did not therefore qualify for our study. Table 2-1 shows that the largest markets (as of today) that in principle qualified for inclusion, but where we have not yet located suitable data, were Hong Kong (1.7 percent of the world total) and Brazil (0.6 percent).

Ideally, we would like to produce a similar breakdown of stock markets by their capitalization in 1900, to assess the relative importance of the sixteen countries at the start of the

---

Figure 2-3: Importance of the sixteen countries covered in this book in 2000 and in 1900

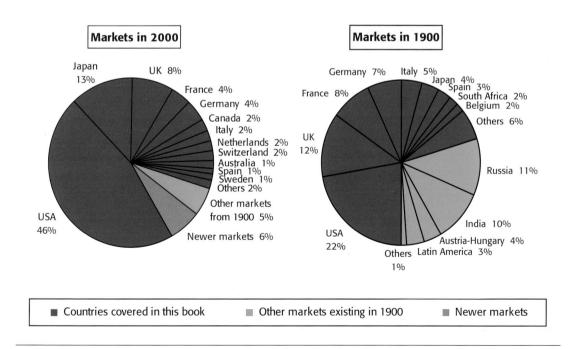

twentieth century. Unfortunately, the data required are not available. Such aggregate data were neither recorded nor even thought about in 1900. The few snippets of historical data that exist are expressed in terms of the nominal value of the shares outstanding rather than the total market value of the shares quoted on each exchange. For the United States and the United Kingdom, we have painstakingly assembled this information from archival sources relating to individual stocks, but we know of no equivalent sources for other markets. For many markets, even the disaggregated archive source data may not have survived from the end of the nineteenth century to the present time.

Given the lack of market capitalization data for 1900, we make comparisons in terms of GDP. The right-hand pie chart of Figure 2-3 shows the relative GDPs of all countries that had stock markets in 1900. These figures were assembled, re-based, and placed on a common US dollar basis by Maddison (1995), but they come with the usual caveats relating to economic data from 1900. Figure 2-3 shows that the sixteen countries covered in this book accounted for 70 percent of the total GDP of all countries with stock markets. Of the balance not covered, the Russian Empire accounts for 11 percent, India for 10 percent, Austria-Hungary for 4 percent, and the five Latin American countries for 3 percent among them.

While India, Austria-Hungary, and the Latin American countries make up 17 percent of the GDP total, this clearly overstates their stock market importance. Austria-Hungary was then a disintegrating dynasty, while the other countries were "emerging markets" and even today are often still viewed as such. The Russian Empire, too, had a relatively low equity market capitalization to GDP ratio of just 18 percent in 1913, versus 109 percent for the United Kingdom (Rajan and Zingales, 2001), suggesting that Russia probably made up less than 2 percent of world equity capitalization. It thus seems very likely, but not proven, that the sixteen countries covered in this book represented at least as high a proportion of the world equity market in 1900 as they do today. The figure may easily have exceeded 90 percent.

Michie (1992) reports one further piece of evidence, namely, that by 1910 UK investors alone owned 24 percent of the outstanding value of securities worldwide, followed by US citizens with 21 percent, French with 18 percent, and Germans with 16 percent. Russians held just 5 percent, Austro-Hungarians 4 percent, and Italians and Japanese, 2 percent each. Most of the balance was held by other western European investors, largely from countries covered in this book. This data relates to ownership and not to where securities were traded, and it covers all securities, including bonds. It nevertheless supports our claims on coverage.

An important feature of markets in 1900 was the prevalence of cross-border investment. Europeans invested heavily in the less developed countries, especially the Americas, Africa, Russia, South-eastern Europe, Turkey, and the Far East. Firms based, or operating, overseas, issued many of the securities traded in London and Paris. Even in such advanced economies as Canada, Europeans owned a large proportion of all securities, and many US stocks and bonds were held abroad. Later in the twentieth century, wars, the Wall Street Crash, the Great Depression, currency restrictions, protectionism, and the Cold War made investors more insular. International investment did not return as a major force until the 1970s.

2.5   The US and UK stock markets: 1900 versus 2000

The two countries for which we have detailed stock- and market-level data for both the start and end of the twentieth century are the United States and the United Kingdom. At the start of the twentieth century, the UK equity market was the largest in the world, dominating even the US market. At end-1899, 783 companies had their shares traded on the London Stock Exchange. This was over six times as many as were then quoted on the NYSE. At the end of 1899, just 123 NYSE stocks are listed in the *Commercial and Financial Chronicle*, the most authoritative data source on the NYSE. This exceeds the figure of only 70 stocks reported by Goetzmann, Ibbotson, and Peng (2001), who used the *New York Herald* and the *New York Times* as their sources. It also exceeds the 87 NYSE stocks covered by Cowles (1938) in 1900.

The market capitalization of London quoted equities at end-1899, using the dollar-pound exchange rate at the time, was $4.3 billion. This was over 50 percent more than the $2.86 billion value of NYSE quoted stocks. At the time, there were over twenty other US stock exchanges, and we estimate that the total value of US stocks across all exchanges in 1900 was $3.5 billion (based on Cowles' (1938) estimate of the size of the NYSE relative to other exchanges). The capitalization of the London Stock Exchange in 1900 was thus over 20 percent greater than the total value of all US equities. Furthermore, this figure is just for London, and, at the time, the United Kingdom had some twenty other regional exchanges.

Early in the twentieth century, the US equity market overtook the United Kingdom, and has since then been the world's dominant equity market. By the end of 2000, there were 6,340 US stocks quoted on the NYSE, Amex, and Nasdaq, with a total capitalization of $14.4 trillion. This compares with a value of $2.7 trillion for the 2,140 UK companies, including Alternative Investment Market (AIM) stocks, traded on the London market.

At end-1899, the largest NYSE stock was the Pennsylvania Railroad, with a capitalization of $373 million, while the smallest was Duluth South Shore and Atlantic Railroad, capitalized at $80,000. In the United Kingdom, the largest stock was London and North Western Railway, with a capitalization of $405 million, while the smallest was the intriguingly named Native Guano, capitalized at just $20,000. At the start of 2001, the largest US stock, General Electric, had a market capitalization of $475 billion, while the largest UK stock, Vodafone, was capitalized at $236 billion. Ignoring differences in purchasing power, General Electric at start-2001 was therefore 134 times larger than the entire US equity market in 1900, while Vodafone was 180 times larger than the then total value of the London Stock Exchange.

2.6   Industry composition: 1900 versus 2000

At the start of the third millennium, many commentators have argued that we are on the verge of a new technological revolution. But as the *Financial Times* editorial of January 13, 2001, argued "the notion that information technology represents the greatest transformation since the Industrial Revolution is historically illiterate. The technological changes between 1880 and 1940 exceeded, in both scope and intensity, all that has happened since."

Those changes included new sources of energy (electricity, petroleum, and gas), new transportation techniques (motor vehicles and airlines), new industries (automobiles and pharmaceuticals), new communications and media (telephone and radio), new products (white goods, mass consumer products, antibiotics), and new leisure pursuits (cinema and television). As the *Financial Times* put it, "These profoundly altered what was produced and how. They also transformed the way people lived."

These changes can be seen in the shifting composition of the types of firms listed on stock markets over the twentieth century. Table 2-4 provides a comparative view of industrial composition for both the United States and the United Kingdom at three points in time: end-1899, 1950, and 2000. It is based on the industrial classification that was in effect in 1900, although a few sectors have been added that, while small in 1900, had become important by 1950. Since the UK equity market was the world's largest back in 1900, the sequencing of the sectors reflects their relative importance in the United Kingdom at that time. For end-1899 and 1950, the UK sector weights are based on the largest 100 stocks, while, for end-2000, they reflect the whole market. The US weightings relate to the entire US market, except at end-1899, when they are based on all NYSE stocks plus New York City banks.

Table 2-4 is dominated by the great importance, at the start of the twentieth century, of railroads. In the United Kingdom, they accounted for nearly 50 percent of the value of the top 100 companies, while in the United States, they made up no less than 63 percent of total market value. In addition, there were also many railroad-related stocks, such as street railways, rail freight companies, and railroad car and wagon manufacturers, and if these are included, the US weighting for railroads rises to 70 percent. 101 years later, railroads have declined in importance almost to the point of stock market extinction, representing just 0.2 percent of the US equity market at the end of 2000, and 0.3 percent of the UK market. The

Table 2-4: Sector weightings within UK and US equity markets using end-1899 classification

Sectors using industry classification from end-1899	United Kingdom			United States		
	1899	1950	2000	1899	1950	2000
Railroads	49.2	0.0	0.3	62.8	4.2	0.2
Banks and finance	15.4	9.7	16.8	6.7	0.7	12.9
Mining	6.7	5.3	2.0	0.0	1.1	0.0
Textiles	5.0	3.3	0.0	0.7	1.3	0.2
Iron, coal, steel	4.5	5.4	0.1	5.2	0.3	0.3
Breweries and distillers	3.9	8.8	2.1	0.3	0.7	0.4
Utilities	3.1	0.2	3.6	4.8	8.3	3.8
Telegraph and telephone	2.5	0.0	14.0	3.9	6.0	5.6
Insurance	1.9	11.5	4.4	0.0	0.4	4.9
Other transport	1.4	1.7	1.5	3.7	0.3	0.5
Chemicals	1.3	6.3	0.9	0.5	13.9	1.2
Food manufacturing	1.0	4.6	2.0	2.5	2.0	1.2
Retailers	0.7	7.3	4.4	0.1	6.7	5.6
Tobacco	0.0	13.1	1.0	4.0	1.5	0.8
Sectors that were small in 1900	3.4	22.8	46.9	4.8	52.6	62.4
Total	**100.0**	**100.0**	**100.0**	**100.0**	**100.0**	**100.0**

other statistic that stands out in Table 2-4 is the high proportion of today's companies whose business is in sectors that were small or non-existent in 1900—62 percent by value of US companies, and 47 percent for the United Kingdom.

Table 2-4 reveals many other differences between the old industrial breakdown and the listed companies of today. But even where sectors are superficially similar, they have often altered radically. For example, compare telegraphy with cellular or WAP phones. Or compare other transport in the 1900 era—such as shipping lines, street railways/tramways, and docks—with their modern counterparts, namely, airlines, airports, and buses.

Interestingly, some sectors that were inconsequential in 1900 grew to prominence by 1950, but declined again by start-2001. Chemicals, for example, grew from a 0.5 to a 13.9 percent weighting in the United States between 1900 and 1950, but then fell back to just 1.2 percent by end-2000; UK chemicals followed a similar pattern, with a five-fold increase in weighting from 1900 to 1950, but then falling to just a tenth of their 1950 weight by start-2001. In the United Kingdom, tobacco presents a similar story. It had zero weight among the top 100 companies of 1900, but accounted for over 13 percent by 1950 (having been even more prominent in the 1930s). By start-2001, it had reverted to a 1 percent weighting. US listed tobacco companies were more important at the start of the twentieth century than their UK counterparts, although over the course of the century, they saw a similar decline. Retailers represent another sector that greatly increased in importance from 1900 to 1950, but subsequently declined—rather more so in the United Kingdom than in the United States.

We find a complementary story in Table 2-5, where the same companies are classified using today's industrial categories, and where sectors are listed in the order of their importance in the United States today. The big six sectors are information technology, banks, pharmaceuticals, telecommunications, retailers, and oil and gas, which together make up almost two-thirds of today's total US market value. Pharmaceuticals and oil and gas were almost totally absent in 1900, while information technology had zero weight in 1900 and 1950. Pharmaceuticals were still small in 1950, while oil stocks had already attained prominence, and have since declined, especially in the United States. Telecommunications, too, was quite a small sector in 1900. By 1950, it had grown to 6 percent of the US market, and has remained around that level since. The UK telecoms industry followed a different path. It operated as a nationalized industry until the 1980s when it was privatized. By end-2000, telecommunications stocks, including cell phone companies, accounted for 14 percent of the UK market.

Table 2-5 shows that, of the US firms listed in 1900, 85 percent of their value was in sectors that are today small or non-existent; the UK figure is 69 percent. Yet similarities are also apparent. The continued importance of the bank and insurance sectors is striking, especially in the United Kingdom. At the start of 1900, UK banks accounted for 15.4 percent of the top 100 stocks, as compared to 16.8 percent of the market today; for the United States, the figures are 6.7 percent in 1900 versus 12.9 percent today. Similarly, UK breweries and distillers have decreased in weighting relative to their 1900 level, but not by much, although their 8.8 percent weighting in 1950 shows that they rose and fell in between. This sector has never been important in the United States, perhaps as a legacy of prohibition. Telecommunications, a high-tech sector in 1900, remains high-tech today. Today's utilities are similar to those listed

Table 2-5: Sector weightings within US and UK equity markets using start-2001 classification

Sectors using industry classification from start-2001	United States			United Kingdom		
	2000	1950	1899	2000	1950	1899
Information technology	23.1	0.0	0.0	4.7	0.0	0.0
Banks and finance	12.9	0.7	6.7	16.8	9.7	15.4
Pharmaceuticals	11.2	0.8	0.0	11.0	0.4	0.0
Telecommunications	5.6	6.0	3.9	14.0	0.0	2.5
Retailers	5.6	6.7	0.1	4.4	7.3	0.7
Oil and gas	5.2	16.4	0.0	11.0	12.9	0.2
Diversified industrials	5.1	2.0	0.0	0.0	1.0	0.0
Insurance	4.9	0.4	0.0	4.4	11.5	1.9
Utilities	3.8	8.3	4.8	3.6	0.2	3.1
Media and photography	2.5	1.0	0.0	5.9	0.4	0.6
Breweries and distillers	0.4	0.7	0.3	2.1	8.8	3.9
Mining	0.0	1.1	0.0	2.0	5.3	6.7
Sectors that are small in 2001	19.7	55.9	84.2	20.1	42.5	65.0
Total	**100.0**	**100.0**	**100.0**	**100.0**	**100.0**	**100.0**

101 years ago, and have roughly the same weighting (although during the century they disappeared from the UK market due to nationalization until being privatized in the 1980s).

Note that the fairly low weighting in traditional manufacturing is not new. A broad definition of manufacturing would include everything we today classify as "basic industries", "general industrials", and "cyclical and non-cyclical consumer goods", but excluding pharmaceuticals and healthcare (see Table 2-6 below). On this definition, manufacturers made up just 18 percent of the US and UK stock markets in 1900. For the United States, the proportion is the same today, while for the United Kingdom it has fallen to 11 percent. By 1950, manufacturing stocks had risen to close to their highest weighting of the century, representing 53 percent of the US and 42 percent of the UK markets. Since 1950, their relative importance has declined, while services, information technology, and financials have been in the ascendant.

Our analysis relates purely to the quoted sector. Some sectors have existed throughout, but have not always been listed. For example, there were many retailers in 1900, but these were often smaller, "Mom and Pop" type stores, rather than the Wal-Mart's of today. Similarly, a higher proportion of manufacturing firms were then family-owned and not stock market listed. In the UK, and many other countries, nationalization and then subsequent privatization programs have caused whole industries—utilities, telecoms, steel, airlines, airports—to be de-listed and then re-listed. In our analysis, we incorporate the value of, for example, railroads, while omitting highways and roads, which remain largely in national or state ownership. Despite these caveats, the comparisons above mostly reflect the industrial evolution that has taken place over the last century, rather than just changes in ownership.

Finally, Table 2-6 provides a more detailed breakdown of the sector weightings of the world's major equity markets at the end of 2000, providing figures for Germany and Japan as well as

Table 2-6: Sector weightings for selected countries and the world as at start-2001

Sector	United States	United Kingdom	Japan	Germany	World
Resources	**5.2**	**13.1**	**0.6**	**0.0**	**6.0**
Mining	0.0	2.0	0.0	0.0	0.6
Oil and gas	5.2	11.0	0.6	0.0	5.4
Basic industries	**2.0**	**2.7**	**7.4**	**8.1**	**3.8**
Chemicals	1.2	0.9	3.4	7.1	1.6
Construction and building materials	0.2	1.6	2.2	0.6	1.1
Forestry and paper	0.4	0.0	0.5	0.2	0.5
Steel and other metals	0.3	0.1	1.3	0.2	0.6
General industrials	**8.6**	**2.5**	**13.1**	**18.9**	**9.2**
Aerospace and defense	1.5	1.3	0.5	0.0	1.0
Diversified industrials	5.1	0.0	0.2	7.1	3.9
Electronic and electrical equipment	1.3	0.6	9.3	8.3	3.0
Engineering and machinery	0.7	0.6	3.2	3.5	1.3
Cyclical consumer goods	**1.3**	**0.4**	**12.1**	**9.4**	**3.1**
Automobiles	0.8	0.4	8.4	8.8	2.0
Household goods and textiles	0.5	0.0	3.8	0.6	1.1
Non-cyclical consumer goods	**20.5**	**17.2**	**9.7**	**5.1**	**15.8**
Beverages	2.2	2.1	0.9	0.0	1.6
Food producers and processors	1.2	2.0	1.5	0.2	1.8
Health	3.1	0.7	0.3	1.0	1.7
Packaging	0.1	0.1	0.2	0.1	0.1
Personal care & household products	1.9	0.3	1.2	1.9	1.4
Pharmaceuticals	11.2	11.0	5.3	1.9	8.5
Tobacco	0.8	1.0	0.5	0.0	0.7
Cyclical services	**10.3**	**14.9**	**12.9**	**6.9**	**10.2**
Distributors	0.1	0.3	2.0	0.3	0.4
General retailers	4.5	2.4	2.4	2.2	3.0
Leisure, entertainment and hotels	2.0	2.4	1.2	0.1	1.4
Media and photography	2.5	5.9	2.3	0.7	3.0
Support services	0.6	2.0	0.9	2.5	0.9
Transport	0.7	1.8	4.1	1.1	1.5
Non-cyclical services	**6.8**	**16.0**	**11.8**	**9.4**	**10.1**
Food and drug retailers	1.1	2.0	1.9	0.2	1.4
Telecommunications services	5.6	14.0	9.9	9.3	8.7
Utilities	**3.8**	**3.6**	**3.5**	**2.0**	**3.7**
Electricity	2.6	2.1	2.9	1.6	2.7
Gas distribution	1.2	0.9	0.6	0.3	0.9
Water	0.0	0.6	0.0	0.0	0.1
Information technology	**23.1**	**4.7**	**11.9**	**8.6**	**15.7**
Information technology hardware	15.0	2.0	8.2	2.6	10.6
Software and computer services	8.1	2.6	3.7	5.9	5.1
Non-financials	**81.7**	**74.9**	**83.0**	**68.3**	**77.5**
Financials	**18.3**	**25.2**	**17.0**	**31.7**	**22.5**
Banks	7.4	15.2	9.4	12.4	11.3
Insurance	4.1	0.7	1.3	18.6	4.3
Life assurance	0.8	3.7	0.0	0.4	1.4
Investment companies	0.0	2.7	0.0	0.0	0.6
Real estate	0.5	1.4	1.0	0.3	1.1
Speciality and other finance	5.5	1.6	5.3	0.0	3.8
All sectors	**100.0**	**100.0**	**100.0**	**100.0**	**100.0**

Source: Thomson Financial Datastream and London Business School *Risk Measurement Service* (Dimson and Marsh, 2001b)

the United States, United Kingdom, and the world equity market, based on 49 different countries. Table 2-6 reveals large differences between countries, and also the world averages. Germany and Japan remain heavily weighted in the three key manufacturing sectors, basic industries, general industrials, and cyclical consumer goods, with these sectors making up around a third of their equity markets—three times higher than in the United States, and six times higher than the United Kingdom. At end-2000, information technology stocks made up nearly a quarter of the value of the US market—twice as much as in Japan and five times higher than the United Kingdom. However, the United Kingdom had the highest weightings in the other "new economy" sectors, media and telecommunications. Pharmaceuticals had an 11 percent weighting in both the US and UK markets, over twice as much as in Japan and six times more than in Germany. The UK weighting in oils was twice that of the United States, and 18 times higher than Japan's, while Germany had zero weight. Meanwhile, insurance companies made up 19 percent of the German market, versus 4–5 percent in the United States and the United Kingdom, and just 1.3 percent in Japan.

These large disparities in country sector weightings are not new. They are one of the reasons for the divergence in past performance—and risk levels—between different countries' equity markets, and they are likely to continue to lead to differential performance in the future. Historically, there have been big differences in the fortunes of different industries. Undoubtedly, investors at the end of 1899 were seeking exposure to the sectors that were destined to grow and prosper, just as investors are today. Those who invested in railroads, the dominant sector in 1900, fared much less well than those who invested in commercial and industrial enterprises. Which of today's big or even nascent sectors will go the way of railroad shares?

2.7 Stock market concentration

An issue of contemporary concern in the United Kingdom and many other national stock exchanges is market concentration. In the United Kingdom, it has been noted that the stock market has become more concentrated recently, and that the biggest companies have grown so large that they dominate the index. This has raised a regulatory concern, since UK mutual funds are not permitted to hold more than 10 percent in a single stock. At start-2001, at least one company, Vodafone, had a weighting of 11 percent in the FTSE 100 Index of the largest 100 UK stocks, while its weighting exceeded 9 percent even in the FTSE All-Share Index. This raised an intriguing issue, namely, that an index fund in one of the world's largest equity markets could be prohibited by the regulators from holding the index portfolio.

Figure 2-4 shows how the United Kingdom compares with other countries. This chart shows the weighting at start-2001 of the largest, and the three largest, stocks, in each of the sixteen countries covered by our database, plus Finland. Countries are ranked from the least concentrated on the left to the most concentrated on the right. The huge US equity market is the world's least concentrated. Here, the largest stock at start-2001, General Electric, accounted for just 3 percent of the market, while the largest three, General Electric plus ExxonMobil and Pfizer, had a combined weight of just 7 percent. The UK market is far more concentrated. The largest stock, Vodafone, had a 9 percent weight, and the three largest, Vodafone, BP, and GlaxoSmithKline accounted for 22 percent of UK equity market value.

Figure 2-4: Concentration of equity markets around the world as at start-2001

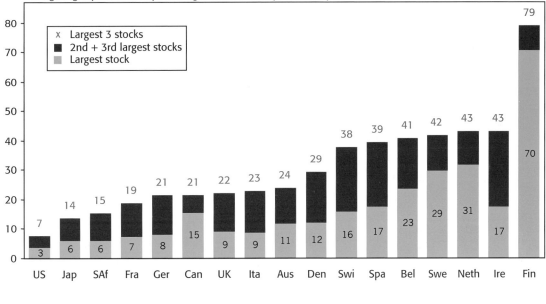

Weighting expressed as a percentage of total country market capitalisation

But despite this apparently high level of concentration, Figure 2-4 shows that the United Kingdom was below average. The majority of markets, especially the smaller ones, were even more concentrated. Finland is the most extreme, where a single stock, Nokia, made up 70 percent of total market value, but Sweden, where Ericsson had a 29 percent weighting, and The Netherlands, where Royal Dutch Shell accounted for 31 percent, are also noteworthy. In the United Kingdom, the recent increase in concentration has arisen from mega-mergers. While this also applies elsewhere, there are other countries where concentration has arisen more from organic growth by a few successful companies, such as Nokia, Ericsson, and Shell.

Besides making international comparisons, we can also check whether today's concentration levels are unusually high by past standards. To examine this for the United Kingdom, we use the historical stock-by-stock data collected in the course of the research for this book. This allows us to assemble a long-term record of market concentration extending back to 1900. Figure 2-5 shows the year-by-year record of the proportion of the value of the top 100 companies that is accounted for by the largest company, the three largest, and the ten largest. On all three measures, UK concentration has risen rapidly over the last six years. Comparing the beginning of 1995 with the beginning of 2001, the weighting of the largest stock has risen from 4.6 percent to 10.9 percent, while the weighting of the ten largest has risen from 33 percent to 52 percent.

The longer-term perspective afforded by Figure 2-5 shows, however, that 1995 was the low point for all three measures of concentration over the 101-year period from 1900–2000. Indeed, until 1995 the long-term trend was downward. Furthermore, concentration on all three measures was higher at the end of the nineteenth century than it is today.

Figure 2-5: Concentration in the top 100 equity index for the United Kingdom, 1900–2000

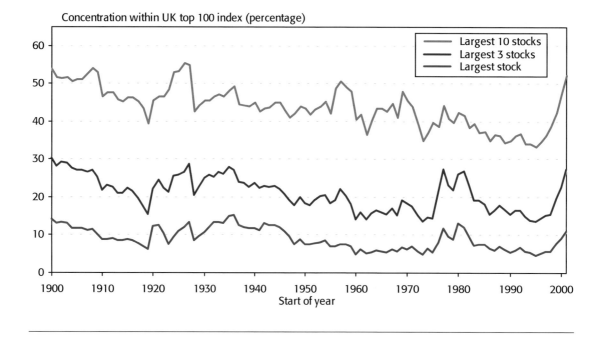

Looking back into history, we can find many years in which the largest stock in the market had a weighting within the top 100 of more than 10 percent, and there were 32 years in which the largest stock had an even greater weighting than Vodafone had at the start of 2001. Similarly, the largest three and the largest ten companies have on several occasions represented a larger proportion of the top 100 than they do today.

The analysis above is based on the proportion of the top 100 index represented by the biggest companies. We have also looked at concentration within the market as a whole, with similar findings. What is striking, however, is the rapidity with which UK concentration ratios increased in recent years. From the mid-1990s onward, the ratios have climbed from almost their lowest levels over the last century to start-2001 levels that are now some 20 percent or so above the averages for the entire period. As yet, however, they are some way off breaching new highs, even on a 101-year view.

Are these patterns of, and recent increases in, concentration unique to the United Kingdom? To investigate this, we repeated our analysis for the US equity market, again calculating the weighting of the largest stock, the top three and the top ten, but in this case, relative to the US market as measured by the universe of stocks covered in the widely used Center for Research in Security Prices (CRSP) database. The CRSP data starts at end-1925, and before this, we have a single data point for end-1899, based on the detailed US stock data we collected from *The Commercial and Financial Chronicle*. The results are plotted in Figure 2-6, with the period 1900–24 shown by a dashed line joining the two known data points for end-1899 and end-1925.

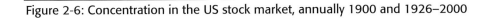

Figure 2-6: Concentration in the US stock market, annually 1900 and 1926–2000

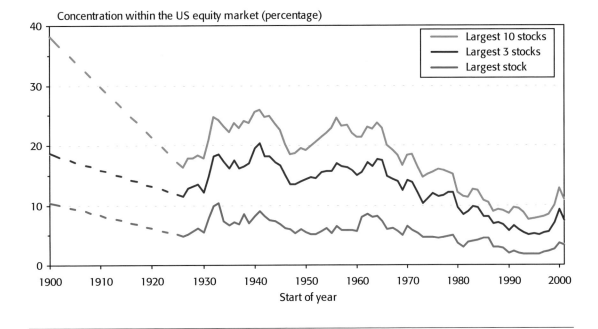

Figure 2-6 shows that the US market was at its most concentrated 101 years ago. At end-1899, the weightings were 10.5, 19, and 38 percent for the top one, three, and ten stocks, respectively. By the 1920s, concentration levels had fallen, and while they have fluctuated since, there has been a downward trend since the mid-1950s. Concentration reached its low-point in 1995, when the weightings were just 1.8, 5.1, and 7.9 percent for the top one, three, and ten stocks. The pattern was thus similar to the United Kingdom, with concentration then increasing sharply from its 1995 low-point. Unlike the United Kingdom, however, concentration fell back in 2000 to levels that were substantially lower than in the United Kingdom (see Figure 2-5).

On the basis of these numbers, it would be hard to get concerned about US trends in concentration. Within more concentrated markets, such as the United Kingdom, however, recent trends in concentration do have consequences. They make life harder for index-trackers if these funds face limits on maximum weightings. They also pose a challenge for active fund managers who are benchmarked against domestic indexes. A decision not to hold or even to underweight a stock such as Vodafone is now a major bet in its own right. But arguably, this simply reveals that the strategic benchmark is wrong. Companies such as Vodafone, BP Amoco, and GlaxoSmithKline are now very much global players, and we should be viewing them in the context of global indexes and adjusting our benchmarks accordingly. As investors, we should also be thinking in terms of internationally diversified, rather than domestically oriented portfolios, which would greatly reduce exposure to the largest stocks. This is a topic to which we return in chapter 8.

Figure 2-7: Concentration within the world equity market as at start-2001

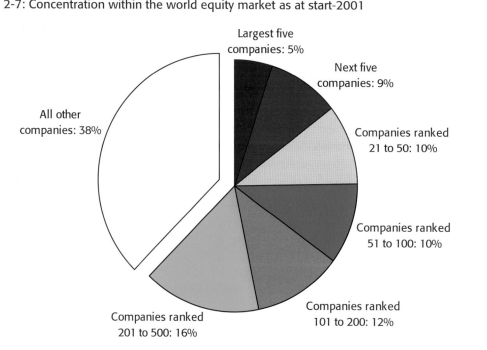

Figure 2-7 shows the degree of concentration in the world equity market portfolio. The world's largest five stocks account for just 5 percent of the sum total of the value of all the world's equity markets. The largest stock, General Electric, has a 1.5 percent weighting, while the largest three make up 3.4 percent of the world total. The 50 largest companies in the world make up less than a quarter of the world total, while the top 100 account for around one third. The largest 500 companies constitute 62 percent of the value of the world equity portfolio, while all other quoted companies worldwide make up the balance. For investors who see the world as their oyster, stock market concentration is not a major issue.

2.8 Summary

In this chapter, we began by looking at world markets as they stand today in terms of their overall size and significance. The sixteen countries covered in this study account for 88 percent of today's world equity market, and 95 percent of the world bond market.

An even more important question is the extent to which these countries were representative of the world stock market in 1900, when our research period began. In 1900, stock markets already existed in no fewer than thirty-three of today's nations, a surprisingly high number. Unfortunately, the data we require to compare the relative market capitalizations of world stock exchanges simply did not exist in 1900. On the basis of the available evidence, however, we conclude that it is very likely, but not proven, that our sixteen countries made up as high a proportion of the world's equity markets in 1900 as they do today.

Finally, the availability of detailed stock level data for both the United States and the United Kingdom enables us to compile some informative snapshots of how the corporate landscape has changed over the twentieth century, particularly in terms of industry composition and stock market concentration. The sector changes that have taken place between 1900 and 2001 reflect huge technological advances that have taken place. Yet despite the changes, we have also been able to identify some interesting similarities between the sector composition of stock markets in 1900, 1950, and 2001.

In terms of stock market concentration, we have shown that concentration levels vary greatly across countries, and have fluctuated considerably over time. While recent increases in concentration have caused concern in countries such as the United Kingdom, we have seen that current UK concentration levels, while well above those in the United States, are actually below average relative to the other countries in our database. Furthermore, we have seen that on a longer-term view, markets have quite often become concentrated in the past, and that the United Kingdom's current concentration levels are still some way off their 101-year highs. More importantly, we have argued that the concern expressed in many countries about concentration levels is misplaced since it arises from a focus on domestic benchmarks at a time when investors should be thinking in terms of global portfolios.

Chapter 3 Measuring long-term returns

Good measures of long-run returns should accurately reflect the outcome of an implement-able investment strategy. The strategy should be one that could have been set up in advance, and followed in real life, and which is representative of the asset class and country in question. It is only too easy for researchers to fail to meet these criteria.

This chapter begins in section 3.1 by setting out the principles that need to be followed in constructing long-run return indexes. These provide a benchmark for assessing previous studies, and have been the guiding framework for this book. Given that our data goes back to the beginning of the last century and covers sixteen countries, we have not always been able to adhere to every principle, especially in the earliest years. Nevertheless, these standards have guided our choices, and we indicate where compromises have been necessary.

Next, in section 3.2 we take a closer look at equity index construction and at a bias that has afflicted some previous studies. When an index is compiled retrospectively, a crucial issue is how to avoid tilting its composition toward companies that, with hindsight, are known to have survived and/or to have been successful. In section 3.3, we review other issues that arise in index design, such as dividend reinvestment, index coverage, and index weighting.

In section 3.4 we consider how best to assemble a sample of international indexes. We show that reliance on data that is easy to acquire, such as indexes that start after the end of a war, tends to result in overstated performance. Both success bias and easy-data bias arise from a focus on assets that have survived or prospered over a particular period, and both can lead to overestimates of index returns and risk premia.

In section 3.5, we focus on the special problems that can arise when measuring inflation rates, as well as long-term returns on bonds, bills and currencies. We conclude in section 3.6 with a summary of the chapter.

3.1 Good indexes and bad

There are five guiding principles that underpin our measures of long-term performance. They are to avoid bias in index construction, to focus on total returns, to ensure the widest possible coverage within each market, to apply appropriate methods of weighting and aver-aging, and to maximize the extent to which comparisons can be made across national boundaries.

First, equity indexes should avoid bias. Good indexes follow an investment strategy that could be followed in real life. Apart from dealing costs, an investor should in principle have been able to replicate index performance. Indexes, especially when they are constructed retrospectively, must therefore be free of any look-ahead bias. They must be constructed solely from information that would have been available at the time of investment. Serious bias can arise if index constituents are tilted toward companies that subsequently survived or became large, or toward sectors that later became important. In Dimson and Marsh (1984), for example, we find that this type of bias can inflate long-term stock index returns by a couple of percentage points per year. More recently, Elton, Gruber, and Blake (1996) and Carhart, Carpenter, Lynch, and Musto (2001) demonstrate that survival also inflates mutual fund returns by around one percentage point per year. Agarwal and Naik (2001) and Brown, Goetzmann, and Park (2001) make similar observations in the context of hedge funds.

Second, long-term performance must be measured using total returns. Investment returns comprise income plus capital gains or losses. As Jorion and Goetzmann (1999) recognize, ignoring either leads to serious bias. Yet many early equity indexes measure just capital gains, ignoring dividends. Conversely, but equally seriously, early bond indexes often recorded just yields, ignoring price movements. As we will see in chapter 11, omitting dividends from stock returns imparts a huge cumulative downward bias. Similarly, estimating bond returns simply from promised yields would frequently have overstated achieved returns since bond investors have often been disappointed, and experienced capital losses.

Third, equity indexes need to be representative of their markets, and the ideal would be full coverage. In recent years our data meets or is close to this aspiration for several countries, including the United States and the United Kingdom. For earlier years, fully comprehensive indexes simply do not exist for most countries. Our guiding principle has been to choose the available series with the best coverage. For the United States, we use Wilson and Jones's (2002) recently constructed return series, on the grounds of its very broad coverage. For the United Kingdom, no satisfactory series existed for 1900–54, so we painstakingly constructed an index of the top one hundred companies from original archive data, to produce the new index series described in chapter 32. To ensure our data covers the longest period as comprehensively as possible, we also hand-collected stock price, dividend and market capitalization data for Ireland and South Africa, as described in chapters 24 and 28.

Fourth, long-term return indexes need to use appropriate methods of weighting and averaging. While investors hold stocks in very different proportions, in aggregate all securities are held in proportion to their market capitalizations. For an equity index to be fully representative, therefore, constituents also need to be weighted by each company's market capitalization. Virtually all our index series conform to this principle, although for earlier periods in a couple of countries we have been forced to settle for equally weighted indexes (for details, see Part Two). As pointed out by Brennan and Schwartz (1985), the method of averaging stock returns also matters. Index returns over a particular holding period should be calculated using arithmetic averaging since this measures the investors' actual change in wealth. While certain older indexes employ the inappropriate alternative of geometric averaging, all the series used in this book are based on arithmetic averaging.

Finally, we obviously wish to maximize the extent to which comparisons can be made across countries. In the past, researchers had emphasized the US experience, but it is dangerous to extrapolate from the remarkably successful US economy. That is why many students of the market have also examined the United Kingdom. But the United Kingdom shares much in common with the United States and may also be non-typical. Indexes for other countries have previously been compiled for limited periods, such as Germany and Japan in the decades following the Second World War. However, a focus on the post-war recovery gives a misleadingly favorable impression of the longer-term returns from these markets. How are we to compare post-war returns in these countries with the longer record for the United States or the United Kingdom? Our final guiding principle is, therefore, to assemble as broad a cross-section of countries as possible, all with index series conforming to the four requirements outlined above. To facilitate comparisons, we also, where appropriate, convert all indexes to a standard currency at the appropriate exchange rates.

3.2 Index design: a case study

Our first guiding principle above was the avoidance of bias, which involves following a potential real-life investment strategy. Unfortunately, some published back-histories fail to meet this standard, and are exposed to both survivorship and success bias. This is because the back-histories are too often based on shares that were index members at the date the index went live. Survival bias occurs because the back-history has an almost total absence of companies that had disappeared by the time the index was launched. Success bias can also occur when indexes are designed to cover the largest stocks in the market, such as the top thirty or largest one hundred. This arises because the back-history has an over-representation of companies that grew large enough to enter the index, and an under-representation of companies that underperformed over the interval up to index launch.

Until our research was completed, the most widely used index of long-run UK stock market performance had been the de Zoete index, described by de Zoete and Gorton (1955) and used by Merrett (1963) and many subsequent researchers. This index series, which continues to be used to the present day, contains a misleading back-history. By replicating the construction of earlier index numbers using our own database, we discovered that the de Zoete index used an inappropriate rights issue adjustment. Most of the inaccuracy, however, is from choosing index constituents with hindsight. There were three main problems: survivor bias in shares that comprise the index, survivor bias in sectors, and poor representation of the target segment of the market within the index. In addition, as mentioned above, the choice of start-date also had a significant impact.

The first source of bias was hindsight in share selection. The initial research had been completed in 1955, on a retrospective basis, and then updated. The index constituents were chosen to match, as closely as possible, the composition of the *Financial Times* (*FT*) Ordinary Share Index, which did not come into existence until 1935. The retrospective study incorporated companies that were important at the time the back-history was assembled. It therefore included companies that were destined to become large, but which had previously been much smaller. Consequently, the index had too little exposure to under-performing companies and too much exposure to companies that performed well.

A related problem was hindsight in sector selection. Index constituents were drawn from sectors that were important in the *FT* Ordinary Share Index. The index therefore covered only four out of nineteen stock exchange industry sectors. It incorporated companies from sectors that, at the beginning of the last century, represented about 18 percent of the value of the largest one hundred companies. As we explained in section 2.6, the big sector then was railways, and these companies were omitted, as were telegraphs, banks, utilities and insurance companies, and several other sectors.

A third source of bias arose from the non-representative nature of the de Zoete index. Coverage was restricted to only thirty shares, but these were not the largest ones, even allowing for the sector biases. Index constituents were a curious mixture of a few very large companies, coupled with some quite small stocks. On average, five shares constituted two-thirds of the index's value, and three shares accounted for half its value. In one year, more than 40 percent of the index was invested in just one stock, Imperial Tobacco, which in reality had less than a 7 percent market weighting that year. Although it has been used in a variety of academic studies, this index is too concentrated to represent the year-by-year performance of the UK market.

Finally, the start date for the de Zoete index was 1919. This captured post-war recovery, while omitting wartime losses and the generally lower real equity returns over the early years of the twentieth century.

As part of our research, we reconstructed the de Zoete index using the data we had collected to construct our own UK equity index series. In Table 3-1, we compare the 1919–54 de Zoete index data, which are still disseminated today by a variety of investment advisors, with our own figures for 1900–54. Contrary to popular belief, there is a marked difference between the returns achieved in the first and second halves of the period 1900–2000. Over the first half of the twentieth century, asset returns were much lower, with an especially low relative return from equities. In the period from 1955, which coincidentally marks the end-date of the de Zoete back-history and the start-date of the authoritative London Share Price Database, equity returns were much higher.

Table 3-1: Comparison of pre-1955 returns with previously published estimate

Index calculation (percent per year)	Nominal return	Real return
Original de Zoete estimate of index return 1919–54	**9.68**	**8.79**
Less Bias from incorrect rights-issue adjustment	-0.37	-0.36
Less Bias in choosing companies with hindsight	-1.57	-1.56
Less Bias from choosing sectors with hindsight	-0.21	-0.20
Less Bias from choosing only 30 shares	-0.22	-0.22
Less Impact from electing to start after the First World War	-1.12	-2.62
Authors' estimate of index return 1900–54	**6.19**	**3.83**

Table 3-2: Annualized real returns for UK asset categories, 1900–2000

Real return	1900–54	1955–2000	1900–2000
Equities	3.8	8.1	5.8
Bonds	0.6	2.1	1.3
Bills	0.3	1.9	1.0
Inflation	2.3	6.2	4.1

Since the research for our book was first publicized, Barclays Capital re-collected their thirty-share index back-history, starting in 1900 (see Bond and Adams, 2000). It is interesting to note that they broadly confirm that the original de Zoete equity index was biased by the retrospective procedure used for index construction, as well as by the choice of start date.

As our UK equity index history extends back to 1900, we can now reassess the long-term returns that investors have achieved from the UK market. The de Zoete estimates reported in Table 3-1 indicated erroneously that equities gave a high annualized (geometric mean) real return of 8.79 percent over the period 1919–54, even better than the 8.1 percent reported in Table 3-2 for the period since then.

The full record of returns for 1900–54, 1955–2000 and the entire 101-year period is given in Table 3-2. We noted the success bias in the compilation of the de Zoete index, and the correct real return for 1919–54 is in fact 6.4 percent. In addition, as Table 3-2 shows, with a start-date of 1900 rather than 1919, the annualized real return to 1954 was just 3.8 percent. Real equity returns in the United Kingdom were actually much lower over the period 1900–54 than they have been subsequently. If the US experience is not replicated even in the United Kingdom, there is a particular need to look at financial history around the world. This is our motivation for examining stock market performance in other national markets.

3.3 Dividends, coverage, and weightings

Stock market indexes have for some time been available for measuring the performance of the New York and London stock exchanges during the last century. With the exception of the CRSP index produced by the University of Chicago's Center for Research in Security Prices, these are largely indexes of capital appreciation. The Standard & Poors and FTSE-Actuaries All Share indexes, for example, provided dividend yields that were for most of their history an approximation to the income actually received on the underlying stocks (see Roden, 1983).

Despite the importance of reinvested dividends, highlighted as early as Fisher and Lorie's (1964) pioneering research, index producers were slow to introduce return indexes. In the United Kingdom, the FTSE indexes were not available in a total return version until as late as 1993. Fortunately, our US and UK data are not reliant on commercial sources, and are underpinned by scholarly research based on original stock-level price and dividend data. Similarly, the US and UK bond indexes are constructed from detailed bond-level price and coupon data. For other countries, we have, where possible, used similar series prepared in the same way by academic researchers. For the early years of the twentieth century, however, total equity returns for some countries have been estimated by combining capital gains with published dividend yields. While this provides good estimates when the yield relates to the constituents of the capital gains index, in a few cases (detailed in Part Two) we have had no choice but to use yields for indexes with non-matching constituents.

In terms of coverage, we have systematically favored broader over more narrow indexes. In the case of the United States, for example, we have chosen the Cowles (1938) Index, as amended by Wilson and Jones (2002) for the pre-CRSP period from 1900–26. This provides more comprehensive coverage that the widely used Schwert (1990) index series that is based on stocks that are constituents of the Dow Jones Indexes. For the United Kingdom, as noted above, we constructed our own set of indexes. For equities, we sought to cover as large a proportion of the UK market as possible, and after 1955, we have fully representative coverage of all London Stock Exchange equities. For bonds, too, we base our UK indexes on a portfolio of eligible government bonds, where this is possible. The decision process for other countries involves choosing the best equity index in each country, tracking this index forward from the beginning of the last century, and chain-linking to a superior index as and when a suitable series is initiated. The criterion for superiority is, naturally, based on the accuracy of price and dividend figures; but additionally, we favor broader and more comprehensive indexes as they become available.

Our index calculations are based on end-of-year index levels, unless there is no choice but to use a time-averaged or intra-year index value. On the occasions this has been necessary, it is highlighted in Part Two. As explained earlier, we also emphasize appropriate methods of index weighting and averaging. Within each market, our indexes are wherever possible weighted by market capitalization and based on arithmetic, rather than geometric, averaging. Nevertheless, it should be noted that, in the early years of the last century, value weighted indexes were comparatively rare, and for a number of countries the index series commence with an equally weighted design.

In more recent years, virtually all index compilers have weighted their indexes by the constituent companies' full market capitalizations, even though this may overstate the proportion of the equity which is available for trading, that is, the "free float." More recently, concerns have been raised over cross-holdings and hence double-counting, as well as possible market distortions that might arise from index funds seeking full market capitalization weightings in companies with low free floats. This is causing many index compilers to switch over to weighting by a measure of free equity, and our index series will in due course reflect these developments.

A related issue is the procedure used for averaging returns across markets. If we wish to take a global perspective on equity market performance, we cannot simply average index returns. Annual index returns are denominated in a variety of currencies, are subject to inflation rates that differ internationally, and experience timing differences. We therefore construct a common-currency twentieth century world equity index. Initially, we compute this in dollar terms, from the perspective of a US-based international investor, but the index can readily be converted into any common currency.

The process for constructing this global index is as follows. For each period, we take a market's local-currency return and convert it to a common currency, typically US dollars. This gives the return received by, say, a US citizen who bought foreign currency at the start of the period, invested it in the foreign market throughout the period, and at the end, liquidated his or her position and converted the proceeds back into US dollars. We assume that at the start of each period our investor bought a portfolio of sixteen such positions in each of the countries covered in this book, weighting each country by its size.

Ideally, these size-based weights would be each country's equity market capitalization. Reliable data on capitalizations are available from end-1967 from MSCI. Before end-1967, we use each country's GDP, converted to dollars. Since GDP weights change quite slowly, the world index is rebalanced just once a decade before 1968. This lowers the implicit rebalancing costs and reduces the impact of any bias arising from annual rebalancing using GDP weights. After 1968, the index is rebalanced annually, but since it is then capitalization weighted, the implied rebalancing costs are small. We also construct an index for the world excluding the United States (world ex-US) using the same principles.

The above procedure results in an index expressed in common currency, typically US dollars. To convert this to real terms, we then adjust by the appropriate inflation rate, in this case US inflation. This gives rise to a global index return denominated in real terms, from the perspective of a notional US investor. We also construct a world bond market index. This is also weighted by country size, to avoid giving, say, Belgium the same weight as the United States. Equity capitalization weights are inappropriate here, so the bond index is GDP-weighted throughout the century.

3.4 Easy-data bias in international indexes

Our final guideline in section 3.1 was to maximize the scope for making cross-country comparisons. One approach is to facilitate international comparisons by using a modern series of indexes with a common start date. For example, when Ibbotson Associates measure international risk premia, they select the MSCI Indexes, most of which start in 1970, as the basis for estimating non-US equity premia. This is a rather brief period when equities generally performed well, so it may show equities in an unduly favorable light. Siegel (1998) also follows this route, though he brings in longer horizons by adding Germany and Japan to his sample over the post-1925 period. Similarly, Jorion and Goetzmann (1999) identify four markets, apart from the United States and the United Kingdom, with pre-1970 dividend information, though none of these dividend series commence earlier than the 1920s.

The influential work of Ibbotson and others has inspired researchers in other countries to emulate their colleagues in the United States, and we have uncovered a growing number of single-country studies of long-term stock market returns. This provides a special opportunity to undertake a comparison across national stock markets. This book covers two North American markets, eleven European markets, two Asia-Pacific markets, and the South African market. We can therefore make comparisons between investment performance in different economic and political environments while focusing on whichever time period is of interest.

Our database covers the performance of stocks, bonds, bills, inflation, and currencies across sixteen countries. Drawing on supplementary data sources, we are able to cover the entire period from 1900 onward, for almost all the main asset categories, in all sixteen markets. In this way, we have over 1,600 observations of annual market returns for each of five asset categories. In addition, we have annual GDP and GDP per capita data for all sixteen countries from 1900 onward. Our data series are therefore remarkably comprehensive. As Table 3-3 makes clear, for seventy-nine out of eighty asset/market combinations, we are able to estimate total returns for the full 101-year period from 1900–2000.

An issue that has achieved prominence is the impact of market survival on estimated long-run returns. Markets can experience not only disappointing performance but also total loss of value through confiscation, hyperinflation, nationalization, and market failure. By measuring the performance of markets that survive over long intervals, we draw inferences that are conditioned on survival. Yet, as pointed out by Brown, Goetzmann, and Ross (1995) and Jorion and Goetzmann (1999), one cannot determine in advance which markets will survive and which will perish.

The danger arises if long-term return measures are based only on surviving markets, while other markets, which at some point failed to survive or experienced total losses—Russia, China, Poland, and so on—get omitted from the record. If markets that experienced total losses, that is, returns of minus 100 percent, are left out, this inevitably inflates our estimates

Table 3-3: Period covered for each asset category (✓ denotes 101 years of data)

Country	Equities	Bonds	Bills	Inflation	Currency
Australia	✓	✓	✓	✓	✓
Belgium	✓	✓	✓	✓	✓
Canada	✓	✓	✓	✓	✓
Denmark	✓	✓	✓	✓	✓
France	✓	✓	✓	✓	✓
Germany	✓	✓	✓	✓	✓
Ireland	✓	✓	✓	✓	✓
Italy	✓	✓	✓	✓	✓
Japan	✓	✓	✓	✓	✓
The Netherlands	✓	✓	✓	✓	✓
South Africa	✓	✓	✓	✓	✓
Spain	✓	✓	✓	✓	✓
Sweden	✓	✓	✓	✓	✓
Switzerland	From 1911	✓	✓	✓	✓
United Kingdom	✓	✓	✓	✓	✓
United States	✓	✓	✓	✓	✓

although since then, the new CPI-U covers "all urban consumers." Despite these drawbacks, we show in chapter 7 that our inflation indexes track long-term currency fluctuations quite closely, which provides some comfort when measuring inflation.

Treasury bills are a simple instrument, and it is straightforward to measure their returns. The only problem that arises here is that they have not always existed in every country that we cover. When this is the case, we adopt the closest equivalent we can find, namely, a measure of the short-term interest rate, with minimal credit risk.

For government bond indexes, coverage and weighting matter less than for equities, but issues such as maturity, coupon, callability and tax assume special importance. Once a bond index's target maturity has been chosen, the efficiency of the markets is such that the prices of all bonds with that maturity will tend to move together, apart from issues relating to coupon, callability and tax. Bond indexes are thus usually equally weighted, with constituents chosen to fall within the desired maturity range. In some countries, taxation issues matter, and, where relevant, these are outlined in the country chapters and references in Part Two.

3.6 Summary

In this chapter, we have set out the criteria that equity and bond indexes need to meet. The five guiding principles are avoiding bias, focusing on total returns, obtaining good coverage, applying correct methods of weighting and averaging, and maximizing the scope for international comparisons. Good measures of long-run returns should accurately reflect the outcome of an investment strategy that could have been set up in advance, and followed in real life, and which is representative of the asset class and country in question.

Not all previous studies have adhered to these principles. In particular, before distribution by ABN AMRO of this research, the previously best-known study of the UK market cited the real return on UK shares from 1919–54 as 8.8 percent. In fact, the real return on UK equities over 1900–54 was just 3.8 percent. The discrepancy arose because the index was unrepresentative, subject to survivorship and success bias, and backdated only to the end of the First World War. The real return on equities over the first fifty-five years of the last century was much less than many had previously assumed. This suggests that we should now revise downward our estimates of the equity risk premium (see chapter 13).

Finally, we highlight the prevalence and dangers of easy data bias. This refers to the tendency of researchers to use data that is easy to obtain, excludes difficult periods such as wars and their aftermath, and typically relates to later periods. We identify sixteen standard sources, one for each country, and show that the equity returns over the periods they cover are higher than the returns over the 101-year period from 1900–2000 by an average of three percentage points per year. Easy data bias has undoubtedly led investors to believe that equity returns over this period were higher than was really the case.

Chapter 4 International capital market history

In this chapter we provide an overview of capital market history over the 101 years from 1900 to 2000 for the sixteen countries covered by our study. We examine the performance of the main asset classes—equities, bonds, and bills—in both real and nominal terms, and draw comparisons across countries.

Sections 4.1 to 4.4 deal with the investment performance achieved by our sixteen countries, while sections 4.5 to 4.7 focus on the accompanying risks. Given the importance and dominance of the US capital markets, we begin in section 4.1 by examining the investment returns on US stocks, bonds, and bills. The US record may, however, paint a misleadingly rosy picture of twentieth century investment since the United States has been an especially successful economy. Section 4.2 therefore looks at the corresponding data for the United Kingdom, a nation that was in comparative decline over much of the century, but which, back in 1900, had the world's largest equity and bond markets. We find that UK returns were below those in the United States, but, perhaps surprisingly, by only a small margin. In section 4.3, we broaden our comparisons to embrace all sixteen countries, comparing nominal and real equity returns. Section 4.4 then compares equity returns around the world with the corresponding returns from bonds and bills.

Investment is as much about risk as return, so in sections 4.5 to 4.7 we turn our attention to risk. In section 4.5, we examine the distribution of annual real asset returns for the United States from 1900–2000, and document the risk of US equities, bonds, and bills. Our figures for equity risk are based exclusively on market indexes that represent highly diversified portfolios. Section 4.6 shows that individual stocks tend to be much riskier than this, and demonstrates the importance and power of diversification for equity investors. Finally, in section 4.7 we present risk comparisons both across asset classes and countries. We show that over the long haul, risk and return have gone hand-in-hand.

In the chapters that follow, we then examine each asset class in greater detail—bills and inflation in chapter 5, bonds in chapter 6, currencies and common-currency asset returns in chapter 7, international investment in chapter 8, stock returns in chapters 9–11, and the equity risk premium in chapters 12 and 13.

4.1 The US record

The United States is today's financial superpower. Its equity and bond markets are the largest and most important in the world, and its markets account for nearly half the world's total market capitalization. The US markets are also the best documented and most heavily researched, thanks to the early availability of comprehensive, high quality financial data. The most important contribution here was the founding in the early 1960s of the Center for Research in Security Prices (CRSP) at the University of Chicago's Graduate School of Business.

It seems natural, therefore, to begin our review of international capital market history by looking at the US record. Figure 4-1 shows the cumulative performance of US stocks, bonds,

Figure 4-1: Cumulative return on US asset classes in nominal terms, 1900–2000

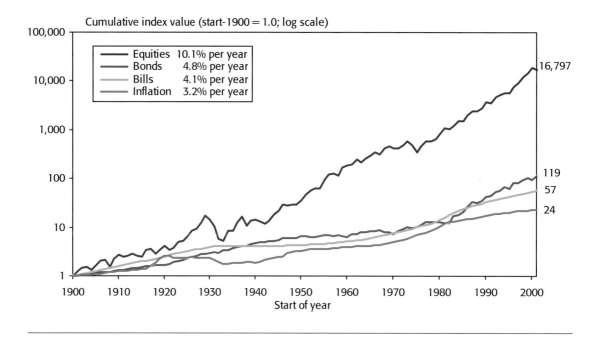

bills, and consumer prices (i.e., inflation) over the 101-year period from 1900 to 2000. It shows the wealth that would have accumulated at each year-end from 1900 through to 2000 from an initial investment of $1 in stocks, bonds, or bills at the end of 1899. It assumes that dividends and interest were reinvested, and that there were no taxes or transactions costs. Figure 4-1 also shows inflation, that is, the increase in consumer prices over time.

For stocks, the investment strategy represented in Figure 4-1 is one of buying and holding the US equity market. Today, this would be most cheaply accomplished by investing in an index tracker fund. Back in 1900, some 70 years before tracker funds were launched, it would have meant investing in all NYSE securities in proportion to their market capitalizations. From 1900–25, we use the capitalization weighted Cowles Index of all NYSE stocks (as modified by Wilson and Jones, 2002); from 1926–61, we employ the capitalization weighted CRSP Index of all NYSE stocks; from 1962–70, we use the extended CRSP Index, which over this period also incorporates Amex stocks; and from 1971 on, the underlying investment is in the comprehensive Wilshire 5000 Index, which, despite its name, now contains over 7,000 US stocks, including, of course, Nasdaq stocks (for further details, see chapter 33).

Figure 4-1 shows that US equities performed best, with an initial investment of $1 growing to a nominal value of $16,797 by the end of 2000. Long bonds and treasury bills gave lower returns, although they beat inflation. Their respective index levels at the end of 2000 are $119 and $57, with the inflation index ending at $24. These terminal wealth levels correspond to annualized returns over the 101-year period of 10.1 percent on equities, 4.8 percent on bonds, and 4.1 percent on bills, while inflation ran at 3.2 percent per year (see the legend for Figure 4-1).

Over this period, consumer prices rose 24-fold, making comparisons in nominal terms hard to interpret. In Figure 4-2, we therefore show the corresponding real (i.e., inflation-adjusted) returns. Over the 101 years, an initial investment in equities of $1 would, with dividends reinvested, have grown in purchasing power to 711 times as much as the initial investment. The equivalent multiples for bonds and bills are a growth in real terms to 5.0 and 2.4 times the initial investment, respectively. These terminal wealth figures correspond to annualized real returns of 6.7 percent on equities, 1.6 percent on bonds, and 0.9 percent on bills.

Figure 4-2 shows that US equities totally dominated bonds and bills. There were setbacks of course, most notably during the First World War; the Wall Street Crash of 1929 and its aftermath, including the Great Depression; and the OPEC oil shock of the 1970s. Each shock was severe at the time. At the depths of the Wall Street Crash, the Dow Jones Industrial Index had fallen by 89 percent. Many investors were ruined, especially those who had bought stocks with borrowed money. The crash lived on in the memories of investors—and indeed, those who subsequently chose to shun equities—for at least a generation. Yet in Figure 4-2, it features as little more than a short-term setback. The October 1987 crash, and the dramatic bursting of the technology bubble in 2000, hardly even register on this long-run graph. The setback in 2000, however, will look more severe when combined with the poor returns in 2001, including the sharp downturn in the wake of the tragic events of September 11.

We should be cautious about generalizing from the United States which, over the twentieth century, rapidly emerged as the world's foremost political, military, and economic power. For a more balanced view, we also need to look at investment returns in other countries.

Figure 4-2: Cumulative returns on US asset classes in real terms, 1900–2000

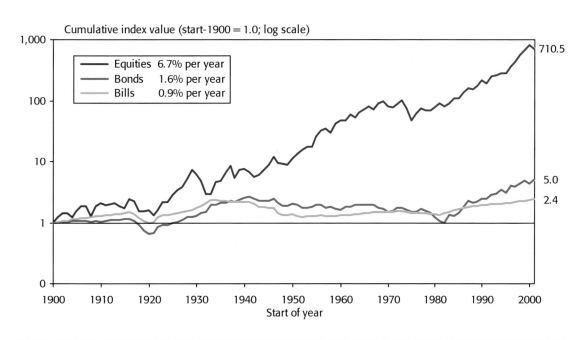

4.2 The UK record

To help set the US record in perspective, the United Kingdom is an obvious comparator. UK markets are also well documented, and with the new data and indexes assembled for this book, we now have high quality data back to 1900 (see chapter 32). Furthermore, in 1900, London was the world's leading financial center. Its equity and bond markets were the world's largest, and its equity market capitalization exceeded that of the NYSE by 50 percent.

Yet for much of the twentieth century, the United Kingdom was in comparative decline. Despite "winning," the United Kingdom was weakened financially by the world wars. De-colonization led to the dissolution of the British Empire. Yet the United Kingdom was slow to come to terms with its diminished role, and continued to overstretch itself, for example, in defense. It also suffered serious economic, labor, productivity, and investment problems, which were not fully addressed until the late 1970s. These were deeply rooted in its past as a mature industrialized nation, and the United Kingdom's early start in industrialization had become an unfortunate legacy. As Eatwell (1982) argued,

> The weakness of the British economy … is the cumulative product … of the entire history of Britain since the end of the nineteenth century, when it first became evident that Britain was unable, or unwilling, to adapt to a competitive world in which her pre-eminence could no longer be taken for granted.

Unlike the United States, the British economy cannot therefore readily be classified as an obvious success story. Despite this, Figure 4-3, which shows the cumulative performance of UK stocks, bonds, bills, and inflation from 1900 to 2000, reveals that the UK investment

Figure 4-3: Cumulative returns on UK asset classes in nominal terms, 1900–2000

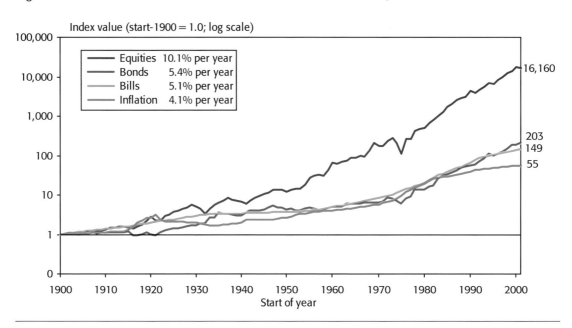

record was not greatly different from that of the United States. Equities performed best, with an initial investment of £1 growing to £16,160 in nominal terms by the end of December 2000. Long bonds and treasury bills gave lower returns, although they beat inflation. Their respective index levels at the end of 2000 are £203 and £149, with the inflation index ending at £55. The nominal returns of each asset category are recorded in the legend for Figure 4-3. UK equities, for example, gave an annualized nominal return of 10.1 percent, which to one decimal place is identical to the annualized nominal return for US equities. However, the United Kingdom's higher inflation rate of 4.1 percent per year compared with a US rate of 3.2 percent means that US equities outperformed in real terms.

Given that UK prices rose 55-fold over this period, it is more helpful to make comparisons in real terms. Figure 4-4 shows the real returns on UK equities, bonds, and bills. Over the 101 years, an initial investment of £1, with dividends reinvested, would have grown in purchasing power to 291 times as much as the initial investment. The corresponding multiples for bonds and bills are a growth in real terms to 3.7 and 2.7 times the initial investment, respectively. As the legend for Figure 4-4 shows, these terminal wealth figures correspond to annualized real returns of 5.8 percent on equities, 1.3 percent on bonds, and 1.0 percent on bills. These equity and bond returns lie below the equivalent US figures of 6.7 and 1.6 percent, but perhaps surprisingly, given the discussion above, by only a small margin.

Figure 4-4 shows that although the real return on UK equities was negative over the first twenty years of the twentieth century, the story thereafter was one of steady growth, broken by periodic setbacks. These occurred at the start of the two world wars and in the early

Figure 4-4: Cumulative returns on UK asset classes in real terms, 1900–2000

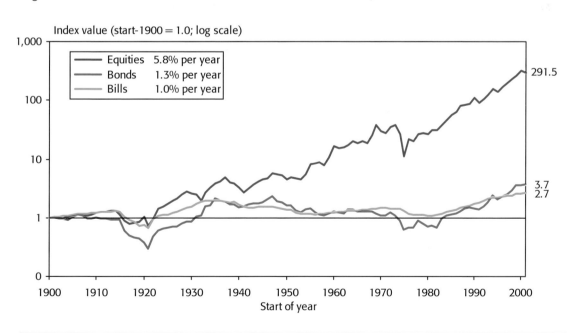

1930s, but unlike the United States, the largest decline in the United Kingdom was not during the 1930s, but instead in 1973–74, the period of the first OPEC oil squeeze following the 1973 October War in the Middle East. Oil prices jumped from around $3 per barrel before the war to $11.65. This drove the world economy into deep recession. In the United Kingdom, the impact was aggravated by poor economic management and monetary policy, which led to inflation spiralling, eventually peaking at 25 percent in 1975. It also coincided with serious labor unrest, political uncertainty, and a secondary banking crisis. Investors who kept faith with equities were eventually vindicated, however, and UK equities rose by 97 percent in real terms in 1975. Since the bottom of this savage UK bear market at the end of 1974, the dollar gains on UK equities have been greater than for any other country in our study.

4.3   Stock market returns around the world

In Figure 4-5 we show how US and UK equity market performance over the 101 years from 1900–2000 compares with the other fourteen countries in this study. This figure shows the annualized equity return for each of the sixteen countries in both nominal and real terms.

Clearly, to make comparisons across markets, it is more meaningful to focus on real (i.e., inflation adjusted) returns. The countries in Figure 4-5 have therefore been ranked by their annualized real returns, with the worst performers on the left and the best on the right. Figure 4-5 shows that the six worst performers in terms of real returns on the left-hand side experienced some of the highest nominal returns across all sixteen countries. (The nominal return for Germany excludes the hyperinflationary years 1922–23; without this adjustment, it

Figure 4-5: Nominal and real equity returns around the world, 1900–2000

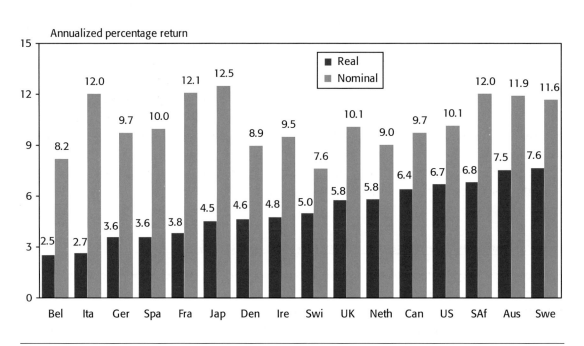

would have been the highest for all countries.) High inflation rates may increase nominal returns but have on average been associated with lower real returns. Equities in the countries on the left-hand side of the chart were thus unable to avoid the negative impact of very high inflation rates.

When we focus on the more economically meaningful real return figures, there is at first sight a degree of similarity in the annualized (geometric mean) real returns of different countries, which can be seen in Figure 4-5. Despite great variation in their endowments, economic development, and wartime experiences, all sixteen countries achieved annualized real returns within three percentage points of the average of 5.1 percent.

Note, however, that because of the power of compound interest, small return deviations represent large differences in terminal wealth; the inter-country differences in annualized returns are therefore important. For example, an investment at start-1900 of one unit of local currency in the Belgian equity market (the worst performing country) would have grown, with dividends reinvested, to a terminal wealth of just 12.3 in real terms. The corresponding investment in Sweden, the best performing country, would have grown to a value of just under 1,700.

Thus, despite the fact that we have confined our study to data series that persist from 1900 to the current time, and therefore omit stock market fatalities, there is noticeable variation across countries in stock market performance. Some national markets have given strikingly good real equity returns, while others have turned in more modest results. It is the differences between each country's capital market experience that makes it worthwhile to compare the US and UK markets with others from around the world.

On the right-hand side of Figure 4-5, we show the countries that achieved the highest real returns over the period 1900–2000. The United States was fourth highest, and the United Kingdom's performance was above the (unweighted) international average. Thereafter, real returns decline as one shifts from the right-hand to the left-hand side of Figure 4-5. Over the 101 years as a whole, it was thus resource rich countries such as Sweden, Australia, South Africa, the United States, and Canada that achieved the best equity market performances. The Netherlands and the United Kingdom also gave good performance, while other countries fared less well. Generally speaking, the worst performing equity markets were associated with countries which either lost major wars, or were most ravaged by international or civil wars. These same countries also experienced periods of high or hyperinflation, typically associated with wars and their aftermath.

4.4 Equities compared with bonds and bills

Figure 4-6 portrays the long-term performance, in real terms, of the three asset categories—equities, bonds, and bills for the United States. Each bar in the diagram displays the average inflation-adjusted return from holding an asset category over the entire 101-year period, and over the most recent seventy five, fifty, and twenty five years. US Equities have outperformed government bonds and bills in all four periods considered.

Figure 4-6: Annualized US real returns over sub-periods to start of 2001

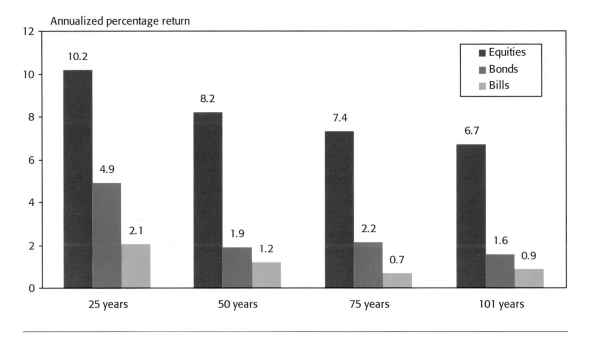

Table 4-1, which shows the real returns on equities, bonds, and bills in different countries, reveals that the US experience of equities outperforming bonds and bills has been mirrored in all sixteen countries. This table shows the annualized real returns over our full 101-year period from an investment in local currency. It is interesting to note that every country

Table 4-1: Annualized real returns on major asset categories around the world, 1900–2000

Country	Equities	Bonds	Bills
Australia	7.5	1.1	0.4
Belgium	2.5	-0.4	-0.3
Canada	6.4	1.8	1.7
Denmark	4.6	2.5	2.8
France	3.8	-1.0	-3.3
Germany*	3.6	-2.2	-0.6
Ireland	4.8	1.5	1.3
Italy	2.7	-2.2	-4.1
Japan	4.5	-1.6	-2.0
The Netherlands	5.8	1.1	0.7
South Africa	6.8	1.4	0.8
Spain	3.6	1.2	0.4
Sweden	7.6	2.4	2.0
Switzerland†	5.0	2.8	1.1
United Kingdom	5.8	1.3	1.0
United States	6.7	1.6	0.9

*Bond and bill figures for Germany exclude the years 1922–23; †Swiss equities from 1911.

achieved equity performance that was better than that of bonds. Over the 101 years as a whole, there were only two bond markets and just one bill market that provided a better return than our *worst* performing equity market.

As can be seen from Table 4-1, US and UK capital market history from 1900–2000 has been relatively benign for investors. Nevertheless, since few investors take a 101-year view on performance, we also need to look at risk, even in these two relatively successful markets. We turn to the question of investment risk in section 4.5. Interestingly, countries that experienced major dislocations still achieved equity market returns that were ahead of inflation. Bond and bill returns in these countries were often markedly negative, however, as these periods of economic turmoil had a more dramatic impact on fixed income than on equity investors.

Figure 4-7 shows the real equity and bond return data from Table 4-1 in bar chart form, in ascending order of equity market performance from left to right. In the bond markets, the five worst performing countries (shown by the blue bars with negative returns) were among those with the lowest equity returns (on the left-hand side of the chart). These are the countries that were hit hard by hyperinflation, which we discuss further in chapter 5. Interestingly, inflation appears to have had a negative impact on both stock and bond markets. This means that when we later consider the equity risk premium relative to bonds (see section 12.3), we may find the risk premium less affected by inflation than the underlying equity and bond returns.

Figure 4-7: Real returns on equities versus bonds internationally, 1900–2000

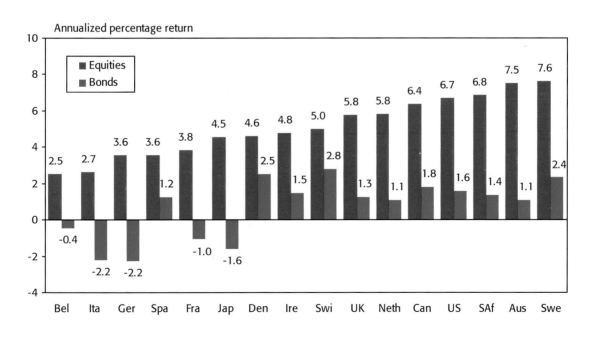

4.5   Investment risk and the distribution of annual returns

So far, we have compared returns across asset classes and countries without taking account of risk. Since investment is as much about risk as return, we now turn to the question of risk. By risk, most investors mean downside risk, that is, the prospect of loss, or of failing to meet some target return. The more variable is an asset's return, the riskier is the asset. In practice, therefore, investment risk is almost always measured by volatility, that is, the standard deviation of returns.

Figure 4-8 provides a visual representation of risk and volatility by displaying the annual real returns on US equities (plotted as bars) and on bonds (the area plot) from 1900–2000. The year-to-year performance of equities was clearly more volatile, and hence riskier, than that of bonds. Equity returns had a volatility (standard deviation) of a little over 20 percent. That is, in roughly one year out of six, equities tend to underperform expectations by 20 percent or more, and in roughly one year out of six, they tend to exceed expectations by 20 percent or more. Long bonds had a volatility of 10 percent. By comparison, the corresponding figure for short-term bills was less than 5 percent.

The real returns shown as a time series in Figure 4-8 can also be regrouped and presented as a histogram. Figure 4-9 shows the distribution of annual real returns on US equities over the period 1900–2000. The distribution is roughly bell-shaped, resembling a normal distribution, with an arithmetic mean (i.e., the average of the 101 one-year returns) of 8.7 percent. As noted above, the standard deviation, which measures the dispersion of the returns around

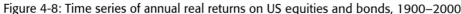

Figure 4-8: Time series of annual real returns on US equities and bonds, 1900–2000

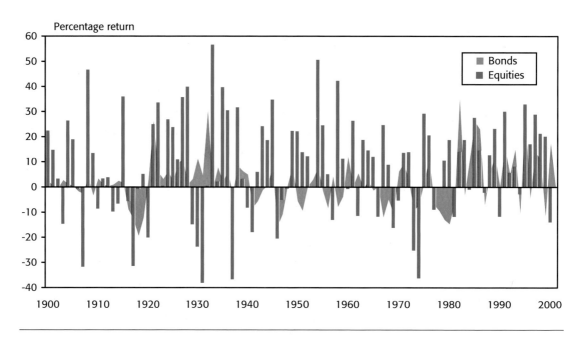

Figure 4-9: Histogram of annual US real equity returns, 1900–2000

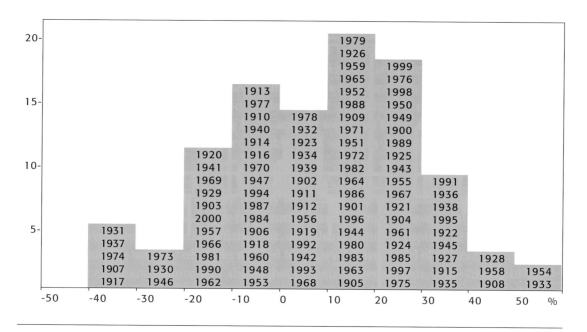

the mean, is 20.2 percent. US equities were clearly far from risk free, and in over a third of the years, real returns were negative. The leftmost column of Figure 4-9 shows that the worst year was 1931, with a real return of -38 percent, followed in sequence by 1937, 1974, 1907, and 1917. The best year was 1933, with a real return of 57 percent, closely followed by 1954, and then 1908 and so on. The distributions of returns for the other countries covered in this study are similar, but for most of them, the extremes are more marked. For example, the nominal equity return in Germany has been as high as 305 billion percent (in 1923) and as low as -87 percent (in 1948).

Figure 4-10 repeats the time series pattern of annual equity returns shown in Figure 4-8, but also displays rolling ten-year annualized real returns as well as the 101-year arithmetic mean real return of 8.7 percent, which is shown by the horizontal line. The rolling ten-year returns are naturally smoother, and there have been relatively few periods when they have fallen below zero. A real return of zero, however, is not the appropriate benchmark since US investors have earned positive real returns from much lower risk investments in bills and bonds. The equity risk premium relative to bills and bonds forms the topic of chapter 12.

The standard deviation of real returns on US equities was 20.2 percent. If returns were normally distributed, we would expect that, one year in six, they would fall outside the range 8.7 ± 20.2 percent. Thus over 101 years, we would expect to find roughly sixteen years when returns fell below -11.5 percent and sixteen when they exceeded 28.9 percent. For the US market, the figures were eighteen years and sixteen years, consistent with a normal distribution. The United States was unusual, however, compared with other countries. Most had fewer than sixteen years falling in the left- and right-hand tails, but the tails contained

Table 4-2: Means and standard deviations of real returns on asset classes around the world

Country	Equities (%)			Bonds (%)			Bills (%)		
	Arithmetic mean	Standard error	Standard deviation	Arithmetic mean	Standard error	Standard deviation	Arithmetic mean	Standard error	Standard deviation
Australia	9.0	1.8	17.7	1.9	1.3	13.0	0.6	0.6	5.6
Belgium	4.8	2.3	22.8	0.3	1.2	12.1	0.0	0.8	8.2
Canada	7.7	1.7	16.8	2.4	1.1	10.6	1.8	0.5	5.1
Denmark	6.2	2.0	20.1	3.3	1.2	12.5	3.0	0.6	6.4
France	6.3	2.3	23.1	0.1	1.4	14.4	-2.6	1.1	11.4
Germany*	8.8	3.2	32.3	0.3	1.6	15.9	0.1	1.1	10.6
Ireland	7.0	2.2	22.2	2.4	1.3	13.3	1.4	0.6	6.0
Italy	6.8	2.9	29.4	-0.8	1.4	14.4	-2.9	1.2	12.0
Japan	9.3	3.0	30.3	1.3	2.1	20.9	-0.3	1.4	14.5
The Netherlands	7.7	2.1	21.0	1.5	0.9	9.4	0.8	0.5	5.2
South Africa	9.1	2.3	22.8	1.9	1.1	10.6	1.0	0.6	6.4
Spain	5.8	2.2	22.0	1.9	1.2	12.0	0.6	0.6	6.1
Sweden	9.9	2.3	22.8	3.1	1.3	12.7	2.2	0.7	6.8
Switzerland†	6.9	2.1	20.4	3.1	0.8	8.0	1.2	0.6	6.2
United Kingdom	7.6	2.0	20.0	2.3	1.4	14.5	1.2	0.7	6.6
United States	8.7	2.0	20.2	2.1	1.0	10.0	1.0	0.5	4.7

*Bond and bill statistics for Germany exclude the years 1922–23.　†Swiss equities are from 1911

at 20.1 percent. The highest volatility markets were Germany, Japan, Italy, and France, which were the countries most seriously affected by the depredations of war and inflation. Table 4-3 also shows that, as one would expect, the countries with the highest standard deviations experienced the greatest range of returns, that is, the lowest minima and the highest maxima. Inevitably, these were also the countries where the annualized rate of return over the 101 years (the geometric mean) differed most from the average annual return (the arithmetic

Table 4-3: Real (inflation-adjusted) equity returns around the world, 1900–2000

Country	Geometric mean %	Arithmetic mean %	Standard error %	Standard deviation %	Minimum return %	Minimum year	Maximum return %	Maximum year
Australia	7.5	9.0	1.8	17.7	-34.2	1974	53.5	1983
Belgium	2.5	4.8	2.3	22.8	-40.9	1947	100.5	1940
Canada	6.4	7.7	1.7	16.8	-32.0	1974	55.2	1933
Denmark	4.6	6.2	2.0	20.1	-28.4	1974	106.1	1983
France	3.8	6.3	2.3	23.1	-37.5	1947	66.1	1954
Germany	3.6	8.8	3.2	32.3	-89.6	1948	155.9	1949
Ireland	4.8	7.0	2.2	22.2	-54.3	1974	69.9	1977
Italy	2.7	6.8	2.9	29.4	-72.9	1945	120.7	1946
Japan	4.5	9.3	3.0	30.3	-84.0	1946	119.6	1952
The Netherlands	5.8	7.7	2.1	21.0	-34.9	1941	101.6	1940
South Africa	6.8	9.1	2.3	22.8	-52.2	1920	102.9	1933
Spain	3.6	5.8	2.2	22.0	-43.3	1977	98.9	1986
Sweden	7.6	9.9	2.3	22.8	-43.0	1918	89.5	1905
Switzerland†	5.0	6.9	2.1	20.4	-37.8	1974	56.2	1985
United Kingdom	5.8	7.6	2.0	20.0	-57.1	1974	96.7	1975
United States	6.7	8.7	2.0	20.2	-38.0	1931	56.8	1933

†Swiss equities are from 1911

Figure 4-14: Standard deviations of real equity and bond returns around the world, 1900–2000

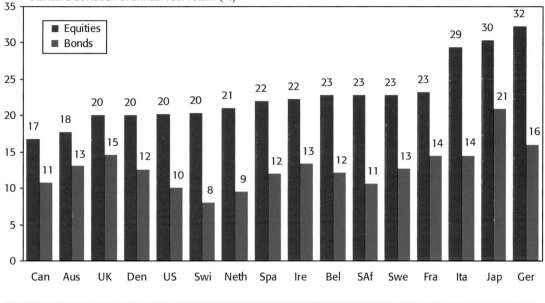

mean). We return to these differences between arithmetic and geometric means in chapter 13. Finally, Figure 4-14 highlights (in red) the comparative historical volatilities of equity markets, with countries ranked from lowest volatility on the left, to highest on the right, with accompanying bond market volatilities (in blue).

4.8 Summary

This chapter has provided an overview of the international evidence on the investment performance of the major asset classes—stocks, bonds and bills—over the 101 years from 1900–2000. The results we have presented provide a foretaste of our more detailed discussion of interest rates, inflation, and bill returns in chapter 5, bond performance in chapter 6, currencies in chapter 7, international investment in chapter 8, stock returns in chapters 9–11, and the equity risk premium in chapters 12 and 13.

This chapter has overviewed risk as well as return. We find a clear ranking of asset risks in all sixteen countries. Stocks are the most volatile investment, followed by bonds and then bills, with the latter most closely approximating a risk free asset. For the United States, which ranked toward the lower end of the country risk spectrum, we find that the standard deviation of real returns on stocks was 20.2 percent, compared with 10.0 percent for bonds and 4.7 percent for bills. This equity risk figure is for the overall US market, and it is far lower than the risk of individual stocks, thanks to the power of diversification. Even for well-diversified portfolios, however, we have seen that the high volatility of equities means that there can be, and indeed have been, periods of large losses.

We have also seen that, over the long run, the risk of investing in stocks has been rewarded. US equities provided a real (inflation adjusted) return of 6.7 percent versus 1.6 percent on bonds and 0.9 percent on bills. We have cautioned against generalizing too readily from the US experience since the US economy has been such an obvious growth and success story over the twentieth century. But while we find that US stocks have performed well, the United States has not been the best performing equity market, nor are its returns especially out of line with the world averages. The real return on equities was positive in all sixteen countries, typically at a level of 4–6 percent compounded over the period 1900–2000.

Bonds performed much worse than equities. In the majority of countries, however, they gave a positive real return, although several markets recorded negative real returns for bonds and bills. The five countries with the worst performing bond markets were also among those with the lowest equity returns. Mostly, this poor performance dates back to the first half of the twentieth century, and these were the countries that either lost major wars, or were most ravaged by war and civil strife. These same countries also experienced periods of high or hyperinflation, typically associated with wars and their aftermath. In spite of this, over the 101 years as a whole, there were only two bond markets and just one bill market that provided a better real return than the *worst* performing equity market.

In summary, we have found that, over the long haul, stocks—the riskiest asset class—have beaten bonds in every single country. At the same time, bonds, which are intermediate in risk between equities and bills, have beaten bills almost everywhere, the main exception being Germany. Our findings thus provide strong support for one of the lasting laws of finance—the law of risk and return.

Chapter 5 Inflation, interest rates, and bill returns

In this chapter, we take a closer look at the returns on two of our five asset classes, consumer goods and treasury bills. The return on—or change in the prices of—consumer goods provides a measure of inflation, while the return on treasury bills is the short-term interest rate. Inflation and interest rates are closely linked, and both are key investment benchmarks.

Investors care not just about the number of dollars they earn from an investment, but also what those dollars will buy. Inflation indexes provide the benchmark needed to compare purchasing power over time. If inflation were low, this would not matter. But from 1900–2000, even in the world's *lowest* inflation country, consumer prices rose by 2.2 percent per year. Inflation was a major force in the last century, and investment outcomes need to be adjusted by the rate of inflation to convert them to real, purchasing power adjusted, returns.

This chapter therefore begins in section 5.1 with an overview of US inflation over the twentieth century, where we compare the US experience with that of the United Kingdom. Section 5.2 extends this comparison worldwide, where we find a wide range of inflationary experiences, ranging from low inflation countries, such as Switzerland, to a number of countries that experienced episodes of very high, and even hyper-, inflation.

The second asset class covered in this chapter is short-term government treasury bills—or their closest equivalent. Bill returns are both interesting in their own right, and also because, like inflation, they serve as an investment benchmark. As an asset class, bill returns tell us the investment return on "cash." And since they are generally regarded as near risk free, they provide the benchmark for the risk free interest rate. They thus play a key role in calculating the risk premium, as discussed in chapter 12.

In examining bill returns, we look first in section 5.3 at the US experience from 1900–2000, comparing this with that of the United Kingdom. In particular, we focus on the inflation-adjusted bill rate, or real rate of interest. In section 5.4, we then compare twentieth century real interest rates across all sixteen countries in our long-run returns database. These comparisons reveal that there have been circumstances when even treasury bills have proved far from risk free. Periods when inflation is exceptionally and unexpectedly high can decimate the value of both bills and, as we will see in chapter 6, bonds.

5.1 Inflation in the United States and the United Kingdom

US inflation averaged 3.2 percent per year over the period from 1900–2000. The line plot in Figure 5-1 gives a decade-by-decade snapshot of price levels. It shows that $1 in 1900 had the same purchasing power as $24 today. It also shows that prices rose far more slowly in the first seventy years (2.4 percent) than in the subsequent period since 1970 (5.1 percent).

The bars in Figure 5-1 show the decline in purchasing power. A dollar bill put under the mattress 101 years ago would today have only 4.2 percent of its 1900 purchasing power, that is, four cents in 1900 had the same purchasing power as $1 in 2000.

Figure 5-1: US inflation from 1900–2000

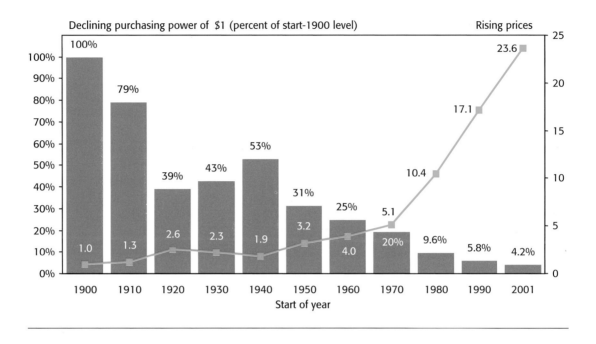

Figure 5-1 shows that there were also periods of deflation, with purchasing power *rising* during the 1920s. By the end of 1920, the price level had risen to 2.64 from its end-1899 level of 1.0. During the subsequent deflation, the price level fell to 1.78 in 1933, a third lower than in 1920. It then took until 1947 for prices to rise back to their end-1920 level.

The deflation in the 1920s and depression years of the early 1930s is very evident in Figure 5-2. The green line, which is plotted against the scale on the left-hand axis, traces out the year-by-year US inflation rates. Clearly, US inflation has varied greatly over time. The average inflation rate was lower in the first half of the twentieth century at 2.4 percent per year, than during the second, when it ran at nearly 4.0 percent per year. However, during the first fifty years, it was also more volatile since this period encompassed high inflation around the two world wars, peaking at 20.4 percent in 1918 and 18.2 percent in 1946, along with the severe deflationary period between the wars. In the subsequent fifty-one years, inflation was generally higher and more pervasive, peaking at 13 percent in 1979, and then mostly trending downward, although not without setbacks, ending the year 2000 at 3.4 percent.

The yellow line in Figure 5-2 shows the corresponding year-by-year inflation rates for the United Kingdom. Until the mid-1960s, UK inflation followed a remarkably similar pattern to the United States. There were some wartime differences reflecting the later entry of the United States into the two world wars, and the deflationary period was more severe in the United Kingdom than the United States, with prices almost halving between end-1920 and 1933, and not regaining their 1920 level until 1952. But the similarities between the countries dominate the differences until the mid-1960s. Thereafter, UK inflation rates were generally

Figure 5-2: US and UK annual inflation rates and cumulative inflation, 1900–2000

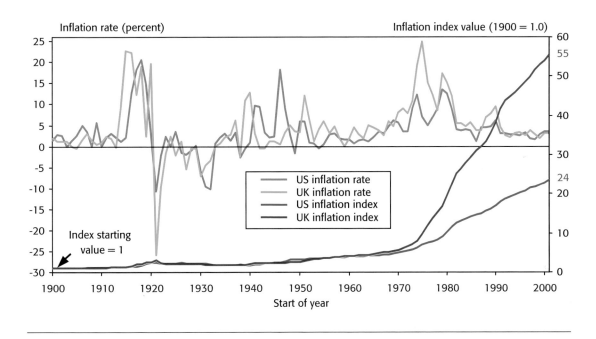

much higher than in the United States, peaking at 25 percent in 1975. The cumulative impact of these higher rates can be seen by comparing the two inflation indexes, which are plotted against the right-hand axis in Figure 5-2. The red line for the United Kingdom and the blue line for the United States are virtually coincident until the mid-1960s. From that point onward, the UK index rises to a value of fifty-five by end-2000, compared with twenty-four for the United States. From 1900–2000, UK consumer prices thus rose 55-fold, a factor of 2.3 times more than in the United States, with the difference almost entirely attributable to the last thirty-five years. Over the full 101-year period, the average annualized UK inflation rate was 4.1 percent per year, versus 3.2 percent for the United States.

5.2 Inflation around the world

While inflation was fairly similar in the United States and the United Kingdom, a number of other countries had quite different experiences. Table 5-1 provides international inflation rate comparisons across all sixteen countries covered in this book, showing the mean inflation rates from 1900–2000. Clearly, there were large differences between countries. At the same time, the standard deviations for each country show that there was also considerable variation in inflation rates over time. Taking the full 101-year period as a whole, there have been four high inflation rate countries, France, Germany, Italy, and Japan; two runner-ups, Belgium and Spain; and one low inflation country, Switzerland. The other countries fall in between, with inflation rates in the region of 3–4 percent per year. Note that the true 101-year means and standard deviations for inflation in Germany are much higher than shown in Table 5-1 since the statistics in the table omit the hyper-inflationary years of 1922–23.

Table 5-1: Inflation rates around the world from 1900–2000

Country	Geometric mean %	Arithmetic mean %	Standard error %	Standard deviation %	Minimum rate %	Minimum year	Maximum rate %	Maximum year
Australia	4.1	4.2	0.5	5.5	-9.9	1921	24.9	1951
Belgium	5.5	5.9	0.9	9.0	-12.4	1904	29.5	1915
Canada	3.1	3.2	0.5	4.9	-15.8	1921	15.1	1917
Denmark	4.1	4.3	0.6	6.5	-15.0	1926	25.9	1916
France	7.9	8.8	1.5	14.6	-23.8	1921	74.0	1946
Germany *	5.1	6.0	1.6	15.8	-9.5	1932	209bn	1923
Ireland	4.5	4.7	0.7	6.8	-16.1	1922	23.6	1915
Italy	9.1	11.7	3.6	36.6	-9.7	1931	344.4	1944
Japan	7.6	11.0	4.0	40.2	-18.7	1930	317.1	1946
The Netherlands	3.0	3.1	0.5	5.0	-13.4	1921	18.7	1918
South Africa	4.8	5.1	0.8	7.8	-17.2	1921	47.5	1920
Spain	6.1	6.4	0.7	7.2	-6.7	1928	36.5	1946
Sweden	3.7	3.9	0.7	6.8	-25.2	1921	35.7	1918
Switzerland	2.2	2.4	0.6	6.0	-22.2	1921	25.7	1918
United Kingdom	4.1	4.3	0.7	6.9	-26.0	1921	24.9	1975
United States	3.2	3.3	0.5	5.0	-10.8	1921	20.4	1918

* For Germany, the means, standard deviation and standard error are based on 99 years, excluding 1922–23

Over the full 101-year period, Germany is a high inflation country largely because of the first quarter of the last century, notably 1922–23, although German inflation was high from 1914 onward. Figure 5-3 shows how inflation rates in each country changed between the first half of the twentieth century and the subsequent fifty-one years. Germany had the highest inflation rate in the first fifty years, although this does not show up in Figure 5-3 as 1922–23 is excluded. During the subsequent fifty-one years, it enjoyed the lowest inflation rate. This was no doubt the result of economic learning as well as acquisition of a deep-seated national fear of inflation.

German inflation in 1922–23 was so extreme that, in Table 5-1 and all other tables in this and the next chapter, we choose to exclude these two years when calculating German means and standard deviations. In 1922, inflation was 3,442 percent. In January 1923, there were 20,000 marks to the dollar; this increased to 630 billion marks to the dollar by early November. During this period, 300 paper mills and 150 printing works with 2,000 presses worked day and night to keep up with the demand for banknotes (Stolper, Hauser and Borchardt, 1967). There were further staggering rises in inflation until end-1923, when the German government ceased printing money. In 1923, the inflation rate was 209 billion percent. If we were to include 1922 and particularly 1923 in our calculations, the German arithmetic mean annual inflation rate over the 101 years from 1900–2000 would exceed two billion percent.

The German hyperinflation had devastating consequences, wiping out all internal debts almost overnight, and ruining a substantial proportion of Germany's middle class. Savings, bank balances, mortgages, annuities, pensions, bills, bonds, and other paper investments all became worthless. This episode remains as a dreadful warning that government bonds and even bills can, under extreme circumstances, experience a real return of -100 percent.

Figure 5-3: International inflation: first half of twentieth century versus subsequent fifty-one years

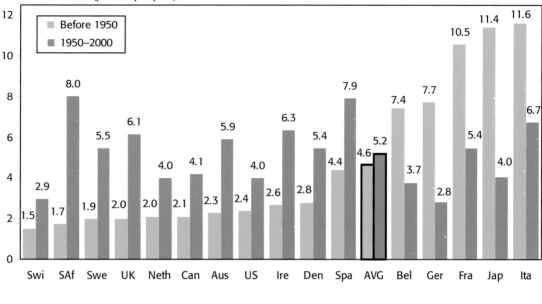

Between 1919 and 1925, four other countries outside our sample, Austria, Hungary, Poland, and Russia, also experienced hyperinflation, although not quite on the German scale. The second Hungarian hyperinflation of 1945–46, however, dwarfed even Germany's, with a compound rate of 19,800 percent *per month.* In more recent memory, there have been very high rates of inflation in several South American and African countries, Israel, and various former members of the Soviet Union.

Within our sample, the maximum inflation rate column in Table 5-1 shows that, although only Germany experienced true hyperinflation, very high inflation rates occurred in several other countries. Annual inflation rates hit a maximum of 344 percent in Italy in 1944; 317 percent in Japan in 1946; and 74 percent in France, also in 1946. For most countries, the inflationary peaks coincided with the world wars, or their immediate aftermath and consequences. The exception is the United Kingdom, where the peak year was 1975. Figure 5-3 shows that, although the United Kingdom had one of the lowest inflation rates from 1900–49, only Italy, Ireland, Spain, and South Africa had higher inflation rates during the subsequent period from 1950–2000.

The first half of the twentieth century was thus characterized by generally low rates of inflation, although the averages were boosted by a few wartime and post-war years of savage inflation especially in Germany, Italy, Japan and France. Furthermore, just as in the United States, all countries experienced a period of negative inflation during the 1920s and early 1930s. Over this period, Table 5-1 shows that all countries (except Belgium) experienced their lowest inflation year of the 101-year period. For nine countries, the inflation low-point occurred in 1921, with deflation ranging from 10 percent in Australia to 26 percent in the United Kingdom.

As Figure 5-3 shows, inflation in the second half of the period from 1950–2000 was more pervasive, although both Germany and Switzerland enjoyed annualized rates of less than 3 percent. As in the United Kingdom, however, inflation in most countries was brought gradually under control from the mid-1970s on. The inflation tables for each country in Part Two of this book show that over the most recent period from 1990–2000 the average inflation rate across the sixteen countries was just 3.0 percent.

5.3   US treasury bills and real interest rates

Treasury bills are short-dated government bonds. They normally have a maturity when issued of three, six, or twelve months. In most countries, they are issued by auction or tender, but there is usually also a very liquid secondary market in which bills can be bought and sold. Bills are non-interest paying discount bonds. The implied rate of interest is given by the difference between the purchase price and the maturity value. Thus if a twelve month bill with a face value of $100 were purchased at issue at $96 and held to maturity, the return would be $100/96 - 1 = 4.167$ percent. For all practical purposes, including taxation, this return is an interest payment.

Treasury bills are issued by governments, and thus have effectively no default risk, at least in developed countries, and under all but the most extreme circumstances. Furthermore, unlike longer-maturity government bonds, where investors face uncertainty about the purchasing power of future interest and maturity payments, short-dated bills have low inflation risk because a rolling investment in, say, one-month bills will expose the investor to only one month's uncertainty at any time. When the next one-month bill is purchased, its price will have adjusted to reflect the latest information on expected inflation. Inflation risk is thus small unless there is runaway hyperinflation.

Treasury bills are not only important in their own right, but as an asset class they tell us the investment return from cash, and provide us with the closest possible approximation to the risk free interest rate. In many of the sixteen countries covered in this book, there was no treasury bill market at the start of the twentieth century. Wherever this is the case, the principle that we adopt is to identify the closest possible proxy for the short-term risk free interest rate. In some cases, this involves using the returns on short-dated government coupon bonds; in other cases, we use high-grade commercial bills, bank deposit rates, central bank discount rates, or call money rates.

Our US treasury bill data from 1926 onward is taken from Ibbotson Associates (2001), and reflects the returns from a rolling investment in the shortest-term bills available, subject to their having at least one month to maturity. US treasury bills were introduced in 1929, but no data are available before 1931. From 1919–31, we use the returns on short-term coupon government bonds, while from 1900–18, we take the returns on short-dated commercial bills. For the United Kingdom, treasury bills existed throughout the entire period, and we use the return on a rolling investment in three-month bills.

The cumulative return from a policy of investing $1 in US treasury bills at the start of 1900 and reinvesting the proceeds in subsequent bills on a rolling basis was shown earlier in Figure 4-1. We saw there that this policy would have generated a terminal value of $57 by end-2000, an annualized return of 4.1 percent. From Figure 4-2, we saw that this was equivalent to 0.9 percent in real terms. UK treasury bills gave a higher nominal return of 5.1 percent (see Figure 4-3), and also a slightly higher real return of 1.0 percent (see Figure 4-4).

Figure 5-4 shows the path of US bill rates over time. From 1900–30, the short-term risk free rate averaged 4.6 percent, with interest rates at their highest around the First World War, peaking at 7.6 percent in 1920. From the early 1930s until the mid-1950s, interest rates were very low, averaging around 0.5 percent. During the 1930s, rates were understandably very low, as this was a largely deflationary period. From late 1941 until March 1951, the US government pegged the yields on treasury bills at low rates, so that the average bill return was just 0.5 percent despite an average inflation rate of 6 percent. From the mid-1950s onward, interest rates rose, peaking at 14.7 percent in 1981. This high rate was attributable both to high inflation, and also to the US government's determination to use high interest rates to combat inflation. From 1981, rates trended downward, but not without setbacks from resurgences in inflation. By the end of 2000, treasury bill yields were standing at 5.9 percent.

Fisher (1930) long ago pointed out that, in free markets, we should expect a close relationship between interest rates and inflation. He asserted that the nominal or "money" interest rate must equal the real interest rate plus the prospective rate of inflation. He argued that a change in the expected inflation rate will cause the same change in the nominal interest rate.

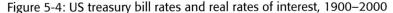

Figure 5-4: US treasury bill rates and real rates of interest, 1900–2000

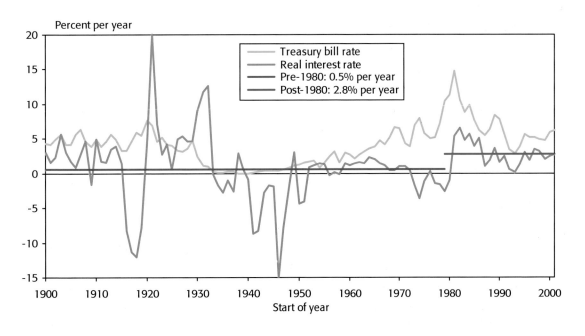

Figure 5-5: Real interest rates internationally pre- and post-1980

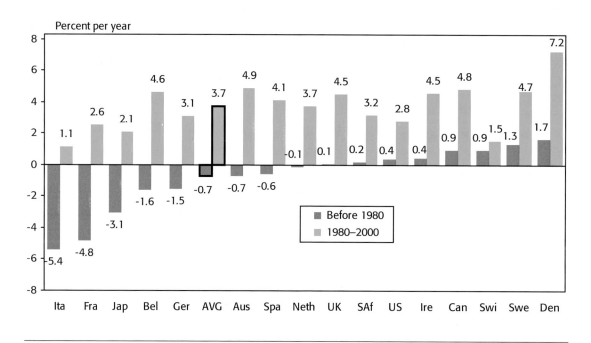

The standard deviation column in Table 5-2 shows the volatility of annual real rates of interest over the 101-year period from 1900–2000. The four countries with the worst inflation experiences, Italy, Germany, France, and Japan, all experienced volatile real rates, mostly during the first half of the century, with standard deviations of 11–15 percent. The remaining countries were somewhat less volatile, with standard deviations in the range 5–8 percent. The United Kingdom was roughly in the middle of this range, while the United States had the lowest volatility of any country.

We noted that for the United States and the United Kingdom, there was a sea change in the real rate of interest at the end of the 1970s. Figure 5-5 shows that this was replicated internationally. In Figure 5-5, the left-hand bars show the average annualized real rate of interest in each country from 1900–79, while the right-hand bars show the annualized post-1980 real rate. In all of the sixteen countries, real rates were appreciably higher over the twenty-one years starting in 1980. The smallest increase was experienced by Switzerland, and even here, although there was no step change, real rates were still 0.6 percent higher after 1980 than before. Across all sixteen countries, the mean real rate of interest over the first eighty years of the twentieth century was negative, at -0.7 percent, while over the twenty-one years since 1980, the mean has been +3.7 percent.

5.5 Summary

Inflation was a major force over the twentieth century, and investment returns clearly need to be adjusted for inflation. In the United States, inflation averaged 3.2 percent over the 101 years from 1900–2000, while in the United Kingdom the figure was 4.1 percent. While these two inflation rates look quite similar, the power of compound interest is such that over the 101-year period examined, US consumer prices rose by a factor of twenty-four, while UK prices rose 55-fold. Prices did not rise steadily throughout the twentieth century, however, and all countries experienced deflation at some stage during the 1920s and early 1930s. US consumer prices, for example, fell by nearly a third in the years after 1920, and did not regain their 1920 level until 1947.

While the United States and the United Kingdom escaped the ravages of hyperinflation experienced by Germany, or the turmoil of very high inflation experienced by many countries at the end of the Second World War, the US inflation rate was still nearly 50 percent higher than that of Switzerland, while UK inflation ran at almost twice the Swiss rate. The average inflation rate for all sixteen countries (but excluding the hyperinflationary period in Germany) was 4.9 percent per year.

After being the highest inflation country in the first half-century, Germany enjoyed the lowest rate (2.8 percent) in the second half. Several countries, including the United Kingdom, South Africa, Sweden, and Australia, moved in the opposite direction: having been among the lowest inflation countries over the first half-century, they ended up in the higher inflation group during the second half-century. Switzerland was a low inflation country throughout the twentieth century. US inflation was higher in the second half of the twentieth century than in the first, although the US inflation rate was below average in both halves of the century.

Treasury bills are an important asset class since they tell us the return on cash, and provide a benchmark for the risk free rate. US bill investors earned an annualized real return of 0.9 percent from 1900–2000, while UK investors earned a virtually identical 1.0 percent. Over this 101-year period, investors in five countries, Germany, France, Italy, Belgium, and Japan, earned negative real returns on bills. In 1923, German bill (and bond) investors lost everything, reminding us that, although we can generally regard short-dated government bills as risk free, in extreme circumstances this ceases to be the case.

During the first half of the twentieth century, there was no discernible relationship between interest rates and inflation in the United States or indeed in the other countries examined. From the 1950s onward, however, there is generally a close relationship between the two. In all sixteen countries, there appears to have been a breakpoint in the real rate of interest at the end of the 1970s, with real rates since 1980 having been appreciably higher than during the first eighty years of the twentieth century.

Chapter 6 Bond returns

Bonds are an important asset class. As we saw in chapter 2, the combined value of the world's bond markets at the turn of the millennium exceeded $31 trillion. In many countries, the size of the bond markets and the volume of trading in bonds exceed those of equities. This is not a new phenomenon. Even at the start of the twentieth century, bonds seemed a natural, and often the preferred, investment for individuals and financial institutions. But sadly, the twentieth century turned out to be a far from benign period for bond investors.

Our focus is mostly on long-term government bonds. These form a key segment of all national and international bond markets, and set the benchmark rates for all other debt instruments. Government bonds, unlike corporates, are normally free of default risk, at least in developed markets. They offer known payoffs, and for an investor who holds a bond to its maturity date, the yield is known in advance, and is thus risk free, at least in nominal terms.

Bond returns are not only important in their own right, but also because they are often used as a benchmark in computing the equity risk premium. But while government bonds are generally default free, they are not "risk free." For although investors know for sure how many dollars they will receive in the future, they do not know their purchasing power. Despite this, we follow common practice when we calculate the equity risk premium relative to bonds as well as bills (for example, in chapter 12). This premium is clearly of interest—whether viewed as a true risk premium or not—since it compares returns on the two most important asset classes available to investors.

In examining bond returns, we look first in section 6.1 at the US experience from 1900–2000, comparing it with the United Kingdom. In particular, we focus on real returns earned by bond investors, and on the progress of long bond yields during the twentieth century. In section 6.2, we compare bond returns across all sixteen countries.

We then look in turn at three bond return premia. Section 6.3 focuses on the bond maturity premium, the premium investors require for holding long-term bonds instead of short-dated bills. We look first at the US experience, and then compare maturity premia across all sixteen countries. Section 6.4 examines the returns on long-dated inflation-indexed government bonds, which offer a guaranteed real return. By comparing their returns with those from treasury bills, we can estimate the real term premium, which is the reward for assuming the risk of changes in the real interest rate over the bond's term. Treasury inflation-protected securities (TIPS) were introduced only recently in the United States, and so our focus here is on UK data, and what this can tell us about the likely future behavior of US TIPS. Section 6.5 examines the default risk premium by comparing the returns from long US corporate and government bonds. We summarize in section 6.6.

6.1 US and UK bond returns

Figure 6-1 shows the progress of real returns on US bonds and bills from 1900–2000. An investment of $1 at start-1900 in long-maturity US government bonds grew to a real value of $5.0 by start-2001, giving an annualized real return of 1.6 percent. A comparable investment

74

Figure 6-1: Cumulative real returns from US bonds, 1900–2000

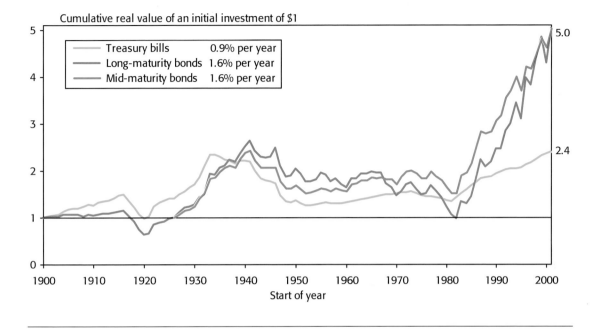

in US government treasury bills grew to a real value of $2.4, equivalent to an annualized real return of 0.9 percent. These treasury bills typically have a very short-term maturity of around one month, while the long-maturity bond index shown in Figure 6-1 is constructed with an approximately 20-year maturity. Figure 6-1 also shows the real return from investing in mid-term US government bonds, with an average maturity of five years. Since this mid-maturity bond index does not start until 1926, we have set its start-1926 value equal to the then value of the long-maturity bond index. Figure 6-1 shows that over the 75-year period from 1926–2000, investors would have ended up with the same terminal wealth whether they had invested in five- or twenty-year bonds.

Figure 6-1 shows that US bond investment over the twentieth century was not a story of steady, unimpeded progress. There were two bear markets, the second of which was especially protracted, and two strong bull phases. In seeking to understand these different phases, it is helpful to look at Figure 6-1 in conjunction with Figure 6-2. The latter shows the path of US inflation rates, short-term interest rates, and the redemption yields on long-maturity bonds over the twentieth century. Clearly, these variables are all closely interrelated since an unexpected rise in inflation or the real interest rate will cause long-bond prices to fall and redemption yields to rise, and vice versa.

Before the 1930s, the absolute low of US bond yields occurred just before the start of our period in 1899. Figure 6-2 shows that, early in the twentieth century, long bonds were selling on a redemption yield of around 2 percent. But the first bear market in US bonds came early. Before the First World War, bond prices generally fell in nominal terms, but inflation was low

Figure 6-2: US Interest rates, inflation and long-maturity bond yields, 1900–2000

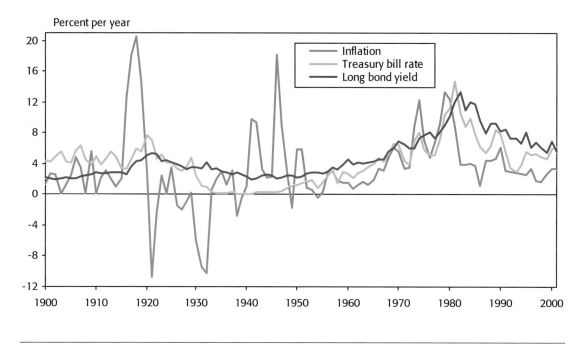

and coupons were high enough to ensure that the real bond returns index scarcely changed. The entry of the United States into the First World War in April 1917 was marked by an immediate decline in the bond market, and the high inflation rates accompanying the war (an average of 16 percent per year over the four years from 1916–19) led to large negative real returns on bonds. From 1900–19, the annualized bond return was 2.6 percent nominal and -2.1 percent real. In contrast, the subsequent deflationary period was good for bond investors, and Figure 6-2 shows that, during the Great Depression of the 1930s, long bond yields fell to a record low of less than 2 percent. During this first great bond bull market from 1920 until 1940, the annualized US bond return was 5.5 percent nominal, and 6.9 percent real.

With hindsight, each of the two world wars occurred just before a turning point in the bond market. The First World War was accompanied by high and rising yields, as was every earlier great war in modern times. Figure 6-2 shows that the point of the highest bond yields up to the 1960s occurred two years after the First World War ended. The Second World War, in contrast, was accompanied by low and declining bond yields. During the war and early post-war years until 1951, the US government maintained low rates through the Federal Reserve's bond support policy. The lowest bond yield in the entire twentieth century—1.93 percent—occurred just one year after the war ended in 1946.

The years following the Second World War saw the great bear bond market. From their low of 1.93 percent in 1946, bond yields climbed to an unprecedented peak of nearly 15 percent during 1981. This period, and particularly the 1970s, saw an unprecedented change in interest rate behavior, driven by inflation rates that reached the low teens by 1979. Since records began, inflation had never been so high for so long. This had a major impact on bond returns. Over the thirty-six years until 1981, US long bonds managed an annualized nominal return of just 2.0 percent. With inflation averaging 4.7 percent a year, this was equivalent to a real return of -2.5 percent per year real.

From the late 1970s, inflation was slowly brought under control, and from the early 1980s, bonds enjoyed a resurgence. As Figure 6-1 shows, the nineteen years from end-1981 to end–2000 saw the most dramatic bull market in bonds yet recorded, with annualized bond returns of 12.6 percent nominal or 8.9 percent real.

Figure 6-3 shows that, over the period from 1900–2000, US long bond returns exhibited substantial year-to-year volatility. Real returns (shown by the bars) were more volatile than nominal returns (shown by the line plot), with a standard deviation of 10.0 percent per year, versus 8.3 percent for nominal returns. These standard deviations are appreciably higher than those reported for bills in chapter 5, where the corresponding figures were 4.7 percent for real bill returns and just 2.8 percent for nominal returns.

Since long bond returns are driven by changes in expectations about both inflation and the real rate of interest, we would expect long bonds to be more volatile than bills, and this has clearly proved to be the case. But given the much higher volatility we have observed for bonds, the 0.7 percent per year margin by which bonds outperformed bills seems quite slim. It seems likely, therefore, that the real returns achieved on bonds over the twentieth century turned out to be lower than investors' *ex ante* expectations. This would have been the case if

Figure 6-3: Annual US nominal and real bond returns, 1900–2000

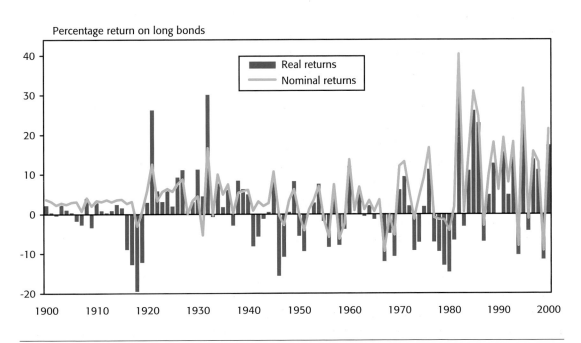

interest rates, and especially the inflation component, had turned out to be persistently higher than expected. Given the evidence above and from chapter 5, this seems plausible.

Figure 6-4 shows that the pattern of UK long bond returns has much in common with the United States. Returns are represented by UK government 2½% consols until 1954, and thereafter by a portfolio of dated bonds with an average maturity of twenty years. This bond index, produced in conjunction with ABN AMRO is described in chapter 32. Figure 6-4 shows that an investment of £1 in this index at start-1900 grew to a real value of £3.7 by start-2001, an annualized real return of 1.3 percent. A comparable investment in treasury bills grew to £2.7 in real terms, a real return of 1.0 percent per year. Figure 6-4 also shows that, from its start-date in 1955, our companion mid-maturity bond index, which tracks the returns on five-year bonds, outperformed long bonds by a noticeable margin.

Figure 6-4 for UK long bonds is strikingly similar to Figure 6-1 for US long bonds, with two bear and bull markets spanning very similar periods. The UK experience was generally more extreme, however, driven by deeper deflation in the 1920s and 1930s, and higher inflationary extremes in the 1970s. This led to even lower real bond returns than in the United States during the bear markets, and rather higher returns during the bull markets. The volatility of real long bond returns was also higher in the United Kingdom at 14.5 percent per year versus 10.0 percent in the United States. The margin by which UK long bonds beat bills was just 0.3 percent per year, compared with 0.7 percent in the United States. We argued above that US investors found this inadequate. If so, then UK bond investors were doubly disappointed.

Figure 6-4: Cumulative real returns from UK bonds, 1900–2000

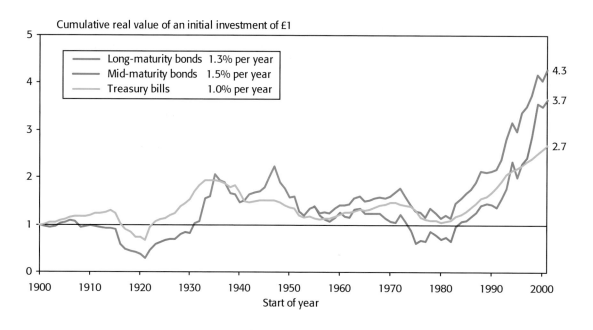

6.2 Bond returns around the world

Table 6-1 provides an overview of real bond returns over the 101 years from 1900–2000 for all sixteen countries. German bonds were the worst performers, and the true position is even worse than revealed in Table 6-1 since the averages in the table exclude 1922 and 1923. In 1923, hyperinflation resulted in a total loss of -100 percent for German bond investors. Nor was this the only dreadful time for bond investors. One of the repercussions of the Second World War was the division of Germany and associated currency reforms. As a result of that process, German bond investors faced a loss of 90 percent in nominal terms in 1948, and the real bond return that year was -92.3 percent.

Five out of the six countries identified in chapter 5 as experiencing the highest inflation rates over the twentieth century, namely, Germany, Italy, Japan, Belgium, and France, experienced negative real returns on bonds. The highest real bond returns came from Switzerland (2.8 percent), which had the lowest inflation rate, and from the two Scandinavian countries, Denmark (2.5 percent) and Sweden (2.4 percent), which were both middle-ranking inflation countries over the twentieth century as a whole. Once again, our results suggest that bond returns in many countries were below investors' prior expectations. The difference between expectations and subsequent experience was naturally greatest in the highest inflation countries.

In the context of the other countries in our study, Table 6-1 shows that the United States was a relatively good performer—ranked fifth out of sixteen—while it had the third lowest volatility.   The United Kingdom was middle-ranked in terms of average real bond returns, but in

Table 6-1: Real bond returns around the world from 1900–2000

Country	Geometric mean %	Arithmetic mean %	Standard error %	Standard deviation %	Minimum return %	Minimum year	Maximum return %	Maximum year
Australia	1.1	1.9	1.3	13.0	-29.9	1951	60.5	1932
Belgium	-0.4	0.3	1.2	12.1	-26.8	1920	40.5	1958
Canada	1.8	2.4	1.1	10.6	-25.9	1915	41.7	1921
Denmark	2.5	3.3	1.2	12.5	-26.3	1919	48.9	1983
France	-1.0	0.1	1.4	14.4	-43.7	1946	49.1	1927
Germany *	-2.2	0.3	1.6	15.9	-100.0	1923	62.5	1932
Ireland	1.5	2.4	1.3	13.3	-34.2	1940	37.9	1993
Italy	-2.2	-0.8	1.4	14.4	-64.3	1944	28.1	1933
Japan	-1.6	1.3	2.1	20.9	-75.1	1946	70.7	1954
The Netherlands	1.1	1.5	0.9	9.4	-18.1	1915	32.8	1932
South Africa	1.4	1.9	1.1	10.6	-32.6	1920	37.1	1921
Spain	1.2	1.9	1.2	12.0	-30.2	1920	53.2	1942
Sweden	2.4	3.1	1.3	12.7	-37.0	1939	68.2	1921
Switzerland	2.8	3.1	0.8	8.0	-16.1	1918	35.9	1921
United Kingdom	1.3	2.3	1.4	14.5	-34.1	1915	61.2	1921
United States	1.6	2.1	1.0	10.0	-19.3	1918	35.1	1982

* For Germany, the means, standard deviation and standard error are based on 99 years, excluding 1922–23

terms of volatility, its standard deviation of 14.5 percent was the third highest, although only marginally ahead of France and Italy at 14.4 percent. Germany experienced the highest standard deviation of annual real bond returns (but does not show as such in Table 6-1 because of the exclusion of 1922–23) followed by Japan at 20.9 percent; Switzerland had the lowest, at just 8.0 percent.

As one might expect from the inflation record documented in chapter 5, there were large differences in real bond returns between the first and second halves of our 101-year period. These are shown in Figure 6-5, where countries are ranked by the left-hand bars, which show the returns during the first half of the twentieth century (excluding 1922–23 for Germany). The right-hand bars relate to the fifty-one years from 1950–2000. There is evidence of regression to the mean and, for some countries, of reversal. The five countries shown in Table 6-1 as having negative real bond returns over the full 101 years, namely, Germany, France, Italy, Belgium, and Japan, were among the best performing bond markets over the period 1950–2000. Their poor overall performance arose entirely from the first fifty years. Figure 6-5 also shows that the five best performers over the first half of the twentieth century, Switzerland, Sweden, South Africa, Australia, and Spain had lower, although still positive, real returns over the following fifty-one years.

For several countries the returns for the first half of the twentieth century reveal the ravages and aftermath of two world wars. Somewhat in contrast, Switzerland and Sweden demonstrate the financial safe-haven benefits of neutrality. The returns for the following fifty-one years reflect the return to peacetime, as well as learning by both governments and investors.

Figure 6-5: Real bond returns: first half of the twentieth century versus the following fifty-one years

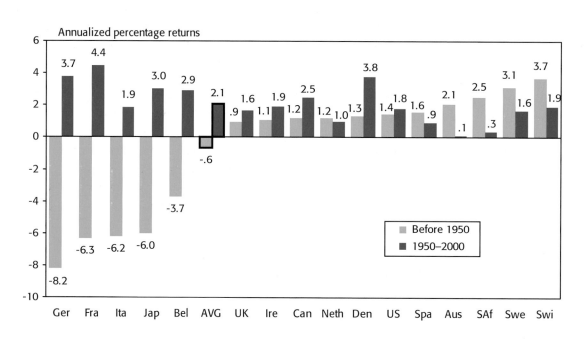

6.3   **Bond maturity premia**

We have seen that long-term bonds behave differently from short-term bills because their prices are more sensitive to interest rate fluctuations. In this section, we compute and compare bond maturity premia. The bond maturity premium is the premium investors require for holding long-term bonds instead of short-dated bills.

One view often expressed is that there is no particular reason to expect a bond maturity *premium.* Bondholders with long-term horizons seeking to match long-term liabilities will view long bonds as the lower risk, since short-term bills have to be regularly reinvested, and there is uncertainty over the reinvestment rate. In contrast, investors with shorter-term horizons and liabilities will view long bonds as the more risky since there is uncertainty about the price at which bonds can be sold. While these arguments are valid, they fail to take account of inflation uncertainty. At times of inflation uncertainty, short-term bonds become the lower risk investment even for investors with long-term (real) liabilities.

We can gain further clues by looking at the yield curve, and at the difference between the redemption yield at which long bonds are trading, and the yield on short-term bills. This data was presented graphically in Figure 6-2, which showed that for the first twenty or so years of the last century, US short-term interest rates were typically above long-term bond yields. Over the eighty years from 1921–2000, however, long bond yields have generally been above short rates by an average of around 1.3 percent per year, with mid-maturity bonds typically lying in between. There has thus normally been an upward sloping yield curve, with yields rising with term to maturity.

There can be at least two reasons for an upward sloping yield curve. First, short-term interest rates may be expected to rise. Alternatively, investors may require some form of liquidity or risk premium for holding long bonds to compensate them for uncertainty about the real interest rate, inflation, or both. Since US interest rates in the early 1920s were similar to those at end-2000, it seems most likely that the tendency for the yield curve to have sloped upward over this period is related to some form of risk premium.

While we cannot measure investors' *ex ante* requirements or expectations relating to this risk premium, we can measure the bond maturity premia actually achieved. The formula for the bond maturity premium is *1 + Long bond rate of return* divided by *1 + Treasury bill rate of return*, minus *1*. The line plot in Figure 6-6 shows the sequence of annual bond maturity premia for the United States from 1900–2000. There has clearly been considerable year-to-year variation, and the standard deviation of annual bond maturity premia has been 7.7 percent, which is somewhat lower than the volatility of 10.0 percent reported above for real bond returns.

Given that the range of bond maturity premia that we observe on an annual basis is quite wide, it is a little misleading to label these annual figures as "maturity premia." For example, US bond investors obviously did not expect the negative maturity premium of -13.6 percent in 1980, otherwise they would have shunned long bonds. All of the negative annual "premia" shown in Figure 6-6 must therefore reflect unpleasant surprises—typically, an increase in inflationary expectations or in the anticipated future real interest rate.

Figure 6-6: US bond maturity premium, 1900–2000

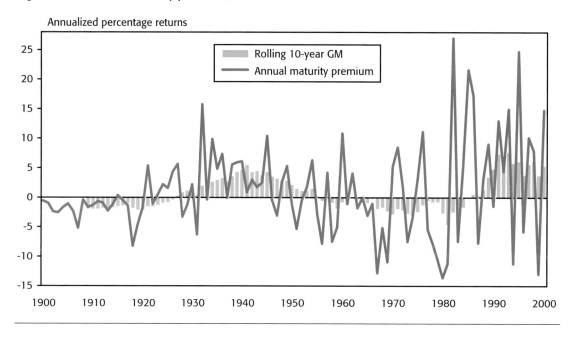

Equally, bond investors could not reasonably have "required" a maturity premium as large as the 27 percent that they obtained in 1982. All of the higher realizations that are plotted in Figure 6-6 must therefore have been pleasant surprises—typically good news on the inflation front, or a fall in the expected level of real interest rates. Strictly speaking, therefore, we should probably refer to the annual maturity premia simply as "excess returns," that is, long bond returns in excess of (or under) the treasury bill rate.

Over long enough periods, however, we might expect the pleasant and unpleasant surprises to cancel each other out, providing us with an estimate of investors' *ex ante* required maturity premium. A common choice of time frame here is a decade, and while this is still too short to produce reliable estimates, it is nevertheless interesting to look at ten-year premia. The bars in Figure 6-6 therefore show the rolling 10-year geometric mean maturity premia. Here, a clearer pattern emerges, with two extended periods when the rolling mean was negative, and two when it was positive. Not surprisingly, these correspond to the two lengthy bear and bull markets in US bonds discussed in section 6.1.

To estimate the required maturity premium, however, we need to look at longer time intervals than a decade. Table 6-2 shows bond maturity premia computed over the entire period from 1900–2000 for all sixteen countries. It shows that for the United States, the 101-year geometric mean bond maturity premium was 0.7 percent, that is, the annualized return on US long bonds exceeded the annualized bill return by 0.7 percent per year. The average geometric mean across all sixteen countries was 0.5 percent, a little below the 0.7 percent for the United States, and not greatly above the 0.3 percent for the United Kingdom. Germany had the lowest premium, and France the highest.

Table 6-2: Bond maturity premia around the world from 1900–2000

Country	Geometric mean %	Arithmetic mean %	Standard error %	Standard deviation %	Minimum premium %	Minimum year	Maximum premium %	Maximum year
Australia	0.7	1.2	1.0	10.4	-23.3	1973	48.2	1932
Belgium	-0.1	0.3	0.9	9.4	-19.6	1914	34.0	1958
Canada	0.1	0.4	0.8	8.1	-26.4	1915	24.1	1982
Denmark	-0.2	0.2	0.9	9.2	-20.0	1986	35.1	1983
France	2.4	2.7	0.8	7.5	-15.8	1914	23.6	1927
Germany *	-1.7	0.2	1.3	13.1	-90.5	1948	48.3	1921
Ireland	0.2	0.8	1.1	10.8	-28.7	1940	37.1	1977
Italy	1.9	2.2	0.8	8.1	-17.5	1935	52.3	1944
Japan	0.5	1.4	1.4	14.1	-45.6	1953	63.0	1954
The Netherlands	0.4	0.7	0.7	7.2	-18.9	1939	25.2	1982
South Africa	0.6	0.9	0.8	7.9	-18.3	1994	30.4	1933
Spain	0.9	1.3	0.9	9.5	-27.0	1920	46.5	1942
Sweden	0.3	0.7	0.8	8.4	-34.1	1939	24.5	1934
Switzerland	1.7	1.8	0.4	4.4	-13.9	1989	15.6	1908
United Kingdom	0.3	0.9	1.1	11.3	-26.6	1974	37.5	1932
United States	0.7	1.0	0.8	7.7	-13.6	1980	27.0	1982

* For Germany, the means, standard deviation and standard error are based on 99 years, excluding 1922–23

As with real bond returns, however, the 101-year averages shown in Table 6-2 conceal a game of two halves. Figure 6-7 shows that of the countries with the lower, and in several cases negative, bond maturity premia in the first half of the twentieth century, several, including Germany, France, Japan, and Denmark, saw substantial rises over the next fifty-one years. Indeed, Germany, France, and Japan, together with Italy and Switzerland, have had the highest premia over the period 1950–2000. Meanwhile, looking at the right-hand side of Figure 6-7, seven of the eight countries with the highest bond maturity premia during the first fifty years of the twentieth century experienced lower maturity premia over the subsequent fifty-one years. The exception was Italy, where the maturity premium was 1.5 percent from 1900–49, and 2.3 percent for 1950–2000. In contrast, for the United States, the United Kingdom, and Canada, the bond maturity premium in the second half-century was very similar to that in the first half.

We saw above that the (unweighted) average bond maturity premium across all sixteen countries over the full 101-year period from 1900–2000 was 0.5 percent. We argued that, given the substantial additional risks faced by long bond investors, this figure seems quite low. Figure 6-7 shows that during the first half of the twentieth century, the average premium was even lower at 0.3 percent, although during the following fifty-one years it rose to 0.8 percent. Given the turbulence of the first half of the twentieth century, it is hard to argue that a maturity premium of 0.3 percent was an adequate reward for long bond investors. Thus even our 50- and indeed our 101-year averages would appear to have been contaminated by bad luck. It seems likely, therefore, that the *ex post* means shown in Table 6-2 underestimate the maturity premium that bond investors were seeking *ex ante*.

Figure 6-7: Bond maturity premia: first half of the twentieth century versus the next fifty-one years

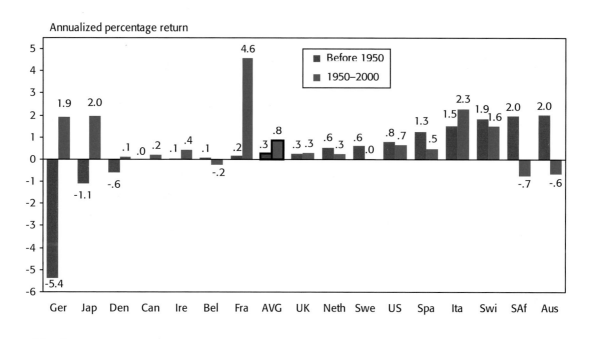

6.4   Inflation-indexed bonds and the real term premium

An asset class that still has considerable novelty even in some of the world's most highly developed markets is inflation-linked bonds. This is curious since instruments of this kind can be traced back to the 1742 loan to the Commonwealth of Massachusetts, which was linked to movements in the prices of a bundle of commodities. Despite this early experimentation, there are still no government bonds of this type in Japan or Germany. In the 1990s, Australia, Canada, Denmark, France, South Africa, Sweden, and several other countries issued inflation-indexed bonds, but mostly, the value of outstanding bonds has remained small. Data from Merrill Lynch indicate that the total capitalization of inflation-linked government bonds around the world at end-March 2001 was some $280 billion, suggesting that bonds of this type account for less than 2 percent of the world government bond market. Not surprisingly, the countries in which inflation-indexed bonds have been most prevalent have been those most troubled by inflation, such as Argentina, Brazil, and Israel, though New Zealand also favors these securities.

In the United States, inflation-indexed government bonds were, for a long time, illegal (see McCulloch, 1980). Despite this, a number of US institutions such as Franklin Savings and Loan Insurance Corporation, Anchor Savings Bank and JHM Acceptance Corporation issued similar securities in 1988 (see Bodie, 1990). Then in January 1997, the United States introduced treasury inflation-protected securities (TIPS). While this asset category has attracted research interest (e.g., Campbell and Shiller, 1996), there is so far only a brief returns history.

In the United Kingdom, however, inflation-indexed government bonds, whose cash flows (coupons plus redemption value) are tied to the level of the Retail Price Index, were introduced as long ago as 1975. They were first issued as non-tradable certificates for restricted categories of investors, but by 1981 they became available as listed securities to all investors. Today, the UK inflation-indexed bond market is large and liquid, there is a wide range of maturities, and it provides the longest history of any major developed market—237 months from April 1981 until December 2000. Though not identical, the structure of US TIPS is similar to their UK counterparts. UK data may therefore provide important clues about how this asset will behave in the United States and other major markets.

Inflation-indexed government bonds are especially interesting as they offer a guaranteed real return (see Woodward, 1990; Brown and Schaefer, 1994), since both coupon and principal are linked to inflation. As they are also default free, their only risk arises from uncertainty about changes in the real rate of interest over the life of the bond. By comparing the returns on long-dated inflation-indexed bonds with the return from treasury bills, we can therefore derive estimates of the real term premium, which is the reward for assuming the risk of changes in the real rate of interest over the bond's term.

To conduct research into this interesting asset class, we use the inflation-indexed bond index described in chapter 32. This incorporates all indexed-linked UK government bonds with a start-year maturity of between 15½ and 25½ years, and typically has 3–4 constituents. Like the corresponding UK long bond index, it has an average maturity of 20 years.

UK inflation-indexed bonds have performed poorly since they became generally available in 1981. From April 1981 until end-2000, long-maturity bonds gave an annualized real return of 8.4 percent, mid-maturity bonds returned 6.6 percent, treasury bills gave 4.7 percent, while inflation-indexed bonds returned just 3.4 percent per year. Inflation-indexed bonds are in principle low risk securities, and so might be expected to underperform conventional bonds of the same maturity. We would nevertheless expect them to deliver a positive real term premium, defined as the reward for investing in inflation-indexed bonds in preference to treasury bills. In fact, the real term premium was negative, averaging -1¼ percent per year. Figure 6-8 shows the year-by-year returns on bills, long bonds, mid-maturity bonds, and inflation-indexed bonds in every year since the latter became available. It shows that, so far, inflation-indexed bonds have never been the best performing asset over a calendar year.

Inflation-indexed bonds are therefore another example of a bond that has delivered returns below investors' expectations, at least relative to the alternative of investing in treasury bills. The reason for the disappointment was not unexpected inflation, since these bonds are inflation-linked. Instead, their poor performance stems from unexpected increases in the real rate of interest particularly in the early 1980s. Since most inflation-indexed bonds have low coupons, and since there is no capital gains tax on UK government bonds, they are attractive to high-rate taxpayers relative to most conventional bonds. The low returns on inflation-indexed bonds may therefore also partly reflect the influence of tax clienteles (see Brown and Schaefer, 1994).

Figure 6-8: Comparative annual real returns from UK bonds including inflation-indexed bonds

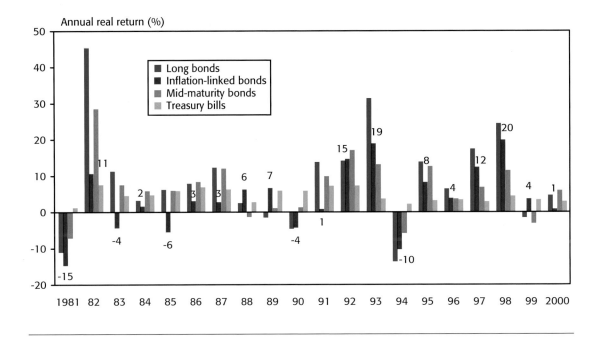

Table 6-3 provides summary statistics on monthly bond returns and inflation over the period since April 1981. The top panel relates to the United Kingdom, and the bottom panel to the United States. The top panel shows that, since their introduction in 1981, the mean real monthly return on UK inflation-indexed bonds has been only 0.29 percent, which is 0.09 percent lower than the treasury bill return. The standard deviation of monthly real returns on UK inflation-indexed bonds has been 2.37 percent, as compared with 0.47, 1.78, and 2.90 percent for treasury bills, mid-maturity bonds, and long-maturity bonds, respectively. UK inflation-indexed bonds have therefore been more volatile than one might have expected, and in terms of risk, have behaved more like conventional long-bonds, and have been only marginally less volatile.

The correlations between monthly asset return are shown in the lower part of each panel. In the United Kingdom, correlations vary from -0.9 (bills versus inflation) to +0.9 (mid- versus long-maturity bonds). The pattern is similar in the United States. The only apparent difference between the two countries is the correlation between the real returns on treasury bills and inflation, which is -0.87 for the United Kingdom, and -0.63 for the United States. UK and US inflation statistics are released at different points in the month, and so this disparity could be attributable to the timing of announcements in the two countries.

The top panel of Table 6-3 is informative for US investors interested in the behavior of TIPS. The similarity between the statistics for UK and US bonds and inflation suggests that, had US inflation-linked bonds existed over this period, they would have performed in a similar way to their UK counterparts. Note, first, the negative correlation (-0.21) between the real returns

Table 6-3: Monthly bond return statistics April 1981–December 2000

Statistic	Inflation	Treasury bills	Mid-maturity bonds	Long bonds	Inflation-indexed bonds
United Kingdom					
Mean real return (%)	.00	.38	.53	.67	.29
Standard deviation of real returns (%)	.00	.47	1.78	2.90	2.37
Serial correlation (nominal returns)	.20	.98	.10	.09	-.02
Correlation with inflation	—	.35*	-.03	-.10	.00
Correlation with treasury bills	-.87*	—	.20	.10	.01
Correlation with mid-maturity bonds	-.31	.37	—	.89	.58
Correlation with long bonds	-.27	.30	.90	—	.53
Correlation with inflation-indexed bonds	-.21	.19	.60	.56	—
United States					
Mean real return (%)	.00	.24	.52	.68	na
Standard deviation of real returns (%)	.00	.25	1.59	3.12	na
Serial correlation (nominal returns)	.45	.95	.21	.06	na
Correlation with inflation	—	.39	-.09	-.18	na
Correlation with treasury bills	-.63	—	.19	.10	na
Correlation with mid-maturity bonds	-.24	.34	—	.91	na
Correlation with long bonds	-.25	.30	.92	—	na

* Correlations in bold are based on monthly nominal returns. Correlations in roman are based on monthly real returns

on inflation-indexed bonds and the inflation rate; and second, the rather high correlation (0.56) between the returns on inflation-indexed bonds and the real returns on conventional long-maturity bonds. In terms of month-to-month price fluctuations, inflation-indexed bonds have behaved more like conventional bonds than might have been expected. While this similarity is likely to carry over to the United States, these relationships could clearly change in an environment where long-bond returns are driven more by changes in inflation and inflationary expectations than by changes in real interest rates.

6.5 Corporate bonds and the default risk premium

So far we have focused on government bonds. We saw in chapter 2 that corporate bonds are also important, accounting for a third of all bonds in issue. The main differences between government and corporate bonds arise from the fact that investors in corporate bonds can experience default if the issuing company encounters financial distress. Corporate bonds are thus of interest in their own right as an important asset class, and also because they provide us with insights into the default risk premium.

The relative quality and default risk of corporate bonds can be judged by the ratings given by agencies such as Moody's and Standard & Poor's. Moody's ratings range from Aaa to C, with bonds below Baa regarded as below normal investment grade or "junk bonds." Aaa and Aa bonds taken together comprise "high grade bonds." Defaults on bonds currently rated as high grade are very rare, but such bonds can be downgraded and later default from a lower rating. Default rates on junk bonds can be very high, and in poor years have exceeded 10 percent. Default can range from having just a minor impact, such as a delayed interest payment, through to a total default on both interest and principal.

Corporate bonds therefore sell at lower prices, and hence on higher yields, than government bonds because of default risk. The expected return on a corporate bond is thus lower than its redemption yield. Part of the yield differential between corporate and government bonds is accounted for by the expected loss from default, while the balance reflects a risk premium that investors demand, and (hopefully) over the long run receive, for bearing default risk. To estimate the magnitude of the default premium, we need to compare the actual returns from corporate bonds, after taking account of any losses from defaults, with the returns from government bonds. The formula for the bond default premium is *1 + Long corporate bond rate of return* divided by *1+ Long government bond rate of return*, minus *1*.

Figure 6-9 shows the cumulative real return and default premia for high grade US corporate bonds from 1900–2000. The data from 1926–2000 are from Ibbotson Associates (2001), who in turn use the Salomon Brothers Long-term High-grade Corporate Bond Index from 1969–98, and Ibbotson and Sinquefield (1976) data from 1926–68. Global Financial Data supplied the pre-1926 data. The two lines plotted against the right-hand axis show the cumulative real return from an initial investment of $1 at start-2000 in either long-term corporate or government bonds. The blue line shows that the investment in government bonds grew to $5 by

Figure 6-9: Cumulative real returns and default premia from US corporate bonds, 1900–2000

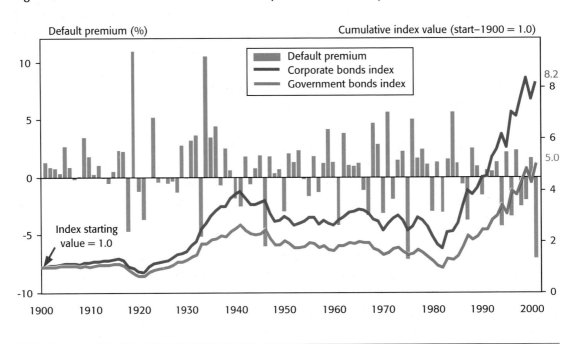

start-2001, an annualized real return of 1.61 percent. The red line shows that a comparable investment in corporates grew to \$8.2, an annualized real return of 2.11 percent. Corporates thus indeed gave a higher return, and the annualized (geometric mean) default risk premium was 48 basis points per year. High-grade corporates typically trade on redemption yields about one percentage point higher than on government bonds. This suggests that about half the "promised" yield differential fails to materialize because of defaults, downgrades, and early calls, while around half represents the achieved risk premium.

The green bars plotted against the left-hand axis in Figure 6-9 show the year-by-year default risk premium. On average, the premium is positive, with an arithmetic mean of 53 basis points. It is quite variable, however, with a standard deviation of 3.0 percent, and in many years it is negative. The latter could represent years in which returns were depressed by defaults, but normally, these negative premia occur in years when there are downgrades, and/or when the yield differential with corporates widens. By the same logic, the years with large positive premia tend to be those when the yield differential narrowed greatly.

Unfortunately, we have been unable to obtain good quality corporate bond returns data spanning the twentieth century for any country other than the United States. Were such data to exist, however, our best guess is that it would mirror the government bond returns in each country, plus a default risk premium similar to that found in the United States.

6.6 Summary

Taken as a whole, the 101 years from 1900–2000 were not especially kind to bond investors. In the United States, the annualized real return on long-term government bonds was 1.6 percent. While this was 0.7 percent higher than on bills, bonds had much higher risk. Across all sixteen countries, the average annualized real bond return was just 0.7 percent. In five countries, Germany, Italy, Japan, France, and Belgium, the real return on bonds was negative. These findings suggest that bond returns in many countries were below investors' prior expectations. The difference between expectations and subsequent experience was naturally greatest in the countries with the highest inflation.

Particularly in the first half of the twentieth century, many countries experienced extreme and disappointingly low returns arising from the ravages of war and extreme inflation. This resulted in a degree of reversal, with the countries experiencing the lowest returns in the first half of the twentieth century being among the best performing bond markets over the subsequent fifty-one years.

The average maturity premium across all sixteen countries over the period from 1900–2000 was 0.5 percent. During the first half of the twentieth century the average was 0.3 percent, while during the following fifty-one years, it rose to 0.8 percent. Given the substantial additional risks faced by long bond investors, and the fact that the fifty-one years from 1950–2000 were by no means uniformly favorable for bonds, it seems likely that even the higher of these two figures still understates investors' *ex ante* expectations.

Even inflation-indexed government bonds have proved a disappointment, at least in the United Kingdom, where they have the longest history. These bonds were first introduced in 1981, partly in response to high UK inflation rates during the 1970s, which seriously eroded conventional long bond returns. Ironically, the period since their introduction has seen a bull market for conventional bonds because of rapidly declining inflationary expectations. Meanwhile, inflation-indexed bonds have performed poorly, and the real term premium has negative rather than positive because, over this period, real interest rates turned out to be higher than expected. On other dimensions, including their risk, inflation-indexed bonds have performed more like conventional bonds than might have been expected. Their behavior is informative for US investors interested in the likely long-term behavior of TIPS, which were not introduced until 1997.

Finally, we examined the return on high-grade, long-maturity US corporate bonds. These differ from government bonds in that there is a possibility that the issuer may default. Over the period from 1900–2000, we found that holders of US corporate bonds have received an annualized default risk premium of 54 basis points to compensate for this extra risk.

Chapter 7 Exchange rates and common-currency returns

So far, we have examined long-run investment from the perspective of domestic investors in our sixteen countries. For example, in chapter 4, when we looked at long-run equity and bond returns, the international comparisons we drew were between the real returns earned by US investors from investing in US equities and bonds, UK investors holding UK equities and bonds, and so on. Our numeraire was local purchasing power, measured in local currency, such as dollars, pounds, and marks.

For the international investor, fluctuations in asset prices must be converted from the local currency into the currency in which portfolio performance is evaluated. For example, a US-based investor who purchases UK equities will not simply earn the local UK pound sterling return, but will also need to convert these pound returns back into dollars by adjusting for the exchange rate movement.

Exchange rate changes are therefore central to measuring and comparing the returns from different countries. In this chapter, we report on the exchange rate fluctuations that were experienced by our sixteen countries over the 101 years from 1900–2000. During this period, these countries experienced multiple exchange rate regimes, and individual currencies had periods of maintained value, revaluation, devaluation, and extreme debasement. Our database thus provides a unique opportunity to observe a series of natural experiments. Over this long interval, we examine the impact on exchange rates of transitory and sustained inflation differentials. We then take the perspective of an international investor and analyze common-currency investment returns, measured using a common numeraire such as dollars, or dollars adjusted for changes in purchasing power.

We start in section 7.1 with a survey of exchange rate behavior over the 101 years from 1900–2000, followed in section 7.2 by a review of the evolution of the international monetary system. In section 7.3 we turn to evidence on long-run purchasing power parity, and discuss deviations from purchasing power parity in section 7.4. In section 7.5 we examine the volatility of real exchange rates. We then present real, common-currency returns on equities and bonds in section 7.6. We then summarize our discussion of exchange rates, purchasing power parity, and common-currency returns in section 7.7.

7.1 Long-run exchange rate behavior

Figure 7-1 compares the exchange rates against the US dollar for our sample of countries. On the left-hand side of the graph we record the dollar value of 5.21 Swiss francs, £0.20 sterling, and the equivalent sums in other currencies that equate, at that date, to US$1.00. That is, we re-base the exchange rates on January 1, 1900 to a value of one. The vertical axis displays the number of dollars required to purchase one local currency unit (after re-basing), so a depreciating currency trends downward while an appreciating currency trends upward in the chart.

Figure 7-1: Nominal exchange rates against the US dollar (rebased to 1900 =1)

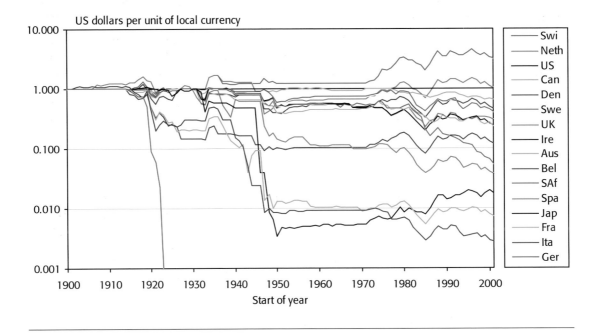

As Figure 7-1 shows, by the middle of the German hyperinflation of 1922–23, that country's currency debasement had taken the German mark off the vertical scale of the graph. Other currencies took longer to move by a smaller margin. By the start of 2001, the currencies depicted in Figure 7-1 had depreciated to the point where the number of lira that could be bought for one US dollar was 358 times as large as in 1900; the number of French francs was 135 times larger; the number of yen was 56 times larger; the number of Spanish pesetas was 26 times larger; and the number of British pounds was 3.3 times larger. The strongest currency in our study, the Swiss franc, had by 2001 appreciated to the point at which the number of dollars required to buy one franc had more than tripled relative to the 1900 level.

Table 7-1 provides exchange rate comparisons across all sixteen countries in our study. It shows the mean rates of currency appreciation or depreciation, in terms of the dollar value of local currency units, measured over the entire period of 101 years. An appreciating currency, such as the Swiss franc, is shown in the table by a positive rate of change—more dollars are needed to buy one franc. A weak currency, such as the Italian lira, has a negative mean—fewer dollars are required to buy one lira. The standard deviations in the table reveal the considerable variation in exchange rates that have been experienced within each of the countries. Five currencies stand out for their extreme annualized (geometric mean) loss of value, and also their volatility (standard deviation), relative to the dollar: France, Germany, Italy, Japan, and Spain. Two countries had strong and stable currencies relative to the dollar: The Netherlands and Switzerland. Other currencies experienced annualized losses in their dollar value of around -1 or -2 percent. Finally, note that where volatilities are large, the arithmetic mean exceeds the geometric mean by a big margin, notably, for Germany.

Table 7-1: Nominal exchange rate changes against the US dollar, annually 1900–2000

Country	Geometric mean %	Arithmetic mean %	Standard error %	Standard deviation %	Minimum change %	Minimum year	Maximum change %	Maximum year
Australia	-1.5	-1.0	1.0	10.0	-39.6	1931	56.0	1933
Belgium	-2.1	-1.1	1.3	13.3	-40.0	1919	56.9	1933
Canada	-0.4	-0.3	0.4	4.3	-17.2	1931	16.1	1933
Denmark	-0.7	0.0	1.2	12.0	-40.9	1946	41.0	1925
France	-4.7	-2.0	2.0	20.3	-85.3	1946	91.3	1943
Germany*	-3.0	9.6	11.0	109.9	-100.0	1923	1046.3	1948
Ireland	-1.4	-0.8	1.1	10.8	-31.7	1949	56.0	1933
Italy	-5.7	-3.7	1.7	17.4	-64.8	1946	60.9	1933
Japan	-3.9	-0.8	1.8	17.8	-91.5	1945	48.5	1933
The Netherlands	0.1	0.9	1.2	12.2	-59.1	1946	56.4	1933
South Africa	-2.8	-2.4	0.9	9.2	-38.6	1984	19.0	1921
Spain	-3.2	-1.6	1.7	17.6	-62.2	1946	99.2	1939
Sweden	-0.9	-0.4	1.0	10.3	-30.2	1931	47.3	1933
Switzerland	1.2	1.7	1.1	11.3	-29.2	1936	57.7	1933
United Kingdom	-1.2	-0.6	1.1	11.0	-30.5	1931	56.0	1933

*For Germany, the means, standard deviation and standard error are based on 99 years, excluding 1922–23

7.2 The international monetary system

These histories of currency appreciation and depreciation reflect the wars and bouts of inflation that took place over the century. To delve further into currency fluctuations since 1900, we need to review the changing nature of the international monetary system.

During the last century, currencies were strongly influenced by the changing exchange rate systems that were prevalent around the world. The gold standard was well established by the start of the twentieth century. Although central and private banks issued paper money and created bank deposits, under the classical gold standard governments backed their notes with a fixed amount of gold and commercial banks maintained a fixed ratio of gold to their liabilities. As Figure 7-1 shows, this kept exchange rates stable until the gold standard broke down in 1914 at the start of the First World War. It was briefly reinstated from 1925–31 as the Gold Exchange Standard. However, competitive devaluations, beggar-thy-neighbor trade policies, and the destructive effects of wars punctuated the first half of the twentieth century.

In 1944 at Bretton Woods, New Hampshire, the Allied nations created the International Monetary Fund (IMF) and the World Bank to instigate a new post-war monetary system. Implemented in 1946, the Bretton Woods Agreement required each government to peg its exchange rate to the dollar or gold. Since one ounce of gold was priced at $35, and the US Treasury stood ready to exchange dollars for gold, exchange rates were fixed against the dollar. They were to fluctuate only within 1 percent of the stated value of the currency, and central banks were to intervene in foreign exchange markets to defend currencies from temporary pressures. Rates were to be changed only in cases of fundamental disequilibrium. By 1971 these "fixed" rates had in fact been changed at some point by all twenty-one major industrial countries except the United States and Japan. Though infrequent, devaluations and revaluations were often large. When the United States devalued the dollar in 1971, the Bretton Woods System collapsed. After some last-ditch attempts to set new fixed rates, the world turned in 1973 to the floating exchange rate system that persists to the present day.

There were thus four exchange rate regimes over the twentieth century. During 1900–14 the gold standard was in effect. After that, apart from a brief return to the Gold Exchange Standard, the period 1914–45 contained the two world wars. The Bretton Woods fixed-rate system then operated from 1946–71. Finally, the period since has been one of floating exchange rates. Currencies went through an adjustment to the Bretton Woods system until 1949. It is therefore helpful to start by dividing our period into two: 1900–49 and 1950–2000. Figure 7-2 shows how exchange rates moved in each of the two halves of our 101-year period.

Germany's hyperinflation after the First World War and currency reform after the Second World War take the Deutschemark to the top of the list of depreciated currencies in the period before 1950, although Germany subsequently had a strong currency. Japan's exchange rate behavior also reversed over the two halves of the century, and the yen was the strongest of the sixteen currencies during the second half-century. Italy, France, and Spain had weak currencies in both halves of the century. South Africa had the weakest currency in the second half of the century. The Swiss franc was strong throughout the entire period.

The century-long average therefore masks secular changes and cross-sectional variation in the strength and weakness of international currencies. Often, exchange rates appear to fluctuate because of changes in the purchasing power of the currency. The gold standard

Figure 7-2: Exchange rate changes vs. US dollar: first half of twentieth century vs. 1950–2000

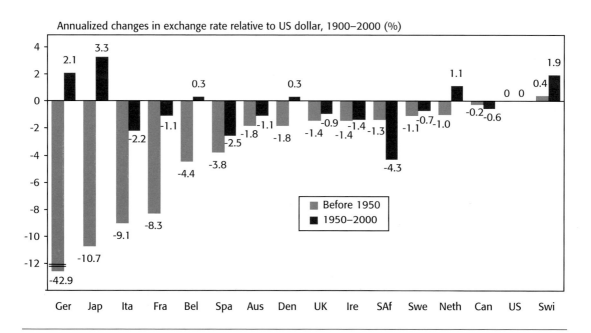

imposed a rigid control on inflation. But the potential for periodic devaluations under the fixed exchange rate system, and for parity fluctuations under the floating rate system, make it appropriate to look in more detail at the evolution of exchange rates over the last century.

7.3 Long-run purchasing power parity

Figure 7-3 plots the exchange rate between US dollars and British pounds. The vertical axis shows the number of dollars required to purchase £1: a decline in the exchange rate denotes a stronger dollar (fewer dollars needed to buy £1) and a weaker pound. The nominal exchange rate plotted in Figure 7-3 shows that at start-2001, the number of dollars needed to buy £1 was 70 percent lower than it was in 1900. Comparison with the inflation rates discussed in chapter 5 shows that the fall in sterling accompanied higher inflation in the United Kingdom than in the United States. We therefore adjust the exchange rate for inflation in the United Kingdom relative to the United States. The inflation-adjusted, or real, exchange rate in each year is defined as the nominal exchange rate multiplied by the ratio of the two countries' inflation indexes. Figure 7-3 shows that over the long run, the real dollar/pound exchange rate has been roughly constant.

There has been much debate about the extent to which exchange rates reflect inflation rates. An extreme viewpoint would be that purchasing power parity (PPP) holds absolutely. That is, exchange-adjusted prices for goods and services are identical all over the world, and a unit of local currency should therefore have the same purchasing power in all countries. It is

Figure 7-3: Nominal and real dollar/pound exchange rate

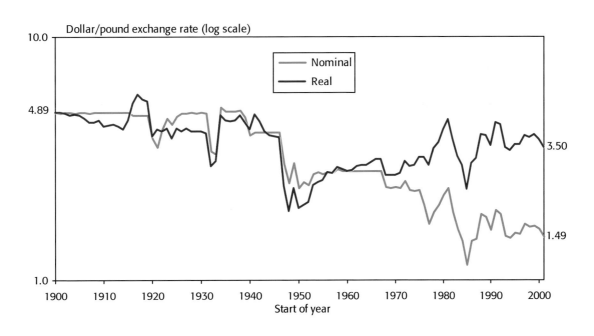

Figure 7-4: Purchasing power parity over the period 1900–2000

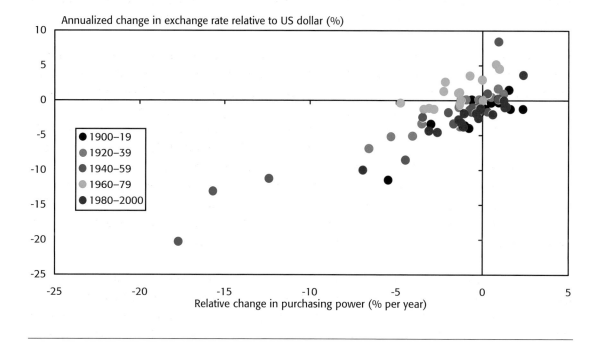

more common to focus on relative PPP, which asserts that an exchange rate will change to reflect movements in the two countries' price levels. This version of PPP asserts that the exchange rate change over an interval should be equal to the inflation differential over the same period. If PPP held over the twentieth century, then we would expect the real exchange rate in Figure 7-3 to remain constant.

Transportation costs, tariffs, trade restrictions and product differentiation make the strictest version of PPP manifestly false. Nevertheless, especially over the long run, there is a clear tendency for currencies with a high rate of inflation to devalue relative to currencies with lower rates of inflation. This can be seen in Figure 7-4, which plots changes in the nominal exchange rate (on the vertical axis) against changes in relative purchasing power (on the horizontal axis). Exchange rates and purchasing power are calculated for each of fifteen countries relative to the US dollar and US inflation. The time periods over which these changes are measured are 1900–19, 1920–39, 1940–59, 1960–79 and 1980–2000, so the scatter diagram contains seventy-five observations.

7.4   Deviations from purchasing power parity

Although most tests of relative PPP support its validity over the long term, departures from parity often last for quite a number of years. Such misalignments do not necessarily indicate mispricing. In the earlier years, inflation indexes were narrow and non-representative, with substantial variation across countries in the composition and weighting of the price index, and parity deviations can easily reflect mismeasurement of inflation. Turning to more recent years it is difficult to believe that, in a world of floating currencies and liquid foreign exchange markets, currencies can remain at a disequilibrium level for years on end.

When deviations from PPP appear to be present it is likely that exchange rates are responding not only to relative inflation but also to other economic and political factors. For example, an oil-producing nation that becomes wealthier through discovery of new reserves, or an increase in the relative price of oil, can expect its currency to appreciate. Changes in productivity differentials, such as Japan's post-war productivity growth in the traded-goods sector, can bring similar wealth effects, with domestic inflation that does not endanger the country's exchange rate. Different weightings in non-traded goods and services—education, healthcare, defense and so on—can yield misleading indicators of a country's competitiveness. Relative changes in the real interest rate between countries can also lead to capital flows and wealth effects. As Taylor (2001) notes, however, in spite of this, real exchange rates have in the main been stable over the long term, as shown in Figure 7-5.

Figure 7-5 presents the real exchange rates for selected countries over the period from 1900 to 2000. As with the dollar/pound rate discussed above, these inflation-adjusted currency values have been comparatively stable over this 101-year period. There have been a few very major short-term fluctuations, however, mostly in Germany. Figure 7-5 shows that for Germany, there were two large downward spikes that reversed themselves within a few years.

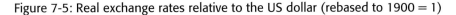

Figure 7-5: Real exchange rates relative to the US dollar (rebased to 1900 = 1)

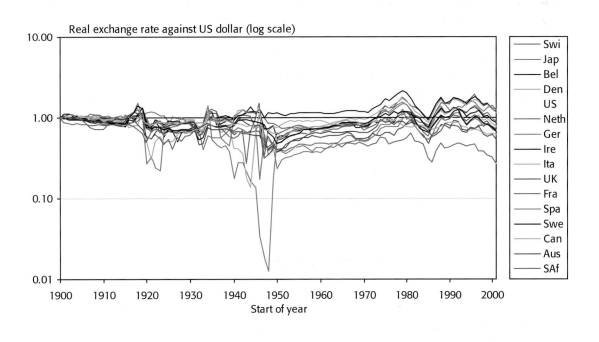

Table 7-2: Real exchange rate changes against the US dollar, annually 1900–2000

Country	Geometric mean %	Arithmetic mean %	Standard error %	Standard deviation %	Minimum change %	Minimum year	Maximum change %	Maximum year
Australia	-0.6	-0.1	1.1	10.7	-39.0	1931	54.2	1933
Belgium	0.2	1.0	1.3	13.3	-32.1	1919	54.2	1933
Canada	-0.5	-0.4	0.5	4.6	-18.1	1931	12.9	1933
Denmark	0.1	1.0	1.3	12.7	-50.3	1946	37.2	1933
France	-0.4	2.5	2.4	24.0	-78.3	1946	141.5	1943
Germany	-0.1	15.1	13.4	134.8	-75.0	1945	1302.0	1948
Ireland	-0.1	0.5	1.1	11.2	-37.0	1946	56.6	1933
Italy	-0.2	4.0	3.9	39.5	-64.9	1946	335.2	1944
Japan	0.2	3.2	2.9	29.5	-78.3	1945	253.0	1946
The Netherlands	-0.1	0.8	1.3	12.6	-61.6	1946	55.7	1933
South Africa	-1.3	-0.7	1.0	10.5	-35.3	1946	37.3	1986
Spain	-0.4	1.1	1.9	18.8	-56.4	1946	128.7	1939
Sweden	-0.4	0.2	1.1	10.7	-38.0	1919	43.5	1933
Switzerland	0.2	0.8	1.1	11.2	-29.0	1936	53.3	1933
United Kingdom	-0.3	0.3	1.2	11.7	-36.7	1946	55.2	1933

The second, and larger of these, was from the Second World War through the currency reforms of 1948. This is probably accentuated by the fact that wartime inflation calculations in Germany were controlled, while German exchange rates during this period may not always have been meaningful.

While real exchange rates do not appear to exhibit a long term upward or downward trend, they are clearly volatile, and on a year-to-year basis, PPP explains little of the fluctuations in foreign exchange rates. The annual rates of change and the standard deviation of the annual changes in real exchange rates are reported in Table 7-2. Some of the extreme changes reflect exchange rates or inflation indexes that are not representative, typically (as in Germany) because of wartime controls, and this may amplify the volatility of real exchange rate changes. Given the potential measurement error in inflation indexes, and the fact that real exchange rates involve a ratio of two different price index series, it is all the more striking that, with the exception of South Africa, all real exchange rates appreciate or depreciate annually by no more than a fraction of one percentage point.

7.5 Volatility of exchange rates

At the time floating exchange rates were adopted in 1973, it was asserted that exchange rates would become free to adjust to international differences in inflation. Countries with price levels that were rising fast would see their currencies depreciate, and countries with relatively low price inflation would see their currencies appreciate. While nominal exchange rates would be free to fluctuate, real exchange rates were expected to become less volatile. We quantify the post-war volatility of real exchange rates in Figure 7-6. This chart shows the standard deviation of annual changes in the real exchange rate, relative to the dollar, from

Figure 7-6: Volatility of annual changes in the real exchange rate: 1950–71 vs. 1972–2000

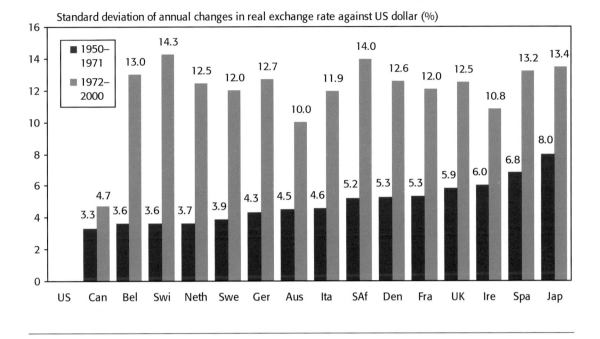

1950 to 2000. We break the time period since the middle of the last century into two halves: the fixed-rate period 1950–71, and the floating-rate period 1972–2000. There is a pervasive tendency for real exchange rates to have been more volatile in the recent floating-rate period, than in the earlier Bretton Woods era as demonstrated more formally by Taylor (2001).

Increased currency volatility has come as a disappointment to the proponents of floating rates and to those who had accepted their arguments. On average, the fifteen non-US countries had a volatility of exchange rates relative to the dollar that was 2.4 times as large during the floating rate period, as compared to the Bretton Woods period. The average volatility of the fifteen non-UK countries' sterling exchange rates was 2.1 times as large as in the Bretton Woods period (not shown in the chart), while that of the non-Japanese countries' yen exchange rate, and of the non-German countries' Deutschemark exchange rate were also much increased. It appears that currency volatility turned out to be high over the floating-rate period because of increased uncertainty over real exchange rates, rather than because of the impact of inflation differentials.

Looking to the future, nearly half the countries in our study entered the Eurozone in the late 1990s. For these countries, intra-Eurozone currency volatility has declined to zero. However, there has not been a corresponding, drastic reduction in the volatility of exchange rates relative to other countries outside the Eurozone. In making international comparisons of investment returns, the importance of exchange rate fluctuations has not diminished. We therefore turn in the next section to looking at common-currency returns.

7.6　Common-currency returns on bonds and equities

In chapter 4, we looked at real bond and equity returns around the world. These returns, which were displayed in Figure 4-7, were the real returns to a domestic investor, based on local purchasing power. We therefore compared a US citizen's real return from investing in US equities with, say, a Dutch citizen's real return from Dutch equities.

When considering cross-border investment, we also need to take account of exchange rate movements. For example, consider the simple case of bilateral international investment with a US citizen buying UK equities and a UK citizen acquiring US stocks. Each citizen now has two investments, one in foreign equities and the other in foreign currency. The annualized real return on equities from 1900–2000 was 6.72 percent in the United States and 5.78 percent in the United Kingdom. Each of our two investors, however, wishes to know the real return in their own local currency. To convert real returns in one currency into real returns in another, we simply adjust them by the change in the real exchange rate. Were we to convert nominal returns, we would use changes in the nominal exchange rate.

The historical real exchange rates against the US dollar were shown in Table 7-2. Over the period 1900–2000, the UK pound sterling was weaker than the US dollar by 0.33 percent per year. Thus, the US citizen who invested in UK equities had a return of 5.78 percent (from UK equities) less 0.33 percent (from sterling compared to the dollar), giving an overall return of $(1 + 5.78\%) \times (1 - 0.33\%) - 1 = 5.43\%$. In contrast, the UK investor who purchased US stocks had a return of 6.72 percent (from US equities) plus 0.33 percent (from the dollar compared to sterling), which equals $(1 + 6.72\%) \times (1 + 0.33\%) - 1 = 7.07\%$.

Rather than just comparing domestic returns, an alternative way of making cross-country comparisons is thus to translate all countries' returns into real returns in a common currency using the real exchange rate. The choice of currency does not affect the ranking of returns across markets, so for illustrative purposes we will work initially in terms of the US dollar.

Figure 7-7 shows the currency translation process for equity returns around the world. The blue bars show the annualized real domestic currency returns from 1900–2000 presented earlier in Figure 4-7. The green bars show the annualized real exchange rate movement over the same period, with positive values indicating currencies that appreciated against the dollar, and vice versa. The red bars are then the common-currency returns, in real US dollars, from the perspective of a US investor. The chart shows very clearly that the adjustment from local currency real returns (in blue) to dollar real returns (in red) is affected simply by (geometric) addition of the real exchange rate movement (in green). In the case of the United Kingdom, for example, the domestic real return (blue bar) is 5.78 percent, the real exchange rate movement (green bar) is -0.33 percent, giving a real dollar return (red bar) of 5.43 percent—exactly the same values as in the sample calculation shown above.

Figure 7-7 shows that, thanks to PPP, we obtain broadly the same ranking of equity markets, whether we rank them by domestic real returns (blue bars), or by their real dollar returns (red bars). Typically, countries change positions only at the margin. Thus in dollar terms, Belgium

Figure 7-7: Real equity returns in US dollars and local currency, 1900–2000

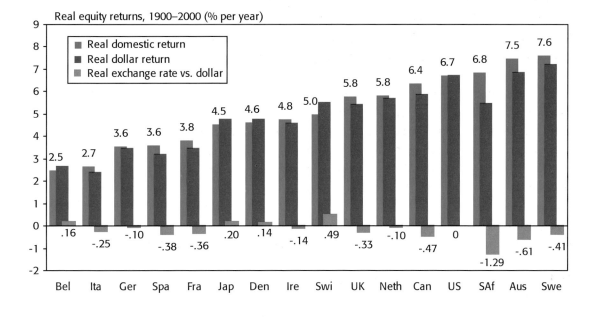

edges ahead of Italy because of its stronger currency over the last century. Similarly, Switzerland moves ahead of the United Kingdom, again because of the relative performance of the Swiss franc versus the pound. The biggest loser is South Africa, which slips back from third place in domestic terms to seventh in dollar terms because of the extreme weakness of the rand, especially during the second half of the twentieth century.

Figure 7-8 shows real equity and bond returns for our sixteen countries in dollar terms, from the perspective of a US investor, that is, denominated in US inflation-adjusted dollars. The equity returns are identical to those shown in Figure 7-7, but countries are now ranked in ascending order of their dollar equity returns. For US-based equity investors, their US home market gave a hard-to-beat real return of 6.7 percent per year, with just two countries, Sweden and Australia, providing higher returns. US bonds ranked in fourth place, after Switzerland, Denmark, and Sweden. All bond markets (with the exception of Germany) achieved a real, inflation-adjusted return in a range running from around -2 percent to around +3 percent. Even though PPP appears roughly to hold in the long run, the bond maturity premium was simply not large enough to generate a uniformly positive return in real terms for international bond investors over this period.

For comparisons such as this, the common currency does not, of course, have to be the US dollar. We can obtain common-currency real returns from the perspective of an investor based in any country simply by adjusting by the cross-rates inferred from Table 7-2. For example, the annualized real returns denominated in UK inflation-adjusted sterling from the point of view of a UK investor are obtained by adjusting by the real sterling-dollar exchange rate movement of -.33 percent per year. In a pound sterling equivalent version of Figure 7-8,

Figure 7-8: Equity and bond returns in real dollar terms, 1900–2000

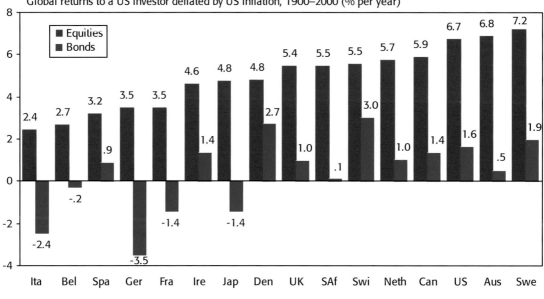

would therefore find that all returns would be about 0.3 to 0.4 percent larger than the dollar returns currently shown. Since the same sterling-dollar exchange rate would be applied to all returns, the ranking of the countries would remain unchanged, and this remains true whichever common currency is chosen.

This is confirmed by Table 7-3, which provides annualized common-currency real returns for equities, bonds, and bills from the viewpoints of both a US and a UK investor. As can be seen, the sterling returns are all between 0.3 and 0.4 percent higher than the dollar returns, and the choice of currency does not affect the country rankings. This table also serves as a summary of the quantitative evidence presented in this section. Equities have provided a substantial real return, markedly above bonds, and with a cross-country average of some 5 percent per year. Though the real return on long-term bonds has been positive, it has been low, and several countries have had bond markets that failed to keep pace with inflation. The cross-country average of the real bond returns has been around ½ percent per year. Short-term deposits provided a real return that was, on average, barely different from zero.

The returns above were presented from the viewpoint of a US or UK investor. The final column of Table 7-3 provides a set of real exchange rate conversion factors for the 101-year period from 1900–2000. These can be used to translate returns from real US dollars into real currency terms for an investor from any other country. For a country whose currency is the pengo, the formula is: *Real pengo return* is equal to *1 + Real dollar return* multiplied by *Country factor*, minus 1. To illustrate this, consider the real pound sterling return to a UK-based individual who had invested in US equities. The real exchange rate factor shown for the United Kingdom in the final column of Table 7-3 is 1.0033, while the real dollar return for

Table 7-3: Annualized returns on equities, bonds, and bills in real dollars and pounds, 1900–2000

Country	Equity returns		Bond returns		Bill returns		Real exchange rate factor against US $ (1900–2000)
	Real $s	Real £s	Real $s	Real £s	Real $s	Real £s	
Australia	6.8	7.2	0.5	0.8	-0.2	0.1	1.0061
Belgium	2.7	3.0	-0.2	0.1	-0.2	0.2	0.9984
Canada	5.9	6.2	1.4	1.7	1.2	1.6	1.0048
Denmark	4.8	5.1	2.7	3.0	2.9	3.3	0.9986
France	3.5	3.8	-1.4	-1.1	-3.7	-3.4	1.0036
Germany*	3.5	3.8	-3.5	-3.1	-1.8	-1.5	1.0010
Ireland	4.6	5.0	1.4	1.7	1.1	1.4	1.0014
Italy	2.4	2.8	-2.4	-2.1	-4.3	-4.0	1.0025
Japan	4.8	5.1	-1.4	-1.1	-1.8	-1.5	0.9980
The Netherlands	5.7	6.1	1.0	1.3	0.6	0.9	1.0010
South Africa	5.5	5.8	0.1	0.4	-0.5	-0.2	1.0131
Spain	3.2	3.5	0.9	1.2	0.0	0.3	1.0039
Sweden	7.2	7.6	1.9	2.3	1.6	1.9	1.0041
Switzerland	5.5	5.9	3.0	3.3	1.3	1.6	0.9978
United Kingdom	5.4	5.8	1.0	1.3	0.6	1.0	1.0033
United States	6.7	7.1	1.6	1.9	0.9	1.2	1.0000

*The bond and bill return figures for Germany exclude the years 1922–23

the United States is 6.7 percent. The real pound sterling return was thus $1.067 \times 1.0033 - 1 = 7.1$ percent, which corresponds to the figure shown for the real pound return on US equities in the bottom row and third column of the table. Similarly, the real Swiss franc return to a Swiss investor who had invested in Australian bonds would have been $1.005 \times .9978 - 1 = 0.3$ percent.

7.7 Summary

Currency values have fluctuated considerably over the 101 years from 1900–2000. This period was marked by four different exchange rate regimes, and these exerted a strong influence on currency movements. Most currencies weakened against the dollar, with five countries standing out for the extreme loss of value in their currencies: Germany, Japan, and France, where the weakness occurred in the first half-century, and Italy and Spain, whose currencies were relatively weak in the second half-century as well. Only the Swiss franc and the Dutch guilder proved stronger than the dollar, and the guilder by only a slight margin.

Purchasing power parity (PPP), which asserts that goods and services will have a similar price experience in different countries, is a poor description of year-to-year foreign exchange fluctuations. The short-run real exchange rate has been quite volatile, and there has been a pervasive tendency for real exchange rates to be more volatile in the recent floating-rate period than in the earlier Bretton Woods era. Over the long run, however, changing relative price levels do tend to be reflected in changes in exchange rates, and real exchange rates tend to be relatively stable.

This tendency for PPP to hold in the long run has important implications for international investors. It means, for example, that a long-run US investor buying UK securities can expect a change in the exchange rate between the dollar and the pound to be offset by the difference in inflation rates between the two countries. Perhaps our notional investor is unsure whether to retire in Florida or Oxfordshire. The investor can seek comfort in the fact that our best guess is that, over the long haul, the dollar value of her UK investments will change in a way that compensates for changes in the cost of living between these two locations.

PPP also matters when comparing investment returns internationally. Earlier, in chapter 4, we made international comparisons on the basis of real, inflation-adjusted returns within each country. By focusing on the purchasing power of the investment return that had been achieved, this approach takes account of the fact that investors in each country have experienced differing levels of price inflation. This approach also has the advantage that it focuses on the primary group of security holders within a country—local investors.

Our emphasis in this chapter is the perspective of an international investor, for whom it may be inappropriate to compare returns in different countries by adjusting every country's return by a different, local inflation index. Real returns may spuriously appear to vary across countries because of the differing goods and services, and their inconsistent weightings, within each country's inflation indexes. The procedure that we adopt is thus to convert all asset returns to real, common-currency returns, using the real exchange rate. This yields the real return that would have been achieved by an investor resident in a particular country.

Are these common-currency returns the best way to compare international capital market returns? There is no clear-cut answer, because adjusting via the real exchange rate also poses problems. First, investors' costs of living may not adequately be represented by our inflation adjustments. The inflation index we use may not match the consumption pattern of investors in the market under consideration. Second, we are implicitly assuming that investors could invest globally throughout the twentieth century, yet markets were segmented for a significant part of this period. And third, as in our domestic comparisons, we are ignoring taxes, fees, or adverse selection costs, and this may matter more when the international comparison presumes transnational investing. We discuss the issue of the barriers to, and costs of, international investment in section 8.6 of the next chapter.

With a common numeraire, we are nevertheless able to make comparisons across markets with added confidence. Comparing the real, common-currency returns in Figure 7-8 with the local-currency real returns presented earlier in Figure 4-7 shows that the same group of countries has underperformed, and the same has done well. This is precisely what we would expect given our finding that, to a first approximation, PPP has held over the long run for most of our sixteen countries. Our rankings of real returns are thus relatively robust, and do not seem to be an artifact of the inflation indexes used in particular countries.

Chapter 8 International investment

Today, the United States has the world's largest equity market. Even so, US equities comprise less than half the world's total. US investors who restrict themselves to their home market are thus ignoring over half the world's opportunity set, and foregoing the risk reduction benefits from international diversification. The case for international investment seems even more compelling for investors from smaller markets such as the United Kingdom, France, or Denmark.

While these arguments may seem persuasive, what is the historical evidence? This chapter addresses the question of how investors from around the world, including the United States, would have fared from foreign investment. In doing so, it recognizes that international investors are concerned not just with the returns from investing abroad, but also the risks.

Cross-border investment typically involves taking stakes not only in foreign markets but also in their currencies, and hence entails exchange risk. We begin in section 8.1 by taking a closer look at the risk of the common-currency returns documented in chapter 7, on a country by country basis. We investigate how the total risk breaks down into local market risk and currency risk, and examine the impact and wisdom of hedging against currency risk.

In section 8.2, we create benchmarks for assessing the risk and return from international diversification by constructing a twentieth century world index for both equities and bonds. These two indexes correspond to a policy of diversifying across all sixteen countries in proportion to their size. In section 8.3, we use the Sharpe ratio, which measures the reward per unit of risk, to analyze whether investors in the United States and elsewhere, would, with hindsight, have been better off investing in these world indexes rather than domestically.

International diversification reduces risk because different countries' markets and currencies are less than perfectly correlated. Section 8.4 provides evidence on the correlations among markets, and how these have changed over time. Section 8.5 then takes a closer look at the risk reduction achievable from international diversification. We examine how rapidly risk is reduced as we move from single country through to full worldwide investment.

Despite the potential benefits from risk reduction from international diversification, investors in most countries still hold portfolios that are heavily weighted toward domestic assets. In section 8.6, we document this home bias puzzle. We discuss the costs and impediments to international investment that existed at various stages during the twentieth century, some of which remain in place today. Section 8.7 then provides a brief summary.

8.1 Local market versus currency risk

International investors care about risk as well as return. Investing abroad involves exchange risk as well as local market risk—US investors who buy UK shares are also buying a stake in the pound. As we saw in chapter 7, currencies have been quite volatile. This raises the concern that currency risk may greatly amplify the risks of overseas investment. In chapter 7, we analyzed the common-currency returns from investing in different countries. This section focuses on the risks by presenting the standard deviations of those returns and decomposing them into local market risk and currency risk. We begin by taking the perspective of a US-based international investor, and focus on risk in real dollar terms.

Figure 8-1 shows the standard deviations and their breakdown over the period 1900–2000. There are two bars for each country. The lower part of the left-hand bar shows the standard deviation of real, local currency equity returns, while the right-hand bar shows the standard deviation of that country's real exchange rate against the dollar (as tabulated in Table 7-2). The total height of the left-hand bar shows the standard deviation of that country's equity returns in real, dollar terms. The top part of the left-hand bar thus shows the contribution that currency risk makes to total risk for a dollar-based international investor.

Figure 8-1 shows that currency risk did not add greatly to a US-based investor's risk, despite the high currency volatility during the twentieth century. The total dollar risk was generally less than the sum of the local market and currency risks because the correlation between the two returns was such that they often offset one another. The correlations are shown in Table 8-1. The top part covers equities, and the bottom half covers bonds. The left-hand side relates to the full period from 1900–2000, and the right-hand side to 1950–2000. The data for Figure 8-1 is thus taken from the first three columns of the top left quadrant. The fourth column in this quadrant shows the correlations between local currency real returns on each country's equity market and that country's real exchange rate against the dollar.

Figure 8-1: Standard deviations of real, US dollar returns on world equity markets, 1900–2000

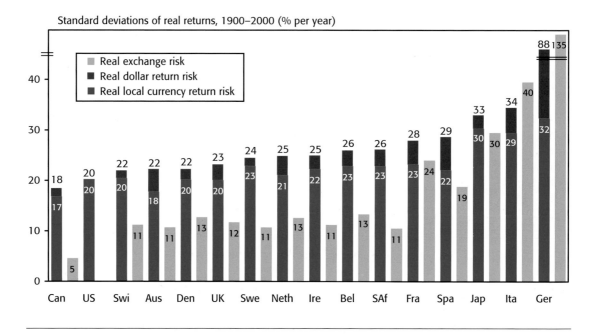

Table 8-1: Standard deviations of real, US dollar returns on world equity and bond markets

	1900–2000				1950–2000			
	Standard deviation of real returns (% per year)			Correlation between local currency real returns and real exchange rate changes	Standard deviation of real returns (% per year)			Correlation between local currency real returns and real exchange rate changes
Asset and country	Local currency	Real exchange rate	Dollar returns		Local currency	Real exchange rate	Dollar returns	
Equities								
Australia	17.7	10.7	22.2	0.06	21.9	8.2	22.2	-0.18
Belgium	22.8	13.3	25.9	-0.13	18.2	10.0	20.5	-0.14
Canada	16.8	4.6	18.4	0.18	15.9	4.2	17.1	0.11
Denmark	20.1	12.7	22.2	-0.15	25.3	10.1	23.5	-0.36
France	23.1	24.0	27.9	-0.27	23.9	9.6	26.0	-0.13
Germany	32.3	134.8	87.8	-0.19	27.3	10.0	30.0	-0.11
Ireland	22.2	11.2	24.9	-0.09	28.5	9.0	29.9	-0.14
Italy	29.4	39.5	34.4	-0.33	27.9	9.4	31.6	0.05
Japan	30.3	29.5	32.9	-0.23	30.6	11.3	35.4	0.10
The Netherlands	21.0	12.6	24.8	-0.04	20.7	9.7	20.0	-0.37
South Africa	22.8	10.5	26.1	0.02	21.6	11.0	26.7	0.20
Spain	22.0	18.8	28.6	-0.07	26.4	10.8	30.7	-0.01
Sweden	22.8	10.7	24.4	-0.06	23.1	9.5	22.1	-0.32
Switzerland	20.4	11.2	21.9	-0.22	21.7	11.0	22.9	-0.28
United Kingdom	20.0	11.7	23.1	-0.10	23.4	10.1	24.5	-0.18
United States	20.2	0.0	20.2	na	17.3	0.0	17.3	na
Bonds								
Australia	13.0	10.7	18.4	0.03	11.7	8.2	12.1	-0.36
Belgium	12.1	13.3	18.1	0.03	9.9	10.0	15.0	0.05
Canada	10.6	4.6	11.7	0.00	10.7	4.2	10.8	-0.17
Denmark	12.5	12.7	19.0	0.04	13.0	10.1	16.0	-0.18
France	14.4	24.0	23.0	-0.10	6.8	9.6	12.5	0.03
Germany*	15.9	134.2	36.5	-0.55	6.1	10.0	12.2	0.02
Ireland	13.3	11.2	17.7	-0.06	14.6	9.0	18.1	-0.02
Italy	14.4	39.5	22.6	-0.45	7.6	9.4	12.9	0.10
Japan	20.9	29.5	24.0	-0.25	19.4	11.3	23.1	0.00
The Netherlands	9.4	12.6	16.0	0.04	8.7	9.7	13.0	-0.06
South Africa	10.6	10.5	14.8	-0.04	10.6	11.0	16.1	0.10
Spain	12.0	18.8	21.9	0.05	10.8	10.8	15.4	-0.05
Sweden	12.7	10.7	16.4	-0.10	9.4	9.5	12.3	-0.21
Switzerland	8.0	11.2	13.4	-0.11	6.1	11.0	12.7	-0.01
United Kingdom	14.5	11.7	18.4	-0.06	13.7	10.1	16.6	-0.10
United States	10.0	0.0	10.0	na	11.4	0.0	11.4	na

* The standard deviations and correlations for bonds for Germany for the period 1900–2000 exclude the years 1922–23

These correlations are typically small and slightly negative, averaging -0.11 across the fifteen "foreign" (from a US perspective) equity markets. This is why currency risk has generally added only modestly to the dollar risk of foreign investment. Investors are taking a stake in two assets—a country's equity market and its local currency—the returns from which tend to move largely independently, and if anything, to act as a modest natural built-in hedge.

Exchange risk can sometimes offset local equity market risk by so much that the risk in dollar terms ends up below the local market risk. The figures in the top right-hand quadrant of Table 8-1 show that between 1950–2000, there were several countries with negative correlations large enough to ensure this was the case. Consider in particular a US holder of equities in The Netherlands, Denmark, or Sweden. Such an investor would have experienced less volatility in dollar terms than domestic investors in those countries would have faced in local currency terms.

The lower half of Table 8-1 shows the matching data for bonds. Bonds were less volatile than equities, so exchange rate volatility generally exceeded (1900–2000), or was of a similar magnitude to (1950–2000), local bond market volatility. Apart from this, the same pattern emerges as with equities. The correlations between each country's local currency real bond returns and its real exchange rate against the dollar were mostly small and slightly negative. From 1900–2000, the average correlation across the fifteen "foreign" markets was -0.10, while from 1950–2000, the average correlation was -0.06.

International investors can, of course, choose to hedge currency risk. We have seen, however, that even for single country investments, exchange risk does not greatly increase portfolio risk, and its impact is even smaller in the context of internationally diversified portfolios (see section 8.2). Indeed, unhedged international portfolios might even have lower long-term variability than their hedged equivalents when measured in real terms.

8.2   A twentieth century world index for equities and bonds

Up to this point, we have focused on the real dollar returns (see section 7.6) and the risks (see section 8.1) that would have been experienced by an investor based in the United States investing in each individual bond, bill, and equity market around the world. The main benefits of international investment, however, arise from international diversification across markets.

There is a clear parallel here with domestic diversification. In our initial discussion of risk, in section 4.6, we saw how quickly diversifiable risk is reduced as the number of stocks in a portfolio is increased (see Figure 4-11). We concluded that an investor with no stock selection skills should hold as widely diversified a portfolio as possible, thus avoiding exposure to diversifiable, and hence unrewarded, risk. This effectively means holding a stake in the overall market. The same principle holds when investing internationally. Risk can be reduced as the returns on different markets and currencies are less than perfectly correlated. Investors with no special insights about the prospects for different markets and currencies should, like their domestic counterparts, hold as widely diversified a portfolio as possible. If it were not for market imperfections and differences in tastes, they should hold the "world market portfolio."

How would investors in a world market portfolio have fared over the 101 years from 1900–2000? To answer this, we construct a world equity market index. Initially, we compute this in dollar terms, from the perspective of a US-based international investor. The index comprises sixteen positions, one in each country, and is based on the real dollar returns for each country (see section 7.6), weighted by country size (see section 3.3).

Figure 8-2 plots the cumulative return on the world equity index from 1900–2000. It shows that $1 invested in this sixteen-country index in 1900 would have grown in real, US purchasing power terms, to $295 by end-2000, an annualized real return of 5.8 percent. As Figure 8-2 shows, this was less than from investing in the US equity market, where $1 grew to $711 in real terms, an annualized real return of 6.7 percent. When the US returns are stripped out of the world index, the world excluding the United States (world ex-US) naturally performs worse still, with $1 growing to just $162 in real terms, an annualized return of 5.2 percent.

We saw earlier in Figure 7-8 that only two of the fifteen non-US equity markets beat the United States. Given this excellent "solo" performance by US equities, it is not surprising to find that they outperformed the world ex-US, and hence the world index. One of the key arguments put forward for investing internationally, however, is diversification of risk. The "equities" panel on the left-hand side of Table 8-2 gives statistics on the risks as well as the returns from investing in the world equity index. The top section of the table gives the figures for 1900–2000, which show that both the world ex-US and the world indexes had lower standard deviations than the United States, with the world index some 15.8 percent below the United States. This is despite the fact that US equities on average made up around half the world's total during the twentieth century, and in spite of the United States proving to be one of the lowest risk equity markets.

Figure 8-2: Cumulative returns (in real dollars) on the world equity index, 1900–2000

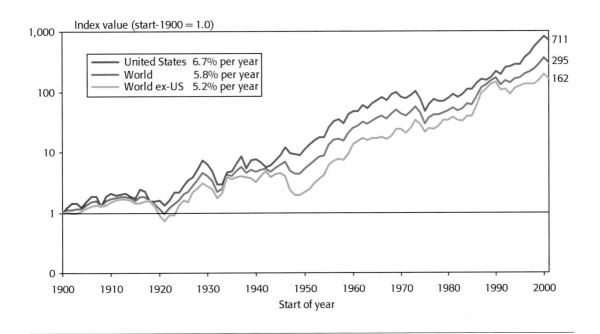

returns in recognition of the fact that investors can blend an investment in equities with lending or borrowing at the interest rate to achieve any desired level of risk.

To illustrate use of the Sharpe ratio, we compare the risk/return trade-off for US equities versus the world index. From 1900–2000, US real equity returns had a standard deviation of 20.16 percent per year, versus 17.04 percent for the world portfolio (see Table 8-2). A US investor could have achieved the same risk as on the world portfolio by starting each year with a proportion 17.04/20.16 = 84.5 percent in US equities and the remaining 15.5 percent in risk free bills. Over this period, the annualized bill return was 0.875 percent, so the investor would have received a return of approximately 84.5% × 6.72 + 15.5% × 0.875 = 5.81 percent. This compares with the 5.79 percent attained on the world portfolio. By coincidence, after adjusting for risk, US investors would have earned virtually identical returns from both domestic and international equity investment over this period, with domestic investment having the slight edge. This ignores any barriers and costs to foreign investment, and also ignores some of the complexities of multiperiod investment (see Sharpe, 1994).

Equivalently, we could just have compared the two Sharpe ratios. The excess return for the United States is 1.0672/1.00875 − 1 = 5.79 percent, so the US Sharpe ratio is 5.79/20.16 = 0.287. For the world, the excess return (relative to US treasury bills) is 1.0579/1.00875 − 1 = 4.87 percent, so the Sharpe ratio is 4.87/17.04 = 0.286. This leads to the same conclusion, namely, that over the twentieth century, US citizens who invested in the world equity portfolio would have achieved almost exactly the same reward-to-risk ratio as those who restricted themselves to US equities. These Sharpe ratios are shown in Figure 8-4, which also

Figure 8-4: Comparative reward-to-risk ratios for US citizens investing in world versus US equities

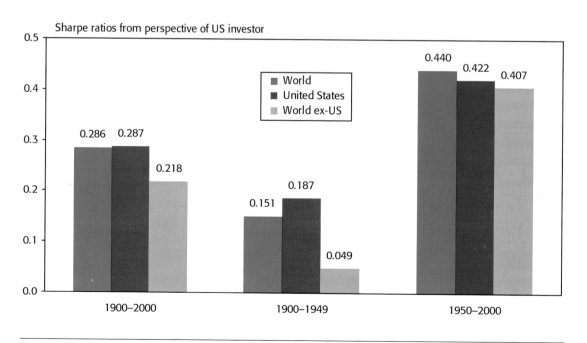

gives the comparative ratios for the two halves of the twentieth century. Clearly, reward-to-variability ratios were much higher in the second half-century. Furthermore, over this period, US investors would have earned a higher reward for risk from investing worldwide.

So far, we have viewed international investment mostly from a US perspective. Over this period, the US equity market was one of the world's most successful, while having quite low risk. This low risk arose partly because the US market was large and highly diversified in its own right—arguably equivalent to considering all the European markets as a single block. We would thus expect to find that the gains from investing abroad would generally have been larger for investors from other countries—not least because, for these other countries, this would automatically have included taking a stake in the United States.

To investigate this, we recompile the world equity index in real, local currency terms from the perspective of investors from each of the other fifteen countries. For each country, we compute a relative Sharpe ratio by dividing the Sharpe ratio for an investment in the world index by the equivalent ratio for domestic investment. For example, for the United States, the relative Sharpe ratio based on the data from Figure 8-4 was 0.286/0.287 = 1.00 for 1900–2000, and 0.440/0.422 = 1.04 for 1950–2000. A relative ratio of one indicates that the world index had the same reward to risk ratio as domestic investment; a ratio above one, that the world index dominated; and a ratio below unity, that domestic investment gave the highest reward for risk. Figure 8-5 shows the relative Sharpe ratios for each country. Countries are ranked from lowest to highest ratio over the period 1900–2000, and ratios are also shown for 1950–2000.

Figure 8-5: *Ex post* gains from holding the world equity portfolio relative to domestic investment

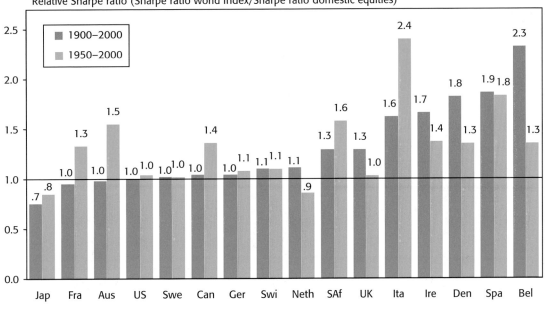

Figure 8-5 shows that, over the full 101 years, investors in three countries, Australia, France, and Japan, would have achieved higher reward-to-risk ratios from staying at home rather than investing worldwide, while for US investors the ratios were virtually identical. These four countries all enjoyed relatively high excess returns and low standard deviations from domestic equity investment. In the other twelve countries, investors would have attained a higher reward per unit of risk by investing worldwide. Part of their gain would have come from risk reduction, and part from the fact that, with hindsight, they would in most cases have targeted part of their funds toward higher return countries. Belgian investors would have gained the most. Over the period 1950–2000, Figure 8-5 shows that equity investors in every country except Japan and The Netherlands would have been better off investing worldwide. Italian investors would have gained the most—largely from risk reduction since Italian equities were median, rather than poor, performers over this period.

Investors in most countries, therefore, would have been better off investing worldwide, but there were exceptions. These were countries that performed very well while enjoying low volatility. Unfortunately, we can spot these markets only with hindsight. If they could be identified in advance, they would be instantly re-rated, thus lowering their expected returns. So looking ahead, and while there are no guarantees, our best guess is that international investment will offer a higher reward for risk due to the risk reduction from international diversification. The next section focuses on the source of these diversification gains.

8.4   Correlations between countries

The risk reduction from international diversification arises because markets are less than perfectly correlated. Table 8-3 shows the correlations between countries. The figures in bold in the lower, left-hand triangle relate to annual, real dollar returns for 1900–2000, and are therefore the correlations that lay beneath the risk reduction figures documented above. Correlations depend on the underlying structural relationship between countries, and these have naturally changed over time. Major shifts have occurred in world power blocks and politics through decolonialization, wars being replaced by peace, economic growth and development, shifting trade flows, economic unions, changing currency regimes, and so on. These 101-year correlations will thus reflect some average of these changing conditions.

Even so, the correlations in Table 8-3 are plausible, and linked to geography and distance. For example, the highest correlation was between the United States and Canada, and the next highest between the United Kingdom and Ireland. Germany had low correlations, reflecting the wars and hyper-inflation, yet its highest correlations were with its neighbors, France, Belgium, The Netherlands, Denmark, and Switzerland. France's highest correlations were with Belgium, The Netherlands, Italy, Ireland, Spain, and Switzerland; Italy's were with France and Switzerland; The Netherlands was most highly correlated with Belgium, followed by France, Denmark, and Switzerland; and Sweden was highly correlated with Denmark, Canada (natural resources), and Switzerland (neutral countries). Australia's highest correlations were with the United Kingdom and Ireland (historical and trade links), and Canada and South Africa (gold, mining, and the British Empire).

Table 8-3: Correlation coefficients between world equity markets[*]

	Wld	US	UK	Swi	Swe	Spa	SAf	Neth	Jap	Ita	Ire	Ger	Fra	Den	Can	Bel	Aus
Wld		.93	.77	.59	.62	.67	.54	.73	.68	.52	.69	.69	.73	.57	.82	.54	.69
US	.85		.67	.44	.46	.53	.46	.57	.49	.40	.66	.56	.56	.46	.78	.45	.57
UK	.70	.55		.58	.44	.63	.31	.71	.42	.39	.73	.58	.59	.57	.57	.59	.56
Swi	.68	.50	.62		.39	.60	.19	.72	.36	.45	.57	.53	.64	.58	.35	.63	.37
Swe	.62	.44	.42	.54		.63	.38	.63	.34	.49	.27	.76	.76	.44	.61	.29	.44
Spa	.41	.25	.25	.36	.37		.35	.63	.32	.64	.50	.64	.75	.56	.51	.55	.54
SAf	.55	.43	.49	.39	.34	.26		.30	.44	.24	.31	.42	.37	.25	.62	.10	.66
Neth	.57	.39	.42	.51	.43	.28	.29		.39	.59	.63	.74	.77	.64	.55	.70	.46
Jap	.45	.21	.33	.29	.39	.40	.31	.25		.18	.33	.25	.36	.24	.50	.17	.59
Ita	.54	.37	.43	.52	.39	.41	.41	.32	.34		.33	.55	.71	.50	.40	.51	.38
Ire	.58	.38	.73	.70	.42	.35	.42	.46	.29	.43		.42	.45	.49	.54	.57	.50
Ger	.30	.12	-.01	.22	.09	-.03	.05	.27	.06	.16	.03		.83	.61	.57	.59	.46
Fra	.62	.36	.45	.54	.44	.47	.38	.48	.25	.52	.53	.19		.63	.60	.66	.48
Den	.57	.38	.40	.51	.56	.34	.31	.50	.46	.38	.55	.22	.45		.55	.54	.30
Can	.80	.80	.55	.48	.53	.27	.54	.34	.30	.37	.41	.13	.35	.46		.30	.65
Bel	.58	.38	.40	.57	.43	.40	.29	.60	.25	.47	.49	.26	.68	.42	.35		.30
Aus	.66	.47	.66	.51	.50	.28	.56	.41	.28	.43	.62	.04	.47	.42	.62	.35	

[*] Correlations in bold (lower left-hand triangle) are based on 101 years of real dollar returns, 1900–2000. Correlations in roman (top right-hand triangle) are based on 60 months of real dollar returns, 1996–2000, from FTSE World (Ireland and South Africa) and MSCI (all others).

Correlations have nevertheless shifted significantly over time, and Table 8-4 provides evidence of this. The table presents the results of estimating correlations over a prediction period from information over an earlier historical period. The top panel shows that when the full set of pairwise correlation coefficients between equity markets are estimated separately for the first and second halves of the twentieth century, there was no discernable relationship between the two. It would not have been possible to predict correlations for 1950–2000 from those estimated from annual data over the first half-century. The slope coefficient was insignificantly different from zero and the adjusted R^2 was negative.

Table 8-4: Regression of correlations between equity markets on earlier historical correlations

Predicted correlations	Historical correlations	Slope	t-value	Adjusted R^2
Annual correlation coefficients (all 101 years)				
1950–2000 (51 years)	1900–49 (50 years)	.07	1.0	-.001
Monthly correlations (post-Bretton Woods)				
1986–2000 (192 months)	1971–85 (180 months)	.08	6.9	.342
Monthly correlations (recent data)				
1996–2000 (60 months)	1991–95 (60 months)	.07	7.1	.296

Goetzmann, Li, and Rouwenhorst (2001) show how correlations between equity markets changed between 1872–2000 over seven successive sub-periods representing distinct economic and political conditions. Their estimates for four core countries, the United States, the United Kingdom, France, and Germany, are shown in Figure 8-6. Correlations have clearly changed over time. For example, the US:UK correlation has varied from near zero to 0.51, while the US:Germany coefficient has ranged from -.36 to +.36. During the two world war periods, several coefficients were negative, as one might expect between opposing sides. While low correlations imply higher diversification benefits, wars are precisely the times when international investment is hardest, and ownership claims most likely to be rescinded.

The final (red) bar for each sub-period in Figure 8-6 shows that the average correlation level also varied over time. Goetzmann, Li, and Rouwenhorst show that these differences in both the level and structure of correlations were statistically significant. The two "early integration" periods before the First World War were statistically indistinguishable. The war periods were quite different, with low average correlations of -0.07 in the First World War and 0.01 in the Second World War. Equity returns in all other periods showed appreciable inter-linkages. Returns were modestly correlated before the First World War, between the wars, and in the 1946–71 Bretton Woods period, and strongly correlated in the "present" period from 1972 on. But while there were some similarities between the "early integration" and Bretton Woods periods, the correlation structures otherwise differed a great deal. The inter-war period, with its post-war boom, hyperinflation in Germany, the Wall Street Crash, and the Great Depression, was unique. Correlations were quite high due to common factors such as the crash and Depression, but the correlation structure differed from all other periods.

Figure 8-6: Correlation coefficients between four core countries over seven successive sub-periods

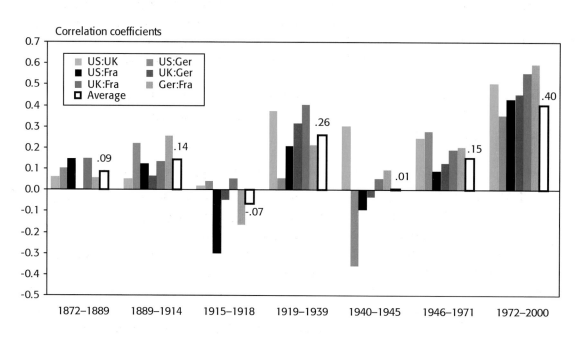

Source: Goetzmann, Li, and Rouwenhorst, 2001

Longin and Solnik (1995) provide further evidence of high correlations during periods of poor performance. They find that markets become more closely related during turmoil such as the 1974 oil shock, the October 1987 crash, the 1990 invasion of Kuwait and the ensuing Gulf War in 1991, or by extension, the aftershock from September 11, 2001. This raises the obvious question of whether international diversification works when it is most needed. Das and Uppal (2001) provide reassurance by showing that the impact of this is small for long-term investors, who should still hold highly international portfolios.

Goetzmann, Li, and Rouwenhorst (2001) find that the "present" period, from the 1970s on, has higher and more stable correlations than any other period. The center panel of Table 8-4 shows that a regression of coefficients for 1986–2000 on those for 1970–85 gave a highly significant slope coefficient and an adjusted R^2 of 34 percent. This suggests quite a high level of underlying stability since there is inevitably estimate error in the individual correlations. Normally, analysts would measure correlations over even shorter periods, with five years of monthly data being typical. The bottom panel of Table 8-4 shows the results of regressing correlations estimated from 1996–2000 on those for 1991–95. Again, there is considerable stability, with a highly significant slope coefficient and an adjusted R^2 of 30 percent.

The top right-hand triangle of Table 8-3 shows recent correlations estimated from monthly data from 1996–2000. These are noticeably higher (mean of 0.50) than the historical estimates for 1900–2000 shown in bold in the lower left-hand triangle (mean of 0.36). Once again, high correlations are associated with trading links, geographical proximity, and other common factors. For example, the United States is most highly correlated with Canada, followed by the United Kingdom and Ireland. Relative to their twentieth century average, German equities today are much more closely correlated with those of other countries, especially France, Sweden, The Netherlands, and Denmark. France has its highest correlations with its immediate neighbors. Italy is most highly correlated with France and Spain. South Africa is most closely correlated with Australia and Canada. Japan is most closely linked (among the countries covered in this book) with the United States, Canada, and Australia.

While recent correlations are reasonably stable and have face validity, they are higher than in earlier periods. The next section examines whether this still leaves scope for risk reduction.

8.5 Prospective gains from international diversification

We drew the parallel above between domestic and international diversification, referring back to Figure 4-11 from section 4.6—the standard textbook diagram showing how rapidly risk declines as we move from a one- to a many-stock equity portfolio. Figure 8-7 shows the equivalent diagram for diversification across countries. The top (red) line shows the risk reduction that could have been achieved by a dollar-based investor over the last century. It assumes equal holdings in each country, and that cross-border investment was possible and costless throughout. The standard deviation of 29.1 percent for a typical single-country investment falls off to 17.3 percent for an equally weighted sixteen-country portfolio. This 41 percent risk reduction is clearly large.

We would expect less risk reduction today, as world equity markets are more integrated, with higher correlations than was typical of 1900–2000. The yellow line in Figure 8-7 is based on standard deviations estimated from recent monthly data from 1996–2000, thus showing the risk reduction we might expect in the early twenty-first century. It lies well below the red line, showing that annualized equity market risk is currently lower than the twentieth century average. The line is also less steep, with standard deviations falling from 20 percent for a typical one-country investment down to 14.6 percent for an equally weighted sixteen-country portfolio. While this risk reduction of 27 percent is more modest than the 41 percent for 1900–2000, it is still quite large.

The above analysis assumes equally weighted investments. This is standard when measuring diversification gains, both domestically (e.g., Campbell, Lettau, Malkiel, and Xu (2001); see Figure 4-11), and internationally, as typified by Solnik's (1974) early research and the recent paper by Goetzmann, Li, and Rouwenhorst (2001). But equally weighted results can be misleading, especially for an investor based in the United States. First, it is unrealistic to assume that investors will hold the same amount in small markets as in large ones. By definition, assets must, in aggregate, be held in proportion to their overall market values. Second, the equally weighted analysis implicitly assumes that the one-country portfolio could, equally plausibly, be any one of the sixteen markets, while the two-country portfolios span all possible two-country pairings, and so on. More realistically, we would expect that for a US investor, the one-country portfolio would be the United States, with other markets then being added to the US core.

Figure 8-7: Historical risk reduction from international diversification of equity portfolios

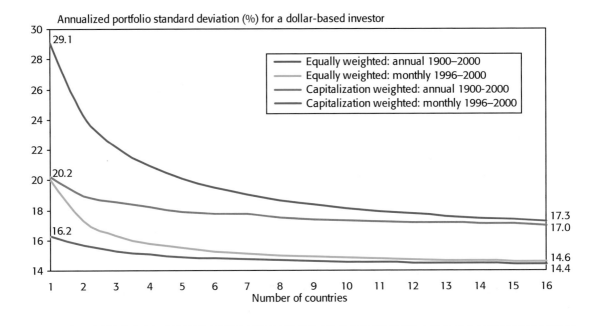

The remaining two lines in Figure 8-7 show the risk reduction achieved by a US investor who started with a single-country holding in the United States and then diversified by selecting the largest markets first, holding each in proportion to its size. Once this portfolio is invested in all sixteen countries, it becomes our world equity index. The green line shows that, from 1900–2000, this strategy would have reduced risk from 20.2 percent, the standard deviation for the United States, down to 17.0 percent for the world index (i.e., the figures presented earlier in Table 8-2). The blue line, which relates to recent data for 1996–2000, shows a lower level of risk reduction from 16.2 percent for the United States down to 14.4 percent for our sixteen-country world index.

The blue line in Figure 8-7 refers only to a US-based investor, and is based on historical standard deviations. Unless suitably adjusted, the latter provide poor forecasts because estimates tend to regress toward the mean. This may arise from estimate error, and/or because risk is truly mean reverting. The net effect is that markets with high standard deviation estimates usually have lower estimates in future periods while still tending to lie above the mean, whereas markets with low estimates tend to regress upward toward the mean.

Figure 8-8 addresses both of these issues, and shows the risk reduction from international diversification that investors in each of the sixteen countries might expect at the start of the twenty-first century. The figures for each country are based on unhedged international equity returns over the period 1996–2000 denominated in each country's home currency, and the standard deviations have been converted into forecasts by means of an adjustment for regression bias. For each country, there are four bars, each showing the percentage reduction in standard deviation from pursuing different levels of international diversification, relative to a policy of purely domestic investment. The first three bars show the risk reduction from investing 20, 50, and 80 percent abroad, while the fourth bar corresponds to a policy of investing the entire portfolio in the world equity index.

Figure 8-8 shows that the prospective gains from international diversification are positive for investors from all countries. It suggests that US investors could expect to reduce risk by 10 percent by investing 20 percent abroad, and by 20 percent by holding the world index. The latter has more than a 50 percent weighting in the United States, and so for US investors, holding 50 and 80 percent abroad would mean under-weighting their home market. No other market is large enough for this to be an issue. Note that for investors in most markets, investment in the world portfolio does not offer the lowest risk, and prospective risk is typically lower with just 50 or 80 percent abroad. This does not imply that lower levels of diversification are superior, since Figure 8-8 focuses just on risk, while ignoring expected returns.

The individual country estimates in Figure 8-8 should be treated with caution. For some countries, especially the United Kingdom, Belgium, and Switzerland, the prospective risk reductions look surprisingly small. These were markets in which domestic risk was low, and/or the exchange risk of foreign investment was high, over the estimation period from 1996–2000. For other countries, the likely gains seem unexpectedly large for precisely the opposite reasons. For Canada, for example, this is because, over this period, exchange rate

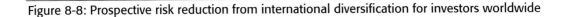

Figure 8-8: Prospective risk reduction from international diversification for investors worldwide

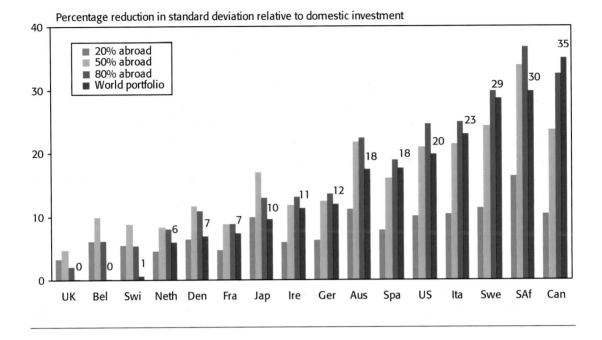

movements actually reduced the risk of investing abroad, making the potential gains from international diversification seem very large. In principle, we could obtain more meaningful estimates of the prospective risk reduction by making more comprehensive adjustments to the historical covariance matrix, including to the currency returns. But while the individual country estimates should be interpreted with care, the overall picture is clear. Investors everywhere stand to gain from international diversification, and the likely risk reduction from moving to a fully diversified global portfolio is around 10–20 percent.

8.6   Home bias and constraints on international investment

For over 30 years, researchers have been advocating the benefits of cross-border investment. Despite this, equity portfolios around the world remain concentrated in their home markets. No one has yet provided a wholly convincing explanation for this home bias puzzle.

Figure 8-9 shows the extent of home bias presented as load ratios. The load ratio is the percentage weighting in a country/region, divided by that region's weighting in the world equity portfolio. For example, a portfolio that is one-quarter invested in a country that comprises one-fifth of the index has a load ratio of 25/20 = 1.25, which we plot as 125 percent. A pair of load ratio bars is shown for each country, although some are missing due to lack of data. The left-hand bars show US investors' load ratios in each country at end-1997, and are from Ahearne, Griever, and Warnock (2001). From the perspective of each country, the left-hand bars signify inward investment by US portfolio investors. The right-hand bars, available for nine countries, show each country's load ratio in foreign stocks. These (except for the United States) are from Cooper and Kaplanis (1995) and relate to 1993. The right-hand bars represent the total of outward investment by portfolio investors from each country.

Focusing first on the left-hand bars, these show the load ratios of US investors in each country. Ratios of 100 percent for all countries would mean that US investors held a fully diversified world portfolio. Ratios above 100 percent for the United States and below 100 percent for foreign markets would indicate home bias. At end-1997, US equity investors held 89.9 percent of their portfolio in the United States, and the US market made up 48.3 percent of the world total. Their load ratio in the United States was therefore 89.9/48.3 = 186 percent. If they had invested nothing abroad, the ratio would have taken its maximum value of 100/48.3 = 207 percent. Foreign markets comprised 51.7 percent of the world total, but US citizens invested only 10.1 percent abroad. Their average loading on foreign markets was 10.1/51.7 = 19 percent, and this is therefore plotted as the value of the right-hand load ratio in Figure 8-9.

For US investors, the most popular foreign market was the United Kingdom, accounting for some 2 percent of their portfolios, followed by Japan and The Netherlands at around 1 percent each. The UK and Japanese markets are much larger than the Dutch market, so the load ratios were 21 and 12 percent for the United Kingdom and Japan and 45 percent for The Netherlands. These, together with the load ratios for the other countries in our study, are shown as the left-hand bars in Figure 8-9. The foreign markets in which US investors have the highest loadings tend either to be those where a few large multinational stocks dominate (e.g., The Netherlands, and also Finland), or where US investor groups exhibit "mother country bias," that is, favor investment in their country of origin (e.g., Ireland, and also Mexico).

Figure 8-9: Home bias: investors' load ratios in equity markets around the world

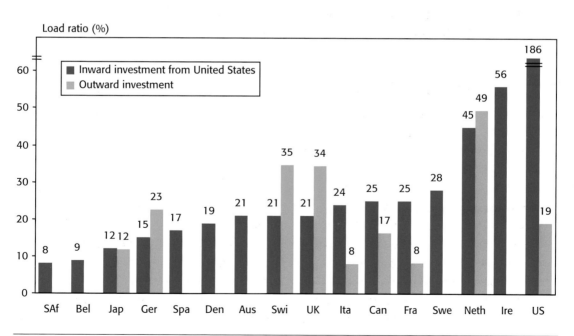

Source: Ahearne, Griever, and Warnock, 2001 (US data) and Cooper and Kaplanis, 1995 (data for other countries)

Switching to the right-hand bars, we have already noted that US investors held 10.1 percent of their equity portfolio abroad, giving a load ratio of 19 percent in foreign stocks. Investors in several countries for which we have data held a higher relative weighting abroad, namely, The Netherlands, Switzerland, the United Kingdom, and Germany. The corresponding load ratios, plotted as the right-hand bars of Figure 8-9, reveal marked under-weighting of foreign markets and a high degree of home bias. Moving to a fully diversified world equity portfolio would require a doubling-up of foreign equity holdings by Dutch investors, a trebling by UK and Swiss investors, a five-fold increase for US investors, an eight-fold increase for Japanese investors, and a twelve-fold increase for French and Italian investors.

Although home bias is still prevalent, there has been a steady trend toward diversifying internationally. US investors followed Solnik's (1974) advice by increasing the percentage of their equity portfolios held abroad from just 1 percent in 1980 to 12 percent by end-2000. Interestingly, there were also earlier periods when home bias was less in evidence. At the start of the twentieth century, there was extensive cross-border investment. London was then the world's leading financial center, and Conant (1908) estimates that in 1900, at least 23 percent, and perhaps as much as 51 percent of UK citizens' securities holdings was invested abroad. Paris ranked second after London, and 32 percent of the value of French owned securities was held in foreign stocks and bonds. For Germany, the figure was 46 percent.

The First World War had a major dampening effect on international investment. Capital controls proliferated, and then in the 1920s, German hyperinflation and the Wall Street Crash crushed confidence. Foreign investment collapsed after 1929, and capital controls and protectionism characterized the period until the Second World War. After the war, the tide turned again, but restrictions continued for many years. The United States imposed interest equalization tax from 1963–74; the Japanese financial markets were effectively closed to foreigners until the 1980s, and the United Kingdom, Germany, and France all had periods of capital control, some continuing until the 1980s.

Home bias until the late 1970s is thus easy to understand. In addition to restrictions on capital movements, there were constraints on cross-border holdings, complex tax barriers, poor information flows, few derivative instruments for hedging, and very limited passive country index investment vehicles. As Cooper (2001) points out, the costs of achieving international diversification may well then have significantly offset the benefits.

Cooper argues that today, most of these costs have been, or are being, swept aside. Barriers to international capital movement have been dismantled. Information is now rapidly and widely available, and in ever greater volume. Accounting, tax, governance, trading and issuance systems are being harmonized. Currency, interest rate and equity market risk can now all be hedged cheaply. Cooper concludes that, in "twenty years or less from now, the challenge will be not 'the case for global investing' but 'why deviate from a globally diversified portfolio?'"

8.7 Summary

Investing internationally expands the opportunity set open to equity and bond investors, and provides risk reduction through diversification across countries, asset classes, and currencies. Exchange risk does not add greatly to the long-run risks of international investment, and anyway can be hedged. Investors with no special insights about the prospects for different world markets should therefore hold as diversified a portfolio as possible. If there were no barriers or costs to international investment, they should hold the world market portfolio.

The evidence from our sixteen-country world indexes is that over the 101 years from 1900–2000, investors in most countries would have been better off investing worldwide. There were exceptions, however, showing that the potential gains do not always materialize, even over long periods. These were countries that performed especially well while enjoying low volatility, most notably the United States. The US bond market provided higher returns for lower risk, while US equities gave higher returns that were almost exactly counterbalanced by the lower risk from the world index. Once the higher costs of investing in foreign equities are factored in, US equity investors would have been better off at home. We should not generalize from this, however, and over the second half-century from 1950–2000, both US bond and equity investors would have gained significantly from investing worldwide.

Many textbooks give a misleading impression of the gains from international diversification by presenting *ex post* efficient frontiers of the risk-return tradeoff based on hindsight about returns. Sadly, we can usually spot the high-return, low-risk markets only after the event, and past performance is a poor guide to the future. So looking ahead, and while we know there is no guarantee, our best guess is that international investment will offer a higher reward for risk than domestic investment, because of the risk reduction from diversification.

Full international diversification was not always possible during the twentieth century. There was a U shaped pattern of globalization, with international investment commonplace at both ends of the century. During the period in between, from the First World War through to the 1970s, many barriers and costs inhibited cross-border investment. More recently, these have been largely swept aside, heralding a new and deeper age of integration. But while cross-border investment has greatly increased, investors still show a strong home bias.

Ironically, as barriers were removed, and markets became more integrated, the correlations between markets rose to a level unmatched in the past, reducing the potential gains from diversification. Despite this, some textbooks still cite quite high potential gains, based perhaps on old data or unrealistic assumptions. Our estimates suggest that global investors in most countries can now expect a more modest, but still useful level of risk reduction of some 10–20 percent. For those willing to invest in emerging markets—which are not considered here—the benefits may be greater. Goetzmann, Li, and Rouwenhorst (2001) argue that the recent period of globalization has had drawbacks and benefits. The higher correlations have attenuated the risk reduction benefits, but the opportunity set has expanded dramatically with many new emerging and re-emerging markets now open to the investor.

Chapter 9 Size effects and seasonality in stock returns

In this and the following two chapters, we focus on three important aspects of equity investment. This chapter deals with the effects of size and seasonality, chapter 10 concentrates on
the performance of value and growth stocks, and chapter 11 is concerned with dividends and
dividend growth.

Why have we chosen to devote a chapter to size and seasonality? The main reason is that the
size effect has over the last twenty or more years become the best-documented stock market
anomaly around the world. As Ibbotson Associates (2000) state, "One of the most remarkable
discoveries of modern finance is the finding of a relationship between firm size and return.
On average, small companies have higher returns than large ones."

Furthermore, this size effect is linked to seasonality, at least in the United States, with
anomalous returns on small stocks tending to occur around the turn of the year and in January. This size-linked seasonality is referred to as the "turn-of-the-year" or "January" effect.

The size effect was first discovered in the US equity market. In section 9.1, we report on the
original US research findings, and document the size effect in the United States over the
period 1926–2000. Research soon followed in other countries, and in section 9.2 we summarize the UK evidence, which is based on a detailed, 46-year record of size-based returns from
1955 to 2000. Using data for the period 1900–54 that was collected as part of the research for
this book, we explore whether there is also evidence of a UK size effect over the earlier part of
the twentieth century. In section 9.3, we examine the evidence on the size effect for numerous other countries around the world.

A frustrating feature of the size effect is that soon after its discovery, the size premium went
into reverse, with smaller companies subsequently underperforming their larger counterparts. In section 9.4, we describe this reversal in the United States and the United Kingdom,
arguing that it was an example of Murphy's Law of perversity. We go on to show that Murphy's Law applied in most other markets around the world.

In the United States, the size effect has been closely associated with the January effect, and
the entire US size effect is in fact attributable to abnormal returns in January. In section 9.5,
we re-examine the evidence on this, and explore whether there is similar seasonality in UK
stock returns. Finally, section 9.6 provides a summary and conclusion.

9.1 The size effect in the United States

The size effect first came to prominence following research on the US market by Banz (1981).
In his influential article, Banz demonstrated that for companies quoted on the New York
Stock Exchange (NYSE), there had been a significant negative relationship between stock
returns and company size, with smaller companies providing higher returns. Although he

found that investment in smaller US stocks typically involved greater risk, his findings were robust, and persisted even after adjustment for risk.

The return premium from investing in smaller stocks was large. After adjusting for risk, Banz found that the difference in returns between the largest fifty and smallest fifty stocks was 1.01 percent *per month*. He also found that the size effect extended throughout the market, with the very smallest stocks performing best of all. The size premium was not evident every year, nor even over every five-year subperiod, but it was nevertheless a strong and significant effect over the full 45-year period spanned by his research.

Banz also constructed size deciles of NYSE stocks. He formed these by ranking all NYSE stocks (excluding investment companies and foreign stocks) from largest to smallest market capitalization, and then dividing them into ten size portfolios, each containing an equal number of companies. CRSP has since regularly updated these size portfolios, rebalancing them quarterly and computing value-weighted returns. These decile returns are reported in Ibbotson Associates (2001). Deciles 9 and 10, containing the very smallest companies, are referred to as micro-cap stocks; deciles 6–8 are labeled small-caps; while deciles 1–5 contain the larger-cap stocks. Figure 9-1 shows the cumulative performance of micro-, small-, and larger-caps over the period since 1926 covered by the CRSP database.

Over this 75-year period, $1 invested in large-cap US stocks would have grown in nominal terms to $1,948, an annualized return of 10.6 percent. This is marginally below the all-NYSE stocks value weighted return of 10.7 percent. These two returns are close because although

Figure 9-1: Performance of small-cap and large-cap stocks in the United States, 1926–2000

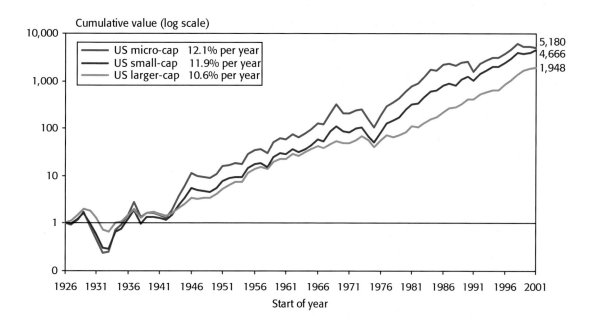

deciles 1–5 comprise half the stocks on the NYSE, they account for some 95 percent of the NYSE's total market value. The small stocks in deciles 6–8 accounted, on average, for only just over 4 percent of the NYSE's value. Figure 9-1 shows that $1 invested in small-caps at start-1926 would have grown to $4,666, an annualized return of 11.9 percent. An equivalent investment in micro-caps would have grown to $5,180, an annualized return of 12.1 percent.

Clearly, small-caps have outperformed large-caps, and micro-caps have performed best of all. The figures above have not been risk-adjusted, and in the United States, small-caps have generally had higher systematic risk. Banz found, however, that the small-cap premium persisted even after risk adjustment. A closer inspection of Figure 9-1 shows that from the start date of the CRSP database in 1926, small stocks initially performed poorly, especially during the Great Depression, and did not catch up with large-caps until the early 1940s. By 1975, although micro-caps were ahead, small-caps were still only marginally beating large-caps. Then, from 1975–83, small-caps raced ahead. Siegel (1998) argues that if this period is left out, large-caps beat small-caps over the period 1926–97. While drawing conclusions from returns data where the very best or worst years have been excluded is potentially misleading, Siegel's observation nevertheless helps underline what he refers to as the "streakiness" of small stock returns. Figure 9-1 also shows that small- and micro-cap returns since 1983 have been relatively disappointing, an observation to which we return in section 9.4.

9.2   The size effect in the United Kingdom

Banz's (1981) findings raised the obvious question of whether the size effect was limited to the United States or also occurred elsewhere. This stimulated research in many other countries (see section 9.3), most notably the United Kingdom (Dimson and Marsh, 1986), where the small firm premium came to prominence with the launch of the Hoare Govett Smaller Companies Index (HGSC) in early 1987. This index covers the bottom tenth by market capitalization of the UK equity market. Made available as an ABN AMRO product, the HGSC has been produced live from 1987 onward, and has a pre-launch back-history from 1955–86 (see Dimson and Marsh, 1987). It thus spans most of the second half of the twentieth century. In addition to the HGSC, an index of micro-capitalization stocks is produced for ABN AMRO at London Business School. The MicroCap™ Index covers the bottom 1 percent of the market, on an ex-investment companies basis, and runs from 1955 to the present time. These indexes are described in Dimson and Marsh (2001a).

Figure 9-2 compares the performance of UK small- and micro-cap stocks with that of the UK equity market as a whole from 1955–2000. Since our UK equity market index is capitalization weighted, and hence dominated by large-caps, these comparisons are effectively between small-cap and large-cap performance. Figure 9-2 shows that despite a setback in the 1990s, UK small-caps still handsomely outperformed the market over the period as a whole. £1 invested in the UK equity market at the start of 1955 would, with dividends reinvested, have grown to a nominal value of £592 by the beginning of 2001, an annualized return of 14.9 percent. An identical investment in small-caps (the HGSC) would have grown to £1,676, almost three times as much, giving an annualized return of 17.6 percent. Micro-caps performed

Figure 9-2: Cumulative performance of UK small-caps versus the market, 1955–2000

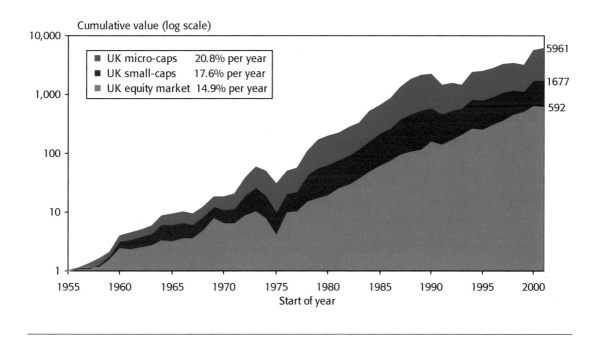

even better, with their annualized return of 20.8 percent producing a terminal value of £5,961, three and a half times more than on the HGSC.

It is common practice in research on the size effect to report the arithmetic difference between small-cap and equity market returns. We follow this convention in this chapter, starting with Figure 9-3, which shows how the size effect has varied over time. The bars show the micro-cap premium (the percentage differences between the MicroCap™ Index and the market), while the line plot shows the small-cap premium (the percentage difference between the HGSC Index and the market). While the size premium has been quite volatile, small-caps beat the market in thirty-two of the forty-six years. Seven of the fourteen years when they underperformed came from the setback of the late 1980s and early 1990s, which we analyze in section 9.4. Figure 9-3 shows that in most years when small-caps outperformed, the MicroCap™ Index outperformed the HGSC, while in years of small-cap underperformance, the MicroCap™ tended to underperform the HGSC. This is further evidence that the size effect tends to extend right across the range of size bands within the market. This was first noted by Banz, and has since been verified by many others.

The key question is whether the size premium will continue in the future. This is unanswerable, since we cannot travel forward in time. However, we can at least travel farther back and look at virgin data for earlier decades, before 1955. As a result of the research for this book, we now have reliable UK stock returns data for the first half of the twentieth century, but unfortunately only for the largest one hundred stocks. This may nevertheless be enough to provide a pointer. Given that the size effect tends to operate across the entire size spectrum, if there were a size effect, we would expect to find evidence even among the biggest stocks.

Figure 9-3: Annual performance of UK small-caps relative to the market

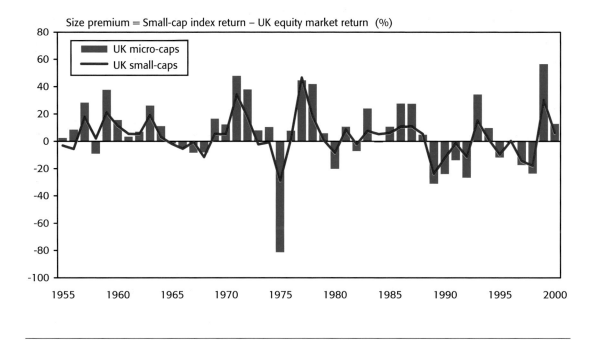

Figure 9-4 provides some tentative evidence on the existence of a size effect over the first half of the twentieth century. We base this evidence on the 100-stock equity index compiled by us with the support of ABN AMRO (see chapter 32). For the 1900–54 period, when the equity index was based on the largest one hundred stocks, we have also computed the index on an equally weighted basis. This equally weighted version will exceed the capitalization weighted index when the size premium is positive, that is, when the smaller companies within the top 100 outperform their larger counterparts. This is because capitalization weighting, by definition, gives more weight to the larger stocks, while equal weighting gives relatively more weight to smaller stocks.

Each bar in Figure 9-4 shows the difference between the equally weighted and capitalization weighted returns on the largest one hundred stocks in the market. After 1955, the equity index moved to fully comprehensive coverage, and so to continue the series from 1955 onward, we have estimated what the equally- and capitalization weighted returns would have been if we had continued to base our index on just the top one hundred shares. The bars in Figure 9-4 plot the difference between these two estimates.

There is a reasonable, but by no means perfect correlation, between the post-1955 data in Figure 9-4 and the actual size effect as plotted earlier in Figure 9-3. Indeed, it would have been possible to predict the differential return between the HGSC and the market (Figure 9-3) from the difference between the equally and capitalization weighted returns on the top one hundred stocks (Figure 9-4), albeit with a degree of inaccuracy. The correlation between the two was 0.62.

Figure 9-4: UK size effect within the top 100 stocks, 1900–2000

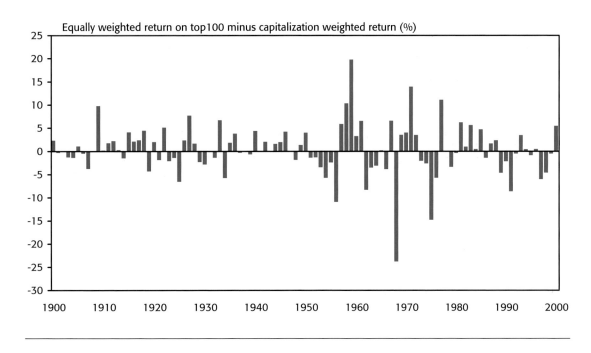

We can therefore be reasonably confident that when we examine the first half of the century in Figure 9-4, we are looking at a realistic proxy for the size effect. Figure 9-4 shows that, from 1900–54, just as in the period since, there was a size effect in the sense that there were years in which the smaller stocks among the top one hundred did best, and years when the larger stocks outperformed. However, there is no overwhelming impression of a size premium, since there were almost as many years when our size effect proxy was positive as negative. Nor were there quite as many runs of good and bad years from 1900–54.

Over the first fifty-five years of the last century, the annualized return on the equally weighted top one hundred index was 6.68 percent, or just ½ percent a year higher than on its capitalization weighted counterpart. This suggests that there may have been a small, but positive size premium. A fuller answer to this question, however, will have to await further data collection focused on genuinely small UK stocks during the first half of the last century.

9.3   The size effect around the world

With the discovery of the size premium in the United States, and its confirmation in the United Kingdom, researchers around the world set out to investigate whether there was a similar premium in other countries. Their research, published mostly in the 1980s and early 1990s, confirmed that the size premium had been present in most other countries. Dimson (1988) and, more recently, Hawawini and Keim (2000) summarize this research, which now spans seventeen countries, including eleven of the sixteen countries covered in this book.

Figure 9-5: International evidence on the size effect

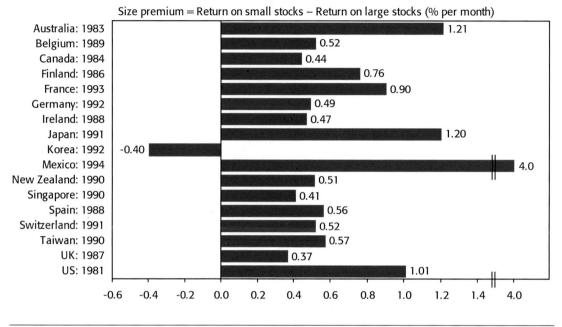

Source: Hawawini and Keim (2000), Banz (1981), and Dimson and Marsh (1987)

Figure 9-5, which is taken (mostly) from Hawawini and Keim, shows the magnitude of the size effect reported in each of these seventeen countries. For each country, this chart shows the results of the first (and in most cases only) published study on the size effect. Hawawini and Keim (2000) give further details on, and full citations for, each study. The only exceptions are the United States and the United Kingdom, where we have replaced Hawawini and Keim's selected studies with the original research in each country, namely, Banz (1981) in the United States and Dimson and Marsh (1987) in the United Kingdom. In Figure 9-5, the size premium is measured as the difference between the average monthly returns on the smallest and the largest stocks. Each study defines "smallest" and "largest" differently, but typically, stocks are ranked by size, and then assigned to between two and ten size portfolios, depending on the study.

Differences in the definition of "small" can give rise to large variations in the size premium, since when small stocks do well, the smallest normally do best. For example, Banz (1981) found that if he took the smallest and largest ten stocks, rather than the top and bottom fifty, his estimate of the US size premium rose from the 1.01 percent shown in Figure 9-5 to 1.52 percent. Similarly, the UK figure shown in Figure 9-5 is the small-cap premium based on the HGSC (see section 9.2), but if we instead take the micro-cap premium, it rises from the 0.37 percent shown to 0.67 percent.

The time periods covered by each study also vary enormously, with start dates ranging from 1931 to 1984 and periods typically ending in the mid-to-late 1980s. The average number of years covered is just seventeen, which is low for estimating long-term stock market returns, and some of the studies span periods as brief as five years. These differences in research periods, methodologies, and definitions of "smallness" mean that the premia shown in Figure 9-5 are not directly comparable. In particular, it would be unwise to make inferences about the magnitudes or significance of any apparent size premium differences between countries.

In spite of this caveat, Figure 9-5 paints a very clear picture, namely, that the size premium was not restricted to the United States but was present in almost every country studied by the researchers. The sole exception was Korea, where a negative premium was reported, although this study used just five years of data. Furthermore, in most countries, researchers also looked at risk differences. They concluded, like Banz (1981), that the size premium could not be explained away by risk.

The pervasiveness and magnitude of the size effect, and the striking outperformance of smaller companies in most countries around the world, meant that the size effect rapidly became recognized as the premier stock market anomaly.

9.4   The reversal of the size premium

The "discovery" of the size effect in the United States by Banz (1981) and Reinganum (1981), and the publication and dissemination of their research, led to considerable interest in small-caps among investors in the United States. This spurred the launch of significant new small-cap investment vehicles led by Dimensional Fund Advisors, who raised several billion dollars within a couple of years of their 1981 launch. This honeymoon period lasted for approximately two years, until the end of 1983, and during this period, US small-caps continued to outperform. But subsequently, and over much of the period since, US small-caps have underperformed.

The UK experience was remarkably similar. When the HGSC was launched in 1987, its back-history showed that smaller companies had outperformed the UK market by 5.2 percent per year. This dramatic outperformance attracted substantial media attention, and there were over two hundred follow-up articles in the UK press. By the end of 1988, at least thirty open- and closed-end funds had been launched to exploit the perceived outperformance of small-caps, and numerous investment institutions developed a strategy of investing in smaller companies as a distinct asset class. Again, the honeymoon lasted just two years. In the decade that followed, smaller companies were to underperform by a large margin.

This reversal in the fortunes of US and UK small-cap stocks led us to write an article in 1999 entitled "Murphy's Law and Market Anomalies." Murphy's Law is often summarized as "bread always falls with the buttered side down." Figure 9-6 shows the performance record of US and UK small-caps at the time of our article, and shows why this appeared like a classic case of Murphy's Law. The left-hand side of Figure 9-6 shows the historical small- and micro-cap premia for the United States and the United Kingdom from the start date of the original research studies until the end of the post publication honeymoon period (i.e., 1926–

Figure 9-6: Murphy's Law and the small-cap reversal in the United States and the United Kingdom

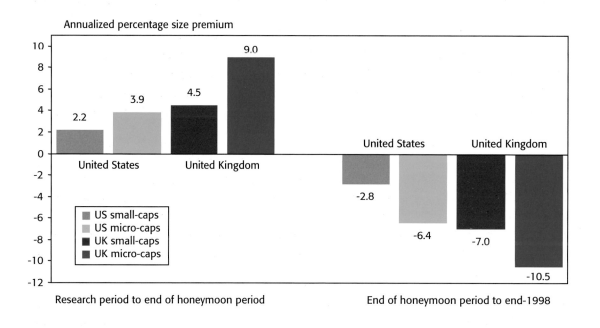

83 for the United States and 1955–88 for the United Kingdom). These premia were all large and positive, with micro-caps performing best of all. The right-hand side of the figure shows the corresponding performance in the years following the honeymoon period until end-1998, the last year before the publication of our Murphy's Law article. It shows that for the United States, the historical small- and micro-cap premia of 2.2 and 3.9 percent had turned into size *discounts* of 2.8 and 6.4 percent. Similarly, for the United Kingdom, the size premia of 4.5 and 9.0 percent for small- and micro-caps turned into negative premia of -7.0 and -10.5 percent, respectively. We noted above that the size effect tends to extend across the whole market, and that when small stocks outperform, it is usually a case of "the smaller the better." We can see here that the corollary is also true, and that when the size effect goes into reverse, it becomes a case of "the bigger the better."

One small irony of our Murphy's Law article was that we were writing about the demise of size just as UK small-caps were poised for a record year. During 1999, the HGSC Index had its best year since launch and its second best on record, with small-caps returning 54 percent. Meanwhile, the UK MicroCap™ Index recorded a return of 81 percent. This was followed in 2000 by a second year of outperformance, albeit by a smaller margin. Had we waited two years to write our article, the UK small-cap discount shown on the right-hand side of Figure 9-6 would have shrunk appreciably from 7.0 to 4.3 percent. The 1999–2000 repeal of Murphy's Law was a classic example of Mrs Murphy's Corollary: "One cannot determine beforehand which side of the bread to butter." Interestingly, though, even this cannot be relied upon, since US small-caps did not perform especially well in 1999–2000.

Our subsequent research has shown that the small-cap reversal extended beyond the United Kingdom and United States, and was a worldwide phenomenon. The line of investigation we followed here was to revisit all of the research studies that have been conducted into the size effect in different countries, and to estimate the size premium over the years since the research was published. These studies were discussed earlier in section 9.3 and their findings were summarized in Figure 9-5. We found that they showed evidence of a significant size premium in every country examined, with the sole exception of Korea, where the research covered just a five-year period. Most of these research studies were published in the 1980s.

To update these studies, we estimated the size premium in each country over the period since each study was published. For consistency, we again measured the size premium as the difference between the average monthly returns on the smallest and the largest stocks. For the United States, we use the CRSP NYSE Decile 10 and Decile 1 returns as our respective measures of small and large stock returns, as this most closely approximates Banz's (1981) earlier research, and gives results close to his over his earlier period. Similarly, for the United Kingdom we adopt the same definition as was used in Figure 9-5, namely, the difference between HGSC returns and overall UK equity returns.

For all other countries, we use the size-based indexes published by either Independence International Associates (IIA) or by FTSE International. IIA publish large- and small-cap indexes for a number of countries starting in 1975. They define small as the bottom 30 percent by capitalization of their universe, and large as the top 70 percent. FTSE publish a similar set of large and medium-small-cap indexes for a larger population of countries, but only from 1987, with some countries starting even later. FTSE define medium/small-cap as the bottom 25 percent by capitalization, and large-cap as the balancing 75 percent. For countries where we had a choice between both IIA and FTSE Indexes, we have used the IIA series since they provide a longer time series and generally have somewhat wider coverage.

The results of our research are shown in Figure 9-7. Countries are listed in alphabetical order, and for each country, the size premium reported by the original research studies and plotted earlier in Figure 9-5 in shown in green. Alongside this, the yellow bar shows the size premium calculated over the period since the original research was published, that is, over the period starting at the beginning of the year immediately following publication and ending at New Year 2001. No size-based indexes were available for Korea or Taiwan, so we omitted these countries. We have, however, included the four countries covered in this book, but which did not feature in Figure 9-5 due to the absence of any research study on the size premium. For these countries, we have omitted the "initial research" bars in Figure 9-7, while the "subsequent period" bars show the size premium over the period from 1990–2000.

It is clear from Figure 9-7 that there was a global reversal of the size effect in virtually every country, with the size premium not just disappearing but going into reverse. Researchers around the world universally fell victim to Murphy's Law, with the very effect they were documenting—and inventing explanations for—promptly reversing itself shortly after their studies were published. The only country experiencing a size premium, as opposed to a size discount, in the period subsequent to the original research was Switzerland. However, the Swiss size premium was statistically insignificant, and its magnitude was just 0.05 percent.

Figure 9-7: Murphy's Law and the international small-cap reversal

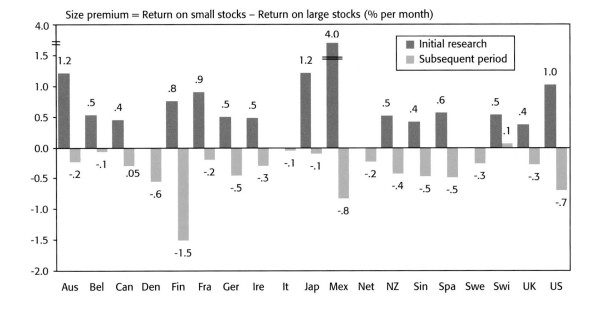

It is also worth noting that the lower bars in Figure 9-7 showing the size discount over the subsequent period almost certainly underestimate the true size discount. This is because both the IIA and FTSE universes are biased heavily toward large-cap stocks since these tend to be the securities of interest to international investors. In practice, both the IIA "small-caps" and the FTSE "medium-small-caps" are really mid-cap companies. Given that the size effect typically operates continuously right across the market, if we observe a size discount for mid-caps, we can be fairly confident that the size discount for true small-caps was even larger. In both the United States and the United Kingdom, where we have a range of size-based indexes spanning the entire market, we certainly observe that this was the case.

Why did the small-cap premium become a small-cap discount virtually everywhere around the world? In our Murphy's Law article, we sought to answer this question, at least for the United Kingdom and the United States. We showed that the earlier periods of small-cap outperformance in both the United Kingdom and United States coincided with superior real dividend growth from small-caps, while the subsequent underperformance coincided with inferior dividend growth. This suggests that the reversal was related to fundamental performance rather than sentiment. We also showed that approximately half of the performance difference in recent years could be explained by differences in the sector composition of small versus large companies. Given the extent to which world equity markets are now integrated, it seems likely that these same factors help explain the poor performance of small-caps in other countries during much of the 1990s.

The experience of the 1990s means that it has become more useful to talk of the size effect as the tendency for small-caps to perform differently from large-caps. It appears inappropriate to use the term "size effect" to imply that we should automatically expect there to be a small-cap premium.

9.5 Seasonality and size

Investors have long been fascinated by whether there are good or bad times to buy or sell shares. Old adages like "Sell in May and go away" are lost in the mists of time. Academic researchers were initially hostile to the idea that there could be simple, calendar-related ways to make money. But since the 1980s, they have joined in the hunt, helping to fuel investors' fascination by documenting ever more puzzling "empirical regularities."

Many calendar anomalies have been reported. These include the January or turn-of-the-year effect; a summer effect (basically the sell in May story, known in the United States as the Halloween indicator because that is when one should "buy back"); a time-of-the month effect (higher returns at the start of the month); a holiday effect (higher returns around holidays); a day-of-the-week or weekend effect (lower returns on Mondays); and a time-of-the-day effect (higher returns at the start and end of trading); and even a Presidential death effect. Popular books such as Schwartz (1997) are devoted to listing statistics such as "the percentage of time prices rise each trading day in June's second quarter."

While an analysis of these anomalies is beyond the scope of this book, one, namely, the January effect, is of relevance. There are three reasons for this. First, of all the calendar anomalies, the January effect is by far the most important, and is more famous than all the others. Second, it is closely intertwined with the size effect since in the United States the entire historical outperformance of smaller stocks is attributable to their returns in January. And third, most previous research on the January size seasonal has been US-based, due to the lack of suitable long-run size-based indexes elsewhere. Our new equity indexes, compiled in association with ABN AMRO, provide high quality monthly data from 1955 onward. They make it possible to check whether there is a similar effect in the United Kingdom, and to test out US theories on a novel database.

The theory most often put forward for the outperformance of US small-caps in January is tax-loss selling. It is argued that stocks that have fallen during the year face downward price pressure near year-end as investors sell them to realize capital losses to minimize tax payments. After the year-end, the pressure is removed, and prices revert to fair values. An alternative theory is that fund managers engage in year-end "window-dressing," ridding their portfolios of losers, thereby artificially depressing their year-end prices. Both effects impact most on smaller stocks because stocks whose prices have fallen have by definition become smaller. Small stocks are also more volatile, and thus more likely to feature among the year's extreme performers. Both theories are hard to square with market efficiency, and neither is fully supported by the evidence, but both are widely cited.

When applied across countries, both theories need adapting since the turn of the tax year and year-end "window dressing" can occur at different dates depending on the fiscal and financial reporting systems. In the United Kingdom, the tax year for individuals starts on April 6 and many firms report on an April–March cycle, though others work to an end-December tax and reporting year-end. If there is a small-cap turn-of-the-year effect in the United Kingdom, we should observe it during April as well as, or instead of, January.

Figure 9-8 shows the average return on US large-cap stocks for each calendar month from 1926–2000. For US large-caps, there is no turn-of-the-year effect. Returns are not low in December, and January does not have the highest returns, but ranks fifth. In contrast, the UK data reveal much larger differences. January has the highest mean return of 3.2 percent; but if we exclude the January 1975 outlier of 50 percent, the January mean falls to 2.2 percent, relegating it to third place behind April and December. It is tempting to interpret the high April average as a turn-of-the-tax-year effect, and the high January, and arguably December, averages as being linked to turn-of-the-calendar-year reporting.

The reason we find no US January effect in Figure 9-8 is because this effect is exclusively a small stock phenomenon. Figure 9-9 confirms this by showing the monthly pattern of the micro-cap premium. For the United States, we adopt Ibbotson Associates' definition of the micro-cap premium as the difference between the returns on CRSP NYSE deciles 9 and 10 (micro-caps) and deciles 1 and 2 (large-caps). For the United Kingdom, drawing on our work with ABN AMRO, it is the difference between the returns on the MicroCap™ Index and our UK equity index.

Figure 9-8: The pattern of monthly equity returns in the United States and the United Kingdom

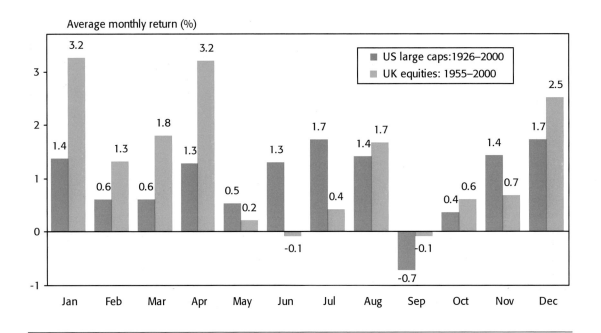

Figure 9-9 shows that the US January effect is very large. The average January premium is 7.1 percent, seven times higher than February, the next highest month. The mean for all other months (February–December) is -0.5 percent, indicating that, without January, the US size premium was negative over the last 75 years. Furthermore, although we saw in section 9.4 that the US size premium has on average been negative since its discovery, the January size premium has stayed positive. Since Keim's (1983) original analysis of the January effect, the micro-cap premium has reversed, with an arithmetic mean of -0.34 percent per month, yet January has continued to be the best month, with a mean premium of 2.95 percent.

Figure 9-9 also shows that in sharp contrast to the United States, there is no evidence of a UK year-end size effect, regardless of whether we look at the tax- or calendar-year-end. Of the twelve monthly premia, January, while positive at 0.9 percent, ranks as only the fourth highest, while the April mean is negative at -0.3 percent and ranks tenth. The highest premium is May, followed by February and July. These results suggest that if there are tax- or calendar-year-end seasonals in the United Kingdom, they relate to the overall market rather than the size premium. This is the opposite of the United States.

In the United States, the January effect has gained considerable acceptance as an explanation for the size premium—even though it really only replaces one puzzle with another. UK smaller companies have outperformed over the long haul, just as in the United States, but there is no evidence of a January size seasonal. Previous US research may therefore have been somewhat misdirected since it is now clear that turn-of-the-year seasonality has slim prospects of providing a validated international explanation of the small firm effect.

Figure 9-9: The pattern of the monthly size premium in the United States and the United Kingdom

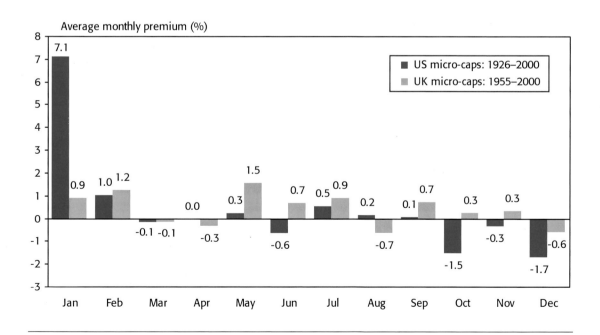

A cow for her milk
A hen for her eggs
And a stock by heck
For her dividends.

In this spirit, Litzenberger and Ramaswamy (1979) documented a marked historical return premium from US stocks with an above-average dividend yield. O'Shaughnessy (1998) demonstrates that this superior reward to high yield stocks persisted over the second half of the twentieth century. To verify this tendency for high yield stocks to provide a higher long-run return, we look at the longest period for which comprehensive data is available for the United States. Figure 10-1 shows the performance since 1926 of US stocks that rank each year in the highest- or lowest-yielding 30 percent of companies, and draws comparison with the overall market (represented by the CRSP value weighted equity index). Returns are in nominal terms.

The annualized return on the high yield companies is 12.2 percent, compared with 10.4 percent for the low yield stocks. There is, of course, a greater tax burden associated with the return from high-yielders in the United States compared with the more favorable tax treatment of stocks whose return arises largely from capital gains. The impact of tax is controversial, but tax alone cannot explain this large value premium. Further, if tax were the major factor, alternative definitions of value and growth stocks would discriminate less well between high and low subsequent performers, but in fact there are alternative measures that do an even better job.

Figure 10-1: Cumulative return from high and low dividend yield US common stocks, 1926–2000

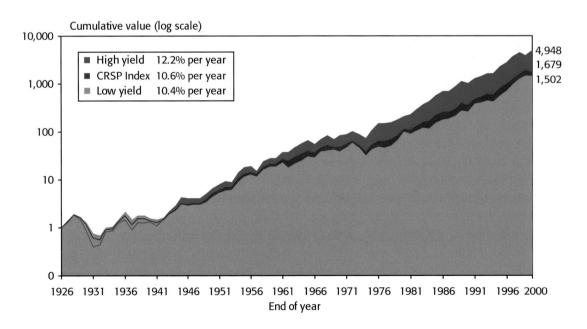

Source: Returns provided by Ken French for portfolios comprising the 30 percent lowest yield and 30 percent highest yield stocks.

The pre-eminent measure of value is at present the book-to-market ratio. Some two decades ago, work by Stattman (1980) and Rosenberg, Reid, and Lanstein (1985) encouraged the view that there may be above-average returns to high book-to-market stocks. The recent interest in value investing was nurtured by Fama and French (1992), who document the relation between company size and book-to-market and subsequent stock returns. Fama and French (1993, 1995) show how size and value can be used to predict portfolio returns; they interpret the predictive power of these portfolios as an indication of their risk exposure.

Figure 10-2 shows the performance of US stocks sorted annually by their book-to-market ratios. The high book-to-market portfolio contains the 30 percent of stocks that rank highest on this criterion; the low book-to-market group contains the 30 percent of stocks that rank lowest. The performance gap between the value and growth portfolios is even larger here than in Figure 10-1. The annualized return from 1926–2000 is 13.7 percent for value stocks and 10.2 percent for growth stocks. Based on the book-to-market criterion, the annualized value-growth premium over this period was therefore 3.2 percent.

Why have value stocks outperformed growth stocks? There are three schools of thought. One is that investors become enthused about companies with good prospects, and bid their prices up to an unrealistic level (see, for example, Lakonishok, Shleifer, and Vishny, 1994). Another possibility is that since value stocks are often distressed companies, their higher returns are simply a reward for the greater risks they impose on investors (see, for example, Fama and French, 1993, 1995). The third possibility, promoted by Black (1993), is that the outcome was simply a chance event: Siegel (1998) attributes the post-1963 value-growth

Figure 10-2: Cumulative return from high and low book-to-market US common stocks, 1926–2000

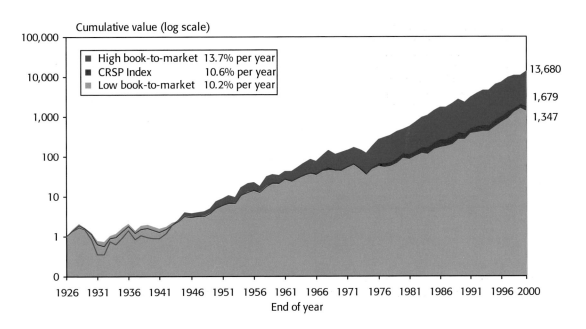

Source: Returns provided by Ken French for portfolios comprising the 30 percent lowest and highest book-to-market stocks.

premium to the 1975–83 oil price rise and its impact on large oil firms, an event that is not recurrent. Many researchers have pored over US stock price databases. To learn more, it is revealing to look at the United Kingdom, and to research as long a period as possible.

10.2 Value and growth investing in the United Kingdom

We now dig deeper into the relative performance of value and growth investing in the UK stock market. We start with the more recent period considered in chapter 9. Our analysis uses a database of balance sheets for all firms listed on the London Stock Exchange since 1953. This data, compiled by Nagel (2001), enables us to look at value effects across the entire population of UK listed stocks over nearly half a century. The source data is free of survivorship bias, and covers some one hundred thousand firm-years of accounting data.

Nagel's database is comparable, and in some ways superior, to the US Compustat data. For example, whereas Davis, Fama, and French (2000) have accounting information on 339 NYSE firms in 1929 and 834 firms in 1955, we have accounting data on some 3,500 UK companies in 1956, and use the UK accounting data in conjunction with the entire stock return series in the comprehensive London Share Price Database (LSPD), covering 1955–2000. The analysis includes all non-surviving companies, but omits foreign companies and closed-end funds. Based on Nagel's data, Figure 10-3 displays the annual value-growth premium. In contrast to the relatively volatile size premium shown in Figure 9-3 in chapter 9, the value premium was remarkably stable and persistent until the late 1970s. Since then, it has been more variable.

Figure 10-3: Annual value-growth return premia based on entire UK market, 1956–2000

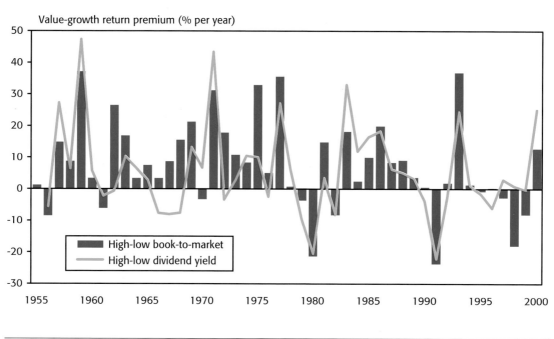

Source: Stefan Nagel

To produce Figure 10-3, we form mid-year portfolios, based on the ratio of the end-June share price to the book value of equity from the end of the preceding December (we omit companies with a non-positive book value). We rank stocks by their book-to-market: the highest 40 percent of companies are designated "value" stocks, while the lowest 40 percent are "growth" stocks. Performance is monitored over the following twelve months, by measuring the return premium of value relative to growth stocks. The process is repeated year by year until 2000, and this value-growth premium is displayed in Figure 10-3 as vertical bars.

The infrequency with which US companies pay dividends has raised questions about the use of the dividend yield as a guide to value (see Fama and French, 2001). In other countries, however, a larger proportion of companies pay dividends, and the dividend yield may be a more useful criterion for value. Dividends are defined here as the sum of dividend payments on a stock over the preceding twelve months (we omit non-dividend paying stocks). We repeat the portfolio formation described above: the 40 percent of firms with the highest yield are regarded as value stocks; the 40 percent with the lowest yield are categorized as the growth stocks. We again monitor performance over the following twelve months, measuring the return premium of value relative to growth stocks for each year until 2000. The premium of high yield stocks relative to low yield stocks is depicted in Figure 10-3 as a line plot.

In Figure 10-3, the annual value-growth premia based on dividend yields (the line plot) are similar to the premia based on book-to-market (the vertical bars). The correlation of the annual premia is 0.82. This suggests that, at least in the United Kingdom, dividend yield also captures much of the cross-sectional variation in returns that is associated with book-to-market. Declining yields and the recent growth in share repurchases have not materially impaired the capacity for yields to capture return differentials. Dividends may therefore give rise to useful measures of value, notably when book values deliver doubtful results or are unavailable. This insight suggests a way of extending our research back to 1900.

Using our record of dividends on UK stocks since 1900, we study the value-growth premium over the full 101 years from 1900–2000. We focus on the hundred companies that comprise our UK equity index over 1900–54, and thereafter on an analogous index of the hundred largest companies. We define value and growth using the top fifty and bottom fifty dividend yields as at each turn of the year. Our results may be regarded as measures of value within the UK's FTSE 100 Index, if the latter had been constructed over the period. The bars in Figure 10-4 show the return premium of high-yielders relative to low-yielders in each year since 1900. For comparison, the line plot on the right-hand half of the chart shows the post-1955 premium computed using book values for the same hundred companies. There is a strong similarity between the two series.

Large-cap stocks represent the majority of the value of the equity market. For institutional investors, and also for individual investors in aggregate, it is necessary to have most of a portfolio invested in large companies. The scale of the value-growth effect within the large-cap sector is therefore of particular interest. Figure 10-4 documents a big performance gap between these two subsamples of the top 100 shares. In some years, value stocks have under-

Figure 10-4: Annual value-growth return premia based on largest 100 UK stocks, 1900–2000

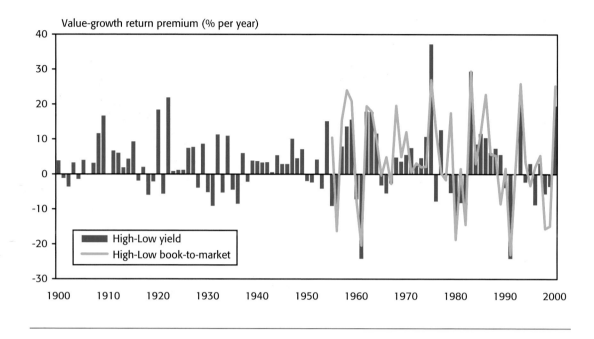

performed by more than 20 percent; in others they have outperformed by at least this margin. Even in the first half of the twentieth century, when the value-growth effect was less volatile, there were several years when the value-growth premium was around twenty percent. This is a more marked degree of variability than we saw in Figure 9-4 for the size effect within the top 100 shares (which is scarcely surprising, given that the top 100 shares exclude all small-caps). Perhaps for this reason, the distinction between value and growth stocks has captured the attention of mainstream fund managers, and has assumed an importance that may even dwarf the celebrated small firm effect.

While the average value-growth premium has in recent decades been undiminished, the volatility of this effect is shown in Figure 10-4 to be greater than it was. Just like the size premium, there has in recent times been more uncertainty about the direction of the value-growth effect. Though the premium for value investing can eventually be substantial, many investors will today regard the choice between a value and a growth strategy as a fundamental active management decision: they will ask themselves whether short-term economic conditions are conducive for value or growth investing. Only a few institutions assert that one should take a permanently overexposed position in the value segment of the market.

Nevertheless, there is a big divergence in return between these two market segments. Figure 10-5 shows the long-term performance of the value and growth indexes described above, together with the performance of the overall UK equity market. The graph shows that value investing has paid off well. An investment of £1 in the value index at start-1900 would have grown in nominal terms to £61,235 by the end of the year 2000. In contrast, the growth index

Figure 10-5: Cumulative return from high and low yielders within top 100 UK stocks, 1900–2000

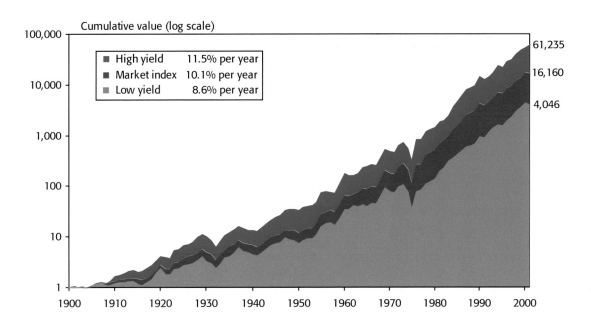

would have stood only at £4,046. The performance of the overall market is somewhat closer to growth than to value, standing at £16,160. This reflects the historical tendency of smaller UK companies to have a value orientation, and of large UK companies to have a growth orientation. Over the 101 years covered by the chart, the annualized return on the value index (containing high dividend yield stocks) is 11.5 percent, while the annualized return on the growth index (containing stocks with a low dividend yield) is 8.6 percent. The annualized value-growth premium over the 101 years is 2.7 percent.

Over the long term, the historical record of value investing has been positive in the United Kingdom as well as the United States. We now know that value stocks did better than growth stocks in the earlier as well as the later parts of the twentieth century. And the value-growth premium appears to be relatively robust to alternative definitions of value. What further evidence can we look for to help us decide whether we can expect value strategies to continue beating growth? There is one more body of evidence that we can examine: the size and consistency of the value-growth premium in countries other than the United States and United Kingdom.

10.3 The international evidence

Although there are fewer studies of other markets, there is a broad literature on value and growth phenomena around the world. Chan, Hamao, and Lakonishok (1991) look at the Japanese experience, and Jog and Li (1995) examine Canada. More comprehensive studies include Capaul, Rowley, and Sharpe's (1993) work covering France, Germany, Switzerland,

and the United Kingdom, and Fama and French's (1998) research on a variety of other markets. These studies use datasets that are limited to large-cap and mid-cap stocks. Nevertheless, they find a substantial value-growth effect across their sample countries, at least over the various periods since 1975 that are covered by these researchers.

Figure 10-6 summarizes the research for all the countries covered in these studies. For each national market, we take the first publication that presented long-run value-growth premia. The basis for computing these premia obviously differs from article to article, so we recomputed all the premia using a uniform dataset, the IIA Index series. Our recomputed index series run from the start-date to the end-date of each study's sample period. We display the monthly value-growth premia in bar-chart form. Italy is the only country in which value was noticeably overtaken by growth. Elsewhere, value investing consistently dominated growth investing. Averaged across all fourteen markets depicted in Figure 10-6, the historical value-growth premium was 0.26 percent per month, which equates to 3.2 percent per year.

The historical superiority of value strategies should not have been a surprise. Since the 1960s, many articles such as Breen (1968) and Basu (1977) had recorded superior returns from buying stocks with low price to earnings ratios. Other measures of value were likely to generate similar results. In those days, deviations from market efficiency were often explained away as a consequence of poor research methods. What was different in the 1990s was that Eugene Fama, the pre-eminent believer in the capital asset pricing model and market efficiency, was the author of much of the research. As Haugen (1999) put it: "The reason the Fama-French study made headlines was that…the Pope said God was dead."

Figure 10-6: International evidence on the value-growth effect based on book-to-market

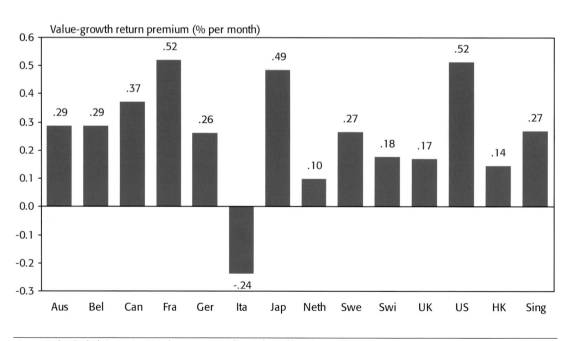

Source: Authors' calculations using IIA Indexes over research periods used in various studies

Despite the contribution of Fama and others to the evidence, and the competing explanations for why one might expect to observe a premium, the robustness of the value-growth premium remains a matter of dispute (see Shleifer, 2000, and Hawawini and Keim, 2000). Recent stock market history has made the phenomenon even more difficult to interpret. This is because the turn of the century coincided with a sharp reversal in sentiment about future growth opportunities.

Value strategies tend to win when economic conditions become more sympathetic to companies that are more likely to be distressed and/or impound less "hope" into their stock prices; and they tend to suffer when latent growth prospects come to be valued more highly by the market. Figure 10-7 compares over three periods the arithmetic mean value-growth premium for the countries we have examined: the research period studied in the previous chart, the interval from then to the end of the first quarter of 2000, and the slightly longer interval from the end of the research period through the fourth quarter of 2000. As noted above, during the first period value beat growth by 0.26 percent per month. During the subsequent interval the results were mixed, but the average premium across all fourteen countries was -0.09 percent per month; in other words, growth stocks did better than value stocks. However, from the end of the research period to the end of 2000, value investing again did better than growth investing.

Value investing looked like a winning strategy over the period spanned by the major published studies. As in other areas of investing, however, the subsequent outcome was for a number of years the opposite of what history was led us to expect, and growth companies

Figure 10-7: The average value-growth premium for fourteen countries over various periods

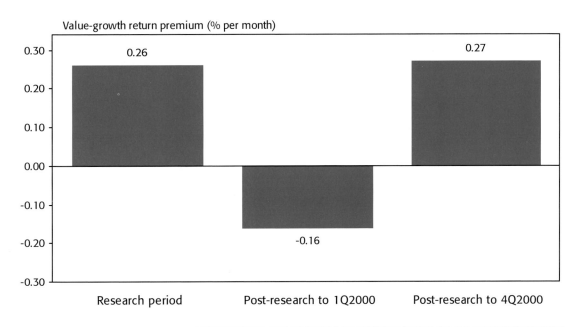

Source: Authors' calculations using IIA Indexes over various periods

surged ahead. Is the year-2000 outperformance by value stocks a sign that long-term relationships are reasserting themselves, and that value strategies will again have superior long-run performance? The volatile markets of 2001 have certainly hurt many growth companies, but we do not know whether value or growth stocks will do better over the next few decades. All we can say is that the variability of the value-growth premium is likely to be important long into the future.

10.4 Summary

Value and growth investing have given rise to dramatically different records of long-term performance. Value strategies typically emphasize stocks with a high dividend yield, or with a high ratio of book value to market value of equity. A large body of US-based evidence shows that there has been a higher long-run return, at least over the period from 1926–2000, from investing in value stocks.

Using a new dataset of accounting information merged with share price data we also find a strong value premium in the United Kingdom. The value premium exists within the small-cap as well as the large-cap universe. We also find that dividend yield as a measure of value produces similar results. The annual return spreads between portfolios sorted by dividend yield are similar to the spreads from portfolios sorted by book-to-market. We research these value-growth effects (based on dividend information) over a full century of UK stock market history. We find that the premium for value stocks was similar in the earlier and later parts of the twentieth century.

We also examine the international evidence. During historical periods for which there was a suitable database covering a reasonably long interval, the value premium was in general positive. Recent periods were more mixed. Over the last few years, different countries had value-growth premia that were sometimes positive and sometimes negative. Only after major turmoil commenced toward the end of the first quarter of 2000, when the technology bubble burst, was there a tendency for value stocks to perform internationally in unison, when they once again reasserted their performance edge over growth stocks.

Chapter 11 Equity dividends

In this chapter, we take a closer look at dividends. We saw in chapter 10 that dividends play a central role in equity investment and valuation. Our focus there was value investing. Our concern here is rather different. We concentrate on the dividend stream itself, namely, the income that is received by long-run investors who hold the overall equity market, without any tilt toward or away from high-yielders.

We begin in section 11.1 by examining the impact of dividend income on US and UK investors' long-run rates of return. We show that although year-to-year performance is driven by capital appreciation, long-term returns are influenced heavily by reinvested income.

Given the importance of reinvested income, it is interesting to examine the time path of dividends in more detail. In section 11.2 we therefore construct dividend income indexes based on the sequence of annual cash dividends that have been reinvested back into the market. From these indexes, we estimate dividend growth rates for the United States and United Kingdom. These growth rates are not only interesting in their own right, but they also play an important role in valuation models, and can provide insights into the magnitude of the cost of capital. In section 11.3, we extend this analysis to all sixteen countries in our database, and compare dividend growth rates around the world and over time.

Many analysts argue that long-run dividend growth should be related to, and ultimately bounded above, by growth in GDP. In section 11.4 we examine the relationship between dividend growth, GDP, and equity returns, and find some surprising results.

Section 11.5 examines how and why dividend yields vary over time and across countries. We note that by end-2000, yields in the United States and worldwide were close to their 101-year low. We also observe that over the last two decades, US dividend growth has been low despite the excellent performance of the US equity market. Part of the explanation for the lower yields and dividend growth could be that companies have shifted away from paying dividends. In section 11.6 we examine the trends toward "disappearing dividends" and increasing stock repurchases. Section 11.7 summarizes this chapter.

11.1 The impact of income

We have seen that equity markets around the world have generally performed well over the long run. But has the return been mostly attributable to price movements and capital gains or to dividends? Certainly, on a day-to-day basis, investors' interest tends to focus mostly on price and market movements. Figure 11-1, which shows the annual capital gain and dividend components of US stock market returns over the 101-year period from 1900–2000, helps illustrate why this is so. The height of each bar represents the capital gain or loss during each year. The area plot shows the dividend income received over each year.

Over a single year, equities are so volatile that most of an investor's performance is attributable to share price appreciation or depreciation. Dividend income adds a relatively

Figure 11-1: Annual US capital gains and dividend impact, 1900–2000

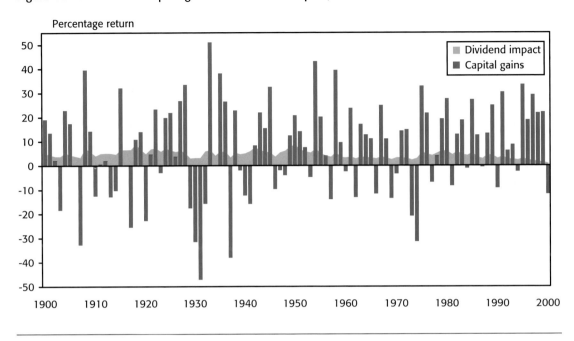

modest amount to each year's gain or loss. Dividends tend to cluster quite closely around a central value, especially if one is focusing on a subperiod of the entire index history.

On balance over the years, capital gains outweigh losses. A US equity portfolio, which started life in New Year 1900 with an initial investment of $1, would have ended 2000 with a value of $198, even without reinvestment of dividends. This represents a compound annualized capital gain of 5.4 percent per year. This significantly outpaced US consumer prices, which ended 2000 at an index level of 23.64, an annual inflation rate of 3.2 percent. The real capital gain was 2.1 percentage points per year.

While year-to-year performance is driven by capital appreciation, long-term returns are heavily influenced by reinvested dividends. The difference in terminal wealth arising from reinvested income is extremely large. Imagine two benefactors, each of whom set up an identically managed equity trust fund at the start of the twentieth century. Their initial investment is in each case $1.

One fund pays out all its income to beneficiaries, while the other reinvests all its income. By the end of the year 2000, we showed in chapter 4 that the latter would have appreciated to $16,797. This represents an annualized nominal return of 10.1 percent, or 6.7 percent in real terms. Over the 101 years the accumulator would have amassed wealth 85 times larger than the spender, who would have ended up with assets worth a mere $198.

The wealth gains from these two different investment strategies are shown in Figure 11-2, which plots the cumulative return from US equities, both with and without reinvested dividends. Even with the logarithmic scale, it is very clear that the total return from equities (the yellow line) grows cumulatively ever larger than the capital appreciation (the blue line).

Figure 11-2: Impact of reinvested dividends on cumulative US and UK equity returns, 1900–2000

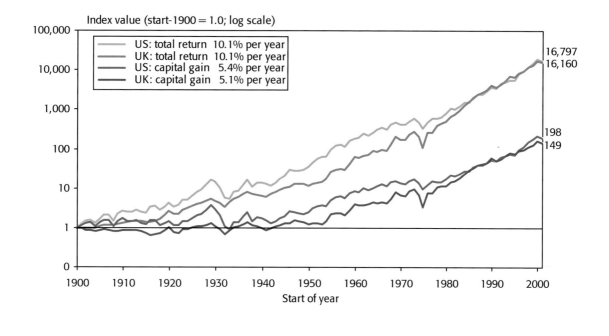

This effect is not specific to the United States but holds true for every equity market around the world. Figure 11-2 shows the equivalent UK returns both with and without dividend reinvestment. With dividends reinvested (the green line), an investment of £1 made at start-1900 in the UK stock market would have grown to £16,160 by the end of 2000. By coincidence, this is very close to the terminal wealth of $16,797 from a $1 investment in the US market. Since UK inflation was higher than US inflation, the United Kingdom had an annualized real return of 5.8 percent compared with 6.7 percent in the United States. If dividends had been spent rather than reinvested, the UK investment of £1 would have grown to just £149 (the red line), a nominal return of 5.1 percent. Over the same period, UK consumer prices rose 55-fold, so this corresponds to a real capital gain of 1 percent per year, compared with 2 percent real in the United States.

The longer the investment horizon, the more important is dividend income. For the seriously long-term investor, the value of a portfolio corresponds closely to the present value of dividends. The present value of the (eventual) capital appreciation dwindles greatly in significance.

The analysis above shows why, throughout this book, we have stressed the importance of dividends in computing total returns. Indexes that record only capital appreciation cannot be used to make comparisons over time since the level of dividend yield fluctuates over the years. Nor can such indexes be used to make comparisons across countries since yields can differ substantially between markets. As we pointed out in section 3.3, many previous long-term performance studies have been hampered by this limitation.

11.2 US and UK dividend growth

Given the importance of reinvested income, it is interesting to examine the time path of dividends in more detail. To do this, we construct indexes of the dividend amounts received over time. Subtracting the capital gain from the total return during any year gives a measure of the dividends paid during that year, expressed as a percentage (or yield) of the start-year index value. The dividend amount is then obtained by multiplying this by the start-year index value, and these annual dividend amounts are then chain-linked to form a dividend or income index. To abstract for the impact of inflation, we convert this index to real terms.

Figure 11-3 shows the real dividend income indexes for the United States and the United Kingdom from 1900–2000. US real dividends fluctuated greatly in the first half of the last century, but made little headway so that by 1949 they had just kept pace with inflation. For the next twenty-one years they grew quite strongly, but thereafter fluctuated with no clear trend. $1 of dividend income received in 1900 grew, after adjusting for inflation, to $1.78 by 2000, an annualized (geometric mean) real dividend growth rate of 0.58 percent. The arithmetic mean annual growth rate was 1 percent higher than this at 1.57 percent, reflecting the high volatility of annual growth rates, which had a standard deviation of 14.3 percent.

The red line in Figure 11-3 shows the UK real dividend index. For the first sixty years of the twentieth century, cumulative UK dividend growth was consistently below inflation. The index hit its low of 0.41 in 1920, returning to 0.42 during the Second World War. After fluctuating around 1.0 during the 1960s, dividends failed to keep pace with the rapidly rising

Figure 11-3: US and UK real dividend income indexes, 1900–2000

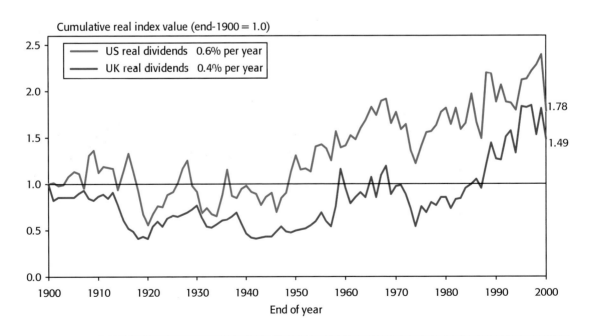

UK inflation of the 1970s, falling to 0.55 in the 1974 bear market. They then grew strongly at nearly 5 percent per year in real terms for the next twenty-five years until falling back in 2000. Over the full period, real dividends rose at an annualized rate of 0.40 percent, with an arithmetic mean of 1.4 percent per year. This was marginally below, but remarkably close to, the United States. The standard deviation of annual dividend changes was also identical in the two countries, although the United States was more volatile in the first half-century while the United Kingdom was more volatile from 1950 on. In both countries, annual dividend growth rates appear to have approximated a random walk. The serial correlation coefficients of -0.07 for the United States and -0.08 for the United Kingdom have a standard error of 0.10, and hence were not statistically significantly different from zero.

Figure 11-4 shows the average (arithmetic mean) real dividend growth rate for each decade. For the United States, average growth was positive in all decades except for the period of the First World War. In the United Kingdom, average growth was negative in three decades, all during the first half-century, while the two best decades were the "Roaring Twenties" and "Nifty Fifties." Note that even over ten-yearly intervals, dividend growth was quite volatile.

One obvious anomaly highlighted by Figure 11-4 is that despite the great bull market of the 1980s and 1990s, US real dividend growth was remarkably low in both decades. UK dividend growth was high over this period but noticeably lower in the 1990s despite higher equity returns. Over this period there has been a tendency, especially by US firms, to pay out less by way of dividends. We look more closely at these "disappearing dividends" in section 11.6.

Figure 11-4: US and UK real dividend growth rates: ten-year averages, 1900–2000

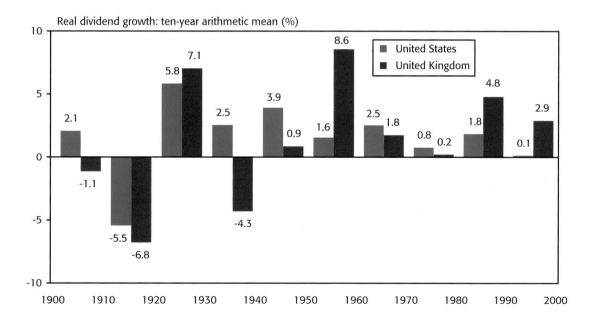

11.3 Dividend growth around the world

We have seen that the United States and the United Kingdom experienced similar real dividend growth, but how does this compare with other countries? To answer this, we have constructed real dividend indexes for all sixteen countries. The blue bars in Figure 11-5 show the annualized (geometric mean) real dividend growth rates from 1900–2000, with countries ranked in ascending order from left to right. Clearly, there has been considerable variation in dividend growth, ranging from Japan, where real dividends *fell* by 3.3 percent per year, to Sweden, where they grew by 2.3 percent per year. US and UK dividend growth ranked fourth and fifth highest behind Sweden, South Africa, and Australia. Only two other countries, Canada and Switzerland, had positive real dividend growth.

Figure 11-5 also shows the real dividend growth rates over both halves of the twentieth century. In most countries, growth was lower in the first half-century. The exceptions were the resource rich countries of Canada, Australia, and South Africa. These, plus two other well-endowed nations, the United States and Sweden, were the only ones with positive real dividend growth over the first half-century. South Africa had the highest growth at 2.5 percent, while Japan and Germany had the lowest growth at around -7 percent. During the second half-century, only four countries had negative growth. Denmark was the lowest at -0.5 percent, and Germany the highest at 5.0 percent. As we have seen in other contexts, there were also some reversals. Some of the lowest growth countries in the first half-century had the highest growth over the next fifty years (e.g., Germany), and vice versa (e.g., Australia). The correlation between the growth rates in the first and second halves of the century was -0.27.

Figure 11-5: Real dividend growth rates around the world: 1900–2000

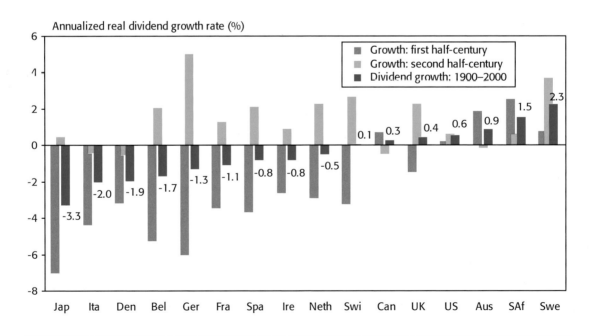

11.4 Dividend growth, GDP growth, and real equity returns

Dividend growth is interesting both in its own right and because of its key role in valuation models. Gordon's (1962) constant dividend growth model, despite its venerability, remains one of the most widely used models for estimating required returns (e.g., Fama and French, 2002). The Gordon model notes that the price of a stock, or the level of an index, equals the present value of future dividends. If these grow at a constant rate, then the required return on equity equals the dividend yield plus the expected future growth rate in dividends.

In applying the Gordon model, the key variable is the expected dividend growth. In seeking to explain the high stock market ratings and low yields of the late 1990s, many analysts and investment bankers assumed quite high real dividend growth rates, in the range of 2–5 percent. Others argued that, in the long run, real dividends cannot grow faster than GDP since otherwise, corporate profits would assume an ever-larger share of GDP.

Figure 11-6 shows the long-run relationship between real dividend growth and real GDP growth. As in the previous figure, the blue bars show real dividend growth from 1900–2000. The yellow bars show growth in real GDP per capita. We focus on GDP per capita to adjust for the large differences in population growth. From 1900–2000, the countries with the lowest population growth were Ireland (19 percent), France (46 percent), Belgium (52 percent), and the United Kingdom (53 percent), while the fastest population growth was in Australia (420 percent), Canada (470 percent), and South Africa (825 percent). The US population grew by 267 percent.

Figure 11-6: Real dividend growth, equity returns, and GDP growth around the world, 1900–2000

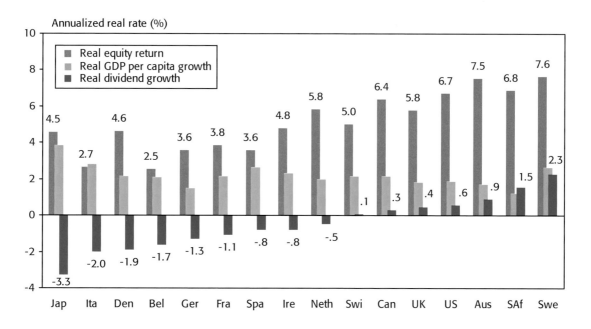

Besides changing over time, Figure 11-7 shows that yields also vary greatly across countries. Despite greater integration of world equity markets, the cross-sectional dispersion of yields at end-2000 remained as wide as in 1900. Yields ranged from 5.2 percent in Spain, down to 2.4 percent in the United Kingdom, 1.1 percent in the United States, and just 0.7 percent in Japan. There are many reasons for this. Differing tax regimes can be especially important. The imputation tax systems in Spain and Australia, for example, may have encouraged higher corporate payout ratios, as was true for UK companies before the 1997 tax changes. Growth opportunities may vary across countries, impacting companies' capital needs and hence their payout policies. Payout differences between countries may also reflect different traditions and conventions, varying attitudes to shareholders, and disparities in the quality of information available to investors. Finally, in any given year countries will be at varying stages in their economic cycles, and this may also be associated with yield differences.

While end-2000 yields varied a lot between countries, yields everywhere were close to their 101-year low point. The average yield across all sixteen countries in 1900 was around 5 percent, and this was still the case in 1950. By end-2000, however, the (unweighted) average yield had fallen to 1.9 percent, while the yield on our capitalization weighted sixteen-country world equity index was even lower at 1.35 percent. There are two plausible explanations for this fall in yields. First, there may have been a downward shift in the capitalization rate or an upward shift in future growth expectations, causing markets to be re-rated. Second, the average payout ratio has fallen so that investors now receive less of their return from dividends. We return to the re-rating argument in chapter 13, but meanwhile the next section looks at the evidence on declining dividends. There is, of course, a third possible explanation for the low yields at the start of the twenty-first century, namely, that these were due to markets having become overvalued thanks to "irrational exuberance" (e.g., see Shiller, 2000).

11.6 Disappearing dividends

We saw above that the yield on US equities fell from 7.2 percent in 1950 to just 1.1 percent by end-2000. Part of this fall is undoubtedly due to a market re-rating, but the balance arises from a decline in dividend payments by US firms. Fama and French (2001) document and analyze the US trend of "disappearing dividends." Figure 11-8 is taken from their article, and shows the proportion of US stocks in different dividend paying groups from 1926–99. The green area shows the percentage of US firms that pay dividends, while the red and blue areas show the percentage of non-payers. In every year, these clearly sum to 100 percent.

Figure 11-8 is based on all stocks on the CRSP database, and the jumps in 1963 and 1973 arise from the addition of Amex and then Nasdaq stocks, fewer of which paid dividends than NYSE stocks. After 1973, when the coverage is fully comprehensive, the graph shows that the percentage of dividend payers initially rose to 67 percent in 1978, and then fell steadily to just 20.8 percent in 1999. The non-dividend-payers are divided into firms that have never paid a dividend (the blue area), and former payers (the red area). The never-paids are always in the majority, making up three-quarters of the non-dividend payers in 1978, and seven-eighths by 1999, when non-dividend-payers represented 79.2 percent of all companies.

Figure 11-8: Percentage of US stocks in different dividend paying categories, 1926–99

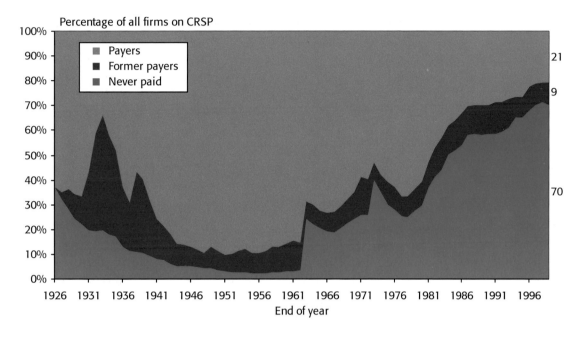

Source: Fama and French (2001)

Fama and French find two explanations for the sharp decline in dividend payers. First, since 1978 there has been an explosion of initial public offerings (IPOs), which tend to be small firms with low profitability and strong growth opportunities—characteristics typical of firms that have never paid dividends. Second, and as important, US firms have become less likely to pay dividends, whatever the company's characteristics. Fama and French suggest that one important reason for this lower propensity to pay is that firms have (finally) become aware of the tax disadvantages of dividends under the US tax system.

Consistent with this view, Figure 11-9, taken from Grullon and Michaely (2000), confirms that share repurchases surged in the United States from the mid-1980s. This change is often attributed to tax. Because capital gains are taxed in the United States at a lower rate than dividends, corporations have an incentive to substitute repurchases for dividends. But this incentive existed long before the mid-1980s, and the US Tax Reform Act of 1986 considerably reduced (although by no means eliminated) the relative advantage of capital gains, so tax cannot be the only explanation (for a fuller discussion, see Grullon and Ikenberry, 2000).

Whatever the explanation, Figure 11-9 shows that repurchases increased from less than 5 percent of earnings in 1980 to 50 percent in 1998. Expressed as a percentage of dividends, repurchases rose from 13 percent in 1980 to 104 percent in 1998, when they actually overtook dividends. Meanwhile, the graph shows that dividend payout has not fallen, although repurchases may have been financed by funds that would otherwise have been used to increase dividends. Another study by Jagannathan, Stephens, and Weisbach (2000) also concludes that repurchases are complementary to, not a replacement for, dividends. Dividends tend to

Figure 11-9: Dividends and repurchases as a percentage of earnings for US firms, 1972–98

Source: Grullon and Michaely (2000); based on Compustat data for 4500 firms (on average); excludes banks, utilities and insurance

be paid from long-run sustainable cash flows, while repurchases serve the corresponding role of paying out temporary cash surpluses. In line with this, Fama and French (2001) find that repurchases are mainly the province of dividend payers and tend to increase their already high cash payouts.

Do these trends in dividends and repurchases extend beyond the United States? The answer is yes, but to a lesser extent. An obvious comparison is with the United Kingdom, the market that normally most closely resembles the United States. From the 1950s until the late 1980s, 90 percent of UK stocks paid dividends. By 2000, this had fallen to 71 percent, and will likely fall further to around 63 percent in 2001. This is still three times higher than in the United States, but the trend is the same direction. As in the United States, it is driven mostly by IPOs, which have typically been small, non-dividend paying, potential growth stocks, often in technology, and usually quoted on the United Kingdom's Alternative Investment Market (AIM), not on the London Stock Exchange. Meanwhile, most large UK stocks still pay dividends. The one hundred largest UK stocks account for 77 percent of total market value, and only nine (3 percent by value) are non-dividend payers.

As in the United States, UK stock repurchases have grown in importance. They were negligible until 1989, but from 1989–98, they averaged 8 percent of dividends (Rau and Vermaelen, 2002). By 1998, this had grown to 16 percent, but while more recent data is not available, there seems to have been little subsequent growth. Rau and Vermaelen show that UK repurchase activity has been strongly influenced by a series of changes in tax rules, but since 1997 the UK tax system has been neutral with respect to the dividend/repurchase decision.

Historically, share repurchases have not been popular in Continental Europe or many other markets around the world. Until fairly recently, they were prohibited in locations such as Germany, France, Japan, Hong Kong, and Taiwan. In other countries, the tax regime provides little incentive for buybacks, while in some, such as The Netherlands, it specifically discourages them. Also, as Rau and Vermaelen point out, buybacks do not fit readily with the European corporate culture, since most continental European countries have traditionally emphasized stakeholder, rather than shareholder, value. There is a gradual process of change, however, and buybacks have become more popular in recent years. Meanwhile, the United Kingdom is the European country where buybacks are most popular, accounting for some 60 percent of the total. Notwithstanding this, even UK repurchase activity remains tiny compared with the United States.

11.7 Summary

This chapter began by showing that dividends are a critical element of long-run gains in wealth. Over the course of the last 101 years, a portfolio of US equities with dividends reinvested would have grown to 85 times the value it would have attained if dividends had been squandered. This explains why, throughout this book, we have stressed the importance of good dividend data when measuring long-run returns. Our study is unique in using total returns for so many markets, rather than using a price index as a performance guide. Many previous studies have been hampered by this limitation.

The availability of total returns as well as capital gains has allowed us to construct long-run dividend growth indexes. We find that real dividend growth has been rather lower than is often assumed. Between 1900 and 2000, US dividends grew at an annualized real rate of 0.58 percent, with an arithmetic mean growth rate of 1.57 percent. This was enough to ensure that the United States ranked fourth out of our sixteen countries. Growth rates varied greatly across countries, ranging from 2.3 percent in Sweden to -3.3 percent for Japan. In most countries, real dividend growth was lower in the turbulent first half of the twentieth century.

Real dividends have generally grown more slowly than real GDP per capita, and real dividend growth does not appear, as is often assumed, to be positively correlated with GDP growth—if anything, the correlation is negative. The same finding applies to the correlation between GDP growth and total equity returns. Over time, the path of real dividend growth rates appears to approximate a random walk, and growth rates have been quite volatile.

Dividend growth is interesting both in its own right and because it plays a key role in valuation models and financial research. For example, in the early literature on excess equity market volatility and speculative bubbles, researchers often assumed that future dividends could proxy for investors' expectations (see Shiller, 1981) or that investors might expect a constant growth rate of dividends to continue indefinitely (e.g., Barsky and De Long, 1993).

Similar assumptions are made in applying classic valuation models such as the Gordon model, where dividend growth is often linked to GDP growth. Our findings suggest that these assumptions are unlikely to be fully appropriate or wholly correct. They also help place in context the debate about the likelihood of future dividend growth greatly outstripping GDP.

In this chapter, we have also looked at how and why dividend yields vary over time and across countries. In particular, we noted that, by end-2000, yields in the United States and worldwide were close to their 101-year low. We also observed that over the last two decades, US dividend growth has been less than might have been expected given the outstanding performance of the US equity market. Part of the explanation for the lower yields and dividend growth could be that companies have shifted away from paying dividends.

In the United States, there has certainly been a sharp decline in the proportion of dividend payers. One reason for this is the changing nature of US firms, caused by the explosion of IPOs by smaller, growth-oriented stocks that seldom pay dividends. But Fama and French (2001) report that US companies of all types now have a lower propensity to pay dividends. They attribute this partly to tax considerations. Consistent with this, there has been huge growth in US stock repurchases since the mid-1980s, with repurchases actually exceeding dividends in 1998.

Interestingly, though, aggregate dividend payouts do not seem to have fallen. Repurchases appear to be a complement to, not a replacement for, dividends. Nevertheless, as Grullon and Michaely (2000) suggest, they may well have been financed by funds that otherwise would have been used to increase dividends. These trends in dividend payment and repurchases therefore go part way toward explaining the relatively low dividend growth rates and yields in the US market. Similar trends have appeared in other countries, most notably the United Kingdom, but even in the United Kingdom they are far less marked than in the United States.

Although repurchases have not replaced dividends, they have become an important source of payouts. Focusing just on cash dividends no longer seems appropriate, and those who argue, for example, that the historically low dividend yield is a sign of stock market overvaluation are not looking at the full picture. In the context of valuation models, or those other areas of finance and financial research which focus on dividends, dividend growth, and yields, we now need to consider total payout as well as cash dividends.

Chapter 12 The equity risk premium

Investment in equities over the 101 years from 1900–2000 has proved rewarding but, as we have seen, has been accompanied by correspondingly greater risks. In this chapter we examine the historical rewards that investors have enjoyed for bearing this risk.

Clearly, investors do not like volatility—at least on the downside—and will be prepared to invest in equities only if there is some expected compensation for their risk exposure. We can measure the reward for risk that they have received in the past by comparing the return on equities with the return from risk free investments. The difference between these two returns is called the equity risk premium. The risk premium is typically measured relative to either government bills or bonds. In sections 12.1 and 12.2 we therefore analyze the risk premium that investors have enjoyed relative to bills, while in sections 12.3 and 12.4 we examine the risk premium relative to long bonds. In each case, we look first at the United States, and then at worldwide comparisons.

The equity risk premium is an extremely important economic variable. An estimate of the premium is central to projecting future investment returns, calculating the cost of equity capital for companies, valuing companies and shares, appraising investment proposals, and determining fair rates of return for regulated businesses. All of these applications require an estimate of the prospective risk premium, whereas, by definition, the only premium that we can measure is the historical risk premium.

In practice, and perhaps because of its measurability, the historical risk premium is often treated as a proxy for the prospective risk premium. It has certainly been by far the most influential variable in conditioning expert opinion about what the future premium might be. It is frequently assumed that if the measurement interval is long enough, the historical risk premium will provide an unbiased estimate of the future premium. In chapter 13 we will consider the extent to which our findings on the historical risk premium differ from prior estimates, and hence challenge established views about the magnitude of the premium. More fundamentally, we will also examine whether the historical premium really provides a reasonable estimate of the prospective premium. In this chapter, however, the focus is on the historical record of the risk premium.

12.1 US risk premia relative to bills

To establish whether equity risk has been adequately rewarded, we need to measure the equity risk premium. This is typically calculated in one of two ways. The first uses treasury bills (very short-term, default-free, fixed-income government securities) as the risk free or "safe" benchmark. The second measures the risk premium relative to long-term default-free government bonds. Of these two, only treasury bills can really be considered risk free, and even here chapter 5 reminded us that hyperinflation can on occasions cause even bill investors to experience large losses in real terms. In this section, we focus on the risk premium relative to bills, while in section 12.3 we contrast this with the premium relative to bonds.

Whether the premium is defined relative to bills or to bonds, we measure it by taking the geometric difference between the equity return and the risk free return. The formula is *1 + Equity rate of return* divided by *1 + Riskless return*, minus *1*. For example, if shares with a one-year return of 21 percent were being evaluated relative to treasury bills yielding 10 percent, the equity risk premium would be 10 percent. This is because $(1 + {}^{21}/_{100})$ divided by $(1 + {}^{10}/_{100})$ is equal to $(1 + {}^{10}/_{100})$. The difference between the equity return of 21 percent and the treasury bill return of 10 percent could also be estimated by subtracting one return from another and the result (11 percent) would be similar.

These measures of the risk premium have no obvious numeraire in terms of currency since the equity risk premium, measured relative to bill or bond returns, is a ratio. It is hence unaffected by whether returns are computed in dollars or (say) pounds, or whether returns are computed in nominal or real (inflation adjusted) terms.

Figure 12-1 shows the year-by-year US risk premium relative to bills. The distribution of out-comes was wide, with the lowest and highest premia occurring, as might be expected, in the worst and best years for stocks. The lowest premium was -45 percent in 1931, when equities returned -44 percent and treasury bills 1.1 percent, while the highest was 57 percent in 1933, when equities gave 57.6 percent and bills 0.3 percent. Figure 12-1 shows that the distribution of annual premia is roughly symmetrical, resembling a normal distribution. The mean is 7.7 percent and the standard deviation is 19.6 percent. On average, therefore, US investors received a positive—and quite large—reward for exposure to equity market risk.

Figure 12-1: Histogram of US equity risk premium relative to treasury bills, 1900–2000

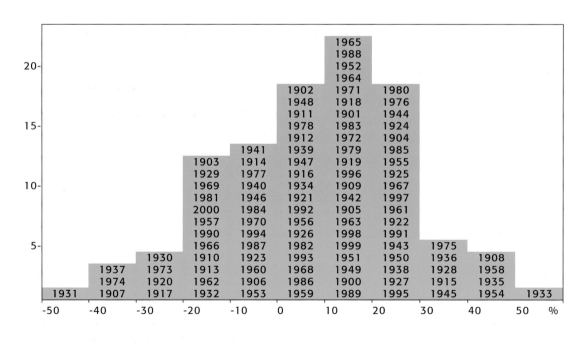

Because the range of premia that are encountered on a year-to-year basis is very broad, it can be misleading to label these as "risk premia." Investors clearly cannot have expected, let alone required, a negative risk premium from investing in equities, otherwise they would simply have avoided them. All the negative and many of the very low premia shown in Figure 12-1 must therefore reflect nasty surprises. Equally, investors could not have "required" the very high premia, such as the 57 percent in 1933. Such numbers are implausibly high as a required reward for risk, and the high realizations must therefore reflect pleasant surprises. To avoid confusion, many writers choose not to refer to these as "risk premia," but instead label them as "excess returns," that is, returns in excess of (or under) the risk free interest rate.

To make sensible inferences about the historical risk premium, it is therefore necessary to look at much longer periods than a single year. Over longer horizons, we might expect good and bad luck to cancel each other out. A common choice of time frame is a decade, and while this is still far too short to produce reliable estimates, we adopt this as our intermediate interval for evaluating risk premia. For long-run comparisons, we use our full 101-year period from 1900–2000.

Over the full 101 years, the annualized (geometric mean) US equity risk premium relative to bills was 5.8 percent, which is 0.9 percentage points lower than the annualized real return on US equities. Figure 12-2 shows the annualized US equity risk premium and US real equity returns, both measured over a sequence of rolling ten-year periods. The two series have tended to track each other. In recent years, the markedly positive real returns on treasury bills have caused the equity risk premium to be lower than the real return on equities.

Figure 12-2: Rolling ten-year US equity real returns and risk premia relative to bills, 1909–2000

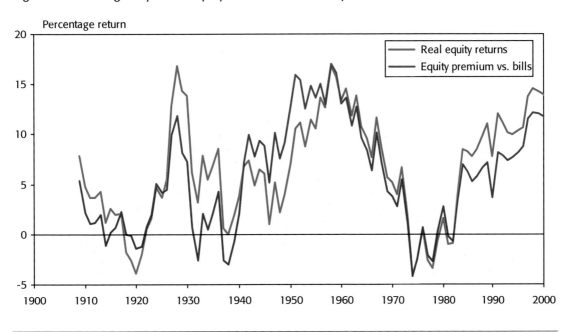

Figure 12-2 shows that even over intervals of a decade, there were periods when the *ex post* US risk premium was negative, most recently in the 1970s and early 1980s. There can be major performance surprises, even over a ten-year interval. It follows that we need very long periods to infer investors' expectations about the reward for exposure to equity market risk. Even then, inference can be problematic, as we will see in chapter 13.

12.2 Worldwide risk premia relative to bills

We have seen that US investors enjoyed a large, positive risk premium relative to bills with a 101-year arithmetic mean of 7.7 percent and a geometric mean of 5.8 percent. The US economy has been especially successful, however, and so we need to set the US record in context.

Figure 12-3 shows the annualized, geometric mean risk premia relative to bills for all sixteen countries over the full 101-year period. The bars plot the equity risk premia relative to bills, while the line plot overlay shows the real rate of return on equities. The chart also shows the "world" risk premium, based on our sixteen-country world equity index, calculated in US dollars, with risk premia and real returns computed relative to US bills and US inflation.

Figure 12-3 shows that while the equity risk premium varies across countries, the 101-year averages fall within a fairly narrow range. The US premium of 5.8 percent, while above average, is not the largest, with five other countries enjoying higher premia. France led the field with a premium of 7.4 percent, while the lowest premium was the 1.8 percent for Denmark. The UK risk premium of 4.8 percent was just below the figure of 4.9 percent on the world index, which, in turn, was 0.9 percent below the premium for the United States.

Figure 12-3: Worldwide annualized real equity returns and risk premia relative to bills, 1900–2000

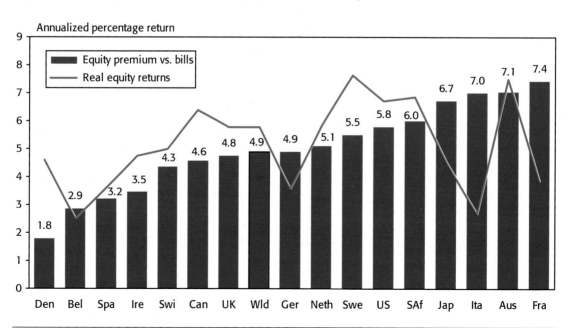

Figure 12-3 shows that the relationship between equity risk premia relative to bills and real equity returns can be complex. In most countries, real equity returns exceeded the risk premium, but in some cases, such as Italy, an above-average risk premium is associated with below-average real returns. The reason for this was identified in chapter 5. In countries like Italy, the returns on cash fell short of investors' *ex ante* expectations due to unexpectedly high inflation. It is therefore possible for an equity market that performs poorly (perhaps also as a consequence of inflation) to have a large *ex post* premium relative to bills.

The equity risk premia relative to bills for the sixteen countries and for the world index are listed in Table 12-1. Note that for Germany the calculations are based on 99, rather than 101 years, since we have excluded 1922–23. While we can calculate a continuous, 101-year real return series for German equities, calculating risk premia is more problematic. The hyperinflation of 1922–23 decimated bill and bond returns, resulting in -100 percent real returns in 1923. We therefore obtain more meaningful statistics by omitting these years.

The first six columns of Table 12-1 provide statistics on the annual risk premia. The geometric means in the first column provided the plotting data for the bars in Figure 12-3. The next five columns show the arithmetic means, standard errors, standard deviations, and maximum and minimum premia. We commented earlier that the distribution of annual risk premia for the United States—displayed in Figure 12-1—was very wide. The standard deviation figures in the fourth column of Table 12-1 show that the dispersion was even greater than in the United States in all but four of the other countries.

Table 12-1: Worldwide equity risk premia relative to bills, 1900–2000

Country	Annual equity risk premium relative to treasury bills						Ten year risk premium		
	Geometric mean	Arithmetic mean	Standard error	Standard deviation	Minimum return	Maximum return	Geometric mean	Arithmetic mean	Standard deviation
Australia	7.1	8.5	1.7	17.2	-30.2	49.4	6.9	7.0	4.2
Belgium	2.9	5.1	2.3	23.5	-38.1	120.6	2.8	3.0	5.4
Canada	4.6	5.9	1.7	16.7	-34.7	49.1	4.6	4.7	4.8
Denmark	1.8	3.4	1.9	19.4	-32.7	87.0	1.4	1.5	3.4
France	7.4	9.8	2.4	23.8	-33.4	78.7	7.5	7.7	7.4
Germany*	4.9	10.3	3.5	35.3	-87.2	165.3	8.1	8.3	8.2
Ireland	3.5	5.4	2.1	20.6	-51.1	73.6	3.2	3.3	4.4
Italy	7.0	11.0	3.2	32.5	-48.6	150.3	6.8	7.2	10.0
Japan	6.7	9.9	2.8	27.9	-48.3	108.6	7.1	7.4	8.7
The Netherlands	5.1	7.1	2.2	22.2	-31.3	126.7	4.7	4.9	6.4
South Africa	6.0	8.1	2.2	22.5	-33.9	106.2	6.6	6.7	5.0
Spain	3.2	5.3	2.1	21.5	-38.6	98.1	2.7	2.9	6.1
Sweden	5.5	7.7	2.2	21.9	-38.3	84.8	4.9	5.1	6.6
Switzerland†	4.3	6.1	2.0	19.4	-37.0	54.8	3.5	3.6	5.2
United Kingdom	4.8	6.5	2.0	19.9	-54.6	121.8	5.0	5.0	3.9
United States	5.8	7.7	2.0	19.6	-44.5	57.1	5.6	5.8	5.4
World	4.9	6.2	1.6	16.4	-39.8	70.9	5.0	5.1	4.7

* All statistics for Germany exclude 1922–23.   † Premia for Switzerland are from 1911.

Note that even with 101 years of data, the standard errors around the risk premia estimates are high, ranging from 1.6–1.7 percent (for the world index, Australia, and Canada) to 3.5 percent (for Germany). The standard error for both the United States and the United Kingdom is 2.0 percent. Strictly, these standard errors relate to the arithmetic mean, but as an approximate guide, we can apply them to the geometric mean. This means that while the US figure of 5.8 percent remains our best estimate, we can be only 68 percent confident that the true geometric mean lies within one standard error of this, that is, within the range 5.8 ± 2 percent, or 3.8 to 7.8 percent. Note that the historical geometric mean risk premia of all but four of our sixteen countries fall within this range.

Political and economic conditions have varied over the last 101 years for every country. Some analysts prefer to emphasize recent data since it reflects the current environment. Others recommend using the longest possible data series since this is more likely to encapsulate unusual events that may have current or future relevance. Parallels have been drawn, for example, between the technology and communications revolution of the late twentieth century and the electricity and the automobile innovations of the early twentieth century; or between the nineteenth century railway bubble and the recent internet bubble; or between the 1990 invasion of Kuwait and ensuing Gulf War of 1991 and the September 11, 2001 attacks on the United States and the subsequent "War on Terrorism." All market analysts agree, however, that repetition of certain historical events is so implausible that the past must be interpreted with care. Extreme hyperinflation is widely regarded as something that will not again afflict major economies, and a world war would be of a different nature if it were to happen in the future.

For these, or perhaps for less dramatic reasons, many people wish to review risk premia over shorter intervals than 101 years. We have selected decades as our intermediate time frame, which although arbitrary, is nevertheless a common choice. The final three columns of Table 12-1 present annualized statistics on premia that have been calculated over ten-year intervals. With 101 years of data, there are ninety-two (overlapping) decades for which we can compute premia. Table 12-1 shows the geometric means, arithmetic means, and standard deviations of these ten-year premia. By definition, the arithmetic mean always exceeds the geometric mean, but the difference between them is small when the measurement interval is as long as a decade. Note that, as with measures based on annual data, the United States ranks sixth while the United Kingdom falls in the middle of the distribution of premia for the countries in our sample.

The last column of Table 12-1 shows that over a ten-year horizon, the dispersion of returns is reduced. This is because there is diversification over time: one poor year is not necessarily followed by another. This gives rise to annualized returns that have a tighter distribution (a smaller standard deviation) than the underlying single-year returns. In the United States, for example, the single-year risk premia have a standard deviation of 19.6 percent while the ten-year premia have an annualized standard deviation of 5.4 percent. Assuming that ten-year annualized risk premia are approximately normally distributed, then in about two decades out of three, the annualized ten-year premium lies within ±5.4 percent of the mean.

12.3 US risk premia relative to bonds

We can also estimate the equity risk premium relative to long-term bonds. As with bills, we take the risk premium relative to bonds as the geometric difference between the equity return and the bond return over the same period. Since by definition the risk premium is the difference between the equity return and the risk free return, we are implicitly assuming here that bonds can be regarded as a risk free asset. This is harder to justify than for bills since long-term government bonds are risk free only in the sense that they normally offer a fixed income, and the likelihood of default is very small. In all other respects, they are appreciably riskier than bills since bond prices are sensitive both to changes in real interest rates and to inflationary expectations. Since bonds are riskier than bills, we would expect the equity risk premium relative to bonds to be lower than the premium relative to bills.

Long-term bonds do have one advantage as a benchmark in that their yields reflect not only today's short-term interest rate but also future expected interest rates. Thus for valuing shares or projects with cash flows extending many years into the future, the promised return on long bonds will encapsulate the expected sequence of returns on short-dated bills over the remaining term of the bond. The corresponding disadvantage is that long-bond prices will also encapsulate a maturity risk premium, the magnitude of which is hard to measure.

With these considerations in mind, we therefore compute both one- and ten-year equity risk premia relative to bonds. In addition, we also compute the average premium relative to bonds over the full 101-year period.   The histogram in Figure 12-4 shows the distribution of

Figure 12-4: Histogram of US equity risk premium relative to bonds, 1900–2000

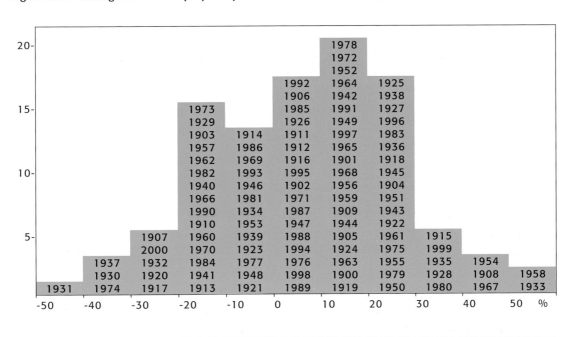

the one-year risk premia relative to bonds for the United States over the 101 years from 1900–2000. The average premium was 5.0 percent, which is below the figure of 5.8 percent relative to bills. The reason for this is that, as discussed in chapter 6, over this 101-year period the return on long-term US government bonds exceeded the return on treasury bills by 0.7 percent. Figure 12-4 shows that there is again a wide dispersion of year-by-year risk premia.

While the one-year equity risk premia in Figure 12-4 summarize historical returns over short periods, it is again helpful to look at longer-term premia. Figure 12-5 plots the rolling ten-year US risk premia relative to bonds over the 101 years from 1900–2000, contrasting this with the equivalent ten-year premia relative to bills. Obviously, over periods when bonds performed poorly, the equity premium relative to bonds has tended to exceed the premium relative to bills, and vice versa. This is especially noticeable over the second half of the twentieth century. During the higher inflation period in the United States from the mid-1950s through until the early 1980s, bond-based premia were consistently higher than bill-based premia. Subsequently, bonds have generally performed well, and from the mid-1980s the ten-year risk premium relative to bonds has been below that on bills.

Note that as with the risk premium relative to bills, there have been periods when the rolling ten-year US risk premium relative to bonds has been negative. Most recently, this occurred in 1990 and 1993. At first sight, this seems surprising since US equities have performed well in recent decades. But over the ten years until the end of 1990, although US equities returned a creditable 12.6 percent per year, US bonds gave an even higher annualized return of 13.7 percent.

Figure 12-5: Rolling ten-year US equity risk premia relative to bonds and to bills, 1909–2000

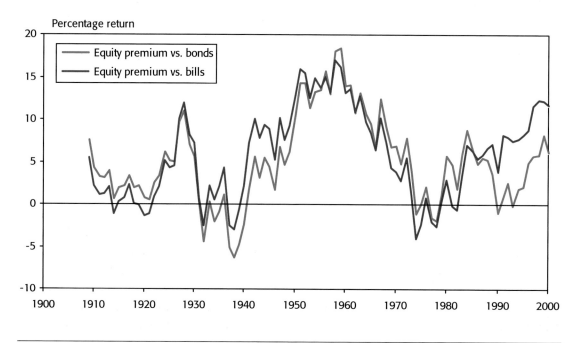

A similar situation has arisen recently in the United Kingdom. By 2000, the rolling ten-year UK risk premium relative to bonds had fallen to just under 2 percent. This led many UK market professionals to conclude that investors now required a risk premium of just 2 percent, and this was frequently used as a justification for the high stock prices at the turn of the millennium. While it may be true that required premia had become low (we address this issue in the next chapter), we cannot infer this from the recent ten-year historical premium relative to bonds. The main reason the ten-year premium is so low is that, over the decade ending in 2000, UK long bonds performed exceptionally well, almost certainly exceeding investors *ex ante* expectations. Over the same period in the United States, the historical ten-year risk premium relative to bonds was 6.1 percent per year, and yet US stocks were if anything more highly rated than their UK counterparts.

The problem that lies at the source of these confusions is that over many periods, even when we look at ten-year returns, the *ex post* returns on bonds appear to have differed markedly from *ex ante* expectations. One option would be to adjust bond returns for unexpected shocks in the bond market, such as unanticipated decreases or increases in inflation. Approximate adjustments might involve computing equity premia relative to each year's starting yield-to-redemption on bonds, or calculating premia relative to the income yield on bonds (excluding capital gains or losses). Although these computations become possible with the availability of our new data series, it can be misleading to compute premia after adjusting bond returns for shocks such as inflation increases or decreases, without also considering the impact of such shocks or other unexpected events on equity prices. The latter is far more challenging, as we will show in the next chapter.

Nevertheless, the experience of the 1980s and 1990s makes it obvious that we should not draw inferences about the expected future risk premium from periods as short as a decade. This is especially true when we have strong reasons to believe that during the decade in question, investors fared much better or worse than they had expected in advance. During the 1930s or mid-1970s, for example, it would have been extremely foolish to conclude that investors required a negative risk premium for investing in equities. These periods when the historical risk premia turned negative simply reflect the poor performance of equities over the previous decade. While less immediately obvious, interpreting the post-1980 era has been equally problematic, since this was a period that turned out to be particularly rewarding for both bond and equity investors.

12.4 Worldwide risk premia relative to bonds

Once again, it is important to set the US findings in their worldwide context. The bars and the line plot in Figure 12-6 show the geometric mean risk premia calculated both relative to bonds (the bars) and to bills (the line plot) over the full 101 years for all sixteen countries plus the world index. This chart shows that for all countries other than Germany, Denmark, and Belgium, the risk premium relative to bonds was lower than the premium relative to bills, consistent with our expectations, given that bonds are higher risk than bills. Figure 12-6 also

Figure 12-6: Worldwide annualized equity risk premia relative to bonds and bills, 1900–2000

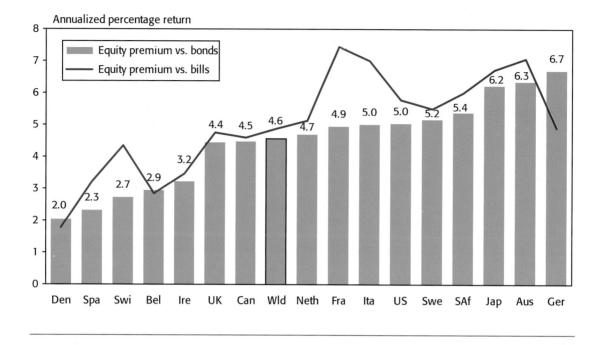

shows that for several countries, in contrast to, say, the United States and the United King-dom, the average risk premium estimated relative to bonds has differed markedly from the premium estimated relative to bills. These include Germany, where the premium relative to bonds is much higher, and France, Italy, and Switzerland, where the premium relative to bonds is much lower. Once again, as was the case with the risk premium relative to bills, the United States ranks in sixth place.

Two of the apparent "winners" in Figure 12-6 are Germany and Japan, which have the high-est and third highest premium relative to bonds. France, on the other hand, has the highest premium relative to bills. But earlier, we saw that Sweden (see Figure 4-7) enjoyed the highest real equity return and the highest return in real dollar terms (see Figure 7-8). These at first sight conflicting accounts of which equity market performed best can be better understood when we recognize that Germany and Japan's high premia relative to bonds arise from their low bond returns rather than high equity returns. Similarly, France's high premium relative to bills largely reflects its low bill returns. This also helps explain why the premium relative to bonds for our world index seems comparatively low at 4.6 percent. This is because several of the higher-ranking countries earned their positions from the relatively poor showing of their bond markets rather than the strength of their equity markets.

A fuller record documenting equity premia relative to bonds is contained in Table 12-2. Note that the unanticipated losses experienced during the century's worst inflation episodes afflicted bondholders more than shareholders. The premia shown in this table for those countries that suffered the worst bond returns are thus subject to caveats (see chapter 6).

Table 12-2: Worldwide equity risk premia relative to long bond returns, 1900–2000

| Country | Annual equity risk premium relative to long-term bonds | | | | | | Ten year risk premium | | |
	Geometric mean	Arithmetic mean	Standard error	Standard deviation	Minimum premium	Maximum premium	Geometric mean	Arithmetic mean	Standard deviation
Australia	6.3	8.0	1.9	18.9	-30.6	66.3	6.3	6.4	4.6
Belgium	2.9	4.8	2.1	20.7	-35.1	76.6	3.0	3.2	5.1
Canada	4.5	6.0	1.8	17.8	-36.8	54.7	4.6	4.7	5.4
Denmark	2.0	3.3	1.7	16.9	-35.9	74.9	1.8	1.9	4.1
France	4.9	7.0	2.1	21.6	-32.7	83.7	4.9	5.1	6.8
Germany [*]	6.7	9.9	2.9	28.4	-38.6	117.6	8.2	8.5	9.1
Ireland	3.2	4.6	1.7	17.4	-37.0	73.3	3.0	3.2	4.8
Italy	5.0	8.4	3.0	30.0	-39.6	152.2	5.0	5.4	9.2
Japan	6.2	10.3	3.3	33.2	-43.3	193.0	6.7	7.2	11.5
The Netherlands	4.7	6.7	2.1	21.4	-43.9	107.6	4.3	4.5	6.5
South Africa	5.4	7.1	2.0	19.7	-29.2	70.9	6.2	6.3	5.0
Spain	2.3	4.2	2.0	20.3	-34.0	69.1	2.2	2.3	5.5
Sweden	5.2	7.4	2.2	22.1	-38.3	87.8	4.8	5.0	7.7
Switzerland [†]	2.7	4.2	1.9	17.9	-34.4	52.2	2.0	2.1	5.1
United Kingdom	4.4	5.6	1.7	16.7	-38.0	80.8	4.8	4.9	4.5
United States	5.0	7.0	2.0	20.0	-40.8	57.7	4.9	5.0	5.2
World	4.6	5.6	1.4	14.5	-31.2	37.4	4.6	4.7	4.8

[*] All statistics for Germany exclude 1922–23.   [†] Premia for Switzerland are from 1911.

In this table, the first six columns give summary statistics for the annual premia, while the last three columns relate to rolling ten-year premia. The first column shows the geometric means that were plotted as bars in Figure 12-6. The fourth column shows the standard deviations. The 20.0 percent figure for the United States is close to the 19.6 percent standard deviation for the premia relative to bills shown earlier in Table 12-1. For some countries, however, the distribution of premia relative to bonds is narrower than relative to bills. For the United Kingdom, for example, the standard deviation is 16.7 percent, compared with 19.9 percent relative to bills. This is because, in the United Kingdom, there was a fairly high correlation between annual equity returns and long bond returns (0.56), while the correlation between equities and bills was lower (0.29). This propensity for good bond years to coincide with good equity years, and vice versa, has tended to lower the annual difference between equity and bond returns in the United Kingdom. This was particularly marked in the best and worst years on record for UK equities, namely, 1975 and 1974 respectively.

12.5 Summary

In this chapter, we have used 101 years of stock market history for sixteen different countries and for the world index to take a fresh look at the equity risk premium. In the past, the historical evidence for the US market, and to a lesser extent for the United Kingdom, has heavily influenced views about the magnitude of the risk premium. For the United States, the most widely cited source is Ibbotson Associates (2000), who estimate a geometric risk premium of

7.3 percent relative to bills for the period 1926–99. Before the publication of the research for this book, the most widely cited sources for the United Kingdom were Barclays Capital (1999) and CSFB (1999), which both started in 1919. Over the period 1919–98, there had been a UK risk premium relative to bills of 6.2 percent.

In recent years, both practitioners and researchers have grown increasingly uneasy about how to interpret these widely cited estimates, largely because they seemed too high. Apart from biases in index construction—a possibility that had not previously been thought important, but which we saw in section 3.2 is material in relation to the UK figure—the finger of suspicion has pointed mainly at success and survivorship bias among countries. The concern over success bias is that inferences about risk premia worldwide were being heavily influenced by the US experience, yet the United States has been an unusually successful economy. The closely related worry over survivorship bias is that previous attempts to place the experience of other countries like the United Kingdom alongside that of the United States may still have overstated the risk premium since they have focused on just a few selected markets that have survived, typically with continuous trading, over a long period.

To provide better estimates of the equity risk premium we therefore need to focus on the experience of all countries, not just the United States and the United Kingdom. If we look at all markets, then survivorship bias ceases to be an issue. Our sample of sixteen countries is by no means comprehensive. However, it does represent a large proportion by value of the world's stock markets in 1900. Fortunately, we are also able to compute total returns, including reinvested dividends, for this remarkably large sample of countries over a full 101-year period. This has allowed us to estimate long-run risk premia over an extended and uniform research period, thus overcoming another important but overlooked factor in previous studies, namely, easy data bias (see section 3.4). In other words, we mitigate the easy-data tendencies of previous researchers who measure a market's performance after a period of growth or recovery, omitting earlier periods of market turmoil.

We have found that from 1900–2000 the annualized equity risk premium relative to bills was 5.8 percent for the United States and 4.8 percent for the United Kingdom. Across all sixteen countries covered by this study, the cross-sectional (unweighted) average risk premium was 5.0 percent, while the risk premium on our size-weighted world equity index was 4.9 percent. Relative to long bonds, the story is similar. The annualized US equity risk premium relative to bonds was 5.0 percent, and the corresponding figure for the United Kingdom was 4.4 percent. Across all sixteen countries, the cross-sectional average risk premium relative to bonds was 4.5 percent, while for the world index it was 4.6 percent.

These figures are, of course, just long-run averages, and this chapter has also highlighted their high standard errors, the wide dispersion of annual equity risk premia, and how premia fluctuate over time as well as across markets. It has also reminded us that premia relative to bills and bonds must be interpreted with care, taking into account the unusual inflationary conditions earlier in the century and increases in the real interest rate more recently.

Nevertheless, two very important conclusions stand out. First, our evidence does not fully support Jorion and Goetzmann's (1999) claim that "the high equity premium obtained for US [and, by implication, UK] equities appears to be the exception rather than the rule." While the United States and the United Kingdom have indeed performed well, especially the United States, there is no indication that they are hugely out of line with other countries. The big differences in long-term stock market performances are between the best and worst countries. The United States and the United Kingdom have experienced somewhat similar long-run equity risk premia, both to each other and to the global average. While US equities have performed very well, and the US risk premium was above the global average, it ranked only sixth out of sixteen countries. The United Kingdom is near the middle of the distribution of worldwide equity premia. Concerns about success and survivorship bias, while legitimate, may therefore have been somewhat overstated. In this sense, investors may not have been materially misled by a focus on the United States and, to a lesser extent, UK experience.

The second important conclusion is that the risk premia estimated in this study and reported in this chapter are around 1½ percent lower than those that have been reported in previous studies of long-term US and UK stock market performance. The differences here arise from previous biases in index construction (for the United Kingdom) and (for both countries) from the use of a rather longer time frame, extending back to 1900.

Chapter 13 The prospective risk premium

In chapter 12, our focus was on the historical risk premium, namely, the premium that investors in different countries have obtained in the past from investing in equities, rather than in less risky assets such as treasury bills or government bonds. In this chapter, we switch from the past to the future, and to the prospective risk premium that investors can reasonably expect to obtain over future years and decades.

In the run-up to the millennial year, there was a series of books with titles like *Dow 36,000*, *Dow 40,000*, and even *Dow 100,000* (see, for example, Elias, 2000, and Kadlec, 1999). Glassman and Hassett (2000), in their book *Dow 36,000*, presented their case for why they believe equities are undervalued. Their view was that investors had come to require an extremely low rate of return on equity investments, and that this required return could get lower still. In short, they agreed that among investors, it was optimists who triumphed—investors in risky securities did well—but Glassman and Hassett believe that, historically, these investors should have done even better. Since stocks therefore remain underpriced in relation to what those authors consider the "perfectly reasonable price," there are further gains still to come. Accordingly, they regard it as likely that in the future optimists will continue to triumph.

Investors' views on the risk premium can be thought of as a tug-of-war. Glassman and Hassett are at one end of the rope. At the other end is Shiller (2000). Shiller's view is essentially that the equity investors triumphed beyond what might reasonably have been expected: they benefited from the stock market moving to irrationally high levels. Shiller and his colleagues are the pessimists.

If everyone were an optimist, the market would climb new peaks. If everyone were a pessimist, the market would collapse right away. The consensus represents an equilibrium between optimists and pessimists. In estimating the consensus of the market, we therefore have to balance the arguments that are put forward by each side in the tug-of-war. We need a view of what premium the market is offering for risks that may be experienced in the future.

The question of what equity premium we can expect has, for years, been a source of controversy (see Kocherlakota, 1996 and Siegel and Thaler, 1997). We therefore start in section 13.1 by reviewing why the risk premium plays such a crucial role in the theory and practice of investment and corporate finance, and why it is the most important contemporary issue in finance. Section 13.2 takes a more theoretical perspective, asking what the alternative points of view are, and how big the premium should be. In section 13.3 we explain that, when we are concerned with the future expected risk premium, our focus should be on the expected arithmetic risk premium. We illustrate in section 13.4 how to derive plausible estimates of the arithmetic risk premium from the historical record presented in earlier chapters.

In section 13.5, we assess the views of academic experts on the likely magnitude of the future arithmetic risk premium. We conclude that the experts have been heavily influenced by the hitherto accepted wisdom on the historical risk premium. Since our current study finds that risk premia appear to be lower than previously believed, we argue that experts might now wish to revise downward their long-term future risk premium forecasts.

We then look in section 13.6 at how using our historical analysis may more deeply inform us about likely future premia. We argue both that twentieth century equity returns almost certainly exceeded investors' *ex ante* risk premium requirements, and that the required risk premium itself fell over time. In section 13.7, by decomposing the historical risk premium into the contribution from unanticipated cash flow increases and the impact of a decline in required returns, we are able to infer the likely magnitude of the equity premium. In our concluding observations, in section 13.8, we summarize what we can learn from the historical record as an indicator of the future equity risk premium around the world.

13.1 Why the risk premium matters

Investors do not knowingly take on risk unless there is some expected recompense for their risk exposure. For taking on the risks of the equity market, this compensation takes the form of the equity risk premium. Why is it that the size of the equity premium has attracted so much attention? Perhaps the most straightforward answer is that the risk premium is fundamental to valuing financial assets, as will be clear with a simple example.

Consider the Gordon model, described in section 11.4. We will use this approach to value an investment such as buying the portfolio that comprises the Dow Index. Just before the World Trade Center tragedy, the Dow stood at a level of around 10,000 and its prospective dividend yield was 1.4 percent. So for a $10,000 investment we expected to receive dividends of $140. Since the dividend yield was much lower than the risk free interest rate, investors were presumably expecting Dow dividends to rise over time.

The Gordon model values this stream of dividends by assuming that dividends grow at a constant rate g and by discounting them at the expected rate of return r. This simplifies to the well-known constant-growth formula: *Value* is equal to *Dividend* divided by $r - g$. This formula makes a number of strong assumptions, such as that growth will continue indefinitely at the same unvarying rate. However, in the interests of pedagogy, we bypass these assumptions, and explore the implications of the Gordon model (Jagannathan, McGrattan and Scherbina (2001) present the multiperiod Gordon model).

Let us assume real dividends are expected to grow indefinitely at the annual rate of $g = 3$ percent, and that the real required rate of return is $r = 4.4$ percent. So $r - g$ is equal to 1.4 percent or 0.014. With these assumptions the valuation of the Dow is 140/0.014 = 10,000, about its level in early September 2001. But what if dividends had been expected to grow at a real rate of 4 percent per year, so that $r - g$ is equal to 0.004? That would give us Glassman and Hassett's valuation of the level for the Dow: $140/0.004 \approx 36,000$. Of course, this valuation of approximately 36,000 could equally well arise from a view that dividends were set to grow annually at 3 percent, while the required rate of return is not 4.4 but only 3.4 percent.

It is clear that given projected dividend growth, the correct value for the Dow depends on the return that investors expect from common stocks. The relationship is shown in Figure 13-1 which shows how the discount rate, which is the return expected by investors, influences the valuation given by the Gordon model. With dividends growing in real terms at 3 percent, valuations vary from infinity (if the expected return, like the dividend growth rate, is also 3 percent in real terms), through 36,000 (when the expected return is close to 3.4 percent) and 10,000 (if the expected return is 4.4 percent), to just 1,000 (if the expected return is 17 percent in real terms) or less. Values depend on the discount rate.

Using these admittedly crude figures, a tiny move of just half a percent in the return currently demanded by investors can shift the Dow a huge amount. A decline in the required return from 4.4 to 3.9 percent would have thrust the Dow upward by 55 percent. An increase in the required return from 4.4 to 4.9 percent would have been expected to precipitate a 26 percent collapse in the Dow, which is larger than the 14 percent fall in the ten days following the World Trade Center attack. The higher the valuation, the more volatile will be the index. So curiously, while low required rates of return drive up valuations, they also increase volatility. Investors are likely to demand a higher reward when the market is especially volatile. This provides a natural floor to required rates of return.

What required rate of return is appropriate? For providing an indication of the value of a stream of future cash flows, virtually no security is safer than a bond issued by the US Treasury. At the time of writing, the US government has to pay around 3 percent in real terms when it issues inflation-protected government bonds. The real redemption yield had been

Figure 13-1: Gordon model valuation of the Dow

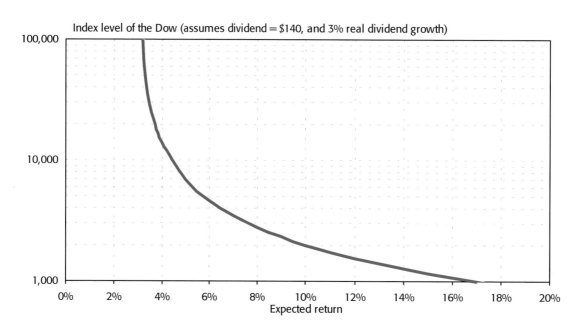

well over 4 percent as recently as late 2000. To the risk free interest rate we may add some additional reward that is expected by investors as compensation for equity market risk. Clearly, the risk premium is the major determinant of asset values. If it is close to zero, the Glassman-Hassett optimists are correct; and if it is large, the Shiller pessimists are correct. This is why most finance professionals and financial economists regard the equity risk premium as the single most important number in finance.

To measure the equity market premium and to establish the reward for risk, we need to look at the markets where equity risk is traded, not only the United States but also other major global stock markets. That was the focus of chapter 12. An unbiased estimate of the *ex ante* risk premium required by investors tells us what equity market returns we can expect in the future relative to bills or bonds. A small risk premium automatically implies higher valuations but lower returns expected in the future from equities; a large risk premium automatically implies lower valuations but higher future returns from equities. If this were not the case, then, as we explained at the start of this chapter, the highly competitive conditions prevailing in the world's leading stock markets would ensure that share prices rapidly rise or fall until promised returns are aligned with required returns.

13.2 How big should the risk premium be?

We have explained the central role that the equity premium plays in determining stock prices. Other things being equal, the higher the required risk premium, the lower the value placed on a stream of cash flows. So when the required risk premium goes up, the realized, or *ex post*, risk premium is reduced over the transition period. Conversely, when the required premium goes down, the historical, *ex post* risk premium will be larger over the transition period. Once transition is complete, of course, equity returns will have an expected return that reflects the new required risk premium. Since transition from a high to a lower required risk premium may occupy many years, the historical, *ex post* premium may overstate consensus expectations. It is therefore important not to extrapolate unadjusted, historical equity premia into the future. Rather, one should use history as a means of informing the quest for a sensible estimate of the *ex ante*, forward looking premium.

We might wish to start with a direct estimate of the prospective risk premium. Unfortunately, we cannot *measure* the prospective risk premium since it relates to the unknown future. The prospective premium is the reward investors require for taking on risk. We could in principle simply ask investors. Indeed, we refer below to the results of investor surveys, but mostly they provide a source of amusement rather than useful information. Private investors' opinions appear to reflect what has happened in the recent past, or even sheer fantasy. Professional money managers seem (at best) to provide answers that reproduce, with some noise, the evidence from long-run historical studies. That approach is unlikely to inform us about the market's expectations.

An alternative approach involves analyzing the earnings, dividend, or cash flow projections of security analysts. The premium is inferred from the discount rate that equates these future cash flows to ruling security prices. This approach, which we discuss in section 13.6, is also fraught with difficulty since there is no evidence that analysts' forecasts are unbiased predictors of the future.

In practice, therefore, we typically measure the historical risk premium, and use this as our starting point for inferences about the future. But to guide us, it is helpful to think about plausible magnitudes for the risk premium. This involves a brief detour into theory.

The starting point is, of course, the capital asset pricing model (CAPM), first formulated by Sharpe (1964). The CAPM was for most of the last three decades the method of choice among finance experts for estimating expected returns. The CAPM asserts that the expected return on a risky asset is the risk free rate of interest plus a risk premium. The latter is equal to the equity market risk premium, scaled up or down by the asset's beta. Beta measures the risk of the asset relative to the market portfolio, and beta estimates are widely available in most stock markets. The average beta for all stocks in a market is, by definition, equal to one. So the equity market risk premium is fundamental in determining CAPM expected returns.

The CAPM links the equity market risk premium to the risk tolerance of investors. The historical reward to equity market investment has, in the United States, looked large. But has it been excessive? The CAPM emphasizes how stock market investments contribute to the level of and uncertainty about an investor's wealth. To say whether the premium has been excessive, we need to look beyond fluctuations in an investor's wealth. What value is wealth unless it is consumed: spent on oneself, spent on others, or given as a bequest? Uncertainty about levels of future wealth leads to uncertainty about levels of future consumption. One variant of the CAPM—Breeden's (1979) consumption CAPM—emphasizes consumption by linking uncertainty about stock returns directly to uncertainty about future consumption.

If equities were to perform well at the same time as consumption peaks, then equities would be a poor hedge against the possibility of low consumption. If equities were to perform well when consumption dips, then equities would be a good hedge against cutbacks in consumption. The equity premium should be large if equities are a poor diversification tool. In other words, the equity premium should be larger when there is a high correlation between stock market returns and consumption.

The equity premium should also be larger when consumers are willing to pay more for insurance against the prospect of reduced consumption. That is, the equity premium should vary positively with the risk aversion of households as well as with the correlation of equity returns and consumption. In reality, however, aggregate consumption changes gradually over time, is not very volatile, and is not obviously correlated with stock market performance. There is a puzzle as to whether the large, historical US equity premium can conceivably be consistent with a focus by households on their potential future consumption. The "equity premium puzzle," first formulated by Mehra and Prescott (1985), thus remains a source of controversy. As Kocherlakota (1996) and Shleifer (2000) point out, traditional finance theory suggests that the equity premium should be much smaller than the (US) historical average.

As one might expect, there are competing theories that suggest differing magnitudes for the risk premium (see Cornell (1999) for a review). Though some writers may give another impression, there is no single figure for the risk premium that theory says is "correct." Stewart (1991) writes: "Is there any fundamental reason why [the] market risk premium should be 6 percent? Not that I can figure. The question is a little like asking why did God make pi the number 3.14159... Don't ask. Just memorize it." If you are not convinced that theory provides a unique constant for you to commit to memory, then you too will wish to read the entrails of capital market history. In the following section, we therefore revert to deeper examination of the historical evidence.

13.3 Measuring the premium

We define the risk premium relative to either bills or bonds. For the sake of concreteness, this chapter emphasizes historical and prospective equity risk premia calculated relative to bills. We select bills because they are the more commonly used basis for defining the equity premium—reflecting the fact that only treasury bills can really be considered close to risk free. Nearly all of our discussion, however, applies equally well to premia relative to bonds. Where it is helpful, we supplement our analysis with premia estimated relative to bonds.

The risk premia reported in chapter 12 were computed as geometric means. This has intuitive appeal from an investment perspective. It corresponds to the annualized performance figures you see every day for mutual funds, for indexes, and for pension plans. When past performance is being considered, the geometric mean summarizes the annualized rate of return over a historical period. Computing the geometric mean requires us to calculate the product of *1 + First return* multiplied by *1 + Second return* and so on up to the nth *return*. We then compute the nth root of this product and deduct *1*. The resulting geometric mean measures the annualized rate of return that equates the initial investment to the final value of a portfolio. The geometric mean risk premium has a similar interpretation. It is the incremental reward from investing in equities in preference to government securities.

We can simplify calculation of the geometric mean return over n years. In practice, all we require is two numbers, the final and the initial values of the portfolio. The geometric mean involves calculating the nth root of *Final value* divided by *Initial value*, and then deducting the value *1*. Think of a portfolio that appreciates over a period, such as 101 years, from $1,000 to (say) $10,000. It will have precisely the same annualized return regardless of whether the intermediate prices are stable or wildly volatile. By construction, the annualized return is the same over every one of the n years for which it has been calculated. We cannot meaningfully talk of the volatility of the geometric mean return. Volatility is a characteristic of the intermediate, year-by-year returns within our 101-year interval.

The year-by-year returns clearly experience considerable variability over time. We can capture this by estimating the average around which returns fluctuate, and the range of these fluctuations, that is, the arithmetic mean and the standard deviation of the annual returns. The arithmetic mean over n periods is the sum of all n returns, divided by n. The arithmetic

The historical arithmetic means in Figure 13-2 are thus clearly influenced by past levels of stock market volatility (among other factors). However, as demonstrated in chapter 8, estimates of the long-term historical standard deviation are not necessarily the best predictors of future volatility. We observed in chapter 12 that repetition of certain historical events is so unlikely that the past must be used with care as a guide to the future. There will be new uncertainties, but we know not what they will be. We therefore need estimates of expected future arithmetic risk premia, conditional on current predictions for market volatility.

It is not clear how investors should ideally adjust historical estimates of the equity risk premium to reflect today's judgments about stock market volatility. The approach we follow is to recalculate the arithmetic means, assuming current projections of early twenty-first century levels of volatility. To do this, we use the result that with lognormally distributed returns, the geometric and arithmetic means are linked by the standard deviation of returns, as described in section 13.3. We bypass some statistical assumptions that underpin our calculations, and which are discussed in Cooper (1996) and Dimson and Marsh (2001). We therefore recalculate the arithmetic mean premium for each country, replacing the historical difference between the arithmetic and geometric means with a difference based on risk estimates that are more contemporary.

For our estimates of arithmetic premia, we illustrate the approach using the same volatility for all national markets. That cannot be correct since markets inevitably expose investors to differing levels of risk. Nevertheless, for simplicity we assume a current volatility level for all sixteen national markets of 16 percent, and for the world index of 14 percent. It follows that our prediction of the difference between the arithmetic and geometric means is $\frac{1}{2} \times$ variance $= \frac{1}{2} \times 0.16^2 = .0128 = 1.28$ percent for each country and $\frac{1}{2} \times 0.14^2 \approx 1$ percent for the world index. At this stage, we adjust the historical record only for volatility changes relative to the past.

Clearly, the volatility of one stock market is not in reality the same as another. Different stock markets have had differing risk levels in the past, and projections for the future should not be uniform. Chapters 4 and 8 show that national stock market risks differ in ways that relate to fundamental attributes, as well as to the impact of political and military history. Some countries are natural resource-based; others are more driven by technology. Some are more highly leveraged; others, less so. Some are concentrated in a narrow range of business activities; others are large, diversified markets which naturally tend to have a lower variability for the risk premium. It is impossible for us to make country-by-country risk predictions that will appear reasonable for the lifetime of this book. We therefore stress that assuming the same projected volatility for all premia is an expositional device, no more.

Given our predicted standard deviation for each country's risk premium, what, then, are our estimates of the arithmetic mean premia? These premia, measured relative to treasury bills, are represented graphically by the line-plot in Figure 13-2. The US equity risk premium is estimated at 7.1 percent, and that for the United Kingdom is 6.0 percent. Arithmetic mean premia range from 3.1 percent (Denmark) to 8.7 percent (France); the worldwide arithmetic mean premium, relative to bills, is 6.2 percent.

The estimates of the adjusted arithmetic mean equity risk premia, relative to government bonds, are not displayed graphically. They are mostly somewhat lower. The US equity premium relative to bonds is estimated at 6.3 percent, and that for the United Kingdom is 5.7 percent; the range runs from 3.3 percent (Denmark) to 7.6 percent (Australia) or higher (Germany). The adjusted worldwide arithmetic mean premium, relative to bonds, is 5.6 percent.

To obtain an estimate of expected equity market returns, we require a forecast of the future arithmetic risk premium. For those who seek to extrapolate from the long-run series of historical premia, the numbers illustrated by the line plot in Figure 13-2 are the ones to use. For our world index, the adjusted arithmetic mean risk premium is 5.9 percent. Hence, the expected return is the risk free rate of interest, plus a premium of 5.9 percent. However, we can do better than simply extrapolate from the twentieth century to the twenty-first. By better understanding the sources of historical performance, we can extract more about investors' consensus expectations. This is the focus of the remainder of this chapter.

13.5 The changing consensus

The key question is whether the worldwide historical risk premium of approximately 6 percent should be our best estimate of the future risk premium. Many leading textbooks advocate the use of the arithmetic mean of historical equity premia, including Brealey and Myers (2000) and Bodie, Kane and Marcus (1999). Until recently, it was widely believed that the best predictor of the equity risk premium was its own past average. Certainly, researchers such as Goyal and Welch (1999) are unable to find variables that robustly predict the equity premium better than simply assuming that the premium will be "like it has been."

Welch (2000) casts light on whether academic finance professionals do, in fact, extrapolate from the historical record into the future. Welch studies the opinions of 226 financial economists who were asked to forecast the arithmetic equity risk premium in the United States. His findings are summarized in Figure 13-3, which shows that the mean forecast of the arithmetic thirty-year equity premium was 7.1 percent. The median was 7.0 percent, and the range ran from 1 to 15 percent. He also finds that the consensus view on a pessimistic outcome (with a 5 percent probability of occurrence) would be an equity premium of 2–3 percent; the consensus regarding an optimistic outcome is for a 12–13 percent premium.

The bars in Figure 13-3 represent the distribution from the Welch survey, while the curved line represents the normal distribution based on the historical mean and the standard error for the US equity risk premium using the full 101 years for which we have data (see chapter 12). An important aspect to grasp is of the inherent spread in both distributions. The uncertainty across financial experts about the risk premium is as large as the uncertainty that arises from statistical analysis of historical returns.

Figure 13-3: Financial economists' risk premium forecasts compared with US capital market history

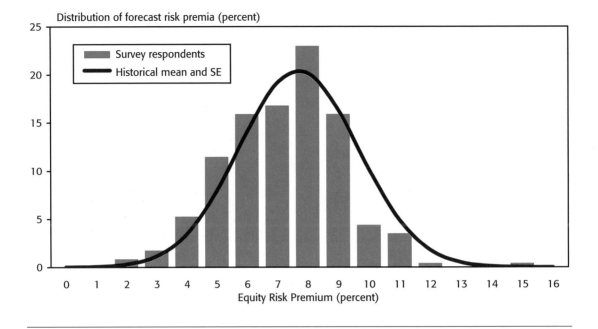

Most respondents to the Welch survey would have regarded the Ibbotson Associates' *Stocks, Bonds, Bills, and Inflation Yearbook* as the definitive study of the historical US risk premium. The first bar of Figure 13-4 shows that, at the time, the most recent long-run arithmetic risk premium computed from Ibbotson data from 1926–98 was 8.8 percent per year. The second bar shows that the key finance textbooks were on average suggesting a premium of 8.5 percent, a little below the Ibbotson figure. The textbook authors may have based their views on earlier, slightly lower, Ibbotson estimates, or else they were shading the Ibbotson estimates downward. The Welch survey mean is in turn lower than the textbook figure, but since respondents claimed to lower their forecasts when the equity market rises, this difference is probably explained by the market's strong performance in the 1990s. Interestingly, the third and fourth bars of the chart show that the survey respondents also perceived the profession's consensus to be higher than it really was. That is, they thought the mean was 0.5 to 1 percent higher than the average revealed in the Welch survey.

These survey and textbook figures represent what is being taught in the world's leading business schools and economics departments. As such, they are also widely used by finance professionals and corporate executives. Similarly, they are cited by regulators and in rate-of-return regulation disputes. Their influence extends from the classroom, to the boardroom, to the dealing room, to the courtroom.

Whether the Welch survey mean of 7.1 percent is appropriate is quite another matter. A large number of the survey respondents were clearly calibrating their forecasts relative to the longest-run historical benchmark available from Ibbotson, and then shading the historical number down based on subjective factors, including their judgment of the impact of recent

Figure 13-4: Alternative estimates of the arithmetic mean risk premium, relative to bills

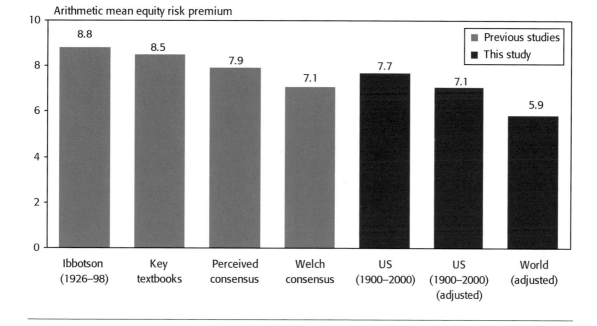

strong market performance in the late 1990s. The Ibbotson Associates risk premium estimates are based on data from the Center for Research in Securities Prices (CRSP) data that
starts in 1926. In the spirit of using the longest possible series of historical data, the fifth bar
in Figure 13-4 shows that the arithmetic mean risk premium over the period 1900–2000, as
estimated in this current study, is 7.7 percent.

The inclusion of twenty-six years of extra data from the start of the twentieth century (plus
adding in 1999 and 2000) lowers the estimated premium by 1.1 percent. To the extent that
their forecasts were anchored in long-run historical data, the Welch survey respondents
might now wish to make a corresponding further downward revision in their forecasts of the
equity risk premium. Welch (2001) is now updating his survey. If his new respondents were
to make a full 1.1 percent reduction in their mean, the revised arithmetic mean would fall to
6.0 percent.

Of course, the 101-year mean of 7.7 percent shown in the fifth bar in our chart is the unadjusted historical mean. We argued above that we are likely to obtain more plausible estimates of the future arithmetic mean risk premium if we adjust the historical estimates
downward to reflect today's current levels of equity market volatility. The sixth and seventh
bars of Figure 13-4 portray the results of making such an adjustment for the United States
and the world index. The adjusted US figure is 7.1 percent, while the world index provided a
risk premium of 5.9 percent. To the extent that the Welch survey respondents were not
already making an adjustment of this kind, this suggests that, in responding to the Welch
(2001) survey, they should further lower their forecasts of the risk premium. This assumes, of
course, that they still wish to use historical means as the anchor for their future forecasts.

13.6　History as a guide to the future

Financial economists may be reluctant to diverge markedly from the historical mean. Decision-makers, on the other hand, need to go beyond using only the past record, and to identify the market's implicit expectation for future performance. This is by no means easy. Recently, a number of researchers have sought to infer expected risk premia from surveys of the financial community, including Claus and Thomas (2001), Fraser (2001), Graham and Harvey (2001a), and Harris and Marston (2001). Unfortunately, such surveys are difficult to interpret. Graham and Harvey find that financial executives underestimate stock market risk substantially, while Brav and Lehavy (2001) and earlier researchers find that investment professionals are over-optimistic about the likely course of stock prices. Despite their wide dispersion, the responses to Welch's (2000) survey are about as usable as any.

The wide dispersion of views reinforces the case for basing estimates on the historical record. However, since history may have been kind to (or harsh on) stock market investors, there are coherent arguments for going beyond raw historical estimates. First, the whole idea of using the achieved risk premium to forecast the required risk premium depends on having a long enough period to iron out good and bad luck. Yet as we noted in section 13.3, even with 101 years of data, standard errors remain high and our estimates of the average are imprecise.

Second, the expected equity risk premium could change over time. This might be because the underlying risk of equity investment has fluctuated, particularly as the variety of exchange-listed sectors has broadened out over the last century (see chapter 2). The corporate sector as a whole may have become more or less risky. The risks faced by investors have been transformed through reduced dealing costs and the advent of pooled investment vehicles. Enhanced diversification opportunities became available, both domestically and internationally. And as many households became wealthier, there may have been systematic changes in investors' levels of risk aversion.

Third, we must take account of the fact that stock market outcomes are influenced by many factors. Some that were important in the past (removal of barriers to international investment, for example) may be non-repeatable. If so, projections of the future risk premium should deviate from the past. The financial history of our sixteen stock markets has been so variable over time that it is worth exploring this argument further.

A comparison between the first and second halves of our 101-year period makes the point. Over the first half of the twentieth century, the arithmetic average US equity risk premium relative to bills was 6.7 percent, whereas over the period 1950–2000, it was 8.6 percent. As is clear from Figure 13-5, this pattern is common to most of the sixteen countries covered in this book, with Australia, Italy, Belgium, and South Africa being the exceptions. The cross-sectional mean for all countries in the first half of the twentieth century was an arithmetic average risk premium of 6.0 percent, versus 8.6 percent for the sixteen-country mean in the next fifty-one years. The corresponding averages for the equity premium relative to bonds are not shown here, but the pattern is similar: a pre-1950 mean of 5.5 percent as compared to 7.5 percent over the following fifty-one years.

Figure 13-5: The equity premium relative to bills: first half-century versus next fifty-one years

Annualized arithmetic risk premium relative to bills (%)

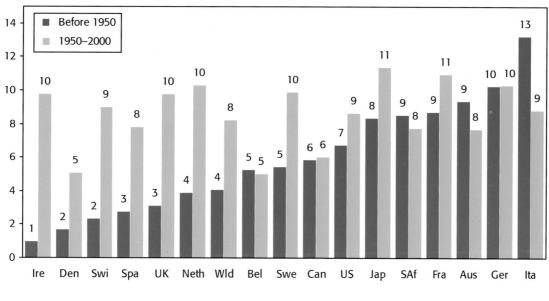

The large risk premia achieved during the second half of the twentieth century are attributable to two factors. First, there was unprecedented growth in productivity and efficiency, acceleration in the pace of technological change, and substantial enhancements to the quality of management and corporate governance. As Europe, North America, and the Asia-Pacific region emerged from the turmoil of the Second World War, expectations for improvement were limited to what could be imagined. Reality almost certainly exceeded investors' expectations. Corporate cash flows grew faster than investors anticipated, and this higher growth is now known to the market and built into higher stock prices.

Second, as noted by Bernstein (1997) and others, stock prices have doubtless also risen because of a fall in the required rate of return due to diminished investment risk. The economic and political lessons of the twentieth century have surely been learned, international trade and investment flows have increased, and the Cold War has ended, leading to a more secure business environment. A further factor that must surely have lowered required returns is that investors now have much more opportunity to diversify, both domestically and internationally, than they had a century ago. Diversification allows investors to lower their risk exposure without detriment to expected return. Transaction costs are also lower now than a century ago. Factors such as these, which led to a reduction in the required risk premium, have contributed further to the upward re-rating of stock prices.

To convert from a pure historical estimate of the risk premium into a forward-looking projection, we need to reverse-engineer the factors that drove up stock markets over the last 101 years. The simplest idea would be to use the Gordon Model (from section 13.1) to infer the impact on returns of the historical changes in dividend yield. But we can go beyond this, as

Figure 13-6: *Ex post* and *ex ante* equity risk premia

Risk premium versus bills

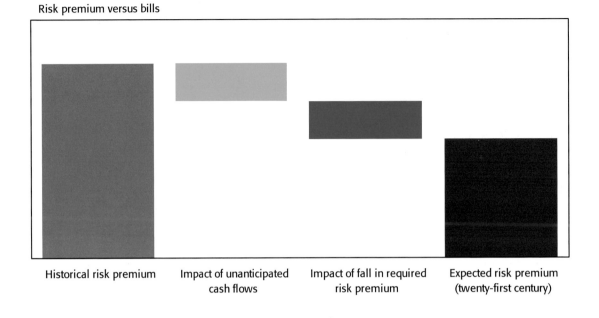

| Historical risk premium | Impact of unanticipated cash flows | Impact of fall in required risk premium | Expected risk premium (twenty-first century) |

illustrated conceptually in Figure 13-6. The left-hand bar in the chart portrays the historical risk premium on the equity market. This includes the contribution from unanticipated growth in cash flows and the gain from falls in the required risk premium. We therefore deduct the impact of these two factors. What remains in the right-hand bar of this chart is an estimate of the prospective risk premium demanded by investors as they look ahead to the remainder of the twenty-first century. The key qualitative point is that this is lower than the raw historical risk premium.

13.7 Expectations of the risk premium

To apply this framework, we need some notion of when cash flows (proxied here by equity dividends) have exceeded or fallen short of expectations. What dividends might investors expect each year? There are a variety of possible approaches (see, for example, Ibbotson and Chen, 2001). Perhaps the simplest approach is one that is commonly used today for forecasting the long-run dividend growth rate, namely, to extrapolate from previous long-term dividend growth. The long-term dividend growth rate is then used to project future real growth. That is, we estimate the product of *1+ Year 1 annual growth* multiplied by *1 + Year 2 annual growth* and so on to year *n*. We then compute the nth root of this product, which is equal to *1 + Projected growth*. To summarize, we calculate the annualized real dividend growth rate to each year-end, over periods that start in 1900. The cumulative real dividend growth rates are illustrated for the United States and United Kingdom in Figure 11-3, and for other countries are summarized in Figure 11-5.

We assume that at every December 31, investors compare the year's real dividend growth to the real growth rate that would have been projected as at January 1 of that year. The difference is defined as *1 + Annual dividend growth* divided by *1 + Projected growth,* minus *1.* This error in projecting dividend growth may be thought of as a naive measure of the unanticipated growth rate in dividends. The unanticipated changes in dividend growth are compounded together to produce an estimate of their annualized impact over the last century. This is clearly a rather unsophisticated measure of unanticipated real dividend growth, but it suffices to illustrate the general idea.

Defined this way, the impact in the United States of unanticipated dividend growth amounts to 0.2 percent per year over the period from 1900 to 2000. For the United Kingdom, the impact of unanticipated dividend growth is 1.7 percent per year. This large difference is explained in chapter 11 and reflects two factors. First, in the early decades of the last century, the United States generated more favorable growth expectations than did the United Kingdom; consequently, there was less scope in the United States for a favorable surprise. Second, over the last quarter-century in the United States, dividends became less important than in the United Kingdom as a result of growing rates of repurchases; this further reduced the scope for unanticipated dividend growth.

Since 1900, there has also been a dramatic change in the valuation basis for equity markets. The price/dividend ratio (the reciprocal of the dividend yield) is much higher now than it was in 1900. In the United Kingdom, for example, the price/dividend ratio at the start of 2001 was 42, as compared to 23 a century earlier. Undoubtedly, this change is in part a reflection of expected future growth in real dividends, so we could in principle decompose the impact of this valuation change into both an element that reflects changes in required rates of return, and an element that reflects enhanced growth expectations. To keep things simple, we assume that the increase in the price/dividend ratio is attributable solely to a long-term fall in the required risk premium for equity investment. Given this assumption, the fall in the required risk premium since 1900 is 1.4 and 0.6 percent per year for the United States and the United Kingdom, respectively. These amounts—which arise from the change in the price/dividend ratio—need to be deducted from the historical risk premium to obtain a measure of investors' *ex ante* expectations.

The remainder of the annualized risk premium represents the expected reward for equity investment. Even though we are deviating from some of its underlying assumptions, we can think of the risk premium in terms of the Gordon model for equity valuation. The Gordon model asserts that the expected equity return is equal to the prospective dividend yield plus the projected long-term dividend growth rate. We have already abstracted for the dividend yield, so for a given yield the Gordon model equates the expected return to the long-term dividend growth rate. It follows that the expected risk premium, measured relative to the riskless interest rate, is the projected dividend growth rate, also measured relative to the real interest rate. That is, *1 + Projected dividend growth* divided by *1 + Riskless rate of interest,* minus *1.* Linking together these premia for each year after 1900, the expected US and UK equity risk premia are respectively 4.1 and 2.4 percent per year.

More complex decompositions of the historical risk premium are possible; see, for example, Arnott and Bernstein (2001) and Ibbotson and Chen (2001). These analyses, however, all point in the same direction. So using our simplistic decomposition of the backward-looking risk premium, we can now show how the historical premium can be broken down into a series of elements. For the United States, United Kingdom and for our sixteen-country world index, the risk premium estimates are depicted in Figure 13-7.

The differences between the estimates for each index should not be taken too seriously, especially since US corporations pay such low levels of dividends that computations based on dividend growth must be interpreted with care (see section 11.2). We acknowledge that our dividend projections are simplistic, and the reader should not put too much weight on cross-country differences. The key point is that the expected equity risk premium, based on the last century, should be lower than our backward-looking, historical averages suggest.

Our estimates indicate a geometric mean premium for the United States of 4.1 percent, for the United Kingdom of around 2.4 percent, and for our sixteen-country world index of about 3.0 percent. This is similar to the Fama and French (2002) estimate for the United States using a related approach. Also based on dividend yields and dividend growth estimates, Fama and French use the Gordon model to compute the US equity premium from 1872–1999. They find a premium of 3.8 percent before 1949, and a premium of 3.4 percent for the subsequent period. They argue that the difference between these estimates and the larger *ex post* risk premium based on historical realized returns is attributable to a reduction, since 1949, in investors' required rate of return. Our analysis is consistent with their assertions.

Figure 13-7: *Ex post* and *ex ante* equity risk premia for selected indexes

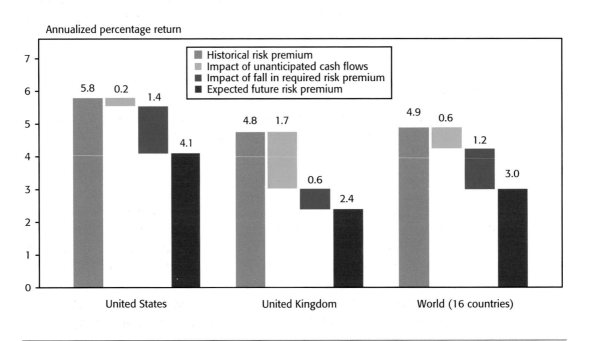

If they are to be used as a prospective risk premium, our annualized figures need to be converted into arithmetic means, as outlined in section 13.4. Using a projected standard deviation for US and UK equities of 16 percent, the prospective *arithmetic* risk premium is 5.4 percent for the United States and 3.7 percent for the United Kingdom. With a slightly lower standard deviation for the world index of 14 percent, the prospective *arithmetic* risk premium for the world index is 4.0 percent. In fact, whichever country one focuses on, our forward-looking predictions for the equity risk premium are lower than the historically based projections reviewed in section 13.4.

There is scope to finesse our estimates of the expected risk premium. Some of the opportunities to enhance our estimates are the following: First, as explained in chapters 18–33, for many countries we use index series that are spliced together, and this presents difficulties when estimating dividend growth rates. Second, we ignore changes in the tax treatment of dividend income, both cross-sectionally and over time. Third, we estimate annual dividends from annual index returns and capital appreciation, rather than using more frequent (say, monthly) data. Fourth, we use a simplified decomposition of equity risk premia that could easily be enriched. Fifth, and very importantly, we use a naive model of investors' dividend expectations, an issue that merits further research (some of which we present elsewhere; see Dimson and Marsh, 2001). We leave these enhancements as a task for future researchers.

Finally, note that the use of historical averages as indicators of current required returns suggests that France may have a higher equity risk premium, while Denmark's risk premium may be lower (see Figure 13-2). There are obviously differences in risk between markets, but this is unlikely to account for cross-sectional differences in historical premia. Indeed, much of the cross-country variation in historical equity premia is attributable to country-specific historical events that will not recur. When making future projections, there is a strong case, particularly given the increasingly international nature of capital markets, for taking a global rather than a country-by-country approach to determining the cost of capital.

13.8 Summary

The equity premium is the difference between the return on risky stocks and the return on safe bonds. The equity market premium is central to investment, financing, and saving decisions. It is often described as the most important number in finance. Yet it is not clear how big the equity premium is today, or how large it has been in the past.

Survey evidence on best practice by corporations and financial advisors, such as Bruner, Eades, Harris, and Higgins (1998), reveals that nearly all respondents estimate the equity risk premium by averaging past data. However, there is considerable variation in their choice of time period and in their method of averaging, whether arithmetic or geometric. Their judgments are usually underpinned by knowledge of one, or at most two, national exchanges: respondents invariably focus on their domestic and/or the US stock market. In this chapter we use evidence from the past to provide a guide to what might be expected in the future.

The chapter addresses four questions: Which historical equity risk premium should one use as the starting point? Why has it typically been so high? What is a good forward-looking predictor for the future? How can one use variables such as the dividend yield to improve forecasts of the risk premium?

We stress the central role in finance of the equity premium. The historical premium is often summarized in the form of an annualized rate of return. This is a geometric mean. It provides information on past performance. For the future, what is required is the arithmetic mean of the distribution of equity premia, which is larger than the geometric mean. For markets that have been particularly volatile, the arithmetic mean of past equity premia may exceed the geometric mean premium by several percentage points. We adjust the arithmetic mean for (i) the differences between the variability of the stock market over the last 101 years, and the variability that we might anticipate today, and (ii) the impact of unanticipated cash flows and of declines in the required risk premium. The result is a forward-looking, *geometric* mean risk premium for the United States, United Kingdom and world of around 2½ to 4 percent and an *arithmetic* mean risk premium for US, UK, and world equities that falls within a range from a little below 4 to a little above 5 percent.

These equity risk premia are lower than those cited in surveys of finance academics. They are also lower than frequently quoted historical averages, such as those from Ibbotson Associates, which cover a somewhat briefer interval. We show that the historical risk premium, even if it embraces countries that have been less successful than the United States, is supported by two factors. Over the second half of the last century, equity cash flows almost certainly exceeded expectations, and the required rate of return doubtless fell as investment risk declined and the scope for diversification increased. Stock markets rose, in both the United States and other countries, for reasons that are unlikely to be repeated. Even after the setbacks of 2001, the prospective risk premium is markedly lower than the historical risk premium.

Chapter 14 Implications for investors

Why are stocks thought to perform so much better, over the long run, than government securities? The explanation is that the equity premium has been large relative to stock market volatility. In *Valuing Wall Street*, Smithers and Wright (2000) define the stable value of the historic real return on common stocks as "Siegel's constant," or *s*. They explain: "We cannot know with certainty what the true value of *s* actually is, but we know that it cannot lie too far from our best estimate of 6¾ percent... Why *s* is, or appears to be, so stable is an important challenge." Siegel's constant is cited more frequently in Smithers and Wright's index than any other word, phrase, or author.

In his foreword to Siegel's (1998) book, *Stocks for the Long Run*, Peter Bernstein writes: "The most powerful part of Professor Siegel's argument is how effectively he demonstrates the consistency of results from equity ownership when measured over periods of 20 years or longer." After noting that even Germany and Japan bounced back after the Second World War, Bernstein continues: "Indeed, he would be on frail ground if that consistency were not so visible in the historical data and if it did not keep reappearing in so many different guises."

Siegel did not invent *s* and would be among the first to agree that its constancy is an empirical question. In this book we present evidence that spans many countries. We show that the equity premium is not constant across markets. More often than not, stock market volatility has been larger in other countries than in the United States. As a result, stock market performance around the world looks like less of a sure thing than historical performance in the US and UK markets. From our global perspective, and looking toward the future, equities are far from risk free even over the long term. This is not to do with a paradigm shift; rather, it reflects the fact that inferences from a single information source are fraught with difficulty. Our new international dataset provides an opportunity to test out the reliability of trading strategies that are predicated on the superiority of equities over fixed-interest investments.

In chapter 13 we interpreted financial market history to extract an indication of expected future risk premia. We now examine the risk of stock market investment, and draw on our analysis to provide a guide for the future. In sections 14.2 and 14.3, we estimate the range of returns that can be expected from investing in the main equity markets. In sections 14.4 and 14.5 we present some *do* and *don't* advice based on our research. Section 14.6 concludes.

14.1 Market risk in the twenty-first century

Predicting the future is difficult; it is easier if we assume the past will repeat itself. But we should be cautious about unthinking extrapolation into the future for at least two reasons: sampling error and survivorship. To understand the issues involved in extrapolating from the historical record, we start by looking at the US record from 1900 to the present day.

Figure 14-1 measures on the vertical axis the risk premia for US equities, annualized over intervals of all possible length from the last 101 years. We show the full range of premia that

Figure 14-1: Annualized US equity risk premium over periods of up to 101 years

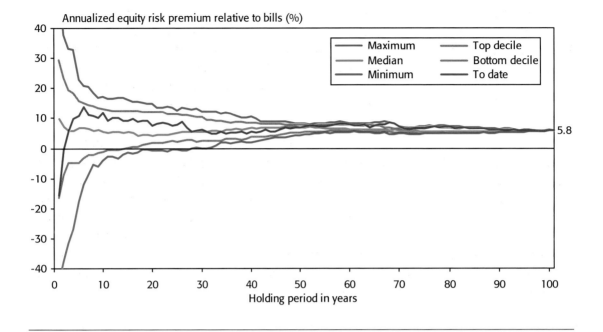

could be computed if data were used as at any year-end between 1900 and 2000. At the left-hand side of the chart, plotted against a value of one year on the horizontal axis, is the range of one-year equity risk premia. The chart embraces 101 estimates of the historical premium, where the latter is based on just a single year of returns. That is, we estimate premia over the years ending at December 31, 1900, 1901, 1902, and so on to 2000. We plot as blue curves the minimum (0th percentile) and maximum (100th percentile) of the distribution of the one-year estimated premia; as grey curves, the bottom decile (10th percentile) and top decile (90th percentile); and as a green curve, the median (50th percentile).

The horizontal axis of Figure 14-1 shows the number of years used to compute the equity premium. When two years are used, we are assuming investors estimate risk premia on a rolling biannual basis. There are 100 two-year investment periods, namely, 1900–01, 1901–02, and so on to 1999–2000. The range of estimated premia is narrower over two years than over one. It narrows further, as a successively larger number of years is used in the calculations. Eventually, at the right-hand side of Figure 14-1, the equity risk premium is the annualized figure over the entire period 1900–2000. This reports the investment experience of a (now rather elderly) investor who bought stocks at the end of 1899 and held them to the end of 2000.

To review, we summarize 5,151 equity premia in Figure 14-1. This comprises 101 annual premia, 100 biannual premia, 99 triannual premia, and so on to two 100-year premia (covering 1900–99 and 1901–2000) and one 101-year premium (covering 1900–2000).

Two features of Figure 14-1 support the opening comments of this chapter. First, over the long haul, annualized real US equity premia converge toward the long-run geometric mean of 5.8 percent. Given the 0.9 percent annualized real return on US treasury bills reported in chapter 5, this premium is consistent with Siegel's "constant" of $s = 6\frac{3}{4}$ percent. Second, for all investment holding periods of around twenty years or more, equity premia have been positive or within a fraction of a percentage point of zero. Allowing for the 0.9 percent real return on bills, Figure 14-1 confirms Siegel's (1998) observation of the superiority of stocks for the long run, where the "long run" is defined as twenty years or more.

To what extent should we rely on such patterns persisting into the future? As we said earlier, one of the critical factors that influences these results is sampling error. Sampling error arises because we observe only a limited number of historical outcomes. Looking to the future, there are an infinite number of possible stock market returns. If we are interested in a one-year investment horizon, we may use the past as a guide, and Figure 14-1 displays a summary of no less than 101 historical one-year premia. We can see the wide dispersion of possible annual premia, ranging from a worst ever premium on US equities of -45 percent to a best ever of +57 percent (note that these two extreme points run off the scale of the chart). The arithmetic mean is 7.7 percent, with a standard deviation of 19.6 percent.

But what if we are interested in the likely performance of US stocks over a century? Our historical record provides only two observations: over the period 1900–99 the annualized premium was 6.0 percent, while over 1901–2000 it was 5.7 percent. As a guide to the future, there might be many other historical one-century records, but our database is too brief to reveal them. More seriously, the number of *independent* observations of the long-term return is limited. There is really only one independent measure, not two, of the century-long risk premium, since our two estimates of the annualized premium share the same data from end-1900 to end-1999. This is why our two century-long premia are similar. Other investors may, of course, be focusing on a shorter period, such as twenty years. But of the eighty-two twenty-year intervals ending between 1919 and 2000, there are only five independent observations. Our sample is too small; the potential error from extrapolating from just five (non-overlapping) twenty-year periods is too large. The narrow range of twenty-year returns in Figure 14-1 is therefore likely to understate the dispersion that might, in the future, occur.

The other critical factor that underpins estimates of long-run risk premia is survivorship and success bias. Many commentators, ourselves included, interpret long-term historical returns to provide a guide to the future. The green median line in Figure 14-1 ends up, at the right-hand side of the graph, at an equity premium (relative to bills) of 5.8 percent per year. This 5.8 percent outcome reflects both what investors might reasonably have expected, plus the impact of chance on US markets. In addition to chance, however, markets are subject to change. Today's stock market is quite different from that of a century ago.

In Figure 12-1 we showed the equity risk premium that would have been computed if, at any time in the last ninety-one years, we had inferred the premium from what was, at those dates, the most recent decade. As confirmed in Figure 14-1, there is a range of historical one-decade premia (relative to bills) that varies between -4 and +17 percent per year. This large gap between high and low decade-long premia was quantified in Tables 12-1 and 12-2. The variation in premia estimated over such brief periods is one reason why analysts tend to use a longer interval for historical estimation. Consultancy firms typically base cost of capital recommendations on the *ex post* premium, choosing between estimates measured from alternative start-dates to the most recent period. Stern Stewart, for example, presents the risk premium over the last 75, 74,…, 2, and 1 years, and expresses a preference for a premium based on data for "the second part of the past century" (Pettit, Gulie, and Park, 2001).

The red line plot in Figure 14-1 provides the history for the annualized equity premium, as at end-2000, computed from previous data covering periods of various durations. The left-most point is the most recent annual equity premium for the year 2000; the next point represents the annualized premium over 1999–2000; and so on to the right-most point, which portrays the long-term geometric mean equity premium over the entire period 1900–2000. It is clear that the premium estimated using recent data is above the median for our historical record. In fact, the premia estimated over periods to end-2000 of 10, 20, 30,…, 90 years are in all cases but one above the median. Despite poor performance in the year 2000, previous stock market returns were so good that most back-calculated premia are flattering to equity markets. The fact that the backward-looking premium converges on the 101-year mean is no consolation, since that is inevitable: there is, after all, only one 101-year history.

The United States is not the only market we can examine. Other markets have provided favorable conditions for long-term equity portfolios. Figure 14-2 presents an analysis for the

Figure 14-2: Annualized UK equity risk premium over periods of up to 101 years

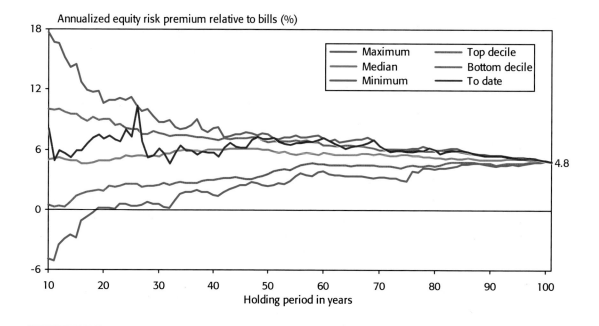

United Kingdom similar to that presented above for the United States, except that we omit data for holding periods of under 10 years. Viewed in retrospect, UK stocks also provided a non-negative premium if held for at least twenty years. Additionally, note the position of the red line, which plots the annualized equity premium for various periods concluding at the end of the year 2000. Most premium-to-date figures are above the median portrayed in Figure 14-2. In other words, the long-term equity premium has again been enhanced by the inclusion of data for relatively recent periods. This favorable long-term mean, coupled with a lower than average volatility, ensures that the annualized premium is positive over periods in excess of twenty years.

It appears that the United States and the United Kingdom have provided a significant reward for equity risk, at least in the sense of Bernstein's favorable remarks about consistency of performance over periods of twenty years or longer. But look again at Figure 14-1 and Figure 14-2. The United States and the United Kingdom have wide dispersions for the twenty-year equity premium around the median. It is clear that if the expected premium were lower, then the outcome could, during a future period, end up on the wrong side of zero. Moreover, if volatility were to be higher, the chance of disappointing performance would be larger still. It is therefore particularly important to look at the entire pool of multi-year equity premia that can be considered. Predictions for the future should take into account the complete range of possible stock market outcomes. To do this, we look at analogous results for other markets.

14.2 Inferences from other markets

Cast your mind back to the very beginning of 1990, before the Japanese bubble burst. Those were the days when, as reported in Ziemba and Schwartz (1991), the grounds of Tokyo's Imperial Palace were worth more than the whole of California, the land value of Japan reached four times the land value of the whole of the United States, and the Japanese telecommunications company NTT was worth more than the entire German stock market. Those were the days when there was near-universal conviction that Japan had reached a permanent plateau of continuing economic success. It was difficult then to visualize the prospect of persistent underperformance. Within a few years, the Japanese equity market was to cease being the largest in the world, declining, as we report in chapter 2, to around one-quarter of the start-2000 value of the US market.

We cannot foretell the future. Until 2000, it seemed bright for the United States, and good for most other countries too. However, just as Japan's rapid collapse came as a surprise to investors, so too might the US or another market be decimated by a downturn in economic and business conditions that persists for a long period. Projections of the risk premium should reflect the experience not of one but of many countries.

To focus on the international dimension, we have looked at the experiences of all sixteen of our countries. Figure 14-3 is a representative case: The Netherlands. This chart follows the same structure as the previous one, and shows the quantiles of the distribution of the Dutch

Figure 14-3: Annualized Dutch equity risk premium over periods of up to 101 years

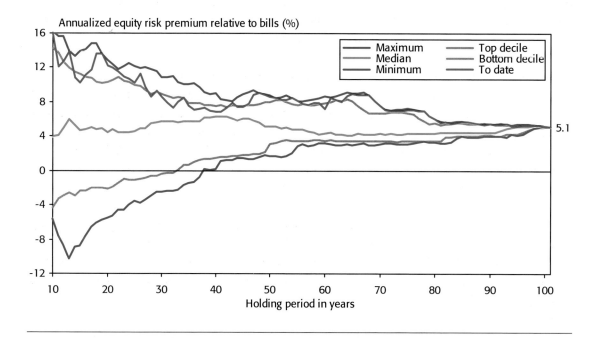

equity premium. As before, the colored lines represent the extremes, the top and bottom deciles, and the median. Note, however, the contrast with the US and UK illustrations discussed in the previous section. While the mean equity premium is not dissimilar from the previous examples, the dispersion of premia is much greater. Furthermore, the red line shows that the premia from earlier dates to end-2000 were all above the median; typically, they are close to top-decile performance. This means that most historical periods did not have the benefit of recent good stock market performance, and hence most of the premia shown in Figure 14-3 are inferior to the premium-to-date figures plotted in red in the chart.

Compare Figure 14-3 with the corresponding charts for the United States and the United Kingdom shown earlier in Figures 14-1 and 14-2. Recall that in the United States and the United Kingdom, every period with a duration of twenty or more years had a risk premium that was within a percentage point of being positive (see the lowest line plots in blue within Figures 14-1 and 14-2). When we look at The Netherlands, the picture is less rosy. Over a twenty-year interval, between one-tenth and one-half of all premia are below zero. Only when we look back at intervals of forty years or longer can we say that the risk premium has always been positive.

While forty years is a very long time, several countries have even longer periods until their historical premium is consistently above zero. We should add that although page constraints preclude going through the details, we have also looked at real (inflation adjusted) returns and at premia relative to bonds rather than bills. The findings are similar, save that the ranking of countries changes (a market with a large premium may nevertheless have a low real return; see chapters 4 and 12). We conclude that stocks may indeed have been attractive investments over the long run. But short-term underperformance can be more severe than has been experienced within the United States. Furthermore, the duration of underperformance may, on past evidence, persist for several decades.

What does this imply for the future? Most individual investors and investment institutions hold a disproportionate part of their funds in a less-than-fully-diversified portfolio of domestic securities. Poor diversification further widens the gap between best- and worst-possible performance. It is clear that domestic investors, in whatever country they are located, should take account of the full range of future possibilities for capital market performance, not simply of the domestic historical record. At the very least, they should allow for the possibility of occasional but severe adverse outcomes.

While future adversity may not resemble past setbacks, there is no doubting that the last century, especially the second half of the twentieth century, was kind to investors in developed economies. Over that period, corporations prospered and share prices went up. Part of that increase reflects what (with hindsight) we now know to be expectations, a century ago, of low profits and high required returns.

Figure 14-4 presents the global evidence on the extent to which stocks can be expected to deliver favorable long-term performance. We retain Siegel's interpretation that twenty years may be considered the long term over which investors make their plans, and hence focus on the twenty-year risk premia. For each country, the red bars show the range of the bottom

Figure 14-4: Percentiles of the distribution of twenty-year risk premia in sixteen countries

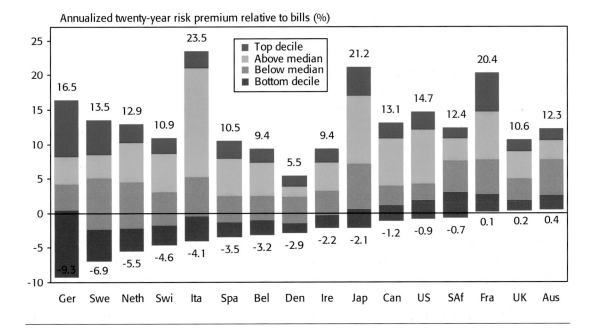

decile of twenty-year premia, with the value of the worst twenty-year outcome shown at the bottom. The blue bars show the range of the top decile, with the value of the best twenty-year outcome shown at the top. The yellow bars show the range of the twenty-year premia that fell above the median but below the top decile, while the green bars show the range that fell below the median but above the bottom decile. The median lies at the point where the yellow bars meet the green bars. Note that the medians are all comfortably above zero. That is, of the eighty-two twenty-year premia, the premium that divides the better forty-one from the worse forty-one periods is an annualized figure of at least 3 percent per year.

However, for half the countries, the lower-decile limit is below zero. For these countries, there was historically a greater than one-in-ten chance of a twenty-year premium on the wrong side of zero. A variety of countries have historical twenty-year premia that, at their minimum, are way below zero. Apart from The Netherlands, the worst offenders here are Germany, Sweden, and Switzerland. This reveals the multiple sources of unexpectedly poor long-term performance: the turmoil of war (Germany), the timing of periods with poor performance (Sweden), or the impact of a generally low premium (Switzerland). In all, there was at least some prospect, historically, of achieving a negative risk premium over twenty years for thirteen out of the sixteen countries studied in this book.

Despite the market declines during 2000 and 2001, considerable optimism is still impounded into stock prices. So in envisioning the future, we should consider not only a more modest expectation for future returns, but also a wider set of return experiences than that of the United States or the United Kingdom over the past. If the "long run" is twenty years, stocks are far from risk free over the long run.

14.3 What does the future hold?

So far in this chapter, we have examined the long run equity premium, drawing inferences from our full global dataset. We now bring this analysis to bear on the expected risk premium that we report in chapter 13. We discuss there the issues involved in making projections from the past into the future, and we noted the large historical rewards from equities: this is Mehra and Prescott's (1985) equity premium puzzle that stocks have provided a higher reward than can be explained by theory. Alternatively, the large ex post risk premium may reflect rewards from bills and bonds that fell short of expectations: this is Weil's (1989) risk free rate puzzle that safe investment has been under-rewarded.

We note in chapter 13 that making inferences from the world equity premium mitigates the impact of measurement errors and market survival. The global equity premium is therefore a good place to start for prediction. In chapter 12 we compute a world geometric-mean equity premium, relative to treasury bills, that historically averaged 4.9 percent. In chapter 13 we estimate the prospective equity premium for this sixteen-country world index to be approximately 3.0 percent (geometric mean) or 4.0 percent (arithmetic mean).

In Figure 14-5 we use the expected geometric mean premium of 3.0 percent to examine the range of risk premia that can be anticipated over various future time horizons. We plot the percentiles of the distribution of risk premium for a national market index whose annual standard deviation is 16 percent (a typical volatility projection for the US and UK), 20 percent (the historical average for the US and UK; see Table 12-1), or 24 percent (which might apply to more poorly diversified portfolios). We assume that the equity premium is lognormally distributed, and plot the first, tenth, fiftieth, ninetieth, and ninety-ninth percentiles of the distribution, over intervals of ten, twenty, thirty, forty, and fifty years.

For each of the three levels of market volatility, we show a set of bars. The red bars plot the range of the bottom decile of ten- to fifty-year premia, with the worst outcome truncated at the first percentile. There is therefore a 1 percent chance of being below the minimum value plotted for each bar. As before, the blue bars display the range of the top decile, with the best outcome truncated at the ninety-ninth percentile. There is therefore a 1 percent chance of being above the maximum value plotted for each bar. The yellow bars show the range of premia that fall above the median but below the top decile, while the green bars show the range that fall below the median but above the bottom decile. The median falls at the point where the yellow bars meet the green bars.

There is clearly a substantial probability of achieving a negative risk premium, even over long investment horizons. With the lowest volatility projection (a standard deviation of only 16 percent) there an 18 percent probability over a period of twenty years of doing worse with equities than with bills. In a smaller market, or with an undiversified portfolio, or if the world

Figure 14-5: Projected percentiles for the distribution of the equity risk premium

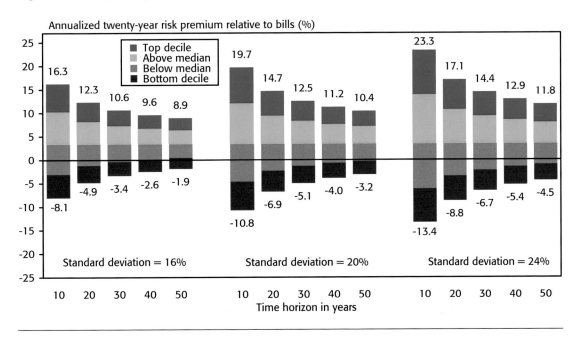

becomes a riskier place, a standard deviation of 24 percent might be realistic, and even over fifty years there would be a 17 percent probability of underperforming.

Arnott and Bernstein (2001) and others analyze the equity premium relative to bonds. The bond maturity premium is around 1 percent above bills (see chapter 6). Hence our 3.0 percent equity premium relative to bills is broadly consistent with the Arnott and Bernstein estimate of 2.4 percent relative to bonds. The probability of a negative equity premium is larger than Figure 14-5 indicates, if premia are defined relative to bonds. Moreover, fat tails in the distribution of returns would further increase the chances of adverse performance.

To sum up, the likely rewards from equity market investing are worth having over the long haul. Yet downside risk is always present. The chance of underperforming government securities shrinks with a longer horizon, but because of the power of compound interest rates, the very worst that could happen to an equity investor worsens as the investment horizon is lengthened. Given the volatility of stock returns, equity investment is not that compelling as a short- or medium-term strategy. This suggests a more subtle set of inferences than those of the "stocks are overpriced" or "stocks are cheap" variety. We explore some of the implications of our research below.

14.4 Implications for individual investors

In every country studied in this book, equities have over the long haul beaten bonds and bills. This outperformance is not simply a pattern from the past; it reflects the theory that risky securities should command a lower price than otherwise similar safe securities. Risky equities can therefore be expected to offer a higher expected return. For risk-tolerant investors, that makes equities a desirable long-term investment. On the other hand, we have provided new estimates of equity risk premia that are, on balance, lower than previous research had suggested. What does this suggest for financial markets? We conclude this chapter with a set of implications of our research for investors.

To highlight the importance of our broad, long-term view we start with the tale of the stockbroker who visits the countryside and sees a shepherd with his flock. "I'll bet you one of your sheep that I can tell you how many are in your field," he says. The shepherd agrees, and the broker responds "320." "Amazing, you win," replies the shepherd. The broker takes an animal and begins to walk away when the shepherd suddenly shouts: "Wait, I'll bet you double or nothing I can tell what your profession is." The broker agrees. "You're a stockbroker," says the shepherd. The broker, stunned, says "How did you know?" The shepherd replies: "Let go of my dog and I'll explain."

Many investors take advice from professionals who, like our stockbroker, still have big gaps in their knowledge. Markets are buffeted by forces that reflect a wide variety of economic, political, social, environmental and business factors, and investment professionals frequently find these forces baffling. Still more confusing, most major fluctuations in the market are reactions to surprises since prices react to the difference between what market participants expect to be revealed and what is revealed. Whether news items viewed in isolation appear to be good or bad is often not the relevant issue. So investment strategy cannot be informed just by a deep knowledge of the individual events that drive markets. We must also look elsewhere. In this book, we look to long-term capital market history as our beacon through the investment haze.

In the remainder of this section, we highlight three areas where we feel our study changes the way individual investors should think about investment. The areas relate to (1) asset allocation, (2) tax management, and (3) mutual fund fees. In section 14.5 we will turn to other issues that are also of relevance to individuals, but which are at the heart of institutional investment strategies. These issues are (4) indexation, (5) active management, (6) anomalies and regularities in stock returns, and (7) international diversification. We start with the implications of our work for asset allocation.

The classic US asset allocation, as described by Loeb (1996) and others, is one-tenth in cash, with risky assets split roughly 60 percent in stocks and 40 percent in bonds. While most advisors will then modify such recommendations in the light of an investor's risk tolerance and investment horizon, many observers have puzzled about this 60:40 stock:bond mix. The fact is, almost any analysis of the historical record suggests allocating more than 60 percent to stocks, and less than 40 percent to bonds. Stocks have displayed a high average return, and low-return bonds have been too volatile to justify a large weighting in an optimized portfolio. Persistently, advisors and investors appear to have selected too little to invest in equities, and too much in bonds. Given the favorable performance of bond markets over the last decade, bonds now offer limited upside potential. Meanwhile, equity prices have declined markedly from their year 2000 all-time highs (see Figure 4-12). One might therefore ask whether, on our evidence, investors should cut back on their weighting to bonds, and increase their exposure to the equity markets?

Far from pursuing a strategy of maximizing asset-class exposure to equities, we draw a different conclusion from the evidence. There is for the first time a more compelling case for regarding the 60:40 guideline as reasonably sensible. The answer is not principally to do with avoiding excess exposure to the risks of equity market investment. Rather, it is to do with the rewards from equity investing. With a smaller equity premium, the opportunity cost from being out of the stock market now looks smaller. One of our students paraphrased to us what she thought we are saying: "You don't like today's equity market risk? Then wait a year. It'll only cost you 3 or 4 percent." That is a part of it. More generally, a smaller equity premium suggests a lower long-term allocation to common stocks. Bonds have more to offer for the future than they provided over the last century.

Our second issue is tax management. It is the marginal investor, not the average investor, who determines market prices. This makes it difficult to assess prices. Does the market largely reflect domestic taxpayers' buying and selling (while tax-exempt investors receive a surplus)? Or are prices determined on a global stage by non-taxpaying institutions, hedge funds, and traders? If so, markets will converge toward prices that are comparable globally, as though nobody pays tax (though taxpayers will still have to pay their annual dues). These are controversial issues. For recent years—and certainly for the early years—of our study we judge that taxes play a small role in the price formation process. Those who do pay tax therefore suffer a deadweight burden on their stock market returns. That burden can be large. Siegel and Montgomery (1995), for example, estimate that the twentieth century annualized real return on US equities is roughly halved if the investor is taxable at the maximum rate on income and capital appreciation—and after tax, real bond and bill returns are transformed from positive to negative. Interestingly, the difference between after-tax stock returns and after-tax bond/bill returns is relatively insensitive to the tax rate since taxes are deducted from bond returns as well as from equity returns. The after-tax equity premium is therefore reasonably robust to tax assumptions.

Taxation does not dampen the case for equity investing. The decimating impact on returns of taxation does, however, highlight the benefits of efficient tax management for *all* asset categories. Provided the associated fees are not onerous, investors should wherever possible seek to hold their assets in tax-exempt, tax-deferred, and tax-managed accounts. This means taking advantage of opportunities such as, in the United States, Individual Retirement Accounts and 401(k) plans; in the United Kingdom, Individual Savings Accounts and personal pension plans; and the equivalent plans around the world. These tax shelters should be used for warehousing bonds, stocks, or a mixture of both. Tax efficiency suggests putting some asset types (e.g., income-producing securities) in a tax-deferred account and other assets (e.g., growth oriented investments) in a taxable account. The precise strategy, of course, will vary with the tax code of the country in question.

Finally, in this section, we turn to the level of mutual fund and portfolio management fees. Mutual funds and other pooled vehicles often charge investors a management fee as high as 1½ or 2 percent per year. We can also include load charges, distribution fees, custody and other charges, brokerage commissions, bid-ask spreads, price impact, relevant taxes, and other expenditures by the manager. Given the relatively high rates of turnover of many mutual fund investors, the deadweight costs can be as much as 3 percent per year, or even more. This verges on our new estimates of the equity premium. The costs born by equity mutual fund investors are not borne by the benchmark. They are largely avoided by tax efficient index funds. It is no surprise that mutual funds around the world tend to underperform on an after fees and costs basis.

Our estimates of the future annualized equity premium, relative to government bonds, are not far from 3 percent. With 3 percent annual cost and performance drag, an equity mutual fund might give a final value that is no greater than direct ownership of government bills or bonds. Nearly all the gains in wealth from equity investment would have been transferred from the investor (who still bears the investment risk) to become a resource for the investment manager, professional advisor and tax-collecting authority. What would happen if investors were to become convinced that the annualized equity premium might indeed be little more than 3 percent? This would impose cost pressure on mutual funds. Many investors are unlikely to be willing, on a continuing basis, to forego a large majority of the reward for investing in the stock market. There will be competitive pressures to control fees and expense ratios. At the same time, retail investors are becoming better informed about the true likelihood of mutual funds outperforming their benchmarks, even on a pre-costs and fees basis. Regulators and those concerned with investor protection are helping to educate investors here, and also to curb the more strident, performance-based advertising claims made by some money managers. We therefore expect a growing appreciation of the advantages of buy-and-hold strategies, and a move toward favoring funds that choose either a demanding outperformance objective or a low cost structure.

To sum up, individual investors now need to adapt their investment strategies to take account of the evidence presented in this book. Today's real interest rates and bond yields are, of course, much higher than the twentieth century average. Compared to the equity risk premium from recent decades, today's forward-looking equity premium is lower. This changing balance in expected rewards has significant implications for individual investors. It highlights the importance of the investor's asset allocation strategy, and puts the spotlight on enhancing net performance by avoiding tax- and cost-drag.

14.5 Implications for investment institutions

It is somewhat artificial to segregate individual from institutional investment strategy. Nevertheless, there are several implications of our research that go straight to the heart of institutional portfolio management. Below, we discuss four of these areas: indexation, active management strategies, anomalies and regularities in stock returns, and international diversification.

We start with a brief look at indexation. It is well known that large plan sponsors and other institutions generally fail to meet their benchmarks. Why is this? Internally, at times of hubris, these organizations often explain their mediocre performance by pointing to their size. They are unable fully to implement their research ideas because as they execute transactions, stock prices tend to move away from them. Treynor (1994) points out that bid-ask spreads and price pressure from the adversarial nature of the trading process give rise to implementation shortfall. This overwhelms the gains that might otherwise have been achieved. A widespread response over the 1980s and 1990s was therefore for plan sponsors and others to index some or all of their portfolios. While active investors, skilled at security analysis and stock selection, continue to trade in the stock market, the large holders of index funds have protected themselves from being "bagged" by well-informed traders.

However, the logic of universal institutional indexation is flawed. If the origin of institutional underperformance were smart individual traders, these individuals would in aggregate have to be exceptionally wealthy and exceptionally active in their trading. Otherwise, their gains could not correspond to the institutions' losses. The reality is that active individual investors underperform by an even larger margin than their institutional counterparts (see, for example, Odean and Barber, 2001). Most individuals have no access to information, analysis, or insights before price-sensitive evaluations are in the public domain. Institutions, on the other hand, often get early access to company meetings, news and announcements, detailed analysis, unpublished research, and the insights of talented investment professionals. Institutions have a research edge that is denied to most people. When investors are concerned that they do not have the skill to beat the market, there is an obvious response— buy index funds. The incremental risk of running an active strategy adds relatively little to equity portfolio volatility, however. So institutions that wish to play the investment game to win need not follow our focus on index investment, and may apply our findings to actively managed portfolios as well.

Treynor and Black (1973) approach investment management as a task in which a high-risk overlay (the "active portfolio") is blended with a low cost, highly diversified index fund (the "passive portfolio"). The active portfolio comprises a decision to hold more-than-index weightings in securities that are perceived to be undervalued, plus a decision to hold less-than-index weightings (or even have a short position) in securities that are perceived to be overvalued. Sometimes the active and passive portfolios are separate entities. Often, however, as is recognized by Grinold and Kahn (1999) and others, the split is a conceptual one—a single, overall portfolio provides broad market exposure accompanied by some stock selection "bets."

When skilled investors consider how much to "bet" on securities that they believe to be mis-priced, they benefit from their prospective gains from stock selection. At the same time, they suffer the extra risk of an imperfectly diversified portfolio. If the equity risk premium is believed to be large, it is less attractive to bet heavily on stocks that appear mispriced. It is preferable to control bets, and to emphasize broad market exposure. When the premium is assessed as large, many so-called active investors will nevertheless appear to run closet index funds. That can be rational since it optimizes the portfolio's reward-to-risk ratio. Our asser-tion in this book, however, is that the equity premium is markedly lower than many people suggest. The reward from passive investing must therefore be lower, in relative terms, than was previously thought. For skilled investors, the size of their portfolio bets should therefore be larger. Our evidence on the small magnitude of the equity risk premium provides encour-agement for active investors to deviate more from benchmark, and to take on more active risk.

Active investors are often interested in anomalies and regularities in stock returns. Stock market researchers have identified a number of persistent patterns in stock returns. Pre-eminent is the size effect: the tendency of smaller companies to perform differently—over the long haul, better—than the market leaders. In recent years, the most talked-about pat-tern has been the differential performance of value and growth stocks. Other anomalies relate to momentum trading, seasonalities and other calendar effects, and various types of apparent over- and under-reaction (see Hirshleifer, 2001). There is little doubt that these phenomena contribute to explaining stock returns, and that the posited relationships some-times persist for quite some time. However, such relationships often break down or turn negative at just the time when statistically meaningful evidence appears to have accumu-lated.

Where these anomalies are indicative of risk exposures that are rewarded by above average expected returns, there can be an expectation of a continuing regularity in stock returns. If that is the case, we would classify the risk-reward relationship as a lasting law: one that is expected to survive indefinitely. Unfortunately, too many anomalies are temporary traits that self-destruct. We have provided extensive illustrations of such tendencies in chapters 9 and 10. We would advise investors to guard against excessive bets on unexplained empirical anomalies. Too often, they do not last long enough to cover the costs of exploiting them.

While stock market anomalies may be illusory, one "free lunch" is still on offer in the investment world—risk reduction through international diversification. Investment risk is lowered in a worldwide portfolio. Global investors can therefore afford to allocate relatively more of their portfolio to risky assets, such as equities. Since riskier assets offer a positive reward for risk, investors' worldwide portfolios have a higher expected return in relation to their risk. Over the 101 years of our study, and from the point of view of investors in most of our sixteen countries, these gains would have been economically meaningful. However, in most countries investors were free to invest globally only in the early and later parts of the twentieth century. The biggest benefits arise during the middle decades of the century, when markets were highly segmented. The greater the barrier to cross-border investment, the larger is the gain from circumventing such restrictions.

In today's markets, it is easier to invest globally. Paradoxically, since that has also enabled companies to extend their business activities beyond their home markets, national stock market returns are now more highly correlated with each other. This has attenuated, but by no means eliminated, the prospective benefits from investing internationally. We estimate in chapter 8 that for investors in most countries, there is a potential risk reduction of 10–20 percent from spreading a portfolio across the mature markets studied in this book. It is plausible that there are larger gains from investing in emerging markets. For many investors, exposure to foreign markets will be by means of mutual funds or exchange-traded index tracking derivatives. With the increasing ease of gaining international exposure, we anticipate a continuing trend toward globalization within equity investors' portfolios.

14.6 Summary

Over the 101 years spanned by our research, stocks have performed better than bonds, but by a narrower margin than was previously surmised. In addition, their returns were enhanced by once-off re-ratings. Taking the evidence of other countries and of a lower prospective equity premium, the apparent superiority of equities will in future years be attenuated. We show that common stocks cannot be regarded as a safe bet for the long haul, even when the investment horizon has a duration of twenty (or more) years.

We explore seven implications of our findings. We explain the potential appropriateness of old-fashioned asset mix guidelines, stress the importance of tax management, and point out the likelihood of mutual fund fee pressure. We then look at the role for indexation, active management strategies, the dangers of anomaly-based trading, and the benefits of international diversification. Readers may now be pondering what our view is of the long-term prospects for equities. Several trends seem likely.

First, as we have seen in the opening years of the twenty-first century, investment in equities will remain risky. This is because business itself is risky, and because the years ahead will bring new forms of disorder and volatility. Instead of—or perhaps in addition to—the disruptions of the past, the new century may herald continuing international terrorism, new diseases, threats of large-scale litigation and corporate liability, environmental disasters, and new pestilences as yet beyond our expectations. The counterparts of the world wars and the Cold War of the twentieth century may be new wars on terror, wars on drugs, courtroom wars, and wars against the forces of nature. The higher the rating at which shares are bought and sold, the more volatile will be stock prices, and the more sensitive they will be to these new threats.

Second, if equities remain risky, as must certainly be the case, equity investors should continue to expect a positive risk premium. This implies that when investors look back a century from now, equities should prove to have been the best performing asset class over the twenty-first century. Nevertheless, we expect that the equity risk premium will turn out to be lower than it has been over the last 101 years. This will be the case even when the premium is calculated, as in this study, to include the turbulent earlier half of the twentieth century.

Third, we favor holding stocks for the very long run. They are not a guaranteed superior performer over the investment horizon of most investors. They should be held as part of a diversified portfolio, including multiple asset classes from more than one country. Security prices incorporate current views about future cash flow growth and current levels of expected returns. Investors who fail to diversify efficiently and/or who overpay for asset management services can expect to erode their reward for equity risk exposure.

These are long-term forecasts. Our accuracy should not, we suggest, be judged for a further one hundred years. Even then, note that with 201 observations the standard error associated with historical equity premium estimates will still be of the order of 1–1½ percent.

Chapter 15 Implications for companies

We have analyzed the long-term performance of the main asset categories in many different national environments, political situations, economic regimes, and historical settings. This has revealed the historical magnitudes of asset returns and their inter-relationships. We have examined returns and premia from the perspectives of an investor in a single country who invests in his or her home market, a domestic investor who holds a portfolio invested in a single foreign market, and an investor whose portfolio is globally diversified. In the process, we have uncovered the long-term record on company size, industry composition, value/growth orientation, and other facets of stock returns. The perspective throughout has been international: not US, not UK, but worldwide.

In chapter 14 we explored some implications of our work for investors. We now ask what our findings imply for the valuation of common stocks and of entire companies. This is of central relevance to investors, but is even more important for corporate managers. Investors care, of course, about the future value of their investments. But corporate managers also make decisions about investing for the future, and their choices often survive to haunt them. Whereas portfolio managers who buy the wrong assets can realize their losses and sell immediately, there may be no escape for the corporate manager who invests in a smelter, warehouse, oilrig, or even a computer game that nobody wants. We therefore start in section 15.1 with a review of the implications of our findings for estimating the cost of capital.

The remainder of this chapter focuses on broader implications for companies. While the issues covered in sections 15.2 and 15.3 are also central to investment, they are discussed here from the corporation's perspective. Questions we address include: How should firms expect regulators to respond to our long-term evidence; has debt lost some of its cost advantage against equity; and should companies pay fewer dividends? In section 15.4 we summarize the main messages of this book for companies and their financial managers.

15.1 The cost of capital

We have seen that the current level of the equity risk premium is likely to be lower than we used to expect. Textbooks have until recently preached an arithmetic equity risk premium of around 7–9 percent. Brealey and Myers (2000), for example, recommend an arithmetic mean of 8½ percent. Similarly, Weston, Chung, and Sui (1997) favor an arithmetic mean premium of 7½ percent. The following advice from Ross, Westerfield, and Jordan (2000) is an example:

> Suppose we had an investment that we thought had about the same risk as a portfolio of large-firm common stocks. At a minimum, what return would this investment have to offer for us to be interested?

> The risk premium on large-company stocks has been 9.4 percent historically, so a reasonable estimate of our required return would be this premium plus the (4.5 percent) T-bill rate, 4.5% + 9.4% = 13.9%. This may strike you as

being high, but, if we were thinking of starting a new business, then the risks of doing so might resemble those of investing in small-company stocks. In this case, the historical risk premium is 13.6 percent, so we might require as much as 18.1 percent from such an investment at a minimum.

Ross, Westerfield, and Jordan use a risk premium of 9.4 percent, or 13.6 percent. These required rates of return are drawn from the Ibbotson Associates *Yearbook*. They are based on the published historical record for US large-cap and small-cap stocks. In the light of our longer-term and broader evidence, such estimates of the equity premium now look high. As we explain in chapter 13, the market is almost certainly building lower risk premia than this into stock prices.

Chapter 5 documented that real interest rates rose from the beginning to the end of the last century. Averaged over our sixteen countries, the annualized real interest rate was below zero over the pre-1980 period, rising to a level during 1980–2000 that averaged 3.7 percent (see Figure 5-5 for details). These are inflation-adjusted returns on treasury bills; the corresponding real return on bonds from 1980–2000 has been even higher (see Figure 6-6). By the mid-1990s, expectations had settled on real interest rates being around the 4–5 percent level for the foreseeable future, though since then real yields have declined.

In January 1997, when the United States started trading TIPS (long-term inflation-indexed bonds), their real yield to redemption turned out to be close to the then current yield on UK inflation-indexed bonds. Toward the end of 2001, the real yield on TIPS was around 3.1 percent, slightly below continental European yields, though above the United Kingdom (whose inflation-indexed bonds are treated favorably for tax purposes). Figure 15-1 shows that although the *ex post* real interest rate had varied considerably across countries, the *ex ante* risk free rate is relatively similar across markets.

To compute the expected return on equity investment, we add the risk premium to the real interest rate. Compared to the position shortly after TIPS were first issued, real yields are a little lower. We do not know what the expected risk premia were in the past, since they cannot be observed, but after publication of the privately distributed predecessor to this book, as well as extensive research by others, it seems that *estimates* of the equity premium also fell. Since both components declined, it follows that the required return on equity capital is lower than it was in the mid-to-late 1990s. With lower inflation and lower real interest rates, the required return on debt has also fallen.

The cost of capital is thus lower in most countries than it was believed to be only a few years ago. This is partly because real interest rates fell, but mostly because the cost of equity was never as high as the historical risk premia, especially over recent decades, had suggested. Many companies, however, are living in the past. They are seeking excessive returns on new investment because of reliance on historical estimates that exaggerate the prospective risk premium. There is a danger, therefore, that once companies recover from the recession that began in 2001, they may under-invest, or delay important projects.

Figure 15-1: Real yields on long-maturity inflation-indexed bonds as at late 2001

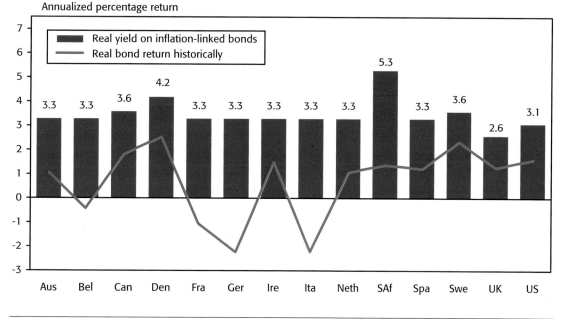

Source: Bloomberg, October 10, 2001. Real yields for Eurozone countries are proxied by French inflation-indexed euro-denominated bonds.

Cancellation or deferral of worthwhile projects erodes a company's competitive position. The biggest losers are likely to be those firms that are overtaken by new competitors who can exploit new technologies, and innovative or re-engineered processes with a lower cost base. The dinosaurs that do not adapt will experience downgrading of their market ratings, and falls in their stock prices. Ironically, the latter may be misinterpreted as an increase in the cost of capital, and may contribute to a vicious circle of continuing loss of shareholder value.

Corporate investment is not automatically a "good thing." To add value, investment must be in worthwhile projects that cover the cost of capital, rather than in expansion, acquisition, or upgrading activities that fail to do so. After the "new economy" bubble burst, and during the setbacks that followed the terrorist outrages of September 11, 2001, many companies have not had sufficient appealing projects to allow them to benefit from today's lower cost of capital. In the fall and winter of 2001, they may also have perceived an upward shock in required risk premia, though this is likely to be transitory. While firms should continue to seek profitable new investments, they may well conclude that the best they can do is to return excess funds to their shareholders. These shareholders then have the option of investing their money in other shares that do offer the normal return from equity investment.

To make the right decision, it is important that managers have insight into the returns that can be expected from investing in the capital market. History can be misleading as a guide to the future, and undoubtedly needs to be interpreted with care. Nevertheless, financial market history provides a starting point. By understanding the capital markets, managers can be empowered to focus on investments that add to the market value of their company.

this section, we look at (1) the danger of under-investment, (2) geography and the cost of capital, (3) allowable returns for regulated businesses, and (4) the impact on pension plans. In section 15.3 we consider some additional issues, namely, (5) capital structure decisions, (6) dividend policy, (7) financial reporting and book values, and (8) the benefits of hedging. We start with a discussion of the danger of under-investment.

We argued in the previous section that, when required rates of return move up or down, corporate decision systems often remain stranded. Criteria for appraising new investment projects tend to be sticky: once a firm has adopted a hurdle rate for capital budgeting, that rate tends to survive until there is an irresistible stimulus for change. Firms set required rates in either nominal or real terms. Nominal rates have in some firms been stranded simply because of the continuing decline in inflation across the developed world. The real risk free rate has fallen back from 4–5 percent in the mid- and late-1990s to the current level of around 3 percent, as revealed in Figure 15-1 by the yield on inflation-indexed bonds. At the same time, the equity risk premium has either fallen or is perceived to have fallen. With a decline in real interest rates, in the estimated equity premium, and in inflation, required returns are likely to be lower than many companies' capital budgeting systems demand.

Large corporations generally claim to base investment decisions on discounted cash flow analysis (Bruner, Eades, Harris, and Higgins, 1998). If the discount rates they use are excessive, they are likely to reject potentially worthwhile projects that should, in fact, be accepted. We have documented a fall in the expected equity risk premium that captures what we believe is really happening in financial markets. If that opinion is accepted, it is probable that some companies will run the risk of underinvesting in profitable projects.

Taken literally, our long-run return estimates might be regarded as indicating a different expected rate of return from equity in each country. For much of the century markets were far from integrated, and for extensive periods many of the countries we look at were at war. It is unlikely that listed companies in major national markets have all had the same expected return. The exchange-listed corporate sector varies from country to country in its risk attributes, exposure to worldwide economic events, financial leverage, industry composition, exposure to global competition, focus on growth businesses, and so on.

On the other hand, there is no reason to regard the attributes of national markets as stationary. *Ex post* risk may not correspond to *ex ante* risk. Moreover, we should not regard *ex post* returns as equating to the fair reward for each country's *ex ante* risk. As explained above, one might interpret the world index as an indicator of risk and reward, with deviations from this global index being attributed to noise. Alternatively, one might estimate the risk premium for just a single country. We find neither approach wholly satisfactory. If we had to choose, however, we would lean toward taking a worldwide approach to setting the cost of capital, while stressing the scope for more research in this area.

As well as being a major factor for investors and managers, the equity risk premium is of fundamental importance to regulators. To company managers, the cost of capital is central to setting minimum hurdle rates for proposed investment projects. Many utilities and other companies face a situation where part or all of their business is subject to price or rate of return regulation. This is designed to ensure that they do not abuse their market power and earn an unfairly high return. The benchmark for judging whether returns are excessive should be the company's cost of capital, which in turn depends on the equity risk premium.

We have seen that the historical risk premium impounds the favorable experiences of the past: the fact that history, at least over recent decades, has been kind to equity investors. It is therefore likely to exceed investors' current required risk premium; the prospective premium is likely to be smaller than many investors might expect. Policy makers and regulators now have new evidence to underpin a review of the rates of return that they regard as acceptable.

For many businesses, one of the largest liabilities is the company's pension plan. It is common to appraise the health of a defined benefit plan by using discount rates that are linked in some way to expected market rates of return; these rates have fallen for equities, and some actuarial valuations still need to adjust to current estimates of the equity premium. Shortfall analysis focuses on setting asset allocation policy in the light of probability limits for long-term performance. Not only is this controversial in its own right (see Bodie, 1995), but our analysis in section 14.2 suggests that shortfall analysis may understate long-term downside risk. For a defined benefit fund (or for the contributor to a defined contribution plan), our research raises questions about the extent to which a tilt toward equities can assist the plan to achieve its objectives.

In summary, our evidence points toward four implications for corporate investment decisions. First, our new estimates of the risk premium, combined with changes in the interest rate environment, suggest that some companies will be using obsolete—typically, excessive—required rates of return. Second, we affirm the importance of estimating risk premia from the global record, and not simply from the history of individual countries. Third, our new (and lower) estimates of the equity risk premium are of direct relevance to regulators. Finally, our research informs strategy for pension plan sponsors.

15.3 Corporate financing decisions

Since our research relates to the cost of capital, it also has relevance to corporate liabilities and company financing strategy. This section therefore looks at capital structure, dividend policy, financial reporting, and currency hedging. We start with capital structure.

We illustrated in chapter 4 and earlier in this chapter that, until recently, there was a consensus that common stocks' high historical return implies a high future required return on equity. The real returns on government bonds and bills had in contrast been poor, suggesting (by extrapolation) that the required return on corporate debt was low. Our study challenges this view, showing that the required return on equity is lower than investors were until recently estimating. At the same time we observe a higher expected return from bonds, in real terms, than would be inferred from long-term capital market history. Moreover, although it has declined since the mid-1990s, today's real yield on inflation-linked bonds is considerably above the 101-year average real return for bonds and bills, so the forward-looking real required return on debt is much increased compared to long-term history.

Finance books—this one included—almost invariably refer to the required returns on equity and debt as the "cost of equity" and "the cost of debt." This terminology is dangerous, since it can lead corporate managers to interpret the changes in the equity premium and real rate of interest documented here as evidence that equity capital is now cheaper, and debt capital more expensive. This may tempt them to reduce their leverage, and finance themselves with equity, which appears to "cost" little more. The Modigliani-Miller (1958) and Miller (1977) propositions and extensions make it clear that changes in the required returns on equity and debt should not, in themselves, influence the choice of capital structure. Financial managers should not base capital structure decisions on the perceived "cost" gap between debt and equity, but instead, should focus their attention on the issues that really matter: tax, the risk of financial distress, informational asymmetries, and agency costs.

A related topic is dividend policy. We have presented the first century-long study on the performance of value and growth stocks. Our evidence suggests that, at least outside the United States, the expected return on stocks with a low dividend yield is smaller than the expected return on high-yield stocks. In other words, high-dividend companies appear to have the higher required return on equity. Does this suggest there is scope for reducing the required return on, or "cost" of, equity by cutting cash payments to shareholders?

If there is a difference between the return that shareholders require from a low- and a high-dividend payout firm, we can be sure this is related to the fundamental attributes of the two companies. Cosmetic changes in dividend policy cannot determine the cost of capital. Indeed, an announcement that henceforth more cash will be retained by a business may provide unintended signals to the market, and is more likely to be greeted with confusion than acclaim. Reduced dividend payout does not of itself signal growth prospects, and hence a reduced required rate of return on equity. Brealey and Myers (2000), for example, conclude, "the effects of dividend policy are too uncertain to justify fine-tuning."

If dividend policy is unlikely to alter corporate valuations, a company that had been exposed to the research of Fama and French (1992), or chapter 10 of this book, might have gained the impression that it could lower its required return by reducing its book-to-market ratio. By looking more like a growth stock, perhaps through judicious financial reporting, the firm might believe its shareholders will require a lower rate of return.

At the end of 2000, Vodafone represented nearly a tenth of the capitalization of the UK market. It was the darling of growth stock investors up to 2000. But after the merger of Vodafone with Airtouch, the firm's book value of equity rose until the stock was classified as a value investment. Did this increase the company's required return, and lead to the subsequent stock price collapse? Of course not: fundamental factors were at work here. Should companies and investors care about accounting conventions that have an impact on book values?

It is difficult to believe that the vagaries of accounting should determine whether, for this one reason, Vodafone is transformed into a value stock. The book-to-market ratio is simply an imprecise proxy for underlying characteristics. For the same reasons as in the case of dividend policy, manipulation of book values is unlikely to reduce the cost of capital, and it may well be misunderstood in the market.

Finally, we reflect on the evidence presented in chapter 7 on purchasing power parity. In the long run, exchange rates can be expected to adjust to reflect relative inflation rates. In integrated global markets, foreign exchange exposure therefore contributes little to expected real returns. Companies might therefore conclude that hedging their currency exposure is unnecessary. On the other hand, short-term currency volatility can represent a significant risk exposure for corporations. The expected *ex ante* cost of hedging is small, but the *ex post* impact of currency volatility is large. Moreover, foreign exchange fluctuations can be a major distraction for management. In order to concentrate on their primary business, and to lower default risk and the associated costs of financial distress, companies may well therefore wish to hedge their currency exposure, and thereby control their short-term risk exposure.

15.4 Summary

In this chapter we examined the implications of our research for corporate financial management. We address three topics: the cost of capital, corporate investment decisions, and corporate financing strategy.

The cost of capital is central to financial decision making. The required return on equity is the risk free interest rate plus a premium for risk. At the time of writing, the size weighted *ex ante* world real interest rate is around 3 percent. This is much higher than the *ex post* historical average real return on bills and bonds over the last century, but it is lower than the real interest rate from the mid- to late-1990s.

At the same time, the equity risk premium for our world index is around 3 percent (geometric mean) or 4 percent (arithmetic mean). This suggests a forward-looking real required return on equity capital of around 6 percent (geometric mean) or 7 percent (arithmetic mean). These projections are based on our sixteen-country world index, and would need to be adjusted for country-specific economic and tax factors. However, one should be cautious about extrapolating into the future from the investment experience of a single national market. There is, for example, no reason to suppose that the market with the lowest *ex post* risk premium has the lowest cost of capital, nor that a country with the highest *ex post* risk premium has the highest cost of capital. We prefer to start with a more global perspective.

We have also drawn inferences for corporate investment and financing strategy. Our new, lower estimates of risk premia and required returns should have a marked impact on investment behavior, ranging from project appraisal through management of the company's pension fund. On the other hand, despite changes in the perceived cost of equity, relative to that of debt, there should be no material impact on capital structure and dividend policy.

Chapter 16 Conclusion

Our book is constructed around prices that are determined in financial markets. Markets are infinitely fascinating to observe but frustrating to analyze. Each time a relationship becomes apparent, there is the danger it may change. Every lasting law may turn out to be a temporary trait. In this chapter we pull together some laws of the market that are likely to pass the test of time, and we draw contrasts with temporary attributes that may be more obvious with the benefit of hindsight than they were before they were noted.

In section 16.1 we summarize the main findings of the book, while in section 16.2 we review the key messages. Section 16.3 concludes not only this chapter, but also the main part of the book. In the remaining chapters, which together comprise Part Two, we provide country-by-country appraisals of the performance of the sixteen national markets that constitute our sample, and of our sixteen-country world index. The book concludes with a comprehensive set of references and a combined subject and author index.

16.1 Long-term returns

In writing this book, we set out to answer four big questions: How have stock markets performed over the twentieth century, domestically and internationally? How has this compared with bonds and bills? What has been the impact of foreign exchange fluctuations? And what toll has inflation taken?

To address these questions, we compile US market indexes, and construct new UK indexes covering equities, bonds, bills, inflation, and exchange rates dating back to 1900. In addition, we assemble a comparable 101-year history for fourteen other countries. Unlike previous studies of global markets, all returns include reinvested income as well as capital appreciation, and our database is more comprehensive, accurate and detailed than any previous research. Our study includes all the main North American, Asia-Pacific, African, and European markets. The sixteen countries we cover account today for over 88 percent of global stock market capitalization. We estimate that they were equally dominant at the start of the twentieth century.

In every country, equities proved to be the best performing investment over the twentieth century. In the United States, equities provided an annualized return of 10.1 percent, or 6.7 percent after adjusting for inflation. In the United Kingdom, equities provided an annualized return of 10.1 percent, or 5.8 percent after adjusting for inflation. The best performing equity market was Sweden, with a real return of 7.6 percent per year, while the worst was Belgium, with an annual real return of 2.5 percent.

This was not the century for bond investors. In the United States, long-term government bonds provided a disappointing return of 4.8 percent per year, or just 1.6 percent after inflation. Risk-free short-dated treasury bills returned 4.1 percent, while inflation was 3.2 percent. UK bill and bond returns were similar. Five countries, Germany, Japan, Italy, France, and Belgium, experienced negative real returns on both bonds and bills over the century taken as a whole.

The poor performance of bonds arose from inflation proving to be higher and more volatile than expected. During the first half of the century, the average US and UK inflation rates were surprisingly low. This was because the years of higher inflation were partially offset by a period in the 1920s and early 1930s when prices actually fell. Deflation was not unique to the United States and the United Kingdom, but was common to all sixteen countries at some stage during this era. For much of the second half of the century, however, UK inflation was pervasive, peaking at 25 percent in 1975.

But while the United Kingdom may view itself as having been afflicted by inflation, the countries identified above as having the lowest real bill and bond returns had worse experiences. In addition to the German hyperinflation of 1922–23, France, Italy, Japan, and to a lesser extent Belgium, all experienced very high inflation around the end of the Second World War. This dramatically affected bill and bond returns. While bills are normally regarded as risk free, German bill investors lost everything in 1923. The same was true of German bond investors, who additionally lost over 92 percent in real terms after the Second World War. Interestingly, however, the countries that had the very worst inflationary experiences and the lowest bond returns over the century taken as a whole, were among the best performing bond markets over the last fifty-one years.

Financial market returns thus reflect the turbulence of the twentieth century. Through the lens of the markets, we can see the decimating impact of wars and their aftermath, inflation, high interest rates, stock market crashes, and the Great Depression. These events affected not only investment returns, but also the volatility of the financial markets.

Although equities gave the highest return in every country, they also proved the riskiest asset class. The real returns on US and UK equities had in both cases a standard deviation of 20 percent, somewhat below the average for the other countries in our study. This compares with a 10.0 (14.5) percent standard deviation for US (UK) bonds and 4.7 (6.6) percent for US (UK) bills. This ranking was common across the world. In every country, equities proved more volatile than bonds, while bonds were more risky than bills.

While real returns on equities have been higher than on bills and bonds, the margin is smaller than many investors have perceived. For the United Kingdom, this stems from shortcomings and biases in previous estimates of long-run UK returns. Before the privately distributed predecessor to this book, the most authoritative UK study indicated a real return on shares from 1919–54 of 8.8 percent. Our analysis shows that this greatly overstates the true return over the first half of the century: the real return from 1900–54 was just 3.8 percent.

Long-run equity returns and equity risk premia are also lower for other countries than has generally been perceived. This arises from "easy data bias," the tendency of researchers to use data that are easy to obtain. Easy data generally excludes difficult periods such as those with breaks in trading activity, times of unrest and upheaval, and wars and their aftermath, and typically relates to more recent periods. Sixteen studies, which might hitherto have been taken as the standard reference for each country, generate a misleading impression of long-term investment returns by reporting equity returns that exceed the actual returns for the last 101 years by, on average, 3 percent per year.

While our international data are superior to that used in previous studies, they still have shortcomings. Although we use the best available sources, for certain assets in some countries the early data fall short of ideal. Since the initial pre-publication editions of this book we have already improved certain data series, and we plan further enhancements in the future. We hope to add one or two more countries, and to undertake further analysis. Meanwhile, we will keep our database current by continuing to calculate the new UK index series and periodically updating the returns for other countries.

We should also sound a cautionary note on our conclusions. The international data used and reported in this book have extensive coverage and a common start date. Despite this, our estimates of long-run returns around the world are still likely to be upward biased. This is in part because of the potential deficiencies referred to above in a small proportion of our international data for earlier years, which may contain some element of retrospective bias. But more importantly, it is because our study is confined to the countries for which total returns can currently be estimated. Our own work, too, thus suffers from easy-data bias.

Recently, there has been much concern in the literature about survivorship bias in markets. The concern is that long-run return studies, such as our own, document returns for surviving markets, and leave out the record for other markets which at some point failed to survive or experienced total losses: Russia, China, Poland, and so on. Omission of markets that experienced returns of -100 percent inevitably inflates our estimates of long-run average returns, though the impact on risk premia is less clearcut.

While these concerns are legitimate, the emerging consensus is that they have been overstated (see, for example, Siegel, 1999). Our study lends weight to this view. While the sizes of stock markets in 1900 can be inferred only indirectly from GDP data, it is likely that the non-surviving markets that suffered total losses made up only a small proportion of the then total world capitalization. Furthermore, Germany, Japan, and other markets are sometimes cited as examples of non-survivors because of the war. Yet the histories we have assembled for these two countries show they experienced positive real equity returns of 3.6 and 4.5 percent per year, respectively. By comparison, the United Kingdom, which is often cited as a classic survivor with favorable returns, experienced equity performance of 5.8 percent, while the hugely successful US economy ranked as the third best performer, with 6.7 percent.

16.2 Key messages

In chapter 1, we remarked that good data is the key to understanding history. We can now leave the starting block. Our new database allows us to make comparisons between investment performance in different economic and political environments, and over different time periods. In the case of the United Kingdom, because our new equity series are based on an underlying, 101-year database of share prices, we have shown that we can also look inside the index. Research on the United States can now be complemented by insights into the UK experience over the long term. We investigate key issues such as changes in industrial structure, value and growth effects in long-run stock returns, the concentration of the equity market, the small-firm effect, stock market seasonality, and the relationship between stock market performance and underlying dividend and GDP growth.

But the single most important variable that we document in this book is surely the equity risk premium. High and volatile levels for the stock market fuelled debate about the expected level of the risk premium, since this is central to the valuation of risky assets. Our research findings have a direct bearing on this debate. We show that the equity risk premium during the first half of the twentieth century was, in fact, lower than in later years. Our view of future market performance should reflect this earlier historical experience as well as the period from the 1950s onward.

The high risk premia achieved during the last fifty-one years are attributable to many factors. First, there have been productivity and efficiency growth, improvements in management and corporate governance, and extensive technological changes. These factors have contributed to, and despite recent setbacks are now built into, stock prices that have risen dramatically over the last half-century.

Second, stock prices have almost certainly also risen over the long haul because of a fall in the required rate of return due to diminished investment risk. The economic and political lessons of the twentieth century have surely been learned, international trade and investment flows have increased, and the Cold War has ended. The developed world is united in seeking a secure business environment. A further factor that may have lowered required returns is that investors now have improved opportunities to diversify, both domestically and internationally, than they did in 1900.

Factors such as these, which led to a reduction in the expected risk premium, contributed to an upward re-rating of stock prices. In chapter 13, we adjust the *ex post* risk premium of our sixteen countries for unanticipated cash flows and for reductions in investors' required rates of return. This suggests that the expected equity risk premium, on an annualized basis, is around 2½–4 percent; and on an arithmetic-mean basis the expected equity risk premium is around 4–5 percent. This is markedly below earlier estimates. For our sixteen-country world index, the *ex ante* risk premia are approximately 3 percent (geometric mean) or 4 percent (arithmetic mean).

Our findings are important for investors and companies alike. The bad news is that some investors may have observed high equity returns in the past and assumed they would continue, when in reality they were due to a gradual re-rating that may now be complete. Returns will certainly not persist at the level of 16 percent annually that was recently cited in the *Financial Times* as the expectation of UK private investors. Nor is the premium likely to be as high as the 9.4 percent arithmetic mean reported recently in the Ibbotson *Yearbook*. Many investors are likely to find that future equity returns fall below the expectations they held until very recently. The bull market of the 1990s is unlikely to recur. Periodic sharp setbacks, such as in 2000–01, will from time to time interfere with the progress of the stock market.

If investors continue to require a relatively low risk premium, then equities can be expected to outperform risk free investments, albeit by a lower margin than over the last 101 years. If instead required returns rise, then share prices will fall, and equities will underperform. Perversely, only if we accept that the expected equity risk premium is now at a permanently low level can high stock prices be justified.

16.3 Conclusion

"An optimist," observed Archy the cockroach, "is a guy that has never had much experience." (Marquis, 1934)

By the middle of the twentieth century, investors with experience had little cause for optimism. Equity returns over the last fifty years had been low. There had been two devastating world wars, the Wall Street Crash and Great Depression, episodes of high and even hyperinflation, and much economic and political turmoil. The Second World War had ended, only to herald in the Cold War and fears of possible future nuclear conflict.

Who but the most rampant optimist would then have dreamt that over the next half-century, the annualized real return on equities would be 9 percent, with most other countries enjoying similarly high returns? Yet this is what happened.

This was a period when most things turned out better than expected. There was no third world war, the Cuban Missile Crisis was defused, the Berlin Wall fell, and the Cold War ended. There was unprecedented growth in productivity and efficiency, improvements in management and corporate governance, and extensive technological change. Corporate cash flows grew faster than expected, and in all likelihood the equity risk premium fell, further boosting stock prices. In short, it was the triumph of the optimists.

Statistical logic tells us that future expectations must lie below today's optimists' dreams. We can hope for, but we cannot expect, the optimists to triumph in the future. Future returns from equities are likely to be lower than those achieved in recent decades. As Archy the cockroach warned us, experience should teach us realism, not optimism. We believe that the experience of sixteen national stock markets over the last 101 years can contribute to a realistic assessment of the future.

PART TWO:

Sixteen countries, one world

Chapter 17 Our global database

In this second part of the book we provide an overview of the long-term performance of each individual market. We list our data sources, covering equities, bonds, bills, currencies, and inflation, and present salient features of the database that we have compiled for each country.

As explained earlier in section 3.4, our data series are remarkably comprehensive. We span five assets in each of sixteen countries. For no fewer than seventy-nine out of eighty asset/market combinations, we are able to estimate total returns for all 101 years from 1900 to 2000, the sole exception being Swiss equities, where the data start in 1911.

In the chapters that follow, each country is represented by an array of five pages. For each market, the first page begins with a description of our data sources. Where possible, we rely on peer-reviewed academic research or, alternatively, highly rated professional studies. Often we compile index series by linking together a sequence of indices. We choose the best available indices for each period, switching when feasible to superior alternatives, as these become available. All indices incorporate reinvested income. Our descriptions of the data sources provide full bibliographic references to our source materials.

Exchange rates are not described separately, as they are all sourced from Global Financial Data (GFD), other than modest corrections for Australia and Spain. Where there is a choice of exchange rates, we use market rather than official rates. Unless stated to the contrary, inflation rates and bill returns are also sourced from GFD.

A summary table follows the data description. This table provides an overview of the asset returns and risk premia for that country. For both nominal and real (inflation-adjusted) asset returns and for three risk premium series, we show the geometric and arithmetic mean return, the standard error of the arithmetic mean (SE), the standard deviation of annual returns (SD), and the lowest and highest annual return, together with the dates in which these extremes occurred. These statistics are based on the entire 101 years of our study.

The second and third pages of each country chapter portray the real returns experienced on each asset class. The second page contains a graph of the real returns achieved on equities, bonds, and bills, together with the real exchange rate against the US dollar. The real exchange rate is defined as the nominal exchange rate against the dollar, adjusted by the inflation rate of the country relative to that of the United States. The lower part of this figure contains a bar chart of the individual yearly percentage returns on equities and on bonds.

The third page of each country chapter, following the graph of real returns, contains a table that provides "return triangles" of the annualized real returns on each of the four asset categories, plus the annualized inflation rate, over all periods of 1, 2,...,10 decades. The table presents returns over individual decades, and returns to date from an initial investment made at the start of 1900, 1910, and so on to the year 2000.

227

The fourth page is a graph plotting the nominal returns from equities, bonds, bills, and inflation, all based at the start of 1900 to a value of one. The lower part of this figure contains a bar chart of the individual yearly percentage nominal returns on equities and on bonds.

The fifth and final page is split into two halves. The top half of the page is a table comprising two "return triangles" for the annualized equity risk premium, measured relative to both bills and bonds over a variety of time horizons. The bottom half of this final page lists index levels for all the asset series in real terms, and also the index level for inflation. The latter enables readers who so wish to calculate a set of asset return indexes in nominal terms. In this table, index values are provided at intervals of one decade from 1900 to 1990, and thereafter on an annual basis.

As mentioned above, our data descriptions indicate for each country the primary information sources we have used. The references to these are at the end of the book. For the United Kingdom, ABN AMRO sponsored us to construct a new set of long-run indexes especially for this book and for its privately distributed precursors. For the United Kingdom, therefore, the description of the primary information sources is built into the country chapter itself. Instead of following the usual five-page format, the data description section for the UK chapter extends over the first three pages, rather than just a single page. As explained in Part One, the UK return series cover equities (total market, small-cap, and micro-cap), bonds (long, mid-maturity, and inflation-indexed), and treasury bills. These indexes are known commercially as the ABN AMRO/LBS indexes. In addition, we analyze the Hoare Govett Smaller Companies (HGSC) Index, which is also an ABN AMRO product. We are grateful to ABN AMRO for their cooperation in making these indexes available for this book.

In chapter 34 we present a seventeenth market. This is based on our world market index for all sixteen countries combined. Since it is computed from the data for other assets, the world indexes have some special attributes that are described in the text at the start of chapter 34.

Finally, the gross domestic product (GDP) estimates used in Part One are sourced from Mitchell (1998) with gaps mostly filled from Maddison (1995, 2001), though for Ireland and South Africa we interpolate from Maddison to estimate missing GDP information.

Chapter 18 Australia

The data for Australian equities are described in Officer's chapter in Ball, Brown, Finn, and Officer (1989). Ball and Bowers (1986) provide a complementary, though brief, historical analysis. We are grateful to Bob Officer for making his database available to us, and also to Ray Ball and John Bowers for providing their own data for Australia.

Officer compiled equity returns from a variety of indexes. The early period made use of data from Lamberton's (1958) classic study. This is linked over the period 1958–74 to an accumulation index of fifty shares from the Australian Graduate School of Management (AGSM) and over 1975–79 to the AGSM value-weighted accumulation index. Subsequently, we use the Australia All-Ordinary index.

Bond returns are based on the yields on New South Wales government securities from the start of the century until 1914. For the period 1915–49 the yields were on Commonwealth Government Securities of at least five years maturity. During 1950–86 the basis is ten-year Commonwealth Government Bonds. From 1987 we use the JP Morgan Australian government bond index.

For 1900–28 the short-term rate of interest is taken as the three-month time deposit rate. From 1929 onward we use the treasury bill rate.

Inflation is based on the GDP deflator (1900–01), retail price index (1902–48) and consumer price index (1949 onward).

The switch in 1966 from Australian pounds to Australian dollars has been incorporated throughout the index history. Note that the exchange rate for the Australian dollar is expressed as the value of that currency in terms of the US dollar.

Table 18-1: Distribution of Australian asset returns and risk premia, 1900–2000

Return	Asset	Mean returns % p.a.			Dispersion of annual returns %				
		Geometric	Arithmetic	SE	SD	Lowest return		Highest return	
Nominal returns	Equities	11.9	13.3	1.8	18.2	-27.3	1952	66.8	1983
	Bonds	5.2	5.8	1.1	11.3	-19.1	1973	53.8	1932
	Bills	4.5	4.6	0.4	4.1	0.7	1951	18.2	1989
	Inflation	4.1	4.2	0.5	5.5	-9.9	1921	24.9	1951
Real returns	Equities	7.5	9.0	1.8	17.7	-34.2	1974	53.5	1983
	Bonds	1.1	1.9	1.3	13.0	-29.9	1951	60.5	1932
	Bills	0.4	0.6	0.6	5.6	-19.4	1951	16.6	1930
	Exchange rate	-0.6	-0.1	1.1	10.7	-39.0	1931	54.2	1933
Risk premia	Equities vs. bills	7.1	8.5	1.7	17.2	-30.2	1974	49.4	1983
	Equities vs. bonds	6.3	8.0	1.9	18.9	-30.6	1990	66.3	1980
	Bonds vs. bills	0.7	1.2	1.0	10.4	-23.3	1973	48.2	1932

Figure 18-1: Returns on Australian asset classes 1900–2000, in real terms

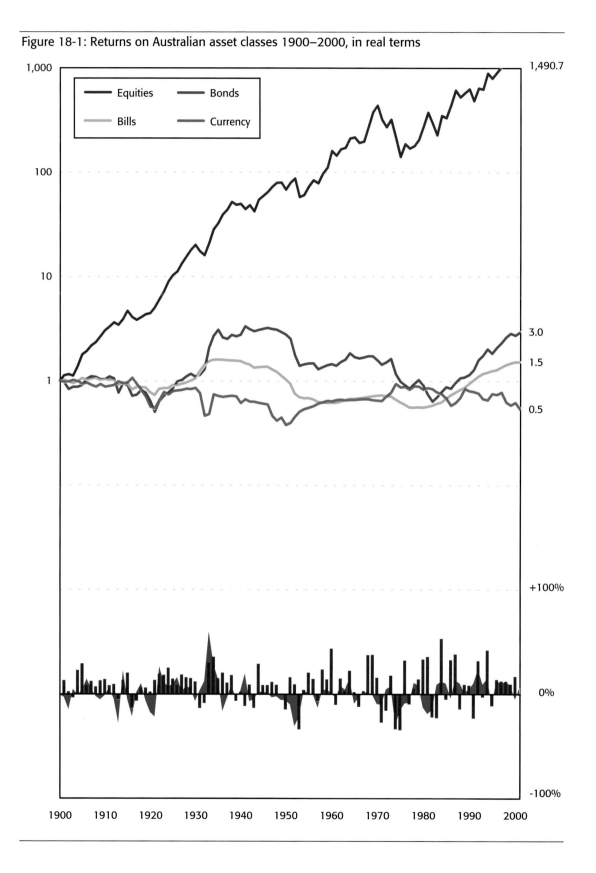

Table 18-2: Australian real rates of return and inflation over various periods, 1900–2000

Return	From ▶ To ▼	1900	1910	1920	1930	1940	1950	1960	1970	1980	1990	2000
Real return on equities	1909	11.8										
	1919	7.8	3.9									
	1929	10.5	9.9	16.3								
	1939	10.3	9.8	12.9	9.5							
	1949	8.8	8.1	9.5	6.3	3.2						
	1959	8.8	8.3	9.4	7.2	6.0	8.9					
	1969	9.1	8.6	9.6	8.0	7.5	9.8	10.6				
	1979	7.3	6.7	7.1	5.4	4.4	4.8	2.7	-4.6			
	1989	7.4	6.9	7.3	5.9	5.2	5.7	4.7	1.8	8.6		
	2000	7.5	7.0	7.4	6.2	5.7	6.2	5.6	4.0	8.3	8.1	-0.7
Real return on bonds	1909	0.5										
	1919	-2.1	-4.7									
	1929	0.4	0.3	5.6								
	1939	2.6	3.3	7.6	9.7							
	1949	2.1	2.5	5.0	4.8	0.1						
	1959	0.6	0.7	2.1	0.9	-3.2	-6.3					
	1969	0.7	0.7	1.8	0.9	-1.8	-2.8	0.9				
	1979	-0.1	-0.2	0.6	-0.4	-2.8	-3.7	-2.3	-5.5			
	1989	0.2	0.1	0.8	0.1	-1.7	-2.2	-0.8	-1.6	2.4		
	2000	1.1	1.2	1.9	1.4	0.1	0.1	1.7	2.0	5.8	8.8	7.1
Real return on bills	1909	0.4										
	1919	-1.3	-2.9									
	1929	0.2	0.1	3.2								
	1939	1.1	1.3	3.5	3.9							
	1949	0.1	0.0	1.0	-0.1	-3.9						
	1959	-0.8	-1.0	-0.6	-1.8	-4.5	-5.1					
	1969	-0.5	-0.6	-0.1	-0.9	-2.5	-1.8	1.6				
	1979	-0.7	-0.9	-0.5	-1.3	-2.5	-2.1	-0.5	-2.6			
	1989	-0.1	-0.1	0.3	-0.2	-1.0	-0.2	1.4	1.3	5.4		
	2000	0.4	0.4	0.8	0.5	0.0	0.7	2.2	2.4	4.9	4.4	0.0
Real exchange rate	1909	-1.3										
	1919	-2.8	-4.3									
	1929	-0.5	-0.1	4.3								
	1939	-1.2	-1.2	0.4	-3.3							
	1949	-1.9	-2.1	-1.3	-4.0	-4.7						
	1959	-0.7	-0.6	0.3	-1.0	0.2	5.3					
	1969	-0.6	-0.5	0.3	-0.7	0.2	2.7	0.2				
	1979	-0.2	-0.1	0.6	-0.1	0.7	2.6	1.3	2.4			
	1989	-0.2	-0.1	0.5	-0.1	0.5	1.9	0.8	1.1	-0.3		
	2000	-0.6	-0.5	-0.1	-0.6	-0.2	0.7	-0.4	-0.6	-2.0	-3.5	-13.1
Inflation rate	1909	1.1										
	1919	3.2	5.3									
	1929	2.3	3.0	0.7								
	1939	1.5	1.6	-0.1	-1.0							
	1949	2.3	2.5	1.6	2.1	5.3						
	1959	2.9	3.3	2.8	3.5	5.9	6.4					
	1969	2.9	3.2	2.8	3.3	4.7	4.4	2.5				
	1979	3.8	4.1	3.9	4.6	6.1	6.3	6.2	10.1			
	1989	4.2	4.6	4.6	5.2	6.5	6.8	6.9	9.2	8.3		
	2000	4.1	4.4	4.3	4.8	5.8	5.9	5.7	6.8	5.3	2.6	5.8

Figure 18-2: Nominal returns on Australian asset classes 1900–2000

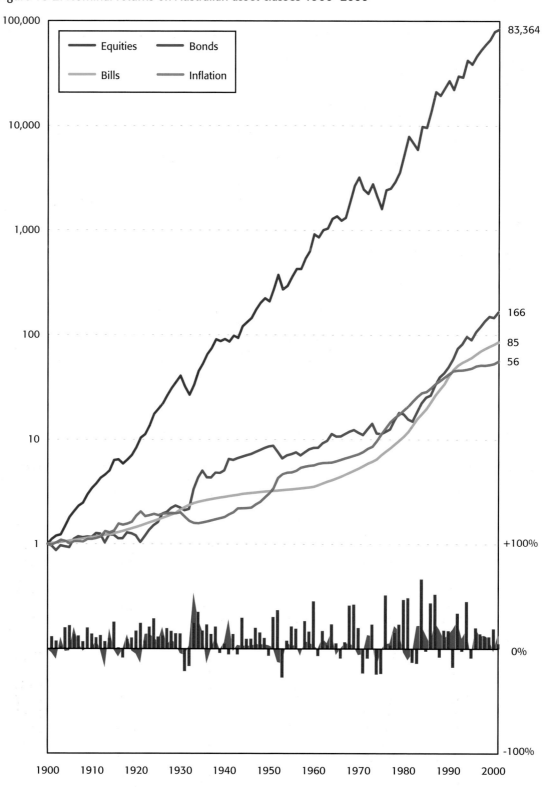

Table 18-3: Australian equity risk premia over various periods, 1900–2000

Premium	From ▶ To ▼	1900	1910	1920	1930	1940	1950	1960	1970	1980	1990	2000
Equity premium versus bills	1909	11.4										
	1919	9.1	7.0									
	1929	10.3	9.8	12.7								
	1939	9.1	8.3	9.0	5.4							
	1949	8.7	8.1	8.5	6.4	7.4						
	1959	9.7	9.4	10.0	9.1	11.0	14.8					
	1969	9.6	9.3	9.8	9.0	10.3	11.8	8.8				
	1979	8.1	7.6	7.7	6.7	7.1	7.0	3.2	-2.0			
	1989	7.5	7.0	7.0	6.1	6.3	6.0	3.2	0.5	3.1		
	2000	7.1	6.6	6.5	5.7	5.7	5.4	3.3	1.5	3.3	3.5	-0.7
Equity premium versus bonds	1909	11.3										
	1919	10.1	9.0									
	1929	10.1	9.6	10.1								
	1939	7.5	6.2	4.9	-0.2							
	1949	6.6	5.4	4.3	1.5	3.1						
	1959	8.1	7.5	7.2	6.2	9.5	16.3					
	1969	8.4	7.9	7.6	7.0	9.5	12.9	9.6				
	1979	7.4	6.9	6.5	5.8	7.3	8.8	5.2	1.0			
	1989	7.2	6.8	6.4	5.8	7.1	8.1	5.5	3.5	6.0		
	2000	6.3	5.8	5.4	4.8	5.6	6.1	3.8	2.0	2.4	-0.7	-7.3

Table 18-4: Australian real index values and inflation index, 1900–2000

Period	Start of	Equities	Bonds	Bills	Currency	Inflation
1900– 1990	1900	1.00	1.00	1.00	1.00	1.00
	1910	3.06	1.05	1.04	0.88	1.12
	1920	4.47	0.65	0.78	0.56	1.87
	1930	20.25	1.12	1.06	0.86	2.01
	1940	50.18	2.81	1.56	0.62	1.81
	1950	68.72	2.83	1.05	0.38	3.05
	1960	161.79	1.47	0.62	0.64	5.68
	1970	441.87	1.61	0.73	0.65	7.25
	1980	277.31	0.92	0.56	0.83	19.03
	1990	635.47	1.17	0.95	0.80	42.26
1991– 2001	1991	490.57	1.30	1.02	0.79	45.15
	1992	648.74	1.62	1.11	0.76	45.83
	1993	631.98	1.78	1.18	0.67	45.96
	1994	901.12	2.06	1.22	0.66	46.85
	1995	802.55	1.87	1.25	0.75	48.05
	1996	918.18	2.13	1.29	0.74	50.47
	1997	1036.46	2.35	1.36	0.78	51.24
	1998	1166.11	2.67	1.44	0.63	51.11
	1999	1281.48	2.90	1.49	0.59	51.92
	2000	1501.71	2.77	1.53	0.62	52.86
	2001	1490.68	2.97	1.53	0.54	55.92

Chapter 19 Belgium

Annaert, Buelens, de Ceuster, Cuyvers, Devos, Gemis, Houtman-deSmedt, and Paredaens (1998) are researching long-term Belgian returns. We are grateful for access to their interim results, which are subject to correction. The background to this study at the University of Antwerp's SCOB center is described in Buelens (2001).

For 1900–14 equity returns and capital gains we use SCOB's stock indexes (see van Nieuwerburgh and Buelens, 2000). The 1914 return runs to July, and equity prices then remain unchanged over the period of the First World War. Data for 1919–25 are from GFD. From 1926 we use the National Bank of Belgium's 80-share index. The market was closed from August 1944 to May 1945, and we take the closing level for 1944 as the year-end value. For 1946–79 we use the all-share index, which covers some four to five hundred stocks, and for 1980–97 the Brussels Stock Exchange index, switching after that to the Datastream Belgian total market index. Over 1914–25 and 1940–51 we assume the pre-war level of dividends remained unaltered in nominal terms. For 1952–97 we add Belgian dividend yields to produce a total return, and thereafter the index is available in a total return version.

Up to 1956, bond returns are based on estimated prices for 4 percent government bonds. During the 1944–45 closure, we take the last available value from 1944 as the year-end level. Over 1957–67 the index is for bonds with a five to twenty year maturity, and for 1968–86 for bonds with a maturity over five years. From 1987, we use the JP Morgan Belgian bond index.

Short-term interest rates are represented over the period 1900–26 by the central bank discount rate, followed during 1927–56 by the commercial bill rate. From 1957 onward, we use the return on treasury bills. Inflation is estimated for 1900–13 using the consumer price index, and for 1914 is assumed unchanged from the previous year-end. Over 1915–20 and 1941–46 we interpolate the Belgian consumer price index from Mitchell (1998). From 1921 inflation is measured using the Institut National de Statistique's consumer price index.

Table 19-1: Distribution of Belgian asset returns and risk premia, 1900–2000

Return	Asset	Mean returns % p.a.			Dispersion of annual returns %				
		Geometric	Arithmetic	SE	SD	Lowest return		Highest return	
Nominal	Equities	8.2	10.5	2.4	24.1	-36.0	1931	123.3	1940
returns	Bonds	5.1	5.6	1.0	10.0	-15.5	1914	40.8	1958
	Bills	5.2	5.2	0.3	3.0	0.7	1944	14.1	1981
	Inflation	5.5	5.9	0.9	9.0	-12.4	1904	29.5	1915
Real	Equities	2.5	4.8	2.3	22.8	-40.9	1947	100.5	1940
returns	Bonds	-0.4	0.3	1.2	12.1	-26.8	1920	40.5	1958
	Bills	-0.3	0.0	0.8	8.2	-19.7	1920	19.3	1921
	Exchange rate	0.2	1.0	1.3	13.3	-32.1	1919	54.2	1933
Risk	Equities vs. bills	2.9	5.1	2.3	23.5	-38.1	1947	120.6	1940
premia	Equities vs. bonds	2.9	4.8	2.1	20.7	-35.1	1930	76.6	1940
	Bonds vs. bills	-0.1	0.3	0.9	9.4	-19.6	1914	34.0	1958

Figure 19-1: Returns on Belgian asset classes 1900–2000, in real terms

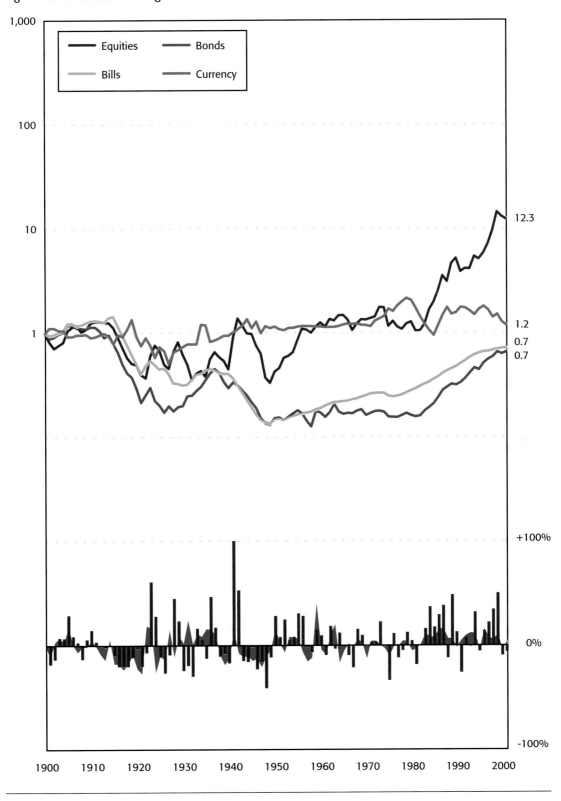

Table 19-2: Belgian real rates of return and inflation over various periods, 1900–2000

Return	To	1900	1910	1920	1930	1940	1950	1960	1970	1980	1990	2000
Real return on equities	1909	2.2										
	1919	-3.5	-8.8									
	1929	-1.6	-3.4	2.3								
	1939	-2.0	-3.3	-0.5	-3.2							
	1949	-1.7	-2.7	-0.5	-1.9	-0.5						
	1959	0.4	0.0	2.4	2.4	5.3	11.5					
	1969	0.4	0.1	2.0	1.9	3.7	5.9	0.6				
	1979	0.3	0.0	1.6	1.5	2.7	3.7	0.1	-0.5			
	1989	1.9	1.8	3.4	3.6	5.0	6.5	4.8	7.0	15.1		
	2000	2.5	2.5	4.0	4.3	5.6	6.8	5.7	7.4	11.4	8.1	-6.0
Real return on bonds	1909	1.4										
	1919	-5.9	-12.7									
	1929	-5.2	-8.4	-3.8								
	1939	-3.0	-4.4	0.1	4.1							
	1949	-3.7	-4.9	-2.2	-1.4	-6.5						
	1959	-2.9	-3.7	-1.3	-0.5	-2.7	1.2					
	1969	-2.6	-3.2	-1.2	-0.5	-2.0	0.3	-0.6				
	1979	-2.3	-2.8	-1.0	-0.4	-1.5	0.2	-0.3	0.0			
	1989	-1.3	-1.6	0.1	0.8	0.1	1.9	2.1	3.4	7.0		
	2000	-0.4	-0.6	1.0	1.7	1.3	2.9	3.3	4.6	6.9	6.8	4.4
Real return on bills	1909	2.6										
	1919	-3.4	-9.1									
	1929	-3.8	-6.9	-4.6								
	1939	-2.2	-3.8	-1.1	2.6							
	1949	-3.8	-5.3	-4.0	-3.7	-9.6						
	1959	-2.7	-3.8	-2.4	-1.7	-3.8	2.5					
	1969	-2.0	-2.7	-1.4	-0.6	-1.6	2.7	2.8				
	1979	-1.6	-2.2	-1.0	-0.2	-0.9	2.1	2.0	1.1			
	1989	-0.8	-1.3	-0.1	0.7	0.3	3.0	3.1	3.3	5.5		
	2000	-0.3	-0.7	0.4	1.2	0.9	3.1	3.3	3.5	4.6	3.8	1.5
Real exchange rate	1909	-1.0										
	1919	-0.4	0.1									
	1929	-1.0	-1.0	-2.2								
	1939	-0.2	0.1	0.1	2.5							
	1949	0.3	0.6	0.8	2.3	2.0						
	1959	0.2	0.5	0.6	1.5	1.0	0.0					
	1969	0.2	0.5	0.5	1.2	0.8	0.1	0.3				
	1979	0.9	1.2	1.4	2.1	2.0	1.9	2.9	5.7			
	1989	0.5	0.7	0.8	1.3	1.0	0.8	1.0	1.4	-2.7		
	2000	0.2	0.3	0.3	0.7	0.4	0.1	0.1	0.0	-2.6	-2.5	-6.9
Inflation rate	1909	1.3										
	1919	8.1	15.3									
	1929	8.6	12.4	9.6								
	1939	6.0	7.6	4.0	-1.3							
	1949	7.4	9.0	7.0	5.7	13.2						
	1959	6.5	7.6	5.7	4.5	7.5	2.1					
	1969	6.0	6.8	5.1	4.1	5.9	2.4	2.8				
	1979	6.1	6.8	5.5	4.7	6.2	4.0	4.9	7.1			
	1989	6.0	6.6	5.4	4.7	5.9	4.2	4.9	5.9	4.8		
	2000	5.5	6.0	4.9	4.3	5.2	3.7	4.1	4.6	3.4	2.1	2.7

Figure 19-2: Nominal returns on Belgian asset classes 1900–2000

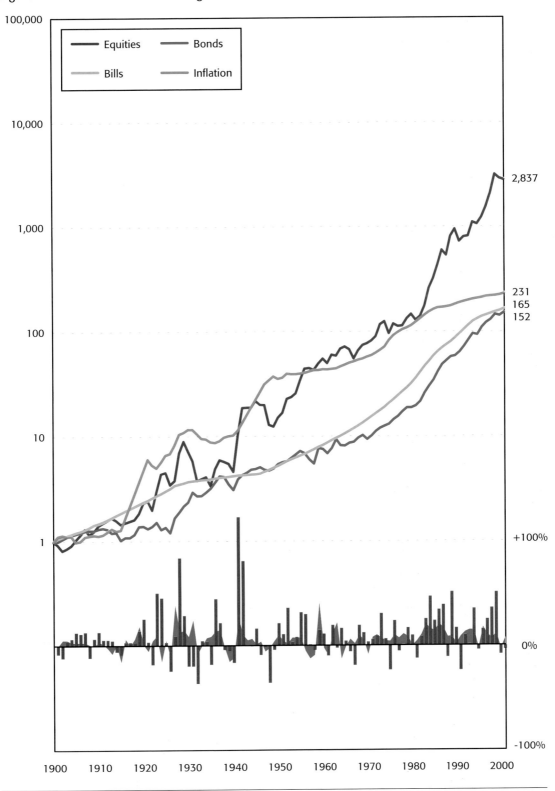

Figure 20-1: Returns on Canadian asset classes 1900–2000, in real terms

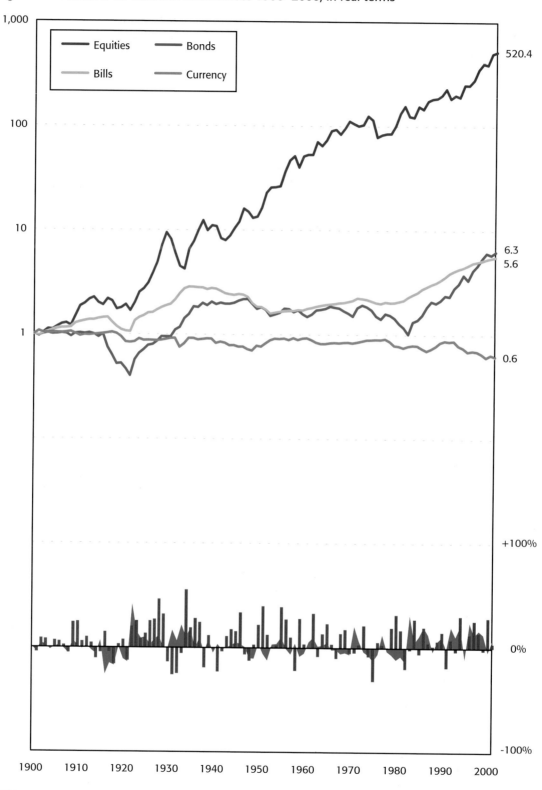

Table 20-2: Canadian real rates of return and inflation over various periods, 1900–2000

Return	From ▶ To ▼	1900	1910	1920	1930	1940	1950	1960	1970	1980	1990	2000
Real return on equities	1909	6.4										
	1919	3.3	0.4									
	1929	7.2	7.7	15.5								
	1939	6.1	6.1	9.0	2.9							
	1949	5.8	5.6	7.4	3.6	4.2						
	1959	6.8	6.9	8.7	6.5	8.3	12.5					
	1969	6.9	7.0	8.3	6.6	7.9	9.8	7.1				
	1979	6.3	6.3	7.3	5.8	6.5	7.2	4.7	2.4			
	1989	6.2	6.2	7.1	5.7	6.3	6.8	5.0	3.9	5.5		
	2000	6.4	6.4	7.2	6.0	6.6	7.0	5.7	5.3	6.7	7.8	4.0
Real return on bonds	1909	0.2										
	1919	-3.7	-7.6									
	1929	-0.2	-0.4	7.3								
	1939	1.7	2.2	7.4	7.5							
	1949	1.2	1.5	4.7	3.4	-0.6						
	1959	0.7	0.8	2.9	1.5	-1.3	-2.1					
	1969	0.6	0.6	2.4	1.2	-0.8	-1.0	0.1				
	1979	0.3	0.3	1.7	0.6	-1.0	-1.2	-0.7	-1.6			
	1989	1.0	1.1	2.4	1.5	0.4	0.7	1.6	2.3	6.4		
	2000	1.8	2.0	3.3	2.7	1.9	2.5	3.6	4.7	7.9	9.3	7.0
Real return on bills	1909	2.8										
	1919	0.4	-2.0									
	1929	2.2	2.0	6.1								
	1939	2.6	2.5	4.8	3.5							
	1949	1.2	0.8	1.8	-0.3	-3.9						
	1959	1.0	0.6	1.3	-0.3	-2.1	-0.3					
	1969	1.1	0.8	1.4	0.2	-0.8	0.8	1.9				
	1979	0.9	0.7	1.1	0.2	-0.7	0.4	0.8	-0.2			
	1989	1.4	1.3	1.7	1.0	0.5	1.7	2.4	2.6	5.5		
	2000	1.7	1.6	2.1	1.5	1.2	2.2	2.8	3.2	4.8	4.1	2.1
Real exchange rate	1909	-0.5										
	1919	-0.9	-1.3									
	1929	-0.3	-0.3	0.8								
	1939	-0.5	-0.5	-0.1	-1.0							
	1949	-0.5	-0.6	-0.3	-0.9	-0.7						
	1959	-0.1	-0.1	0.2	0.1	0.6	1.9					
	1969	-0.3	-0.2	0.0	-0.2	0.0	0.4	-1.1				
	1979	-0.3	-0.3	-0.1	-0.3	-0.1	0.1	-0.9	-0.7			
	1989	-0.2	-0.1	0.1	-0.1	0.1	0.3	-0.2	0.2	1.2		
	2000	-0.5	-0.5	-0.4	-0.5	-0.5	-0.4	-1.0	-0.9	-1.1	-3.1	-3.5
Inflation rate	1909	1.9										
	1919	4.3	6.8									
	1929	2.6	2.9	-0.9								
	1939	1.4	1.3	-1.3	-1.8							
	1949	2.1	2.1	0.6	1.3	4.5						
	1959	2.1	2.2	1.0	1.7	3.5	2.4					
	1969	2.2	2.2	1.4	1.9	3.2	2.5	2.6				
	1979	2.8	3.0	2.4	3.0	4.3	4.2	5.1	7.6			
	1989	3.2	3.4	2.9	3.5	4.7	4.7	5.5	6.9	6.2		
	2000	3.1	3.2	2.8	3.3	4.2	4.1	4.6	5.2	4.1	2.2	3.2

Figure 20-2: Nominal returns on Canadian asset classes 1900–2000

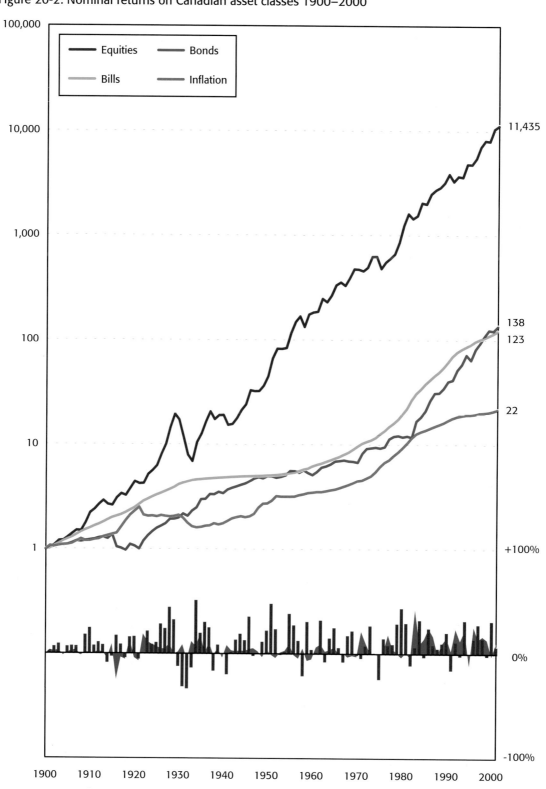

Table 20-3: Canadian equity risk premia over various periods, 1900–2000

Premium	From ▶ To ▼	1900	1910	1920	1930	1940	1950	1960	1970	1980	1990	2000
Equity premium versus bills	1909	3.5										
	1919	2.9	2.4									
	1929	4.9	5.6	8.8								
	1939	3.5	3.5	4.1	-0.5							
	1949	4.5	4.7	5.5	3.9	8.4						
	1959	5.8	6.3	7.3	6.8	10.6	12.9					
	1969	5.7	6.1	6.9	6.4	8.8	9.0	5.2				
	1979	5.3	5.6	6.1	5.6	7.2	6.8	3.9	2.5			
	1989	4.7	4.9	5.2	4.6	5.7	5.0	2.5	1.2	0.0		
	2000	4.6	4.7	5.0	4.5	5.3	4.7	2.8	2.1	1.8	3.5	1.9
Equity premium versus bonds	1909	6.1										
	1919	7.3	8.6									
	1929	7.4	8.1	7.6								
	1939	4.4	3.8	1.5	-4.2							
	1949	4.5	4.1	2.6	0.2	4.9						
	1959	6.1	6.1	5.5	4.9	9.7	14.8					
	1969	6.3	6.3	5.8	5.4	8.8	10.8	7.0				
	1979	6.0	6.0	5.5	5.1	7.6	8.5	5.5	4.0			
	1989	5.2	5.1	4.6	4.1	5.9	6.1	3.4	1.6	-0.8		
	2000	4.5	4.3	3.8	3.2	4.5	4.5	2.1	0.5	-1.1	-1.3	-2.7

Table 20-4: Canadian real index values and inflation index, 1900–2000

Period	Start of	Equities	Bonds	Bills	Currency	Inflation
1900–1990	1900	1.00	1.00	1.00	1.00	1.00
	1910	1.85	1.02	1.32	0.96	1.21
	1920	1.92	0.47	1.08	0.84	2.33
	1930	8.11	0.94	1.95	0.91	2.14
	1940	10.82	1.94	2.74	0.82	1.78
	1950	16.37	1.83	1.84	0.76	2.77
	1960	53.01	1.49	1.78	0.92	3.51
	1970	105.60	1.51	2.14	0.83	4.56
	1980	133.35	1.28	2.10	0.78	9.45
	1990	227.62	2.37	3.60	0.87	17.29
1991–2001	1991	184.56	2.34	3.91	0.86	18.15
	1992	198.49	2.80	4.13	0.87	18.84
	1993	191.35	3.10	4.30	0.79	19.24
	1994	249.10	3.75	4.46	0.75	19.57
	1995	248.02	3.35	4.68	0.69	19.60
	1996	279.12	4.16	4.95	0.70	19.95
	1997	350.63	4.65	5.06	0.69	20.39
	1998	400.00	5.42	5.18	0.66	20.54
	1999	389.54	6.12	5.38	0.61	20.75
	2000	500.26	5.88	5.50	0.64	21.28
	2001	520.44	6.29	5.61	0.62	21.97

Chapter 21 Denmark

We are grateful to Claus Parum for extensive help, and have drawn heavily both on Parum (1999a,b), and also on his more recent research extending back to 1900 (Parum, 2001). We have also referred to the papers by Steen Nielsen and Ole Risager (1999, 2000) and utilized part of Allan Timmermann's (1992) series.

Over the period 1900–14 we use Parum's (2001) equally weighted index of equity returns, which covers some forty to fifty constituents each year. Thereafter, all the studies cited above are based on equity price indexes from Statistics Denmark, though we incorporate Parum's adjustments for capital changes that are not incorporated into the published index numbers. For 1915–20 we employ Timmermann's (1992) equity price series and for 1921–24 we use the Statistics Denmark series (see Lund, 1992), both with dividends from Hansen (1976). For 1925–98 we use the data compiled in Parum (1999a,b) switching thereafter to the Copenhagen KAX Index.

Danish bond returns are estimated from yields on government bonds until 1924. For 1925–98 our data is from Parum (1999a,b) who uses the return on mortgage bonds, a large and liquid asset class throughout the period, in contrast to more thinly traded government bonds, as described in Christiansen and Lystbaek (1994). Starting in 1999, we switch to the Datastream ten-year Danish government bond index.

Short-term interest rates are represented by the central bank discount rate until 1975, and thereafter by the return on treasury bills.

Inflation is measured throughout the century by the consumer price index. The index is provided over the period 1922–99 in Nielsen and Risager (2000) and is supplemented for the interval before that using inflation data from Mitchell (1998).

Table 21-1: Distribution of Danish asset returns and risk premia, 1900–2000

Return	Asset	Mean returns % p.a.			Dispersion of annual returns %				
		Geometric	Arithmetic	SE	SD	Lowest return		Highest return	
Nominal	Equities	8.9	10.7	2.2	21.7	-24.5	1992	120.4	1983
returns	Bonds	6.8	7.3	1.1	11.0	-14.5	1919	59.2	1983
	Bills	7.0	7.1	0.4	4.5	2.5	1933	22.1	1982
	Inflation	4.1	4.3	0.6	6.5	-15.0	1926	25.9	1916
Real	Equities	4.6	6.2	2.0	20.1	-28.4	1974	106.1	1983
returns	Bonds	2.5	3.3	1.2	12.5	-26.3	1919	48.9	1983
	Bills	2.8	3.0	0.6	6.4	-16.6	1916	23.6	1926
	Exchange rate	0.1	1.0	1.3	12.7	-50.3	1946	37.2	1933
Risk	Equities vs. bills	1.8	3.4	1.9	19.4	-32.7	1992	87.0	1983
premia	Equities vs. bonds	2.0	3.3	1.7	16.9	-35.9	1922	74.9	1972
	Bonds vs. bills	-0.2	0.2	0.9	9.2	-20.0	1986	35.1	1983

Figure 21-1: Returns on Danish asset classes 1900–2000, in real terms

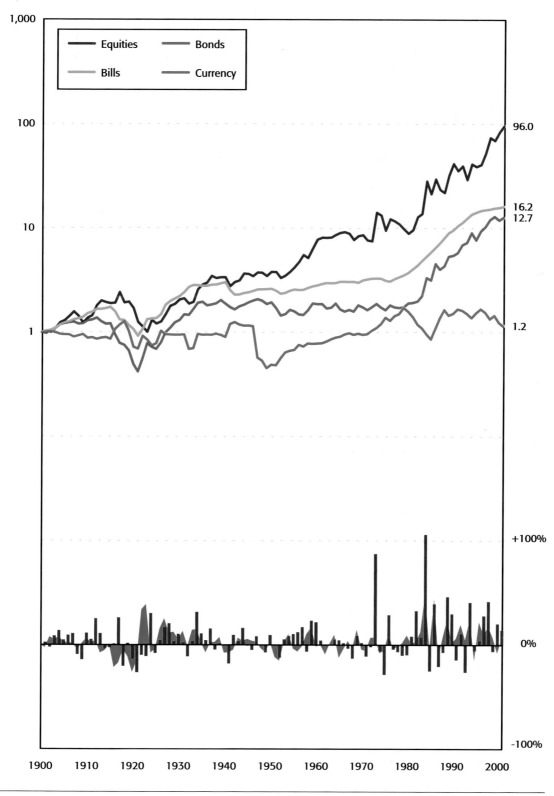

Table 21-2: Danish real rates of return and inflation over various periods, 1900–2000

Return	From ▶ To ▼	1900	1910	1920	1930	1940	1950	1960	1970	1980	1990	2000
Real return on equities	1909	3.2										
	1919	2.7	2.2									
	1929	2.4	2.1	1.9								
	1939	3.1	3.0	3.5	5.0							
	1949	2.7	2.6	2.7	3.1	1.2						
	1959	3.5	3.5	3.9	4.5	4.3	7.5					
	1969	3.1	3.1	3.3	3.6	3.2	4.2	1.0				
	1979	2.8	2.7	2.8	3.0	2.5	2.9	0.7	0.3			
	1989	4.2	4.4	4.7	5.1	5.2	6.2	5.7	8.2	16.7		
	2000	4.6	4.8	5.1	5.6	5.6	6.5	6.3	8.1	12.0	7.9	14.4
Real return on bonds	1909	2.6										
	1919	-3.5	-9.2									
	1929	0.9	0.1	10.3								
	1939	1.6	1.3	6.9	3.7							
	1949	1.3	1.0	4.7	2.0	0.3						
	1959	1.0	0.7	3.4	1.2	0.0	-0.3					
	1969	0.8	0.5	2.6	0.7	-0.3	-0.5	-0.7				
	1979	0.8	0.6	2.3	0.8	0.0	0.0	0.1	0.9			
	1989	1.9	1.8	3.5	2.4	2.2	2.6	3.6	5.9	11.1		
	2000	2.5	2.5	4.1	3.3	3.2	3.8	4.8	6.6	9.5	8.0	6.5
Real return on bills	1909	4.3										
	1919	0.3	-3.4									
	1929	2.7	1.9	7.6								
	1939	2.8	2.3	5.3	3.1							
	1949	1.9	1.4	3.0	0.8	-1.5						
	1959	1.7	1.3	2.5	0.8	-0.3	0.8					
	1969	1.7	1.2	2.2	0.9	0.1	1.0	1.1				
	1979	1.7	1.3	2.1	1.1	0.5	1.2	1.4	1.7			
	1989	2.5	2.3	3.2	2.5	2.3	3.3	4.2	5.7	9.9		
	2000	2.8	2.6	3.4	2.8	2.8	3.6	4.3	5.4	7.2	4.8	2.5
Real exchange rate	1909	-1.3										
	1919	-1.6	-1.9									
	1929	-0.2	0.4	2.7								
	1939	-0.3	0.1	1.1	-0.5							
	1949	-1.4	-1.5	-1.3	-3.2	-5.9						
	1959	-0.4	-0.2	0.2	-0.6	-0.7	4.8					
	1969	-0.1	0.1	0.5	0.0	0.2	3.4	2.0				
	1979	0.6	0.8	1.3	1.0	1.4	4.0	3.6	5.2			
	1989	0.5	0.7	1.1	0.8	1.1	2.9	2.2	2.4	-0.4		
	2000	0.1	0.3	0.6	0.3	0.4	1.7	1.0	0.6	-1.5	-2.5	-7.5
Inflation rate	1909	1.0										
	1919	5.0	9.1									
	1929	2.7	3.5	-1.9								
	1939	2.2	2.6	-0.6	0.8							
	1949	2.8	3.2	1.3	2.9	5.1						
	1959	3.0	3.3	2.0	3.3	4.5	4.0					
	1969	3.3	3.7	2.6	3.8	4.8	4.7	5.4				
	1979	4.0	4.5	3.7	4.9	5.9	6.2	7.3	9.3			
	1989	4.3	4.8	4.2	5.2	6.1	6.4	7.2	8.1	6.9		
	2000	4.1	4.4	3.9	4.7	5.4	5.4	5.8	5.9	4.4	2.1	2.4

Figure 21-2: Nominal returns on Danish asset classes 1900–2000

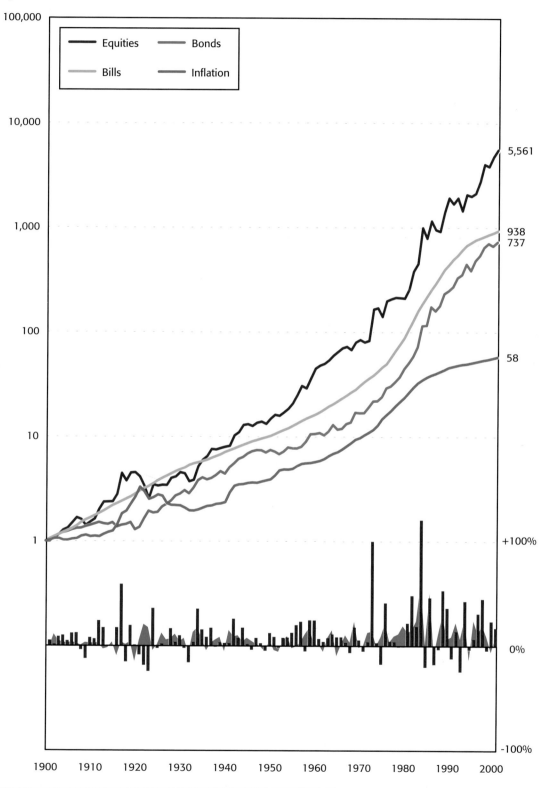

Table 21-3: Danish equity risk premia over various periods, 1900–2000

Premium	From ▶ To ▼	1900	1910	1920	1930	1940	1950	1960	1970	1980	1990	2000
Equity	1909	-1.0										
premium	1919	2.4	5.8									
versus	1929	-0.3	0.1	-5.3								
bills	1939	0.3	0.7	-1.8	1.9							
	1949	0.8	1.2	-0.3	2.3	2.7						
	1959	1.7	2.3	1.4	3.7	4.6	6.6					
	1969	1.4	1.9	1.1	2.7	3.0	3.2	-0.1				
	1979	1.1	1.4	0.7	1.9	1.9	1.6	-0.7	-1.4			
	1989	1.6	2.0	1.4	2.6	2.8	2.8	1.5	2.4	6.2		
	2000	1.8	2.1	1.6	2.6	2.8	2.8	1.9	2.5	4.4	2.9	11.6
Equity	1909	0.6										
premium	1919	6.4	12.6									
versus	1929	1.5	2.0	-7.6								
bonds	1939	1.5	1.8	-3.2	1.3							
	1949	1.4	1.6	-1.9	1.1	0.9						
	1959	2.4	2.8	0.5	3.3	4.3	7.8					
	1969	2.3	2.6	0.7	2.9	3.5	4.7	1.7				
	1979	1.9	2.1	0.5	2.2	2.4	2.9	0.6	-0.6			
	1989	2.3	2.5	1.1	2.7	2.9	3.4	2.0	2.2	5.0		
	2000	2.0	2.2	1.0	2.2	2.4	2.7	1.4	1.4	2.3	-0.1	7.4

Table 21-4: Danish real index values and inflation index, 1900–2000

Period	Start of	Equities	Bonds	Bills	Currency	Inflation
1900– **1990**	1900	1.00	1.00	1.00	1.00	1.00
	1910	1.37	1.29	1.52	0.88	1.11
	1920	1.70	0.49	1.07	0.73	2.65
	1930	2.06	1.30	2.23	0.95	2.19
	1940	3.37	1.88	3.03	0.90	2.37
	1950	3.80	1.93	2.61	0.49	3.90
	1960	7.80	1.86	2.83	0.78	5.76
	1970	8.62	1.73	3.16	0.95	9.75
	1980	8.92	1.91	3.75	1.59	23.65
	1990	41.74	5.46	9.62	1.53	45.93
1991– **2001**	1991	35.78	5.80	10.54	1.68	47.13
	1992	39.78	6.94	11.34	1.63	48.27
	1993	29.41	7.26	12.45	1.53	49.28
	1994	41.47	9.03	13.63	1.39	49.88
	1995	39.20	7.69	14.21	1.54	50.90
	1996	40.87	9.37	14.78	1.69	51.96
	1997	52.33	10.27	15.04	1.57	53.06
	1998	74.25	12.06	15.28	1.36	54.22
	1999	69.63	12.93	15.63	1.47	55.25
	2000	83.91	11.94	15.79	1.25	56.61
	2001	95.98	12.71	16.19	1.16	57.95

Chapter 22 France

The primary studies that we use for France are Laforest and Sallee (1977), for the first half of the twentieth century, followed by Gallais-Hamonno and Arbulu (1995) for the period commencing in 1950. We are grateful to Georges Gallais-Hamonno for sending us his database, which underpins the computations presented here.

The common basis for equities is the index series compiled by the Institut National de la Statistique et des Etudes Economiques (INSEE). The INSEE equity index is a weighted average of price relatives with about three hundred constituents. We use the SBF-250 from 1991 onward.

The bond series for France, also compiled by INSEE, is based on consol yields until we switch in 1950 to the Gallais-Hamonno and Arbulu (1995) series, which is the INSEE General Bonds Index, with coupons reinvested monthly as received. From 1993 we use the JP Morgan French government bond index.

The short-term interest rate for France is based on the central bank discount rate until 1930. The rate is measured by the return on treasury bills starting in 1931.

To measure consumer price inflation, we use the consumption price index that is compiled by the Institut National de la Statistique et des Etudes Economiques.

Table 22-1: Distribution of French asset returns and risk premia, 1900–2000

Return	Asset	Mean returns % p.a.			Dispersion of annual returns %				
		Geometric	Arithmetic	SE	SD	Lowest return		Highest return	
Nominal returns	Equities	12.1	14.5	2.4	24.6	-32.4	1931	82.0	1941
	Bonds	6.8	7.1	0.8	8.4	-12.4	1914	30.1	1927
	Bills	4.3	4.3	0.2	2.3	1.0	1932	10.8	1974
	Inflation	7.9	8.8	1.5	14.6	-23.8	1921	74.0	1946
Real returns	Equities	3.8	6.3	2.3	23.1	-37.5	1947	66.1	1954
	Bonds	-1.0	0.1	1.4	14.4	-43.7	1946	49.1	1927
	Bills	-3.3	-2.6	1.1	11.4	-41.7	1946	38.9	1921
	Exchange rate	-0.4	2.5	2.4	24.0	-78.3	1946	141.5	1943
Risk premia	Equities vs. bills	7.4	9.8	2.4	23.8	-33.4	1931	78.7	1941
	Equities vs. bonds	4.9	7.0	2.1	21.6	-32.7	1931	83.7	1946
	Bonds vs. bills	2.4	2.7	0.8	7.5	-15.8	1914	23.6	1927

Figure 22-1: Returns on French asset classes 1900–2000, in real terms

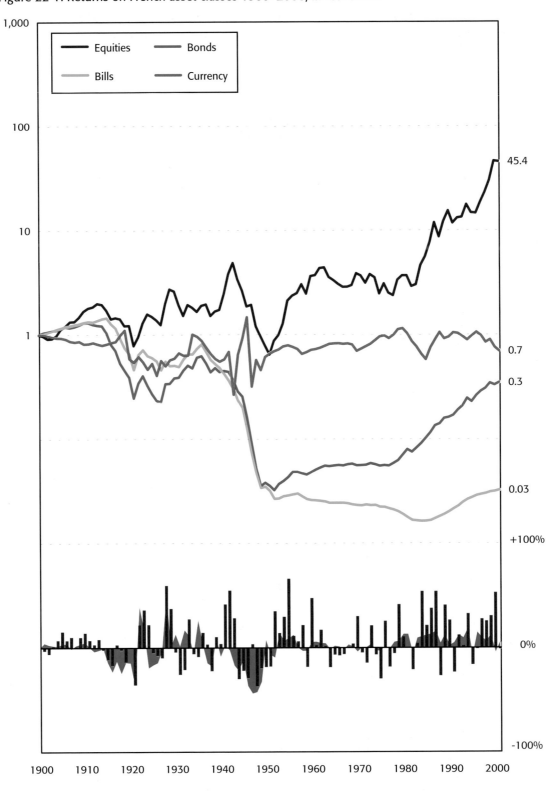

Table 22-2: French real rates of return and inflation over various periods, 1900–2000

Return	From ▶ / To ▼	1900	1910	1920	1930	1940	1950	1960	1970	1980	1990	2000
Real return on equities	1909	5.3										
	1919	1.0	-3.1									
	1929	3.2	2.2	7.9								
	1939	1.4	0.1	1.8	-4.0							
	1949	-0.5	-1.9	-1.5	-5.8	-7.6						
	1959	2.2	1.6	2.8	1.1	3.8	16.5					
	1969	1.9	1.4	2.3	1.0	2.7	8.3	0.6				
	1979	1.6	1.1	1.9	0.7	1.9	5.3	0.1	-0.5			
	1989	3.1	2.8	3.7	3.0	4.5	7.7	4.9	7.2	15.4		
	2000	3.8	3.7	4.6	4.1	5.5	8.3	6.4	8.3	12.7	10.3	-1.6
Real return on bonds	1909	2.7										
	1919	-4.6	-11.4									
	1929	-3.1	-5.9	-0.1								
	1939	-2.0	-3.6	0.6	1.4							
	1949	-6.3	-8.5	-7.5	-10.9	-21.7						
	1959	-4.9	-6.4	-5.1	-6.7	-10.5	2.4					
	1969	-4.0	-5.1	-3.8	-4.7	-6.7	1.9	1.5				
	1979	-3.3	-4.1	-2.8	-3.3	-4.5	2.1	1.9	2.4			
	1989	-2.0	-2.6	-1.3	-1.4	-2.0	3.7	4.1	5.4	8.6		
	2000	-1.0	-1.4	-0.1	-0.1	-0.4	4.4	4.9	6.1	7.9	7.3	5.4
Real return on bills	1909	2.8										
	1919	-2.1	-6.8									
	1929	-2.2	-4.7	-2.5								
	1939	-1.8	-3.3	-1.5	-0.5							
	1949	-6.5	-8.7	-9.3	-12.5	-23.1						
	1959	-5.9	-7.5	-7.7	-9.4	-13.6	-2.9					
	1969	-5.2	-6.5	-6.4	-7.4	-9.6	-2.0	-1.1				
	1979	-4.8	-5.9	-5.7	-6.4	-7.8	-2.0	-1.5	-2.0			
	1989	-4.2	-5.1	-4.8	-5.2	-6.2	-1.4	-0.8	-0.7	0.6		
	2000	-3.3	-4.0	-3.6	-3.8	-4.3	-0.1	0.5	1.1	2.6	4.4	2.6
Real exchange rate	1909	-2.0										
	1919	-2.6	-3.2									
	1929	-1.7	-1.6	0.1								
	1939	-1.5	-1.3	-0.3	-0.7							
	1949	-1.0	-0.7	0.1	0.1	1.0						
	1959	-0.6	-0.3	0.5	0.6	1.3	1.5					
	1969	-0.5	-0.3	0.3	0.4	0.8	0.6	-0.2				
	1979	0.2	0.5	1.1	1.3	1.8	2.1	2.4	5.2			
	1989	-0.1	0.2	0.7	0.8	1.1	1.1	1.0	1.6	-1.9		
	2000	-0.4	-0.2	0.2	0.2	0.4	0.2	-0.1	0.0	-2.4	-2.8	-8.0
Inflation rate	1909	0.3										
	1919	5.9	11.9									
	1929	6.6	9.9	8.0								
	1939	5.7	7.5	5.4	2.9							
	1949	10.5	13.3	13.7	16.7	32.4						
	1959	9.8	11.8	11.8	13.1	18.5	6.0					
	1969	8.9	10.5	10.2	10.7	13.4	5.0	4.0				
	1979	8.9	10.2	9.9	10.3	12.3	6.3	6.4	8.8			
	1989	8.7	9.8	9.5	9.8	11.2	6.4	6.6	7.9	6.9		
	2000	7.9	8.8	8.4	8.5	9.4	5.4	5.3	5.7	4.2	1.8	1.6

Figure 22-2: Nominal returns on French asset classes 1900–2000

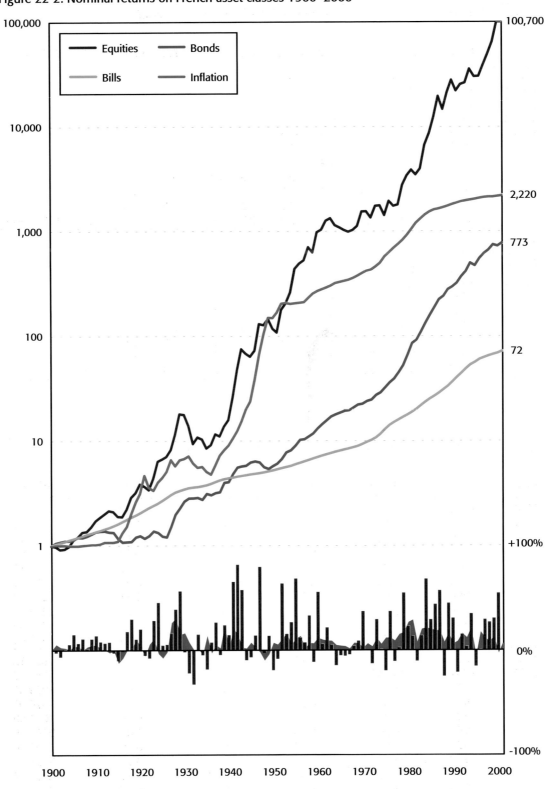

Table 22-3: French equity risk premia over various periods, 1900–2000

Premium	From ▶ To ▼	1900	1910	1920	1930	1940	1950	1960	1970	1980	1990	2000
Equity premium versus bills	1909	2.5										
	1919	3.2	3.9									
	1929	5.6	7.2	10.6								
	1939	3.3	3.5	3.3	-3.5							
	1949	6.4	7.5	8.7	7.7	20.2						
	1959	8.6	9.8	11.4	11.6	20.1	20.0					
	1969	7.6	8.4	9.4	9.1	13.6	10.5	1.7				
	1979	6.8	7.4	8.0	7.5	10.5	7.4	1.6	1.5			
	1989	7.7	8.3	9.0	8.7	11.3	9.2	5.8	7.9	14.7		
	2000	7.4	8.0	8.5	8.2	10.3	8.4	5.8	7.1	9.9	5.7	-4.1
Equity premium versus bonds	1909	2.5										
	1919	5.9	9.3									
	1929	6.6	8.7	8.0								
	1939	3.5	3.8	1.2	-5.3							
	1949	6.2	7.2	6.5	5.7	18.0						
	1959	7.5	8.5	8.3	8.4	15.9	13.8					
	1969	6.2	6.9	6.4	6.0	10.0	6.2	-0.9				
	1979	5.1	5.4	4.8	4.2	6.7	3.1	-1.8	-2.8			
	1989	5.2	5.5	5.0	4.5	6.6	3.9	0.8	1.6	6.2		
	2000	4.9	5.2	4.7	4.3	5.9	3.7	1.3	2.1	4.5	2.9	-6.6

Table 22-4: French real index values and inflation index, 1900–2000

Period	Start of	Equities	Bonds	Bills	Currency	Inflation
1900–1990	1900	1.00	1.00	1.00	1.00	1.00
	1910	1.68	1.31	1.31	0.82	1.03
	1920	1.22	0.39	0.65	0.59	3.16
	1930	2.61	0.39	0.51	0.60	6.82
	1940	1.74	0.44	0.48	0.55	9.11
	1950	0.79	0.04	0.03	0.61	150.51
	1960	3.63	0.05	0.03	0.71	270.68
	1970	3.86	0.06	0.02	0.70	401.36
	1980	3.67	0.07	0.02	1.15	933.54
	1990	15.36	0.16	0.02	0.95	1820.41
1991–2001	1991	11.73	0.17	0.02	1.05	1882.12
	1992	13.13	0.19	0.02	1.03	1940.65
	1993	13.34	0.21	0.02	0.96	1979.08
	1994	17.65	0.25	0.03	0.89	2020.03
	1995	14.74	0.23	0.03	0.98	2051.68
	1996	14.56	0.26	0.03	1.06	2094.50
	1997	18.51	0.29	0.03	0.99	2129.70
	1998	23.19	0.31	0.03	0.85	2153.90
	1999	30.19	0.34	0.03	0.90	2157.24
	2000	46.07	0.33	0.03	0.76	2185.29
	2001	45.36	0.35	0.03	0.70	2220.25

Table 23-2: German real rates of return and inflation over various periods, 1900–2000

Return	From ▶ To ▼	1900	1910	1920	1930	1940	1950	1960	1970	1980	1990	2000
Real	1909	3.6										
return	1919	-4.9	-12.7									
on	1929	-1.5	-3.9	5.8								
equities	1939	0.5	-0.6	6.1	6.5							
	1949	-1.8	-3.1	0.4	-2.2	-10.3						
	1959	2.2	1.9	5.9	6.0	5.7	24.6					
	1969	2.4	2.2	5.5	5.5	5.1	13.8	3.9				
	1979	1.8	1.5	4.1	3.8	3.2	8.1	0.7	-2.5			
	1989	3.1	3.0	5.5	5.5	5.2	9.5	4.9	5.4	14.0		
	2000	3.6	3.6	5.8	5.8	5.6	9.1	5.6	6.1	10.5	7.5	-11.8
Real	1909	-2.3										
return	1919	-11.3	-19.5									
on	1929	-9.1	-12.7	-3.3								
bonds＊	1939	-4.5	-5.3	3.6	9.5							
	1949	-8.2	-9.7	-5.9	-6.9	-20.8						
	1959	-6.2	-7.0	-3.4	-3.5	-9.4	3.8					
	1969	-4.9	-5.3	-2.1	-1.9	-5.4	3.5	3.1				
	1979	-4.1	-4.3	-1.4	-1.1	-3.6	2.9	2.5	1.9			
	1989	-3.1	-3.2	-0.5	-0.2	-2.0	3.4	3.2	3.3	4.7		
	2000	-2.2	-2.2	0.2	0.6	-0.8	3.7	3.7	3.9	4.9	5.1	5.0
Real	1909	1.8										
return	1919	-6.2	-13.6									
on	1929	-6.3	-10.5	-6.5								
bills＊	1939	-3.1	-4.8	0.5	6.4							
	1949	-3.0	-4.2	-0.6	1.9	-2.4						
	1959	-2.1	-2.9	0.1	1.9	-0.3	2.0					
	1969	-1.7	-2.3	0.2	1.6	0.0	1.3	0.6				
	1979	-1.5	-2.0	0.2	1.3	0.0	0.9	0.3	0.1			
	1989	-1.0	-1.3	0.6	1.6	0.7	1.5	1.3	1.7	3.3		
	2000	-0.6	-0.8	0.9	1.8	1.1	1.8	1.7	2.1	3.1	2.9	2.0
Real	1909	-0.5										
exchange	1919	-6.3	-11.8									
rate	1929	-0.4	-0.4	12.4								
	1939	-4.2	-5.5	-2.1	-14.8							
	1949	-1.2	-1.3	2.4	-2.2	12.2						
	1959	-0.5	-0.5	2.5	-0.6	7.3	2.7					
	1969	-0.2	-0.2	2.3	-0.1	5.3	2.1	1.4				
	1979	0.5	0.6	2.8	1.0	5.4	3.2	3.5	5.6			
	1989	0.2	0.3	2.1	0.5	3.9	1.9	1.6	1.7	-2.0		
	2000	-0.1	-0.1	1.5	0.0	2.7	1.0	0.5	0.2	-2.2	-2.5	-7.4
Inflation	1909	1.9										
rate	1919	10.9	20.7									
	1929	157.2	308.6	1283								
	1939	102.1	153.9	268.2	-2.0							
	1949	77.1	103.4	142.0	1.2	4.5						
	1959	61.3	76.9	94.6	1.2	2.8	1.2					
	1969	51.2	61.5	71.2	1.6	2.8	1.9	2.7				
	1979	44.5	51.9	57.9	2.3	3.4	3.0	3.9	5.1			
	1989	39.1	44.7	48.5	2.4	3.2	2.9	3.5	3.9	2.8		
	2000	34.6	38.8	41.2	2.4	3.1	2.8	3.2	3.4	2.6	2.4	2.2

＊ Real returns on bonds and bills exclude 1922–23

Figure 23-2: Nominal returns on German asset classes 1900–2000

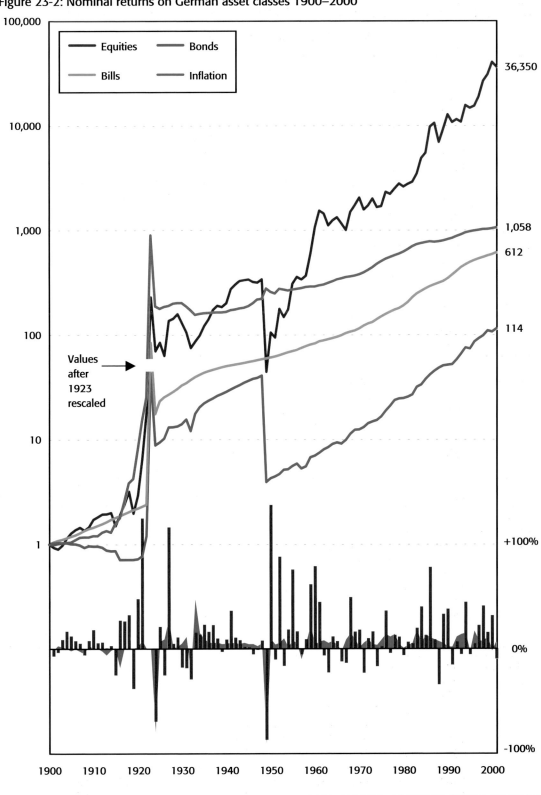

Table 23-3: German equity risk premia over various periods, 1900–2000

Premium[*]	From▶ To▼	1900	1910	1920	1930	1940	1950	1960	1970	1980	1990	2000
Equity	1909	1.8										
premium	1919	1.4	1.1									
versus	1929	7.5	10.8	24.3								
bills	1939	5.5	6.9	10.2	0.1							
	1949	2.5	2.7	3.3	-4.0	-8.0						
	1959	5.7	6.5	8.0	4.0	6.0	22.2					
	1969	5.3	5.9	7.0	3.8	5.1	12.4	3.3				
	1979	4.3	4.6	5.3	2.5	3.1	7.1	0.3	-2.6			
	1989	5.0	5.4	6.0	3.8	4.5	8.0	3.6	3.7	10.4		
	2000	4.9	5.3	5.8	3.9	4.5	7.2	3.8	4.0	7.2	4.4	-13.6
Equity	1909	6.1										
premium	1919	7.2	8.4									
versus	1929	10.8	13.6	20.3								
bonds	1939	7.1	7.4	6.9	-2.7							
	1949	8.3	9.0	9.2	5.0	13.3						
	1959	10.3	11.2	11.9	9.8	16.6	20.0					
	1969	8.8	9.3	9.5	7.5	11.1	10.0	0.8				
	1979	7.0	7.2	7.0	5.0	7.0	5.0	-1.8	-4.4			
	1989	7.3	7.4	7.3	5.6	7.4	6.0	1.6	2.1	8.9		
	2000	6.7	6.8	6.5	5.1	6.4	5.1	1.8	2.1	5.4	2.3	-16.0

[*] Risk premia exclude 1922–23

Table 23-4: German real index values and inflation index, 1900–2000

Period	Start of	Equities	Bonds[*]	Bills[*]	Currency	Inflation
1900–	1900	1.00	1.00	1.00	1.00	1.00
1990	1910	1.43	0.79	1.20	0.95	1.20
	1920	0.37	0.09	0.28	0.27	7.90
	1930	0.64	0.07	0.16	0.87	2.02[†]
	1940	1.21	0.17	0.30	0.18	1.66
	1950	0.41	0.02	0.24	0.56	2.57
	1960	3.67	0.02	0.29	0.73	2.89
	1970	5.40	0.03	0.30	0.84	3.78
	1980	4.19	0.04	0.31	1.45	6.22
	1990	15.57	0.06	0.42	1.19	8.18
1991–	1991	12.80	0.06	0.44	1.31	8.40
2001	1992	13.10	0.07	0.46	1.30	8.75
	1993	11.91	0.07	0.49	1.22	9.08
	1994	16.52	0.08	0.50	1.16	9.46
	1995	15.17	0.08	0.51	1.30	9.70
	1996	15.62	0.09	0.52	1.39	9.87
	1997	18.82	0.09	0.53	1.27	10.01
	1998	26.03	0.10	0.54	1.09	10.19
	1999	29.92	0.11	0.56	1.16	10.24
	2000	38.95	0.10	0.57	0.98	10.36
	2001	34.34	0.11	0.58	0.90	10.58

[*] Real bond and bill index series exclude 1922–23   [†] Inflation series rebased to 1900 = 1.0E-12

Chapter 24 Ireland

The first long-run asset return study for Ireland is by Shane Whelan (1999), who uses Irish Central Statistical Office (CSO) data from 1934, and UK data before that. Thomas (1986) provides some additional early data, but only in graphical form.

We therefore create a new, market capitalization-weighted index of Irish equity prices for 1900–33. Our prices are taken from the *Irish Times*, and we follow the procedure outlined for the United Kingdom in chapter 32, making full adjustments for capital changes. Seventy securities were listed in the *Irish Times* of 1899, and of these, twelve railway and banking stocks account for about 60 percent of the total market capitalization. For 1934–83 we use the Irish CSO Price Index of Ordinary Stocks and Shares. Until this date, we incorporate our estimates of UK dividend yields, based on the indexes described in chapter 32. From 1984 we use the Irish Stock Exchange Equity (ISEQ) total return index.

The bond series for Ireland is from Whelan for 1900–28. For 1929–53 we use the return on Ireland 5 percent, followed during 1954–70 by 3.5 percent exchequer bonds, switching in 1971 to an index of fifteen-year Irish government bonds. For 1979–98, we use Whelan's (1999) return on a twenty-year representative Irish government bond, as estimated by Raida Stockbrokers, turning thereafter to the Datastream ten-year Irish government bond index.

Short-term Irish interest rates for 1900–22 are from Whelan (1999). During 1923–69 we use the yield on Irish central bank deposits. From 1970 we use Irish treasury bills.

Up to independence from Britain, inflation is measured using Bowley's (1937) cost of living index for 1900–13 and the working-class cost of living index for 1914–21. For 1922–52 we use Meghen's (1970) Irish cost of living index, and from 1953, the Irish consumer price index. Note that the exchange rate is expressed as Irish pounds per US dollar.

Table 24-1: Distribution of Irish asset returns and risk premia, 1900–2000

Return	Asset	Mean returns % p.a.			Dispersion of annual returns %				
		Geometric	Arithmetic	SE	SD	Lowest return		Highest return	
Nominal returns	Equities	9.5	11.5	2.3	22.8	-45.1	1974	88.3	1977
	Bonds	6.0	6.7	1.2	12.2	-26.6	1940	48.8	1977
	Bills	5.8	5.9	0.4	3.7	2.3	1908	17.6	1982
	Inflation	4.5	4.7	0.7	6.8	-16.1	1922	23.6	1915
Real returns	Equities	4.8	7.0	2.2	22.2	-54.3	1974	69.9	1977
	Bonds	1.5	2.4	1.3	13.3	-34.2	1940	37.9	1993
	Bills	1.3	1.4	0.6	6.0	-16.2	1915	22.3	1922
	Exchange rate	-0.1	0.5	1.1	11.2	-37.0	1946	56.6	1933
Risk premia	Equities vs. bills	3.5	5.4	2.1	20.6	-51.1	1974	73.6	1977
	Equities vs. bonds	3.2	4.6	1.7	17.4	-37.0	1974	73.3	1972
	Bonds vs. bills	0.2	0.8	1.1	10.8	-28.7	1940	37.1	1977

Figure 24-1: Returns on Irish asset classes 1900–2000, in real terms

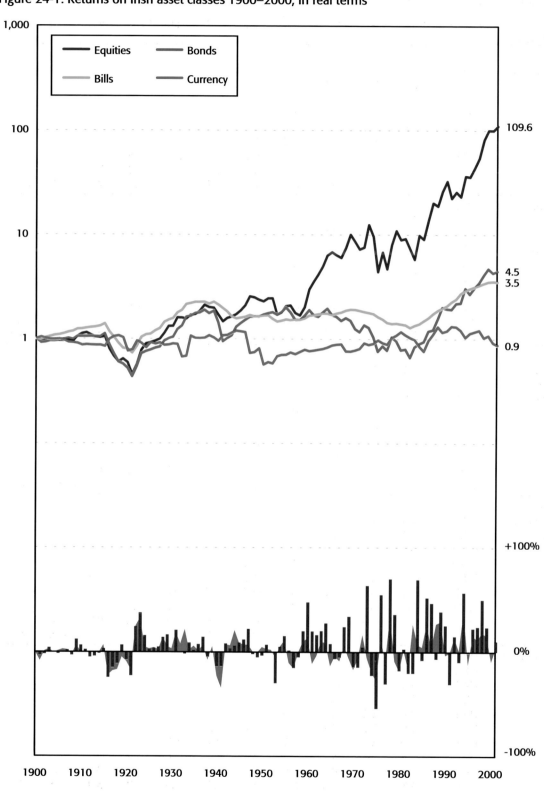

Table 24-2: Irish real rates of return and inflation over various periods, 1900–2000

Return	From ▶ To ▼	1900	1910	1920	1930	1940	1950	1960	1970	1980	1990	2000
Real	1909	1.1										
return	1919	-2.6	-6.2									
on	1929	0.9	0.8	8.4								
equities	1939	1.3	1.4	5.4	2.5							
	1949	1.7	1.8	4.6	2.8	3.0						
	1959	1.8	2.0	4.1	2.7	2.8	2.7					
	1969	3.1	3.4	5.5	4.8	5.5	6.8	11.1				
	1979	2.8	3.0	4.6	3.9	4.2	4.6	5.6	0.5			
	1989	3.9	4.3	5.9	5.5	6.1	6.9	8.3	6.9	13.8		
	2000	4.8	5.2	6.7	6.4	7.1	7.9	9.2	8.6	12.7	11.7	10.1
Real	1909	0.6										
return	1919	-3.2	-6.8									
on	1929	0.2	-0.1	7.1								
bonds	1939	0.9	1.0	5.2	3.3							
	1949	1.1	1.2	4.0	2.5	1.8						
	1959	1.1	1.2	3.3	2.0	1.4	1.0					
	1969	0.3	0.3	1.8	0.5	-0.5	-1.6	-4.1				
	1979	-0.3	-0.4	0.7	-0.6	-1.5	-2.6	-4.3	-4.6			
	1989	0.7	0.8	1.9	1.0	0.6	0.3	0.1	2.2	9.5		
	2000	1.5	1.6	2.7	2.1	1.9	1.9	2.1	4.2	8.7	7.9	4.0
Real	1909	2.2										
return	1919	-1.1	-4.4									
on	1929	1.5	1.2	7.0								
bills	1939	1.9	1.8	5.0	3.1							
	1949	1.0	0.7	2.5	0.3	-2.4						
	1959	0.9	0.6	1.9	0.2	-1.2	0.0					
	1969	0.9	0.7	1.8	0.5	-0.4	0.6	1.3				
	1979	0.4	0.1	0.9	-0.3	-1.1	-0.6	-0.9	-3.1			
	1989	0.8	0.6	1.4	0.5	0.0	0.5	0.7	0.4	4.1		
	2000	1.3	1.1	1.9	1.1	0.8	1.5	1.8	2.0	4.5	4.9	-0.9
Real	1909	-1.5										
exchange	1919	-1.4	-1.3									
rate	1929	-0.4	0.2	1.7								
	1939	-0.1	0.3	1.1	0.6							
	1949	-1.1	-1.1	-1.0	-2.3	-5.0						
	1959	-0.5	-0.3	0.0	-0.5	-1.1	3.0					
	1969	-0.4	-0.2	0.0	-0.4	-0.7	1.6	0.2				
	1979	0.2	0.4	0.7	0.5	0.5	2.5	2.2	4.2			
	1989	0.2	0.4	0.6	0.5	0.5	1.9	1.5	2.2	0.2		
	2000	-0.1	0.0	0.2	0.0	-0.1	0.9	0.3	0.4	-1.4	-2.8	-4.7
Inflation	1909	0.9										
rate	1919	4.7	8.6									
	1929	2.5	3.3	-1.8								
	1939	2.0	2.4	-0.6	0.7							
	1949	2.6	3.1	1.3	2.9	5.2						
	1959	2.8	3.2	1.9	3.2	4.4	3.7					
	1969	3.0	3.4	2.4	3.5	4.4	4.0	4.3				
	1979	4.2	4.7	4.1	5.3	6.5	6.9	8.6	13.1			
	1989	4.7	5.2	4.7	5.9	6.9	7.4	8.6	10.9	8.7		
	2000	4.5	4.9	4.4	5.3	6.1	6.3	7.0	7.8	5.4	2.5	5.1

Table 25-2: Italian real rates of return and inflation over various periods, 1900–2000

Return	From ▶ To ▼	1900	1910	1920	1930	1940	1950	1960	1970	1980	1990	2000
Real return on equities	1909	4.4										
	1919	0.8	-2.8									
	1929	1.3	-0.2	2.4								
	1939	3.3	2.9	5.9	9.6							
	1949	0.2	-0.9	-0.2	-1.5	-11.5						
	1959	3.2	2.9	4.4	5.1	2.9	19.7					
	1969	2.7	2.5	3.5	3.8	2.0	9.5	0.1				
	1979	0.8	0.3	0.8	0.5	-1.6	1.9	-6.0	-11.7			
	1989	2.2	2.0	2.7	2.7	1.4	4.9	0.4	0.5	14.4		
	2000	2.7	2.5	3.1	3.3	2.2	5.2	1.9	2.5	10.1	6.3	4.6
Real return on bonds	1909	4.9										
	1919	-2.1	-8.6									
	1929	-1.6	-4.6	-0.4								
	1939	0.1	-1.5	2.4	5.2							
	1949	-6.2	-8.8	-8.8	-12.7	-27.6						
	1959	-4.8	-6.6	-6.1	-8.0	-13.9	2.3					
	1969	-4.0	-5.4	-4.8	-5.8	-9.2	1.6	0.9				
	1979	-4.1	-5.3	-4.8	-5.6	-8.2	-0.6	-2.0	-4.8			
	1989	-3.4	-4.4	-3.8	-4.3	-6.1	0.2	-0.6	-1.3	2.4		
	2000	-2.2	-3.0	-2.2	-2.5	-3.7	1.9	1.7	2.0	5.4	8.3	4.1
Real return on bills	1909	2.7										
	1919	-2.4	-7.3									
	1929	-2.2	-4.6	-1.9								
	1939	-1.1	-2.3	0.2	2.4							
	1949	-7.6	-10.0	-10.9	-15.1	-29.7						
	1959	-6.5	-8.2	-8.5	-10.6	-16.4	-0.6					
	1969	-5.6	-6.9	-6.8	-8.0	-11.2	-0.3	0.0				
	1979	-5.4	-6.5	-6.3	-7.2	-9.5	-1.5	-1.9	-3.9			
	1989	-4.7	-5.6	-5.4	-6.0	-7.5	-1.0	-1.1	-1.7	0.5		
	2000	-4.1	-4.8	-4.5	-4.8	-5.9	-0.4	-0.4	-0.5	1.1	1.7	1.4
Real exchange rate	1909	-0.8										
	1919	-3.3	-5.6									
	1929	-1.4	-1.8	2.3								
	1939	-2.2	-2.6	-1.1	-4.3							
	1949	-0.9	-0.9	0.8	0.0	4.5						
	1959	-0.5	-0.4	1.0	0.5	3.0	1.6					
	1969	-0.3	-0.2	1.0	0.6	2.4	1.3	1.0				
	1979	0.0	0.2	1.2	0.9	2.3	1.6	1.6	2.1			
	1989	0.1	0.3	1.1	1.0	2.0	1.4	1.4	1.6	1.0		
	2000	-0.2	-0.2	0.5	0.3	1.0	0.4	0.1	-0.2	-1.3	-3.4	-6.9
Inflation rate	1909	0.5										
	1919	5.7	11.1									
	1929	5.5	8.1	5.2								
	1939	4.2	5.4	2.7	0.2							
	1949	11.6	14.5	15.7	21.4	47.0						
	1959	10.1	12.1	12.4	14.9	23.1	3.1					
	1969	9.2	10.7	10.6	12.0	16.2	3.4	3.6				
	1979	9.6	10.9	10.9	12.1	15.3	6.3	7.9	12.4			
	1989	9.7	11.0	10.9	11.9	14.4	7.5	9.0	11.8	11.1		
	2000	9.1	10.1	10.0	10.7	12.5	6.7	7.6	8.9	7.3	4.0	2.8

Figure 25-2: Nominal returns on Italian asset classes 1900–2000

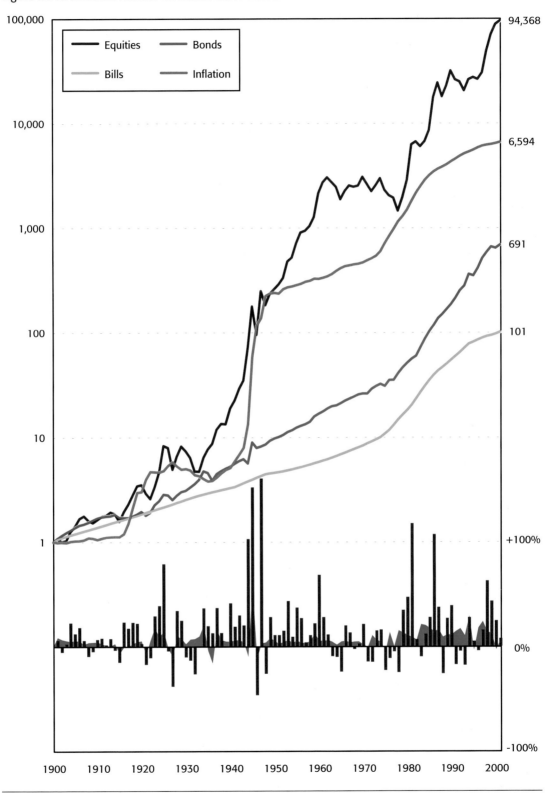

Table 25-3: Italian equity risk premia over various periods, 1900–2000

Premium	From ► To ▼	1900	1910	1920	1930	1940	1950	1960	1970	1980	1990	2000
Equity	1909	1.7										
premium	1919	3.3	4.8									
versus	1929	3.6	4.6	4.4								
bills	1939	4.5	5.4	5.7	7.1							
	1949	8.4	10.2	12.0	16.0	25.7						
	1959	10.3	12.2	14.1	17.5	23.1	20.5					
	1969	8.8	10.0	11.1	12.9	14.9	9.8	0.1				
	1979	6.5	7.3	7.7	8.3	8.6	3.5	-4.1	-8.1			
	1989	7.3	8.1	8.5	9.2	9.7	6.0	1.5	2.3	13.8		
	2000	7.0	7.6	8.0	8.5	8.7	5.6	2.3	3.1	8.8	4.5	3.2
Equity	1909	-0.4										
premium	1919	2.9	6.4									
versus	1929	2.9	4.6	2.8								
bonds	1939	3.2	4.5	3.5	4.2							
	1949	6.8	8.6	9.4	12.8	22.2						
	1959	8.4	10.3	11.2	14.2	19.6	17.0					
	1969	7.0	8.3	8.7	10.2	12.3	7.7	-0.8				
	1979	5.1	6.0	5.9	6.5	7.1	2.5	-4.0	-7.2			
	1989	5.9	6.7	6.7	7.4	8.0	4.7	1.0	1.8	11.7		
	2000	5.0	5.6	5.5	5.9	6.2	3.3	0.2	0.5	4.4	-1.9	0.5

Table 25-4: Italian real index values and inflation index, 1900–2000

Period	Start of	Equities	Bonds	Bills	Currency	Inflation
1900–	1900	1.00	1.00	1.00	1.00	1.00
1990	1910	1.54	1.61	1.31	0.92	1.05
	1920	1.16	0.65	0.61	0.52	3.01
	1930	1.47	0.62	0.51	0.65	4.99
	1940	3.69	1.04	0.64	0.42	5.09
	1950	1.08	0.04	0.02	0.65	239.52
	1960	6.55	0.05	0.02	0.76	324.88
	1970	6.61	0.06	0.02	0.84	464.55
	1980	1.91	0.03	0.01	1.03	1497.41
	1990	7.34	0.04	0.01	1.14	4296.32
1991–	1991	5.71	0.05	0.01	1.28	4558.39
2001	1992	5.12	0.05	0.01	1.30	4850.54
	1993	3.99	0.05	0.01	1.04	5112.93
	1994	4.88	0.07	0.01	0.90	5327.66
	1995	4.93	0.06	0.01	0.97	5546.10
	1996	4.49	0.07	0.01	1.02	5834.49
	1997	4.98	0.08	0.01	1.07	6067.87
	1998	7.94	0.10	0.01	0.92	6189.23
	1999	11.21	0.11	0.01	0.99	6282.07
	2000	13.68	0.10	0.02	0.84	6413.99
	2001	14.31	0.10	0.02	0.78	6593.58

Chapter 26 Japan

Japanese data of good quality is available from the Hamao (1991) database, and from the studies by Schwartz and Ziemba (1991) and Ziemba and Schwartz (1991). However, these data sources require substantial augmentation to cover the century as a whole. We are grateful to Kenji Wada for facilitating provision of pre–First World War equity data.

For 1900–13 we use the Laspeyres price index for the Tokyo Stock Exchange, as published in Fujino and Akiyama (1977). Thereafter, share prices are represented by the Japan National Bank index for 1914–32; the Oriental Economist Index from 1933 until September 1946; the Tokyo Stock Exchange Volume-Weighted Index, based on over-the-counter prices, from October 1946 until April 1949; and the Nikkei-225 from May 1949 to 1951. Dividend data are available for 1900–13, 1921–45 and 1949 on. Dividend payments are therefore interpolated over 1914–20 and 1946–48. During 1952–70 we use the Japan Securities Research Institute total return index, a description of which is provided by Schwartz and Ziemba (1991). From 1971 we use total returns from Hamao and Ibbotson (1989). Returns continue from 1995 with the Tokyo Stock Exchange TOPIX index.

From 1900–57, Japanese government bond returns are estimated from yield data. No yield information is available for the end of 1947, and the yield for 1946 is used instead. The data for 1948–57 represent the yields on newly issued bonds. From 1957–68, the bonds are those issued by Nippon Telephone and Telegraph. From 1968–70, we use government bond data from the Bank of Japan. From 1971 we use the government bond index from Hamao and Ibbotson (1989), followed from 1995 by the JP Morgan Japanese bond index.

The short-term riskless rate is based on call money rates from 1900–59, and on treasury bills thereafter. Inflation is measured by the wholesale price index for 1900, and the consumer price index for 1901 onward.

Table 26-1: Distribution of Japanese asset returns and risk premia, 1900–2000

Return	Asset	Mean returns % p.a.			Dispersion of annual returns %				
		Geometric	Arithmetic	SE	SD	Lowest return		Highest return	
Nominal	Equities	12.5	15.9	2.9	29.5	-44.0	1920	121.1	1952
returns	Bonds	5.9	6.9	1.5	14.9	-42.4	1953	72.8	1954
	Bills	5.4	5.4	0.2	2.0	0.1	1999	9.1	1901
	Inflation	7.6	11.0	4.0	40.2	-18.7	1930	317.1	1946
Real	Equities	4.5	9.3	3.0	30.3	-84.0	1946	119.6	1952
returns	Bonds	-1.6	1.3	2.1	20.9	-75.1	1946	70.7	1954
	Bills	-2.0	-0.3	1.4	14.5	-75.1	1946	29.8	1930
	Exchange rate	0.2	3.2	2.9	29.5	-78.3	1945	253.0	1946
Risk	Equities vs. bills	6.7	9.9	2.8	27.9	-48.3	1920	108.6	1952
premia	Equities vs. bonds	6.2	10.3	3.3	33.2	-43.3	1920	193.0	1948
	Bonds vs. bills	0.5	1.4	1.4	14.1	-45.6	1953	63.0	1954

Figure 26-1: Returns on Japanese asset classes 1900–2000, in real terms

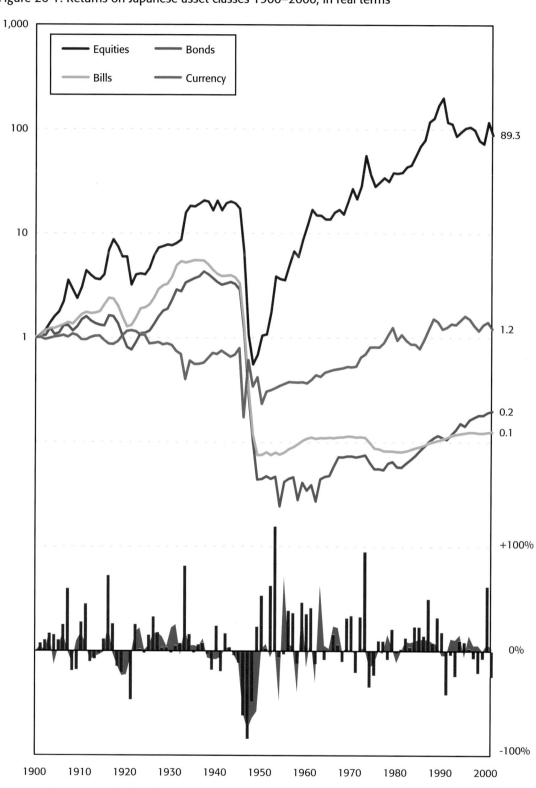

Table 26-2: Japanese real rates of return and inflation over various periods, 1900–2000

Return	From ▶ To ▼	1900	1910	1920	1930	1940	1950	1960	1970	1980	1990	2000
Real return on equities	1909	11.8										
	1919	9.4	7.0									
	1929	7.0	4.8	2.5								
	1939	7.9	6.6	6.4	10.4							
	1949	0.1	-2.6	-5.6	-9.5	-25.7						
	1959	4.2	2.8	1.8	1.5	-2.7	27.5					
	1969	4.8	3.7	3.1	3.2	0.9	17.6	8.5				
	1979	4.7	3.7	3.1	3.2	1.5	12.7	5.9	3.4			
	1989	6.1	5.4	5.1	5.6	4.7	14.0	9.9	10.5	18.2		
	2000	4.5	3.8	3.4	3.5	2.4	9.1	5.0	3.9	4.1	-7.1	-24.5
Real return on bonds	1909	4.1										
	1919	-1.1	-6.0									
	1929	2.8	2.2	11.0								
	1939	3.1	2.8	7.5	4.0							
	1949	-6.0	-8.4	-9.2	-17.9	-35.2						
	1959	-5.5	-7.3	-7.6	-13.1	-20.5	-2.5					
	1969	-3.7	-4.9	-4.7	-8.2	-12.0	2.5	7.9				
	1979	-3.5	-4.5	-4.3	-7.1	-9.7	0.9	2.6	-2.3			
	1989	-2.4	-3.2	-2.8	-4.9	-6.6	2.3	4.0	2.1	6.7		
	2000	-1.6	-2.2	-1.7	-3.4	-4.6	3.0	4.4	3.3	6.0	5.4	2.9
Real return on bills	1909	5.3										
	1919	1.3	-2.7									
	1929	4.6	4.2	11.6								
	1939	3.6	3.0	6.0	0.7							
	1949	-5.0	-7.4	-9.0	-17.8	-32.9						
	1959	-3.6	-5.3	-6.0	-11.2	-16.6	3.7					
	1969	-3.1	-4.4	-4.7	-8.4	-11.3	2.1	0.5				
	1979	-3.1	-4.2	-4.5	-7.4	-9.3	0.2	-1.4	-3.3			
	1989	-2.5	-3.4	-3.5	-5.8	-7.0	0.9	-0.1	-0.3	2.7		
	2000	-2.0	-2.8	-2.8	-4.7	-5.5	1.0	0.4	0.3	2.1	1.5	0.9
Real exchange rate	1909	-0.4										
	1919	0.7	1.9									
	1929	-0.5	-0.6	-3.0								
	1939	-0.9	-1.1	-2.5	-1.9							
	1949	-2.9	-3.5	-5.2	-6.2	-10.4						
	1959	-1.6	-1.9	-2.8	-2.7	-3.1	4.7					
	1969	-0.9	-1.0	-1.6	-1.2	-0.9	4.1	3.6				
	1979	-0.1	0.0	-0.3	0.2	0.8	4.8	4.9	6.1			
	1989	0.2	0.3	0.1	0.6	1.1	4.2	4.1	4.3	2.5		
	2000	0.2	0.3	0.1	0.5	0.9	3.3	3.0	2.8	1.2	0.1	-13.8
Inflation rate	1909	2.0										
	1919	5.5	9.1									
	1929	2.3	2.5	-3.7								
	1939	2.6	2.8	-0.2	3.4							
	1949	11.4	13.9	15.5	26.5	54.8						
	1959	9.9	11.6	12.2	18.1	26.2	2.9					
	1969	9.3	10.6	10.8	14.8	18.9	4.2	5.5				
	1979	9.2	10.3	10.5	13.6	16.3	5.8	7.2	9.0			
	1989	8.5	9.3	9.3	11.7	13.4	4.9	5.6	5.6	2.3		
	2000	7.6	8.2	8.1	9.9	11.0	4.0	4.3	3.9	1.6	0.9	-0.6

Figure 26-2: Nominal returns on Japanese asset classes 1900–2000

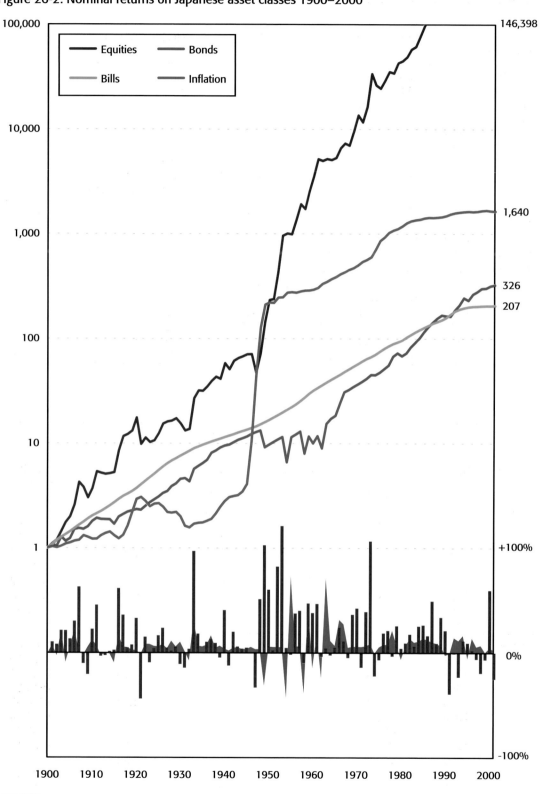

Table 26-3: Japanese equity risk premia over various periods, 1900–2000

Premium	From▶ To▼	1900	1910	1920	1930	1940	1950	1960	1970	1980	1990	2000
Equity premium versus bills	1909	6.1										
	1919	8.0	10.0									
	1929	2.4	0.5	-8.1								
	1939	4.1	3.5	0.4	9.6							
	1949	5.4	5.2	3.7	10.1	10.7						
	1959	8.2	8.6	8.2	14.3	16.7	23.0					
	1969	8.1	8.5	8.2	12.7	13.7	15.2	8.0				
	1979	8.0	8.3	8.0	11.5	12.0	12.4	7.5	6.9			
	1989	8.7	9.1	8.9	12.1	12.6	13.1	9.9	10.9	15.0		
	2000	6.7	6.8	6.4	8.6	8.4	8.0	4.6	3.6	2.0	-8.5	-25.2
Equity premium versus bonds	1909	7.4										
	1919	10.6	13.8									
	1929	4.1	2.5	-7.6								
	1939	4.6	3.7	-1.0	6.1							
	1949	6.5	6.3	4.0	10.3	14.6						
	1959	10.3	10.8	10.1	16.7	22.5	30.8					
	1969	8.8	9.1	8.1	12.5	14.7	14.7	0.6				
	1979	8.4	8.6	7.8	11.1	12.4	11.7	3.2	5.9			
	1989	8.7	8.9	8.2	11.1	12.1	11.4	5.6	8.3	10.7		
	2000	6.2	6.1	5.2	7.1	7.3	5.9	0.6	0.6	-1.8	-11.9	-26.6

Table 26-4: Japanese real index values and inflation index, 1900–2000

Period	Start of	Equities	Bonds	Bills	Currency	Inflation
1900– 1990	1900	1.00	1.00	1.00	1.00	1.00
	1910	3.04	1.49	1.68	0.96	1.22
	1920	6.01	0.81	1.28	1.16	2.91
	1930	7.71	2.29	3.83	0.85	2.00
	1940	20.73	3.41	4.11	0.70	2.80
	1950	1.06	0.04	0.08	0.23	220.50
	1960	12.04	0.03	0.11	0.37	292.62
	1970	27.15	0.07	0.11	0.53	500.98
	1980	38.03	0.06	0.08	0.95	1181.68
	1990	201.74	0.11	0.11	1.22	1487.36
1991– 2001	1991	117.91	0.11	0.11	1.27	1543.63
	1992	113.79	0.12	0.12	1.37	1584.70
	1993	86.65	0.13	0.12	1.35	1602.94
	1994	95.53	0.15	0.12	1.48	1619.68
	1995	103.77	0.14	0.12	1.63	1630.55
	1996	106.36	0.16	0.13	1.52	1624.04
	1997	99.31	0.17	0.13	1.32	1633.81
	1998	78.62	0.18	0.12	1.18	1663.10
	1999	73.03	0.18	0.12	1.34	1672.86
	2000	118.28	0.19	0.13	1.43	1649.44
	2001	89.29	0.20	0.13	1.23	1639.55

Chapter 27 Netherlands

For The Netherlands we use the study by Eichholtz, Koedijk, and Otten (2000), to whom we are grateful for making available their database. We also thank Frans van Schaik for advice on Dutch capital market history.

The equity returns over 1900–18 are based on the Central Bureau of Statistics (CBS) general index of share prices, and historical yield data. For the period 1919–51 returns are based on the 50-stock, CBS weighted arithmetic index. The exchange was closed from August 1944 to April 1946, so the end-year index levels are represented by the intra-year values that are closest to the turn of the year. During 1952–80, returns are based on the CBS All Share index, with dividends estimated by the Dutch central bank. For 1981 onward we use the CBS total return index, which went live in 1989 with retrospective estimation of the impact of income reinvestment. The CBS index currently covers 137 shares.

During 1900–14, Dutch bond returns are represented by 2.5 percent and 3 percent consols. During 1915–73, the Eichholtz-Koedijk-Otten bond index is based on a series of 3.5 percent bonds. From 1974, the index is the JP Morgan Netherlands government bond index.

For the riskless rate, during 1900–40 we use the discount rate on three-month private bills. The rate is assumed unchanged when data were unavailable during August 1914 to December 1918, and from mid-May 1940 to the end of that year. From 1941 to date we use the rate on Dutch treasury bills.

Inflation is measured using the consumer price index.

Table 27-1: Distribution of Dutch asset returns and risk premia, 1900–2000

Return	Asset	Mean returns % p.a.			Dispersion of annual returns %				
		Geometric	Arithmetic	SE	SD	Lowest return		Highest return	
Nominal	Equities	9.0	11.0	2.3	22.7	-30.4	1932	130.1	1940
returns	Bonds	4.1	4.4	0.8	7.6	-18.5	1939	36.1	1982
	Bills	3.7	3.7	0.2	2.4	0.5	1939	12.2	1981
	Inflation	3.0	3.1	0.5	5.0	-13.4	1921	18.7	1918
Real	Equities	5.8	7.7	2.1	21.0	-34.9	1941	101.6	1940
returns	Bonds	1.1	1.5	0.9	9.4	-18.1	1915	32.8	1932
	Bills	0.7	0.8	0.5	5.2	-12.7	1918	19.6	1921
	Exchange rate	-0.1	0.8	1.3	12.6	-61.6	1946	55.7	1933
Risk	Equities vs. bills	5.1	7.1	2.2	22.2	-31.3	1932	126.7	1940
premia	Equities vs. bonds	4.7	6.7	2.1	21.4	-43.9	1932	107.6	1940
	Bonds vs. bills	0.4	0.7	0.7	7.2	-18.9	1939	25.2	1982

Figure 27-1: Returns on Dutch asset classes 1900–2000, in real terms

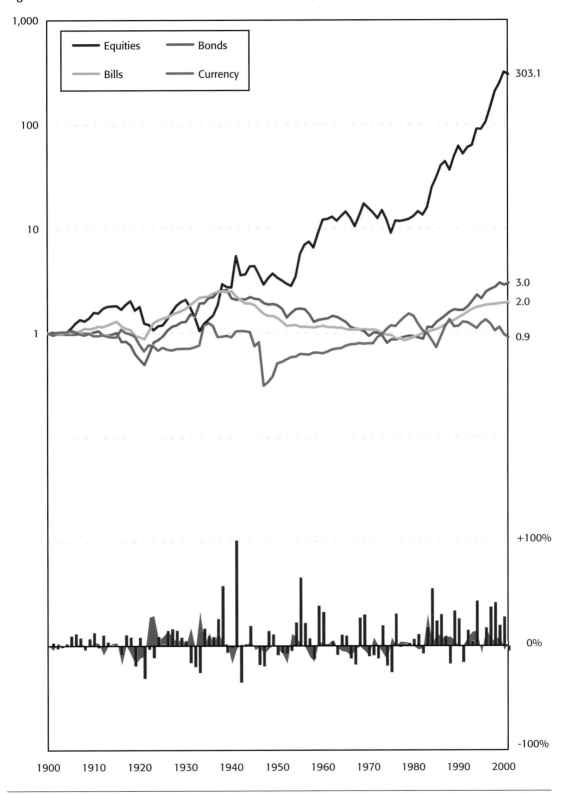

Table 27-2: Dutch real rates of return and inflation over various periods, 1900–2000

Return	From ▶ To ▼	1900	1910	1920	1930	1940	1950	1960	1970	1980	1990	2000
Real	1909	4.8										
return	1919	3.0	1.3									
on	1929	2.5	1.4	1.5								
equities	1939	2.6	1.8	2.1	2.7							
	1949	2.5	1.9	2.1	2.4	2.2						
	1959	4.3	4.2	4.9	6.0	7.8	13.6					
	1969	4.0	3.9	4.4	5.2	6.0	8.0	2.5				
	1979	3.3	3.1	3.4	3.7	4.0	4.6	0.4	-1.8			
	1989	4.7	4.7	5.2	5.8	6.4	7.5	5.6	7.1	16.8		
	2000	5.8	5.9	6.5	7.2	8.0	9.2	8.1	10.0	16.1	15.5	-4.9
Real	1909	0.3										
return	1919	-2.9	-6.0									
on	1929	0.9	1.1	8.8								
bonds	1939	1.9	2.5	7.0	5.2							
	1949	1.2	1.5	4.1	1.8	-1.5						
	1959	0.5	0.6	2.3	0.2	-2.3	-3.0					
	1969	-0.1	-0.2	1.1	-0.8	-2.7	-3.3	-3.7				
	1979	-0.1	-0.1	0.9	-0.7	-2.1	-2.3	-1.9	-0.1			
	1989	0.6	0.6	1.6	0.4	-0.5	-0.3	0.7	2.9	5.9		
	2000	1.1	1.2	2.1	1.2	0.5	1.0	1.9	3.8	5.7	5.6	4.4
Real	1909	1.2										
return	1919	-0.4	-2.0									
on	1929	1.8	2.1	6.5								
bills	1939	2.4	2.7	5.2	3.9							
	1949	0.7	0.5	1.4	-1.1	-5.8						
	1959	0.3	0.1	0.6	-1.3	-3.8	-1.7					
	1969	0.1	-0.1	0.3	-1.2	-2.8	-1.3	-0.9				
	1979	-0.1	-0.3	0.0	-1.3	-2.5	-1.4	-1.3	-1.6			
	1989	0.4	0.3	0.6	-0.3	-1.2	0.0	0.6	1.4	4.5		
	2000	0.7	0.6	0.9	0.2	-0.4	0.7	1.3	2.0	3.7	3.0	1.3
Real	1909	-0.5										
exchange	1919	-1.2	-1.9									
rate	1929	-1.1	-1.4	-0.9								
	1939	-0.2	-0.1	0.8	2.5							
	1949	-1.3	-1.5	-1.4	-1.6	-5.6						
	1959	-0.7	-0.8	-0.5	-0.4	-1.8	2.2					
	1969	-0.3	-0.3	0.0	0.3	-0.5	2.2	2.2				
	1979	0.5	0.6	1.1	1.4	1.2	3.5	4.2	6.3			
	1989	0.2	0.3	0.6	0.8	0.5	2.1	2.0	2.0	-2.2		
	2000	-0.1	-0.1	0.2	0.3	0.0	1.1	0.8	0.4	-2.3	-2.3	-6.7
Inflation	1909	1.9										
rate	1919	3.9	5.9									
	1929	1.7	1.6	-2.5								
	1939	0.7	0.3	-2.4	-2.3							
	1949	2.0	2.1	0.9	2.6	7.7						
	1959	2.3	2.4	1.5	2.9	5.5	3.5					
	1969	2.6	2.7	2.1	3.2	5.1	3.9	4.4				
	1979	3.1	3.3	2.9	4.0	5.6	4.9	5.7	7.0			
	1989	3.1	3.2	2.9	3.8	5.0	4.4	4.7	4.9	2.8		
	2000	3.0	3.1	2.8	3.6	4.6	4.0	4.1	4.0	2.6	2.5	2.9

Figure 27-2: Nominal returns on Dutch asset classes 1900–2000

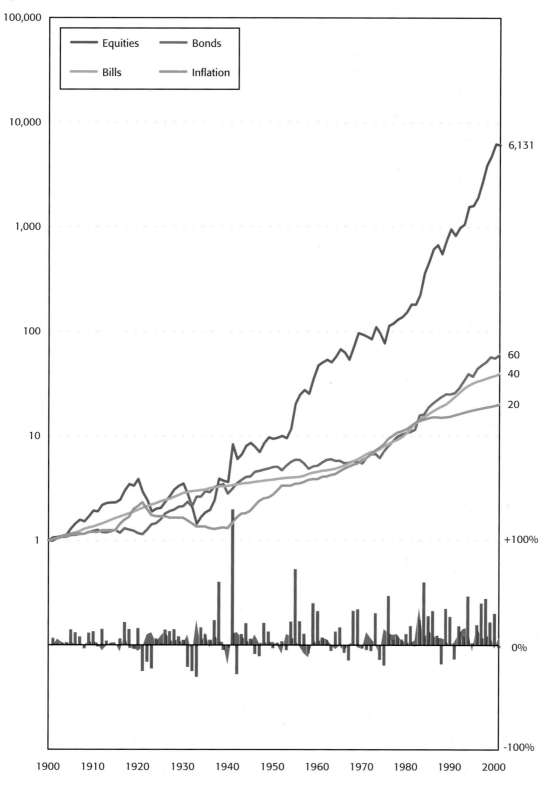

Table 27-3: Dutch equity risk premia over various periods, 1900–2000

Premium	From▶ To▼	1900	1910	1920	1930	1940	1950	1960	1970	1980	1990	2000
Equity premium versus bills	1909	3.5										
	1919	3.4	3.4									
	1929	0.7	-0.7	-4.6								
	1939	0.2	-0.9	-2.9	-1.2							
	1949	1.8	1.4	0.7	3.5	8.5						
	1959	4.0	4.1	4.3	7.4	12.0	15.6					
	1969	3.9	4.0	4.1	6.4	9.1	9.4	3.5				
	1979	3.4	3.4	3.4	5.1	6.7	6.1	1.7	-0.1			
	1989	4.3	4.4	4.5	6.1	7.7	7.5	4.9	5.6	11.7		
	2000	5.1	5.3	5.5	7.0	8.5	8.5	6.8	7.9	11.9	12.1	-6.1
Equity premium versus bonds	1909	4.5										
	1919	6.1	7.8									
	1929	1.7	0.3	-6.7								
	1939	0.6	-0.6	-4.6	-2.4							
	1949	1.2	0.4	-1.9	0.6	3.8						
	1959	3.7	3.6	2.6	5.9	10.3	17.2					
	1969	4.1	4.1	3.3	6.0	9.0	11.7	6.4				
	1979	3.4	3.2	2.5	4.4	6.2	7.0	2.3	-1.7			
	1989	4.1	4.1	3.6	5.4	7.0	7.8	4.9	4.1	10.2		
	2000	4.7	4.7	4.3	6.0	7.4	8.2	6.1	5.9	9.8	9.4	-9.0

Table 27-4: Dutch real index values and inflation index, 1900–2000

Period	Start of	Equities	Bonds	Bills	Currency	Inflation
1900–1990	1900	1.00	1.00	1.00	1.00	1.00
	1910	1.60	1.03	1.13	0.95	1.21
	1920	1.81	0.55	0.92	0.78	2.13
	1930	2.11	1.29	1.73	0.71	1.66
	1940	2.75	2.15	2.54	0.92	1.32
	1950	3.42	1.84	1.39	0.51	2.76
	1960	12.28	1.35	1.18	0.64	3.88
	1970	15.80	0.93	1.08	0.79	5.94
	1980	13.24	0.93	0.91	1.46	11.68
	1990	62.31	1.65	1.42	1.17	15.41
1991–2001	1991	52.53	1.65	1.50	1.28	15.88
	1992	60.57	1.78	1.60	1.26	16.35
	1993	63.55	2.02	1.70	1.19	16.82
	1994	91.04	2.30	1.77	1.11	17.28
	1995	90.63	2.12	1.81	1.25	17.76
	1996	106.54	2.47	1.86	1.34	18.10
	1997	146.56	2.62	1.88	1.23	18.46
	1998	207.87	2.73	1.90	1.05	18.86
	1999	249.26	3.00	1.93	1.14	19.24
	2000	318.80	2.86	1.94	0.97	19.65
	2001	303.14	2.99	1.97	0.90	20.23

Chapter 28 South Africa

Returns for South African stocks, bonds, bills, and inflation since 1925 are presented in Firer and McLeod (1999) who, in turn, draw on the earlier work of Schumann and Scheurkogel (1948) that goes back to 1910. We thank Colin Firer for allowing us to use his database, and for his generous help in accessing South African data sources.

These studies cover industrial and commercial stocks. South African mining and financial companies are also very important, especially early last century. We therefore create a market capitalization weighted index of the thirty to fifty largest mining and financial shares for 1900–59, based on London prices, using the sources and procedures described in chapter 32. This index captures at least 60 percent of the total market. To reflect each sector's relative value, over 1900–59 we blend the mining and financial index with Firer and McLeod's industrial index, using start-decade weights of 100, 95, 90, 85, 80 and finally 75 percent. From 1960–78 we use Firer and McLeod's capital gains, that is the *Rand Daily Mail* Industrial Index and, from 1979, the Johannesburg Stock Exchange (JSE)-Actuaries Equity Index. Dividend yields come from our sample of mining and financial shares and, from 1960, from the JSE.

Up to 1924, bond returns are based on estimated prices for 4 percent government bonds. Subsequently we use the bond returns from Firer and McLeod, based first on market yields together with a notional twenty-year bond prior to 1980, followed by the JSE-Actuaries Fixed Interest Index (to 1985) and thereafter the JSE-Actuaries All Bond Index. Before 1925, short-term interest rates are represented by UK treasury bills. (South Africa was then a British Dominion). Thereafter, we use the bill returns from Firer and McLeod, based on three-month fixed deposits (1925–59), bankers' acceptances (1960–66), and then negotiable certificates of deposits. Before 1925, inflation is measured by the consumer price index and thereafter using the official price index from Central Statistical Services. The switch in 1961 from British pounds to rand has been incorporated throughout the index history.

Table 28-1: Distribution of South African asset returns and risk premia, 1900–2000

Return	Asset	Mean returns % p.a.			Dispersion of annual returns %				
		Geometric	Arithmetic	SE	SD	Lowest return		Highest return	
Nominal returns	Equities	12.0	14.2	2.4	23.7	-29.6	1920	107.7	1933
	Bonds	6.3	6.7	0.9	9.5	-10.7	1915	35.9	1986
	Bills	5.7	5.8	0.6	5.8	0.0	1934	21.8	1985
	Inflation	4.8	5.1	0.8	7.8	-17.2	1921	47.5	1920
Real returns	Equities	6.8	9.1	2.3	22.8	-52.2	1920	102.9	1933
	Bonds	1.4	1.9	1.1	10.6	-32.6	1920	37.1	1921
	Bills	0.8	1.0	0.6	6.4	-27.8	1920	27.3	1921
	Exchange rate	-1.3	-0.7	1.0	10.5	-35.3	1946	37.3	1986
Risk premia	Equities vs. bills	6.0	8.1	2.2	22.5	-33.9	1920	106.2	1933
	Equities vs. bonds	5.4	7.1	2.0	19.7	-29.2	1920	70.9	1979
	Bonds vs. bills	0.6	0.9	0.8	7.9	-18.3	1994	30.4	1933

Figure 28-1: Returns on South African asset classes 1900–2000, in real terms

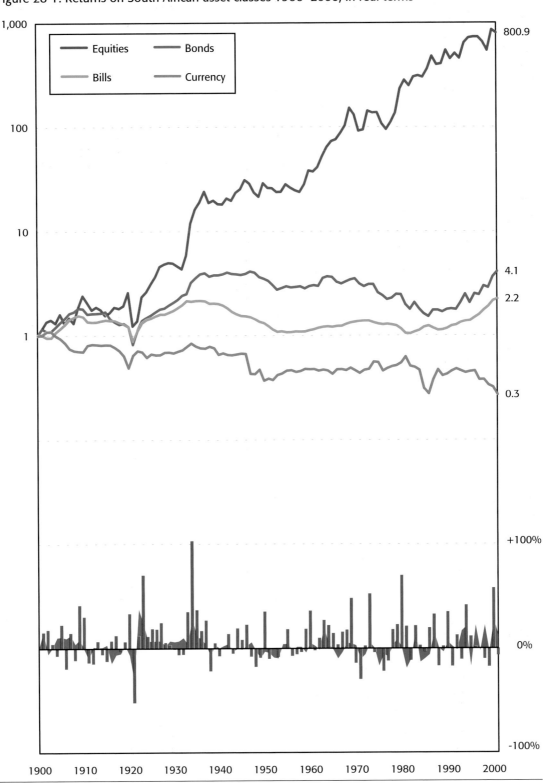

Table 28-2: South African real rates of return and inflation over various periods, 1900–2000

Return	From ▶ To ▼	1900	1910	1920	1930	1940	1950	1960	1970	1980	1990	2000
Real return on equities	1909	9.2										
	1919	4.9	0.7									
	1929	5.5	3.6	6.7								
	1939	7.5	7.0	10.3	14.0							
	1949	7.0	6.4	8.4	9.3	4.7						
	1959	6.3	5.7	7.0	7.1	3.8	2.9					
	1969	7.2	6.9	8.2	8.6	6.8	7.8	13.1				
	1979	7.1	6.7	7.8	8.0	6.6	7.2	9.4	5.9			
	1989	7.3	7.0	8.0	8.2	7.0	7.6	9.3	7.4	8.9		
	2000	6.8	6.6	7.3	7.4	6.4	6.7	7.7	6.0	6.1	3.5	-6.7
Real return on bonds	1909	6.1										
	1919	1.0	-3.9									
	1929	2.4	0.7	5.5								
	1939	3.4	2.5	5.8	6.2							
	1949	2.5	1.7	3.6	2.7	-0.8						
	1959	1.8	1.0	2.3	1.2	-1.2	-1.7					
	1969	1.8	1.1	2.1	1.3	-0.2	0.0	1.7				
	1979	1.1	0.4	1.2	0.4	-1.1	-1.2	-0.9	-3.5			
	1989	0.6	0.0	0.5	-0.2	-1.5	-1.7	-1.7	-3.4	-3.2		
	2000	1.4	0.9	1.5	1.0	0.1	0.3	0.8	0.5	2.4	7.9	12.1
Real return on bills	1909	4.3										
	1919	1.0	-2.2									
	1929	1.9	0.7	3.7								
	1939	1.8	1.0	2.6	1.5							
	1949	0.5	-0.4	0.3	-1.4	-4.2						
	1959	0.2	-0.6	-0.2	-1.4	-2.9	-1.6					
	1969	0.4	-0.2	0.2	-0.6	-1.3	0.1	1.9				
	1979	0.2	-0.4	-0.1	-0.8	-1.4	-0.4	0.2	-1.5			
	1989	0.2	-0.3	0.0	-0.7	-1.1	-0.3	0.1	-0.7	0.1		
	2000	0.8	0.4	0.8	0.4	0.2	1.0	1.7	1.6	3.2	6.1	3.6
Real exchange rate	1909	-3.5										
	1919	-3.5	-3.5									
	1929	-1.3	-0.2	3.3								
	1939	-1.1	-0.2	1.5	-0.4							
	1949	-2.0	-1.6	-0.9	-3.0	-5.5						
	1959	-1.2	-0.8	-0.1	-1.2	-1.6	2.5					
	1969	-1.1	-0.7	-0.1	-1.0	-1.1	1.1	-0.3				
	1979	-0.7	-0.4	0.2	-0.4	-0.4	1.3	0.7	1.7			
	1989	-0.9	-0.6	-0.2	-0.8	-0.8	0.4	-0.4	-0.4	-2.4		
	2000	-1.3	-1.0	-0.7	-1.3	-1.4	-0.6	-1.4	-1.7	-3.3	-4.1	-15.8
Inflation rate	1909	-1.2										
	1919	2.4	6.1									
	1929	1.6	3.0	-0.1								
	1939	1.1	1.8	-0.3	-0.5							
	1949	1.7	2.4	1.2	1.9	4.4						
	1959	2.1	2.7	1.9	2.5	4.1	3.8					
	1969	2.1	2.7	2.0	2.5	3.6	3.1	2.5				
	1979	3.1	3.7	3.3	4.0	5.2	5.5	6.3	10.2			
	1989	4.3	5.0	4.9	5.7	7.0	7.7	9.0	12.4	14.7		
	2000	4.8	5.5	5.4	6.2	7.4	8.0	9.0	11.2	11.7	9.1	7.0

Chapter 29 Spain

Gonzalez and Suarez (1994) present evidence on Spanish stock returns from 1941. Valbuena (2000) provides a longer-term perspective, but his study is as yet incomplete. Santiago Valbuena helped generously with interim estimates that are subject to future amendment.

Valbuena's equity index for 1900–18 is from Bolsa de Madrid. We add a dividend yield that is estimated as the Spanish bond yield minus 0.52 percent, which is the average Spanish yield gap over the period 1919–34. For 1919–36 we use a total returns index from Valbuena (2000) that rectifies some problems in the Sandez and Benavides (2000) index. Trading was suspended during the Civil War from July 1936 to April 1939, and the Madrid exchange remained closed through February 1940, so the 1936 and 1940 returns are each for part of a year. Over the closure we assume a zero change in nominal stock prices. We assume zero dividends during 1936–40. This equates to a real fall in asset values over the Civil War of approximately one-half, as suggested by Valbuena. During 1941–85 we use the Gonzalez and Suarez (1994) data, subsequently linking this to the Bolsa de Madrid total return index.

The bond series for 1900–26 is based on the price of Spanish 4 percent traded in London through 1913 and in Madrid thereafter. For 1926–57 it is based on GFD's estimates for government bonds, with prices kept unaltered during the Civil War. A private bond index is used for 1958–78. From 1989 we use the JP Morgan Spanish government bond index series.

The short-term interest rate over 1900–73 is the central bank discount rate. From 1974 we use the return on treasury bills.

Inflation during 1900–14 is measured using the wholesale price index from Mitchell (1998). For 1915–35 we use the consumer price index from Mitchell (1998; see also Vandellos, 1936). During 1936–40 we revert to the wholesale price index from Mitchell. For 1941–90 we use the Spanish consumer price index from Gonzalez and Suarez (1994).

Table 29-1: Distribution of Spanish asset returns and risk premia, 1900–2000

Return	Asset	Mean returns % p.a.			Dispersion of annual returns %				
		Geometric	Arithmetic	SE	SD	Lowest return		Highest return	
Nominal	Equities	10.0	12.1	2.3	22.8	-29.7	1932	115.9	1986
returns	Bonds	7.5	7.9	1.0	10.5	-23.7	1920	52.4	1942
	Bills	6.5	6.6	0.4	4.0	2.9	1999	21.7	1983
	Inflation	6.1	6.4	0.7	7.2	-6.7	1928	36.5	1946
Real	Equities	3.6	5.8	2.2	22.0	-43.3	1977	98.9	1986
returns	Bonds	1.2	1.9	1.2	12.0	-30.2	1920	53.2	1942
	Bills	0.4	0.6	0.6	6.1	-23.8	1946	12.6	1928
	Exchange rate	-0.4	1.1	1.9	18.8	-56.4	1946	128.7	1939
Risk	Equities vs. bills	3.2	5.3	2.1	21.5	-38.6	1977	98.1	1986
premia	Equities vs. bonds	2.3	4.2	2.0	20.3	-34.0	1932	69.1	1986
	Bonds vs. bills	0.9	1.3	0.9	9.5	-27.0	1920	46.5	1942

Figure 29-1: Returns on Spanish asset classes 1900–2000, in real terms

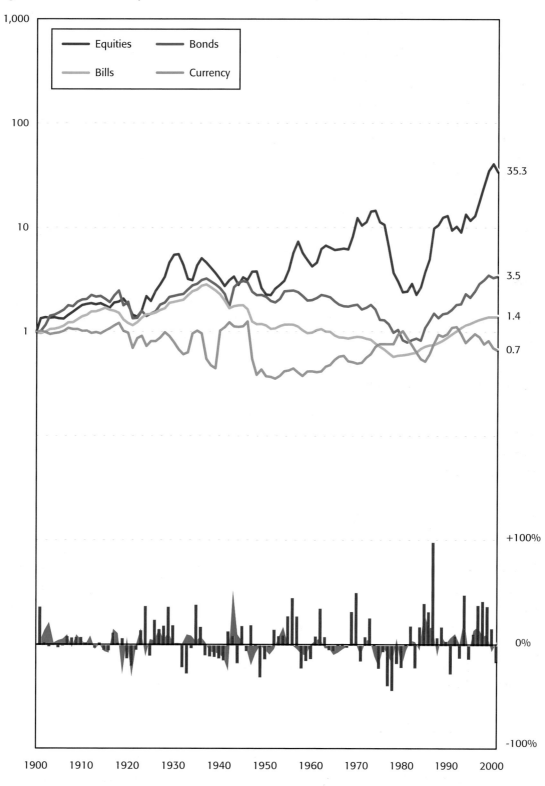

Table 29-2: Spanish real rates of return and inflation over various periods, 1900–2000

Return	From ▶ To ▼	1900	1910	1920	1930	1940	1950	1960	1970	1980	1990	2000
Real return on equities	1909	6.3										
	1919	3.1	0.1									
	1929	5.9	5.7	11.7								
	1939	3.0	1.9	2.9	-5.2							
	1949	1.7	0.6	0.8	-4.3	-3.3						
	1959	2.5	1.7	2.2	-0.8	1.4	6.4					
	1969	3.7	3.3	3.9	2.1	4.6	8.8	11.3				
	1979	1.1	0.4	0.5	-1.6	-0.7	0.2	-2.8	-15.1			
	1989	2.9	2.5	2.9	1.5	2.9	4.5	3.8	0.3	18.4		
	2000	3.6	3.3	3.7	2.6	4.0	5.5	5.2	3.4	13.5	9.2	-16.1
Real return on bonds	1909	7.6										
	1919	3.5	-0.5									
	1929	2.7	0.4	1.3								
	1939	2.5	0.8	1.5	1.7							
	1949	1.6	0.2	0.4	-0.1	-1.8						
	1959	1.2	0.0	0.1	-0.3	-1.3	-0.7					
	1969	0.9	-0.2	-0.1	-0.5	-1.2	-0.8	-1.0				
	1979	-0.2	-1.3	-1.4	-1.9	-2.8	-3.1	-4.3	-7.6			
	1989	0.5	-0.4	-0.3	-0.6	-1.1	-0.9	-0.9	-0.9	6.2		
	2000	1.2	0.6	0.7	0.6	0.4	0.9	1.3	2.0	6.9	7.6	2.9
Real return on bills	1909	3.7										
	1919	1.1	-1.5									
	1929	2.3	1.6	4.8								
	1939	2.2	1.6	3.2	1.7							
	1949	0.3	-0.5	-0.2	-2.5	-6.6						
	1959	0.0	-0.7	-0.5	-2.2	-4.1	-1.6					
	1969	-0.1	-0.7	-0.6	-1.9	-3.1	-1.2	-0.9				
	1979	-0.6	-1.2	-1.2	-2.3	-3.3	-2.2	-2.4	-4.0			
	1989	-0.1	-0.6	-0.4	-1.3	-1.9	-0.7	-0.4	-0.1	3.9		
	2000	0.4	0.0	0.2	-0.5	-0.8	0.4	0.9	1.4	4.1	4.3	0.1
Real exchange rate	1909	0.3										
	1919	0.0	-0.4									
	1929	-0.7	-1.2	-2.1								
	1939	0.1	0.0	0.2	2.6							
	1949	-1.9	-2.5	-3.1	-3.7	-9.5						
	1959	-1.4	-1.7	-2.1	-2.1	-4.4	1.1					
	1969	-1.0	-1.2	-1.3	-1.1	-2.4	1.4	1.7				
	1979	0.1	0.0	0.1	0.5	0.0	3.4	4.5	7.4			
	1989	0.0	-0.1	0.0	0.3	-0.1	2.4	2.8	3.3	-0.6		
	2000	-0.4	-0.5	-0.5	-0.2	-0.7	1.1	1.1	0.9	-2.0	-3.3	-5.7
Inflation rate	1909	0.5										
	1919	3.3	6.1									
	1929	2.3	3.2	0.4								
	1939	2.7	3.4	2.1	3.8							
	1949	4.4	5.4	5.1	7.6	11.4						
	1959	4.6	5.5	5.3	7.0	8.6	5.9					
	1969	4.8	5.5	5.4	6.7	7.7	5.8	5.8				
	1979	6.0	6.8	6.9	8.2	9.4	8.7	10.1	14.7			
	1989	6.4	7.2	7.3	8.5	9.5	9.0	10.0	12.2	9.8		
	2000	6.1	6.8	6.9	7.8	8.5	7.9	8.4	9.3	6.8	4.1	4.1

Figure 29-2: Nominal returns on Spanish asset classes 1900–2000

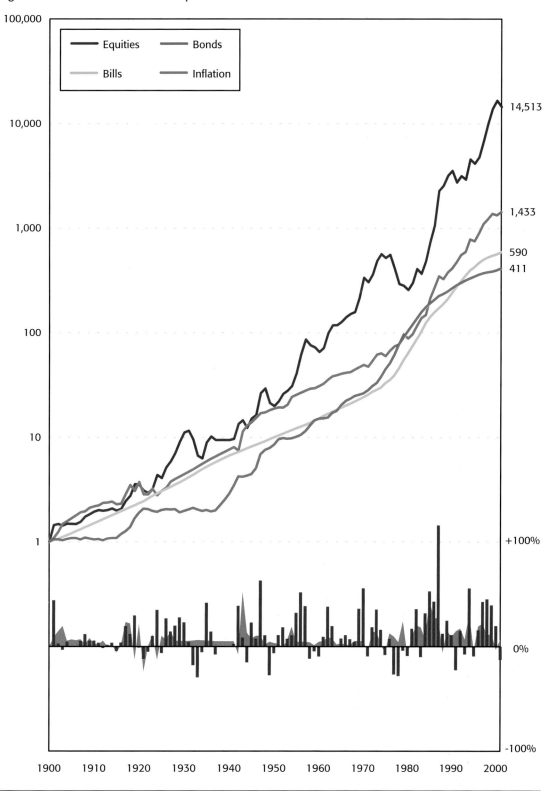

Table 29-3: Spanish equity risk premia over various periods, 1900–2000

Premium	From▶ To▼	1900	1910	1920	1930	1940	1950	1960	1970	1980	1990	2000
Equity premium versus bills	1909	2.5										
	1919	2.0	1.6									
	1929	3.5	4.0	6.6								
	1939	0.8	0.3	-0.3	-6.8							
	1949	1.4	1.1	0.9	-1.8	3.5						
	1959	2.5	2.5	2.7	1.4	5.8	8.2					
	1969	3.8	4.0	4.5	4.0	7.9	10.2	12.3				
	1979	1.7	1.6	1.7	0.7	2.7	2.4	-0.4	-11.6			
	1989	3.0	3.1	3.3	2.8	4.8	5.2	4.2	0.4	13.9		
	2000	3.2	3.3	3.5	3.1	4.8	5.1	4.3	1.9	9.0	4.7	-16.2
Equity premium versus bonds	1909	-1.2										
	1919	-0.3	0.6									
	1929	3.1	5.3	10.3								
	1939	0.5	1.1	1.3	-6.9							
	1949	0.1	0.4	0.4	-4.2	-1.5						
	1959	1.2	1.7	2.0	-0.6	2.7	7.2					
	1969	2.8	3.4	4.0	2.5	5.9	9.8	12.4				
	1979	1.3	1.7	1.9	0.3	2.2	3.4	1.6	-8.1			
	1989	2.4	2.9	3.2	2.1	4.0	5.4	4.8	1.2	11.5		
	2000	2.3	2.7	3.0	2.0	3.5	4.5	3.9	1.3	6.2	1.5	-18.5

Table 29-4: Spanish real index values and inflation index, 1900–2000

Period	Start of	Equities	Bonds	Bills	Currency	Inflation
1900– 1990	1900	1.00	1.00	1.00	1.00	1.00
	1910	1.84	2.08	1.44	1.04	1.05
	1920	1.85	1.97	1.24	1.00	1.90
	1930	5.61	2.25	1.99	0.81	1.98
	1940	3.27	2.68	2.34	1.04	2.87
	1950	2.33	2.22	1.19	0.38	8.49
	1960	4.35	2.07	1.01	0.43	15.02
	1970	12.69	1.88	0.92	0.51	26.40
	1980	2.47	0.85	0.62	1.04	103.74
	1990	13.39	1.56	0.91	0.98	265.13
1991– 2001	1991	9.72	1.68	0.97	1.12	282.92
	1992	10.59	1.87	1.04	1.15	298.55
	1993	9.31	1.90	1.12	0.98	314.52
	1994	13.83	2.38	1.20	0.80	329.99
	1995	12.03	2.20	1.24	0.89	344.30
	1996	13.34	2.51	1.30	0.98	359.19
	1997	18.48	2.98	1.35	0.92	370.72
	1998	26.33	3.24	1.40	0.78	378.20
	1999	36.21	3.59	1.43	0.84	383.49
	2000	42.12	3.39	1.43	0.72	394.61
	2001	35.33	3.49	1.44	0.68	410.79

Chapter 30 Sweden

The authority for Sweden is Per Frennberg and Bjorn Hansson's (1992a,b, 2000) database of returns on stocks, bonds, bills, and inflation over the period 1919–99. We are grateful to both authors for making their data available, and also to Adri de Ridder for advice on the Swedish equity risk premium.

The Swedish stock market was founded at the end of 1900, and we assume that stock prices did not move over 1900; thereafter we use the index values of the Swedish *Riksbank*. Although Moller (1962) provides some early data on Swedish equity dividends, this is limited in scope. Over the period 1900–18, Swedish equity dividends are therefore estimated from contemporaneous bond yields adjusted upwards by 1.33 percent (the mean yield premium over 1919–36). From the start of 1919, the Swedish equity series is based on the share price index published in the journal *Affarsvarlden*, plus the dividend income estimated by Frennberg and Hansson (1992b). De Ridder (1989) provides further information on the Swedish equity premium.

The government bond series uses data for 1900–18 from *The Economist*. For 1919–49 the returns are for perpetuals, and after that the series measures the return on a portfolio of bonds with an average maturity of ten years. We use the Datastream ten-year Swedish government bond index for 2000.

The short-term riskless rate of interest from 1900 is represented by the official discount rate of the Swedish *Riksbank*. Frennberg and Hansson (1992b) switch in 1980 to the return on short-term money market instruments, and from 1982 to treasury bills.

Inflation is represented by the cost of living index (as modified by Frennberg and Hansson) and the Swedish consumer price index.

Table 30-1: Distribution of Swedish asset returns and risk premia, 1900–2000

Return	Asset	Mean returns % p.a.			Dispersion of annual returns %				
		Geometric	Arithmetic	SE	SD	Lowest return		Highest return	
Nominal	Equities	11.6	13.9	2.3	23.5	-34.5	1931	94.1	1905
returns	Bonds	6.2	6.6	0.9	9.2	-32.5	1939	29.6	1993
	Bills	5.8	5.8	0.3	3.1	2.5	1937	15.2	1981
	Inflation	3.7	3.9	0.7	6.8	-25.2	1921	35.7	1918
Real	Equities	7.6	9.9	2.3	22.8	-43.0	1918	89.5	1905
returns	Bonds	2.4	3.1	1.3	12.7	-37.0	1939	68.2	1921
	Bills	2.0	2.2	0.7	6.8	-21.2	1918	42.7	1921
	Exchange rate	-0.4	0.2	1.1	10.7	-38.0	1919	43.5	1933
Risk	Equities vs. bills	5.5	7.7	2.2	21.9	-38.3	1990	84.8	1905
premia	Equities vs. bonds	5.2	7.4	2.2	22.1	-38.3	1990	87.8	1905
	Bonds vs. bills	0.3	0.7	0.8	8.4	-34.1	1939	24.5	1934

Figure 30-2: Nominal returns on Swedish asset classes 1900–2000

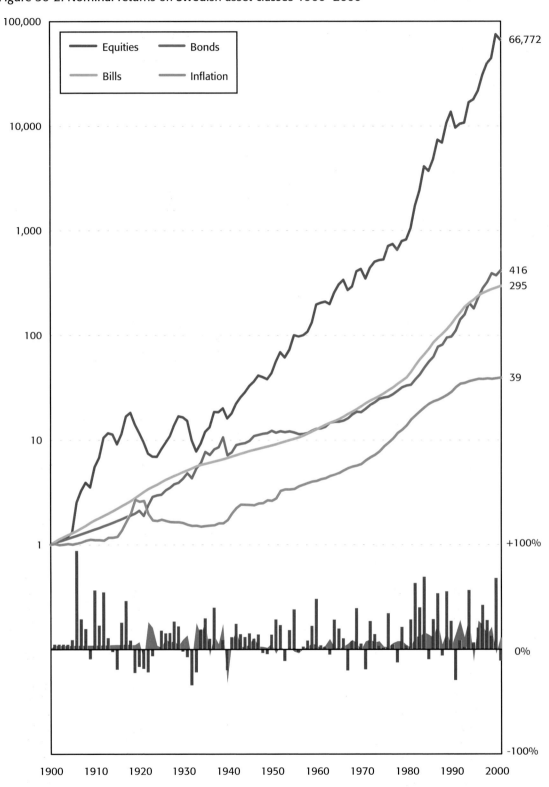

Table 30-3: Swedish equity risk premia over various periods, 1900–2000

Premium	From ▶ To ▼	1900	1910	1920	1930	1940	1950	1960	1970	1980	1990	2000
Equity premium versus bills	1909	12.4										
	1919	7.1	2.0									
	1929	4.1	0.2	-1.7								
	1939	2.2	-1.0	-2.5	-3.3							
	1949	3.2	1.0	0.7	1.9	7.4						
	1959	4.7	3.2	3.5	5.3	9.8	12.3					
	1969	4.4	3.1	3.4	4.7	7.4	7.4	2.8				
	1979	3.9	2.7	2.8	3.7	5.6	4.9	1.4	0.1			
	1989	5.3	4.5	4.8	5.9	7.9	8.0	6.6	8.6	17.7		
	2000	5.5	4.8	5.1	6.1	7.7	7.8	6.7	8.0	12.0	7.1	-14.2
Equity premium versus bonds	1909	14.7										
	1919	8.9	3.4									
	1929	4.6	-0.1	-3.5								
	1939	2.0	-1.9	-4.4	-5.3							
	1949	2.6	-0.3	-1.5	-0.4	4.7						
	1959	4.7	2.8	2.6	4.7	10.1	15.8					
	1969	4.6	3.0	2.9	4.6	8.1	9.9	4.3				
	1979	4.1	2.7	2.5	3.8	6.2	6.7	2.4	0.6			
	1989	5.7	4.6	4.7	6.2	8.6	9.6	7.7	9.4	19.0		
	2000	5.2	4.2	4.2	5.4	7.3	7.8	5.9	6.4	9.3	1.2	-20.2

Table 30-4: Swedish real index values and inflation index, 1900–2000

Period	Start of	Equities	Bonds	Bills	Currency	Inflation
1900–1990	1900	1.00	1.00	1.00	1.00	1.00
	1910	4.98	1.26	1.54	0.88	1.11
	1920	4.54	0.82	1.15	0.81	2.57
	1930	10.20	2.63	3.07	0.70	1.61
	1940	9.34	4.16	3.91	0.81	1.71
	1950	16.56	4.66	3.38	0.47	2.62
	1960	48.58	3.15	3.11	0.73	4.05
	1970	72.74	3.11	3.54	0.84	5.90
	1980	59.79	2.40	2.87	1.19	13.76
	1990	473.98	3.35	4.45	1.02	28.81
1991–2001	1991	301.88	3.46	4.60	1.17	31.97
	1992	303.96	4.10	4.78	1.24	34.47
	1993	306.82	4.49	5.35	0.96	35.02
	1994	461.33	5.59	5.58	0.83	36.49
	1995	479.07	4.82	5.86	0.93	37.44
	1996	565.27	5.99	6.25	1.04	38.28
	1997	808.95	7.38	6.65	0.97	38.11
	1998	1017.04	8.26	6.81	0.84	38.75
	1999	1161.84	10.14	7.19	0.82	38.32
	2000	1927.60	9.58	7.31	0.75	38.83
	2001	1695.93	10.56	7.50	0.66	39.37

Chapter 31 Switzerland

Our data for Switzerland rely predominantly on the series spliced together by Daniel Wydler (1989, 2001) and on extra data he kindly provided to us.

Our equity returns commence at the end of 1910. Over 1911–17 we use the Swiss National Bank index. The Swiss exchanges were closed during September 1914 to December 1915, so for end-1914 and end-1915 we use the index at the date closest to the year-end. We add a dividend yield for 1911–17 that is estimated as the Swiss short-term interest rate plus 1.21 percent, which is the average yield difference between Swiss equities and bills during 1918–25. For 1918–25 we continue with the Credit Suisse General Index, adding in OECD estimates of the annual dividend yield. For 1926–59 Ratzer (1983) estimates total returns. For 1960–83 Huber (1985) computes the returns from index levels and dividends on the SBC index. Over 1984–91 we use the Pictet return index, and then the Datastream Swiss total market index.

For Switzerland only, and solely for the period 1900–15, we estimate bond returns from the short rate. We use the latter as a proxy for the yield on seven-year bonds, and infer the annual returns for this series. This provides very rough estimates of bond returns for 1900 onward. For 1915–25 we use annual data from the *Statistischen Bureau*. The interval 1926–59 employs Ratzer's (1983) estimates based on redemption yields for new Swiss bond issues. The 1960–80 period is represented by Huber's (1985) bond index based on actual trading prices. From 1981 we use the Datastream ten-year Swiss government bond index.

During 1900–55 short-term rates are represented by the central bank discount rate, and for 1956–79, by the return on three-month time deposits. From 1980 onward, we use the return on treasury bills.

Nominal returns are adjusted for inflation using movements in the Swiss consumer prices index.

Table 31-1: Distribution of Swiss asset returns and risk premia, 1900–2000

Return	Asset	Mean returns % p.a.			Dispersion of annual returns %				
		Geometric	Arithmetic	SE	SD	Lowest return		Highest return	
Nominal	Equities[*]	7.6	9.3	2.1	19.7	-33.1	1974	61.4	1985
returns	Bonds	5.1	5.2	0.4	4.5	-8.1	1989	20.8	1908
	Bills	3.3	3.3	0.2	1.7	0.6	1978	8.6	1990
	Inflation	2.2	2.4	0.6	6.0	-22.2	1921	25.7	1918
Real	Equities	5.0	6.9	2.1	20.4	-37.8	1974	56.2	1985
returns	Bonds	2.8	3.1	0.8	8.0	-16.1	1918	35.9	1921
	Bills	1.1	1.2	0.6	6.2	-16.5	1918	34.4	1921
	Exchange rate	0.2	0.8	1.1	11.2	-29.0	1936	53.3	1933
Risk	Equities vs. bills[*]	4.3	6.1	2.0	19.4	-37.0	1974	54.8	1985
premia	Equities vs. bonds[*]	2.7	4.2	1.9	17.9	-34.4	1974	52.2	1985
	Bonds vs. bills	1.7	1.8	0.4	4.4	-13.9	1989	15.6	1908

[*] Equity and equity risk premia statistics are from 1911

Figure 31-1: Returns on Swiss asset classes 1900–2000, in real terms

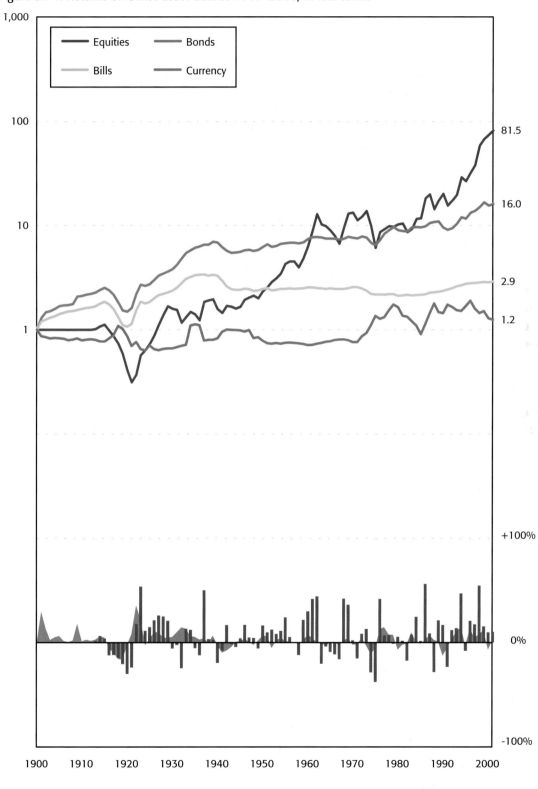

Table 31-2: Swiss real rates of return and inflation over various periods, 1900–2000

Return	To	1900	1910	1920	1930	1940	1950	1960	1970	1980	1990	2000
Real return on equities (from 1911)	1909	na										
	1919	na	-9.4									
	1929	na	2.5	14.4								
	1939	na	1.6	6.9	-0.1							
	1949	na	2.2	5.9	1.9	4.0						
	1959	na	3.8	7.0	4.7	7.2	10.4					
	1969	na	4.5	7.2	5.4	7.3	9.1	7.7				
	1979	na	3.4	5.5	3.8	4.8	5.1	2.5	-2.5			
	1989	na	3.9	5.7	4.3	5.2	5.6	4.0	2.1	7.0		
	2000	na	5.0	6.7	5.7	6.7	7.2	6.5	6.0	10.4	13.5	10.3
Real return on bonds	1909	7.8										
	1919	2.0	-3.4									
	1929	4.6	3.0	9.8								
	1939	4.9	4.0	7.9	6.0							
	1949	3.7	2.7	4.9	2.5	-1.0						
	1959	3.4	2.5	4.1	2.2	0.4	1.8					
	1969	2.9	2.2	3.3	1.7	0.4	1.0	0.3				
	1979	2.8	2.1	3.0	1.7	0.7	1.2	1.0	1.7			
	1989	2.5	1.9	2.7	1.5	0.7	1.1	0.9	1.1	0.6		
	2000	2.8	2.3	3.0	2.0	1.4	1.9	1.9	2.4	2.8	4.8	3.1
Real return on bills	1909	4.8										
	1919	0.4	-3.8									
	1929	2.9	2.0	8.3								
	1939	3.0	2.5	5.8	3.3							
	1949	1.8	1.1	2.8	0.2	-2.9						
	1959	1.6	0.9	2.2	0.2	-1.3	0.3					
	1969	1.4	0.8	1.8	0.2	-0.8	0.2	0.1				
	1979	0.9	0.4	1.1	-0.2	-1.1	-0.5	-0.9	-1.9			
	1989	1.0	0.5	1.1	0.0	-0.7	-0.1	-0.3	-0.4	1.1		
	2000	1.1	0.7	1.2	0.3	-0.2	0.3	0.3	0.4	1.5	1.9	1.3
Real exchange rate	1909	-2.3										
	1919	-0.7	1.0									
	1929	-1.4	-0.9	-2.7								
	1939	-0.5	0.1	-0.3	2.2							
	1949	-0.5	0.0	-0.3	0.9	-0.5						
	1959	-0.6	-0.2	-0.5	0.2	-0.8	-1.0					
	1969	-0.4	-0.1	-0.3	0.3	-0.3	-0.2	0.7				
	1979	0.6	1.0	1.1	1.8	1.7	2.5	4.3	8.0			
	1989	0.4	0.7	0.7	1.3	1.1	1.5	2.4	3.2	-1.3		
	2000	0.2	0.5	0.4	0.9	0.7	0.9	1.4	1.6	-1.3	-1.3	-3.0
Inflation rate	1909	-0.1										
	1919	4.3	8.8									
	1929	1.4	2.2	-4.1								
	1939	0.7	1.0	-2.7	-1.3							
	1949	1.5	1.9	-0.4	1.6	4.5						
	1959	1.4	1.7	0.0	1.5	2.8	1.2					
	1969	1.7	2.0	0.7	1.9	3.0	2.2	3.2				
	1979	2.1	2.4	1.4	2.5	3.5	3.1	4.1	5.0			
	1989	2.2	2.5	1.7	2.6	3.4	3.2	3.8	4.2	3.4		
	2000	2.2	2.5	1.7	2.6	3.2	2.9	3.4	3.4	2.7	2.1	1.5

Figure 31-2: Nominal returns on Swiss asset classes 1900–2000

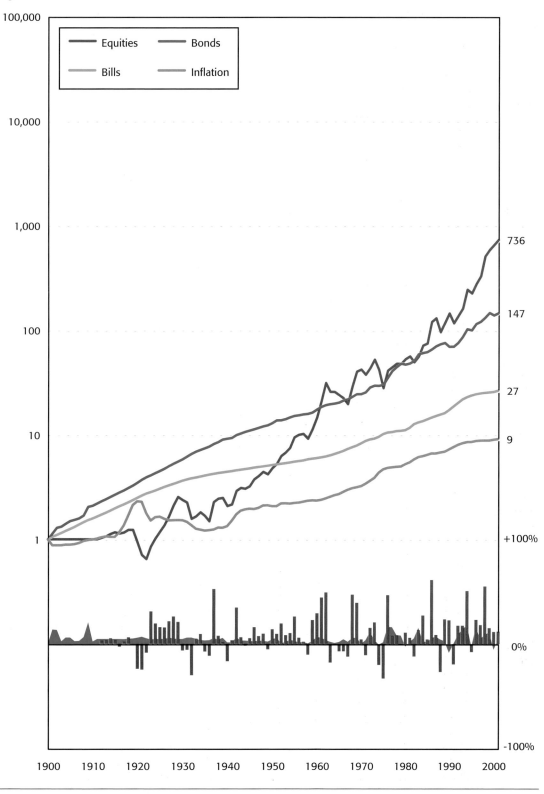

Table 31-3: Swiss equity risk premia over various periods, 1900–2000

Premium	From ▶ To ▼	1900	1910	1920	1930	1940	1950	1960	1970	1980	1990	2000
Equity	1909	na										
premium	1919	na	-5.1									
versus	1929	na	0.4	5.7								
bills	1939	na	-0.9	1.1	-3.3							
(from	1949	na	1.1	3.1	1.7	7.0						
1911)	1959	na	2.9	4.8	4.4	8.5	10.1					
	1969	na	3.7	5.3	5.2	8.2	8.9	7.7				
	1979	na	3.0	4.3	4.0	6.0	5.6	3.4	-0.6			
	1989	na	3.4	4.5	4.3	5.9	5.7	4.2	2.6	5.9		
	2000	na	4.3	5.5	5.4	6.9	6.9	6.1	5.6	8.7	11.4	8.9
Equity	1909	na										
premium	1919	na	-5.6									
versus	1929	na	-0.5	4.2								
bonds	1939	na	-2.4	-0.9	-5.7							
(from	1949	na	-0.5	1.0	-0.5	5.0						
1911)	1959	na	1.3	2.9	2.4	6.7	8.5					
	1969	na	2.3	3.7	3.6	7.0	8.0	7.4				
	1979	na	1.3	2.4	2.0	4.1	3.8	1.5	-4.1			
	1989	na	1.9	3.0	2.8	4.5	4.4	3.1	1.0	6.4		
	2000	na	2.7	3.7	3.6	5.2	5.3	4.5	3.5	7.4	8.3	6.9

Table 31-4: Swiss real index values and inflation index, 1900–2000

Period	Start of	Equities	Bonds	Bills	Currency	Inflation
1900–	1900	na	1.00	1.00	1.00	1.00
1990	1910	1.00[*]	2.12	1.59	0.79	0.99
	1920	0.41	1.50	1.08	0.87	2.32
	1930	1.59	3.83	2.38	0.66	1.53
	1940	1.58	6.87	3.30	0.83	1.34
	1950	2.33	6.22	2.47	0.79	2.08
	1960	6.28	7.43	2.55	0.71	2.35
	1970	13.24	7.65	2.57	0.76	3.23
	1980	10.26	9.03	2.12	1.64	5.24
	1990	20.21	9.58	2.36	1.44	7.29
1991–	1991	15.49	9.12	2.44	1.73	7.68
2001	1992	17.32	9.44	2.50	1.65	8.08
	1993	19.70	10.41	2.61	1.54	8.35
	1994	28.99	12.00	2.67	1.51	8.56
	1995	26.66	11.68	2.77	1.68	8.60
	1996	32.19	13.24	2.79	1.90	8.77
	1997	37.77	13.81	2.82	1.59	8.84
	1998	58.39	14.97	2.85	1.44	8.87
	1999	67.36	16.68	2.88	1.51	8.87
	2000	73.95	15.55	2.86	1.29	9.03
	2001	81.54	16.04	2.90	1.25	9.16

[*] Real equity values start at 1.00 in 1911

Chapter 32 United Kingdom

For the United Kingdom, it was clear that there was a need for a long and consistently compiled equity return series. With support from ABN AMRO, we therefore created a new index that adheres to the guidelines presented in section 3.1. The basis for our study of the UK market is a database that comprises two elements. To compile share prices for the period starting in 1955, we use the fully representative record of equity prices maintained by London Business School. This database covers several thousand shares, and is described in Dimson and Marsh (1983). The London Share Price Database (the LSPD) provides reliable measures of stock market returns, which cover most of the second half of the century. We refer the reader to our article in the *Journal of Business* (Dimson and Marsh, 2001) for details on our comprehensive UK index histories for the period from 1955 to date.

The period from 1899 to 1954 presented a rather different challenge. Rather than accepting a standard back-history at face value, we took on the painstaking process of collecting share prices from old issues of the *Financial Times* from 1899 onward. This enabled us to calculate an index of the returns from the top 100 companies over the period from New Year 1900 to the end of 1954. The companies that enter the index are included without reference to whether they survive after entering the index. The index resembles the FTSE 100 in its method of construction. Our new value-weighted equity index contains the hundred companies that, before the start of each year, have the largest market capitalization for their ordinary or deferred shares. For the entire 101 years, we follow the same criteria for index membership: inclusion of UK companies with ordinary or deferred shares, and omission of companies with non-UK registration/head office. We exclude preference shares.

The first stage was to identify a list of shares that were eligible for investment. To avoid any upward returns bias, this had to be a set of firms that existed at each point in time, and which had not been screened for subsequent survival. Our definition of the companies eligible for inclusion was based on those with stock prices published in the *Financial Times* (*FT*) for 1899–1954, and in the *Stock Exchange Daily Official List* (*SEDOL*) for 1955–99.

For the earlier period, we constructed a cross-section of all shares with prices quoted in the *FT* on the last trading day of 1899, 1909, 1918, 1927, 1936, and 1945. Despite omission from the end-1899 and end-1909 *FT*s, the banking and insurance sectors were included in our index series, based on *SEDOL* prices. The reason for doing this is that the banking and insurance sectors appeared regularly, though not daily, in the *FT*. Note also that in 1899 and 1909 smaller mining shares were excluded. The number of shares in our pre-1955 cross-section rose from 247 in 1899 (when *SEDOL* contained 783 shares) to 604 in 1954 (when *SEDOL* contained 3,789 shares). Compared to the full list of companies in *SEDOL*, our sample covers a minority by number but a substantial majority by value of all quoted companies.

Share prices before 1955 were taken as the average of bid and offer prices for the last trading day of the year as quoted in the *FT*. Very occasionally, where necessary, other prices were taken from *SEDOL*. Year-end prices for 1914 were taken from January 4, 1915, the first day of trading after the closure of the Stock Exchange following the outbreak of the First World War.

From 1955 onward, our database is the LSPD, which provides full monthly share price and ancillary information taken from *SEDOL*, Exshare, and other sources.

The share capital of index constituents was checked against the annual *Stock Exchange Official Yearbook* throughout the period up to 1955, to identify capital changes and acquisitions. The timing of rights issues and nearly all bonus issues was identified to the specific month. Market capitalizations were calculated as the product of number of shares and market price. Typically, ordinary and "A" ordinary shares (with similar share prices) were combined. Where there were two different classes of ordinary shares, as was the case for certain banks and insurance companies, the one with the larger market capitalization was chosen.

Before 1955, all cash flows are assumed to occur at the end of each year, including dividends, special dividends, returns of capital, and cash from acquisitions. Where companies are acquired for shares, or when they merge during the year, we base returns on the end-year share price of the acquirer or merged entity, taking account of the exchange ratio. Before 1955, the primary source of information regarding dividend cash flows was the *Stock Exchange Ten-Year Record* published by Mathiesons. After 1955, we use monthly data from the LSPD, reinvesting dividends at the end of the ex-dividend month. Cash from acquisitions and similar sources is reinvested at the end of the month the acquisition is consummated.

Returns are calculated in three ways: raw price movements, capital returns and total returns including reinvested dividends. The price returns reflect annual price changes, adjusted for capital changes. Capital returns add returns of capital (such as special dividends, the distribution of shares in other companies and the distribution of non-ordinary shares as a bonus to ordinary shareholders) to the price returns. Total returns add income returns (dividends received during the year) to the capital returns. We report both capital returns, namely the capital appreciation or loss, and total returns including reinvested income.

A benefit of our bottom-up approach to creating a UK equity index is that we are now able to study the performance of segments of the market that are of interest. Groups based on company size, dividend yield or industry sector may now be investigated. We can also look at secular trends in market concentration, and at the risks of investing in ordinary shares.

We also compiled a new set of UK government bond indexes especially for this study. First, we constructed an index of the returns on default-free long bonds. For the 1900–54 period the returns are based on perpetual bonds issued by the UK government. At the start of 1900, there was only one true UK gilt-edged stock (UK government stocks are referred to as "gilts"), the 2¾ percent (later 2½ percent) Consol. This was an undated, or "perpetual", stock. Early in the century this was joined by another perpetual, War Loan. Over time, further perpetuals, as well as dated stocks, joined the list. But for much of the first half of the last century, the government bond market, and market liquidity, was dominated by the perpetuals.

Our new long bond index therefore tracks the returns (coupon plus capital gains) on 2½ percent Consols for the first half of the twentieth century, until end-1954. By then, Consols had declined in importance and liquidity, while the UK government bond market had broadened sufficiently to enable the construction of an index of dated long bonds. From 1955–2000 our long bond index thus measures the return on a portfolio of government bonds with a mean maturity (at mid-year) of twenty years. It is designed to measure returns to a tax-exempt investor, and historically, this has implied a high-coupon strategy. From start-1955, the long bond index is thus based on high coupon bonds, defined as those that fall within the top third of all coupons for the long bond maturity range. On average, there are four constituents in the index each year. We also constructed an index of intermediate term bonds, starting in 1955. This mid-maturity bond index follows the same design principles as the long-bond index, but has a maturity (at mid-year) averaging five, rather than twenty, years. On average, this index contains two constituents per year.

Finally, we also constructed an index of inflation-indexed long bonds. In the United Kingdom, inflation-indexed government bonds, whose coupons and redemption values are tied to the level of the retail price index, were first introduced in 1975. Initially, they were issued as non-tradable certificates, but by 1981, they became available as listed securities to all investors. Our inflation-indexed bond index thus starts in April 1981, and incorporates all inflation-indexed UK government bonds that have a maturity of between 15½ and 25½ years at the start of each calendar year. Typically, this index has 3–4 constituents, and like our corresponding index of long conventional bonds, it has an average maturity of twenty years.

Throughout the century, treasury bills are used to measure the UK short-term riskless rate of interest. Inflation is calculated using the retail price index and, before 1962, the index of retail prices. Rather than the more usual format of dollars per pound, for consistency with other currencies the exchange rate is expressed as pounds per dollar.

As noted in chapter 17, the equity, bond, and bill series presented here are known commercially as the ABN AMRO/LBS indexes.

Table 32-1: Distribution of UK asset returns and risk premia, 1900–2000

Return	Asset	Mean returns % p.a.			Dispersion of annual returns %				
		Geometric	Arithmetic	SE	SD	Lowest return		Highest return	
Nominal	Equities	10.1	11.9	2.2	21.8	-48.8	1974	145.6	1975
returns	Bonds	5.4	6.1	1.2	12.5	-19.1	1915	53.1	1982
	Bills	5.1	5.1	0.4	3.9	0.5	1946	17.2	1980
	Inflation	4.1	4.3	0.7	6.9	-26.0	1921	24.9	1975
Real	Equities	5.8	7.6	2.0	20.0	-57.1	1974	96.7	1975
returns	Bonds	1.3	2.3	1.4	14.5	-34.1	1915	61.2	1921
	Bills	1.0	1.2	0.7	6.6	-15.4	1915	42.4	1921
	Exchange rate	-0.3	0.3	1.2	11.7	-36.7	1946	55.2	1933
Risk	Equities vs. bills	4.8	6.5	2.0	19.9	-54.6	1974	121.8	1975
premia	Equities vs. bonds	4.4	5.6	1.7	16.7	-38.0	1974	80.8	1975
	Bonds vs. bills	0.3	0.9	1.1	11.3	-26.6	1974	37.5	1932

Figure 32-1: Returns on UK asset classes 1900–2000, in real terms

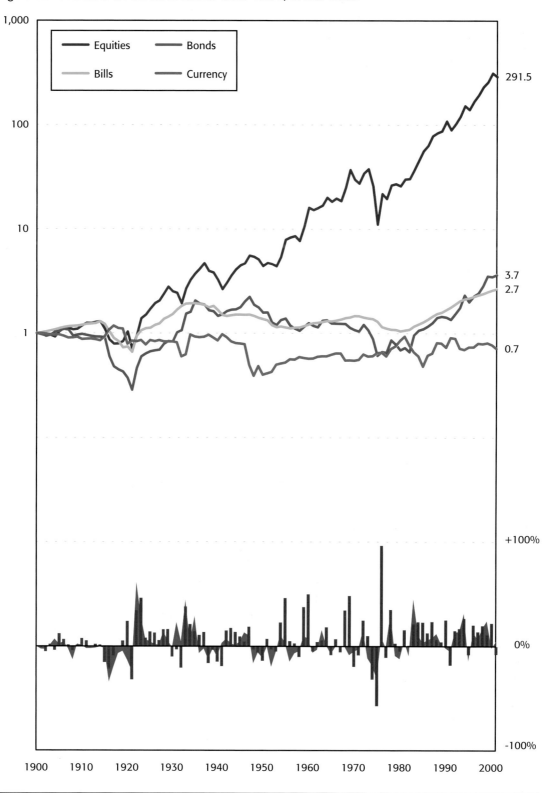

Table 32-2: UK real rates of return and inflation over various periods, 1900–2000

Return	From ▶ To ▼	1900	1910	1920	1930	1940	1950	1960	1970	1980	1990	2000
Real return on equities	1909	1.8										
	1919	0.2	-1.3									
	1929	3.1	3.8	9.3								
	1939	3.0	3.4	5.9	2.6							
	1949	3.0	3.3	4.9	2.9	3.1						
	1959	4.7	5.3	7.1	6.4	8.3	13.7					
	1969	5.0	5.5	7.0	6.4	7.7	10.0	6.5				
	1979	4.2	4.5	5.5	4.8	5.3	6.1	2.5	-1.4			
	1989	5.4	5.8	6.9	6.5	7.3	8.3	6.6	6.7	15.4		
	2000	5.8	6.2	7.2	6.9	7.6	8.6	7.3	7.6	12.2	9.3	-7.6
Real return on bonds	1909	-0.2										
	1919	-4.8	-9.2									
	1929	-0.6	-0.8	8.3								
	1939	1.0	1.4	7.1	5.9							
	1949	0.9	1.2	4.9	3.3	0.7						
	1959	0.4	0.5	3.1	1.4	-0.8	-2.3					
	1969	0.1	0.2	2.1	0.7	-1.0	-1.9	-1.5				
	1979	-0.5	-0.5	1.0	-0.4	-1.9	-2.7	-3.0	-4.4			
	1989	0.4	0.5	1.9	0.9	-0.1	-0.3	0.4	1.4	7.5		
	2000	1.3	1.5	2.9	2.1	1.5	1.6	2.6	4.0	8.2	8.9	4.5
Real return on bills	1909	1.9										
	1919	-1.4	-4.7									
	1929	1.4	1.2	7.5								
	1939	1.3	1.1	4.1	0.9							
	1949	0.6	0.3	2.1	-0.5	-2.0						
	1959	0.3	0.0	1.2	-0.8	-1.6	-1.2					
	1969	0.6	0.3	1.4	-0.1	-0.4	0.4	1.9				
	1979	0.1	-0.2	0.6	-0.7	-1.2	-0.9	-0.7	-3.3			
	1989	0.6	0.4	1.2	0.2	0.0	0.5	1.1	0.7	4.8		
	2000	1.0	0.9	1.6	0.8	0.8	1.3	1.9	1.9	4.5	4.3	3.0
Real exchange rate	1909	-1.3										
	1919	-1.1	-1.0									
	1929	-0.6	-0.3	0.5								
	1939	-0.4	-0.1	0.4	0.3							
	1949	-1.8	-1.9	-2.2	-3.6	-7.2						
	1959	-0.9	-0.9	-0.8	-1.2	-2.0	3.6					
	1969	-0.9	-0.8	-0.7	-1.0	-1.5	1.6	-0.4				
	1979	-0.2	0.0	0.1	0.0	0.0	2.5	2.0	4.5			
	1989	-0.3	-0.2	-0.1	-0.2	-0.3	1.5	0.8	1.5	-1.5		
	2000	-0.3	-0.2	-0.1	-0.2	-0.3	1.1	0.5	0.9	-0.8	-0.2	-7.7
Inflation rate	1909	1.1										
	1919	4.9	8.9									
	1929	2.2	2.8	-2.9								
	1939	1.8	2.0	-1.3	0.4							
	1949	2.0	2.2	0.1	1.6	2.8						
	1959	2.3	2.6	1.1	2.4	3.5	4.1					
	1969	2.5	2.8	1.6	2.7	3.5	3.9	3.7				
	1979	3.8	4.2	3.4	4.7	5.8	6.9	8.3	13.1			
	1989	4.1	4.5	3.9	5.1	6.1	6.9	7.8	10.0	6.9		
	2000	4.1	4.4	3.8	4.8	5.6	6.1	6.6	7.6	5.1	3.4	2.9

Figure 32-2: Nominal returns on UK asset classes 1900–2000

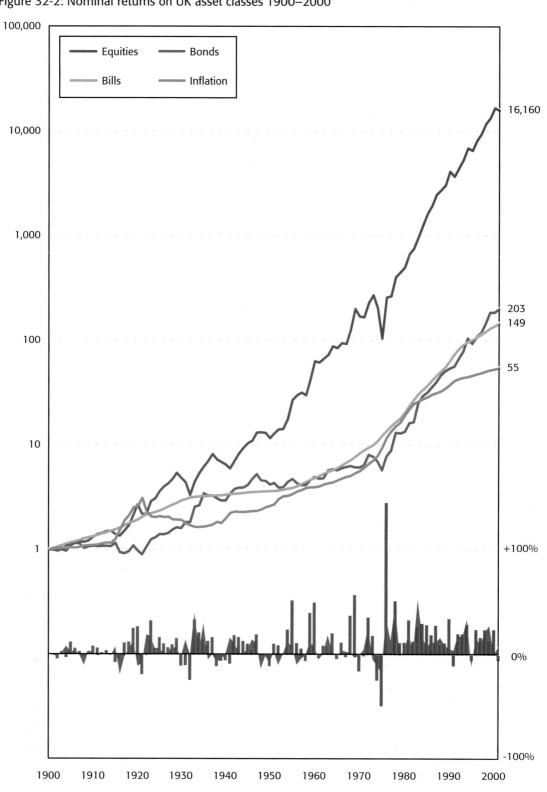

Table 32-3: UK equity risk premia over various periods, 1900–2000

Premium	From ▶ To ▼	1900	1910	1920	1930	1940	1950	1960	1970	1980	1990	2000
Equity premium versus bills	1909	-0.1										
	1919	1.7	3.5									
	1929	1.7	2.6	1.7								
	1939	1.7	2.3	1.7	1.7							
	1949	2.4	3.0	2.8	3.4	5.1						
	1959	4.4	5.3	5.8	7.2	10.0	15.1					
	1969	4.4	5.2	5.5	6.5	8.1	9.6	4.5				
	1979	4.1	4.7	4.9	5.6	6.5	7.0	3.2	2.0			
	1989	4.7	5.4	5.6	6.3	7.3	7.8	5.5	6.0	10.1		
	2000	4.8	5.3	5.5	6.1	6.8	7.1	5.3	5.6	7.3	4.8	-10.3
Equity premium versus bonds	1909	2.0										
	1919	5.3	8.6									
	1929	3.8	4.7	0.9								
	1939	2.0	2.0	-1.1	-3.1							
	1949	2.1	2.1	0.0	-0.4	2.3						
	1959	4.3	4.8	3.9	4.9	9.1	16.4					
	1969	4.9	5.3	4.7	5.7	8.8	12.2	8.1				
	1979	4.6	5.0	4.4	5.2	7.3	9.1	5.6	3.1			
	1989	4.9	5.3	4.8	5.5	7.3	8.6	6.2	5.2	7.3		
	2000	4.4	4.7	4.2	4.7	6.0	6.8	4.6	3.5	3.6	0.4	-11.6

Table 32-4: UK real index values and inflation index, 1900–2000

Period	Start of	Equities	Bonds	Bills	Currency	Inflation
1900– 1990	1900	1.00	1.00	1.00	1.00	1.00
	1910	1.19	0.98	1.21	0.88	1.12
	1920	1.04	0.37	0.75	0.79	2.62
	1930	2.53	0.83	1.54	0.83	1.94
	1940	3.28	1.48	1.68	0.85	2.01
	1950	4.44	1.59	1.38	0.40	2.66
	1960	16.07	1.26	1.23	0.57	3.99
	1970	30.08	1.08	1.48	0.55	5.72
	1980	26.13	0.69	1.06	0.85	19.54
	1990	109.51	1.44	1.69	0.73	38.24
1991– 2001	1991	89.72	1.37	1.79	0.91	41.82
	1992	103.32	1.56	1.93	0.89	43.68
	1993	121.03	1.78	2.07	0.72	44.81
	1994	153.33	2.33	2.14	0.70	45.68
	1995	141.18	2.01	2.19	0.74	47.00
	1996	170.15	2.29	2.26	0.74	48.51
	1997	194.11	2.44	2.34	0.80	49.70
	1998	232.64	2.86	2.41	0.79	51.51
	1999	258.48	3.56	2.52	0.81	52.93
	2000	315.59	3.50	2.60	0.78	53.86
	2001	291.51	3.66	2.68	0.72	55.44

Chapter 33 United States

The standard study for the United States, covering the period since 1926, is the Ibbotson and Sinquefield (1976) article and subsequent Ibbotson Associates updates. The broadest index of US stock market returns prior to 1926 is the one presented in Wilson and Jones (2002), and we use the latter for this study. We are grateful to Jack Wilson for providing us with his database.

Earlier sources are described in Goetzmann, Ibbotson, and Peng (2001). Our series, however, commences with the Wilson-Jones index data over 1900–25. For 1926–61 we use the University of Chicago's Center for Research in Security Prices (CRSP) capitalization-weighted index of all New York Stock Exchange stocks. For 1962–70 we use the CRSP capitalization-weighted index of NYSE and Amex stocks. From 1971 onward we employ the Wilshire 5000 index, which by end-2000, included over 7,000 US stocks listed on the NYSE, Amex, Nasdaq, and other exchanges. All indexes include reinvested dividends.

The government bond series for 1900–18 is based on 4 percent government bonds. Over 1919–25 we use the Federal Reserve ten-to-fifteen year bond index. After that bond returns are based on Ibbotson Associates' long bond index.

The bill index uses commercial bills during 1900–18. From 1919 onward, the series is based on US treasury bills.

Inflation is based on the consumer price index.

Table 33-1: Distribution of US asset returns and risk premia, 1900–2000

Return	Asset	Mean returns % p.a.			Dispersion of annual returns %				
		Geometric	Arithmetic	SE	SD	Lowest return		Highest return	
Nominal	Equities	10.1	12.0	2.0	19.9	-43.9	1931	57.6	1933
returns	Bonds	4.8	5.1	0.8	8.3	-9.2	1967	40.4	1982
	Bills	4.1	4.1	0.3	2.8	0.0	1938	14.7	1981
	Inflation	3.2	3.3	0.5	5.0	-10.8	1921	20.4	1918
Real	Equities	6.7	8.7	2.0	20.2	-38.0	1931	56.8	1933
returns	Bonds	1.6	2.1	1.0	10.0	-19.3	1918	35.1	1982
	Bills	0.9	1.0	0.5	4.7	-15.1	1946	20.0	1921
Risk	Equities vs. bills	5.8	7.7	2.0	19.6	-44.5	1931	57.1	1933
premia	Equities vs. bonds	5.0	7.0	2.0	20.0	-40.8	1931	57.7	1933
	Bonds vs. bills	0.7	1.0	0.8	7.7	-13.6	1980	27.0	1982

Figure 33-1: Returns on US asset classes 1900–2000, in real terms

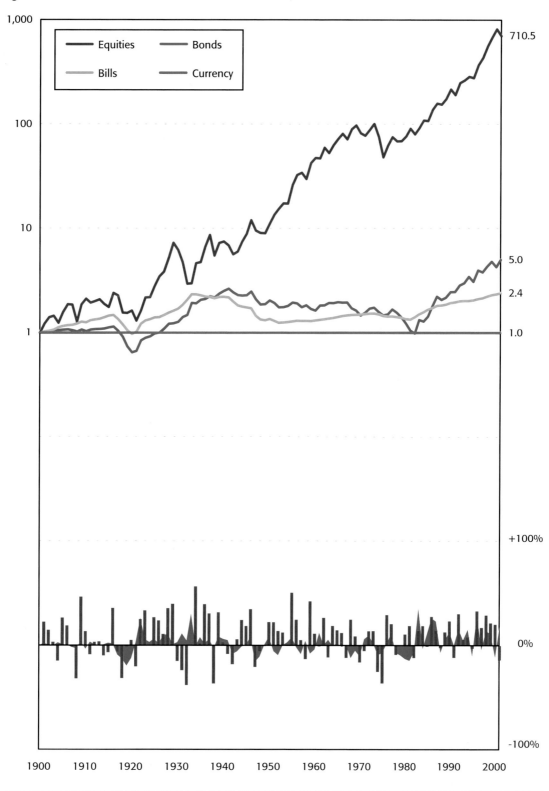

Figure 34-1: Returns on World asset classes 1900–2000, in real dollar terms

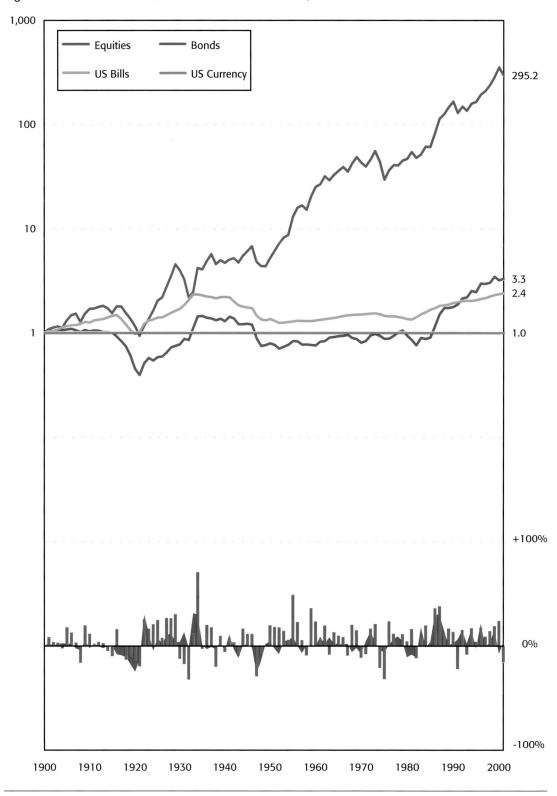

Table 34-2: World real rates of return and US inflation over various periods, 1900–2000

Return	From ▶ To ▼	1900	1910	1920	1930	1940	1950	1960	1970	1980	1990	2000
Real return on equities	1909	5.4										
	1919	0.8	-3.7									
	1929	4.7	4.3	13.0								
	1939	3.9	3.4	7.2	1.7							
	1949	3.3	2.8	5.1	1.4	1.0						
	1959	5.5	5.5	8.0	6.4	8.8	17.1					
	1969	5.5	5.5	7.5	6.1	7.7	11.2	5.5				
	1979	4.9	4.9	6.4	5.1	5.9	7.6	3.1	0.9			
	1989	5.8	5.9	7.3	6.4	7.4	9.1	6.5	7.0	13.5		
	2000	5.8	5.8	7.1	6.3	7.0	8.2	6.2	6.4	9.2	5.4	-16.0
Real return on bonds	1909	0.3										
	1919	-3.9	-7.9									
	1929	-0.9	-1.4	5.5								
	1939	0.6	0.8	5.4	5.3							
	1949	-0.5	-0.7	1.9	0.1	-4.8						
	1959	-0.5	-0.6	1.3	-0.1	-2.7	-0.4					
	1969	-0.3	-0.4	1.2	0.1	-1.6	0.1	0.6				
	1979	-0.1	-0.1	1.2	0.4	-0.8	0.6	1.1	1.6			
	1989	0.6	0.7	2.0	1.4	0.6	2.0	2.9	4.0	6.6		
	2000	1.2	1.3	2.5	2.1	1.5	2.8	3.7	4.7	6.2	5.8	3.6
Real return on US bills	1909	2.3										
	1919	-0.1	-2.5									
	1929	1.8	1.5	5.8								
	1939	2.0	1.9	4.2	2.7							
	1949	0.6	0.2	1.1	-1.1	-4.7						
	1959	0.5	0.1	0.8	-0.9	-2.6	-0.3					
	1969	0.6	0.3	0.9	-0.3	-1.3	0.5	1.3				
	1979	0.4	0.1	0.6	-0.4	-1.2	0.0	0.2	-1.0			
	1989	0.7	0.5	1.0	0.2	-0.3	0.9	1.3	1.3	3.6		
	2000	0.9	0.7	1.1	0.5	0.1	1.1	1.5	1.5	2.8	2.0	2.4
Real exchange rate	1909	0.0										
	1919	0.0	0.0									
	1929	0.0	0.0	0.0								
	1939	0.0	0.0	0.0	0.0							
	1949	0.0	0.0	0.0	0.0	0.0						
	1959	0.0	0.0	0.0	0.0	0.0	0.0					
	1969	0.0	0.0	0.0	0.0	0.0	0.0	0.0				
	1979	0.0	0.0	0.0	0.0	0.0	0.0	0.0	0.0			
	1989	0.0	0.0	0.0	0.0	0.0	0.0	0.0	0.0	0.0		
	2000	0.0	0.0	0.0	0.0	0.0	0.0	0.0	0.0	0.0	0.0	0.0
Inflation rate (US)	1909	2.4										
	1919	4.8	7.3									
	1929	2.9	3.1	-1.0								
	1939	1.6	1.4	-1.5	-2.0							
	1949	2.4	2.4	0.7	1.6	5.4						
	1959	2.3	2.3	1.1	1.8	3.8	2.2					
	1969	2.4	2.4	1.4	2.0	3.4	2.4	2.5				
	1979	3.0	3.1	2.4	3.0	4.4	4.0	4.9	7.4			
	1989	3.2	3.3	2.7	3.4	4.5	4.3	5.0	6.2	5.1		
	2000	3.2	3.3	2.8	3.3	4.2	4.0	4.4	5.1	4.0	3.0	3.4

Figure 34-2: Nominal US dollar returns on World asset classes 1900–2000

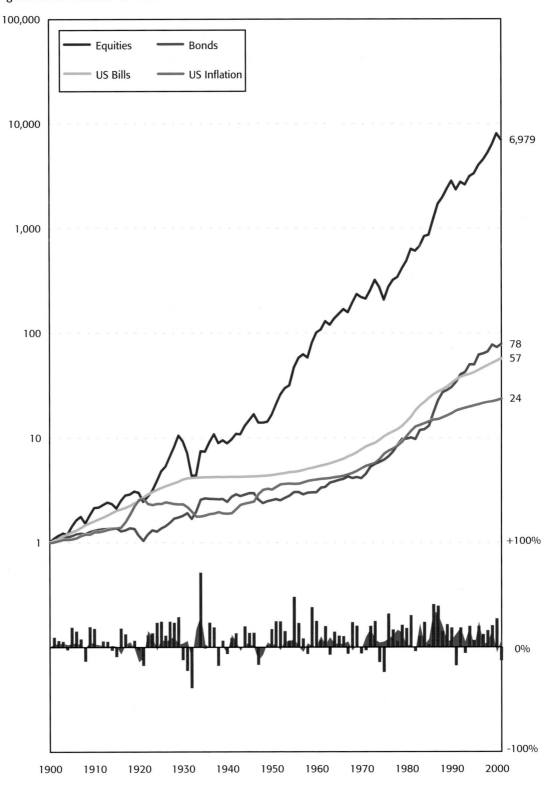

Table 34-3: World equity risk premia over various periods, 1900–2000

Premium	From ▶ To ▼	1900	1910	1920	1930	1940	1950	1960	1970	1980	1990	2000
Equity premium versus US bills	1909	3.1										
	1919	0.9	-1.2									
	1929	2.9	2.8	6.9								
	1939	1.9	1.5	2.9	-1.0							
	1949	2.7	2.6	3.9	2.5	6.1						
	1959	5.0	5.4	7.2	7.3	11.7	17.5					
	1969	4.9	5.2	6.6	6.5	9.1	10.6	4.1				
	1979	4.5	4.7	5.8	5.5	7.2	7.6	3.0	1.9			
	1989	5.1	5.3	6.3	6.2	7.7	8.1	5.1	5.6	9.6		
	2000	4.9	5.1	5.9	5.7	6.9	7.0	4.6	4.8	6.2	3.3	-17.9
Equity premium versus bonds	1909	5.2										
	1919	4.9	4.6									
	1929	5.6	5.8	7.1								
	1939	3.3	2.7	1.7	-3.4							
	1949	3.8	3.5	3.2	1.2	6.1						
	1959	6.0	6.2	6.6	6.4	11.8	17.7					
	1969	5.9	6.0	6.3	6.0	9.4	11.1	4.9				
	1979	5.0	5.0	5.1	4.7	6.8	7.0	2.0	-0.7			
	1989	5.2	5.2	5.3	5.0	6.7	6.9	3.5	2.8	6.5		
	2000	4.6	4.5	4.5	4.1	5.4	5.3	2.4	1.7	2.8	-0.4	-18.9

Table 34-4: World real index values (in real US dollars) and US inflation index, 1900–2000

Period	Start of	Equities	Bonds	US Bills	Currency	US Inflation
1900– 1990	1900	1.00	1.00	1.00	1.00	1.00
	1910	1.70	1.03	1.26	1.00	1.27
	1920	1.16	0.45	0.97	1.00	2.57
	1930	3.96	0.77	1.71	1.00	2.33
	1940	4.68	1.29	2.22	1.00	1.90
	1950	5.19	0.79	1.36	1.00	3.21
	1960	25.23	0.75	1.32	1.00	3.99
	1970	42.97	0.80	1.50	1.00	5.12
	1980	46.79	0.93	1.36	1.00	10.43
	1990	166.18	1.76	1.94	1.00	17.13
1991– 2001	1991	129.00	1.87	1.97	1.00	18.18
	1992	148.45	2.14	2.02	1.00	18.73
	1993	135.78	2.18	2.03	1.00	19.28
	1994	158.64	2.52	2.04	1.00	19.81
	1995	164.68	2.44	2.06	1.00	20.34
	1996	192.99	2.95	2.12	1.00	20.85
	1997	209.65	2.93	2.16	1.00	21.55
	1998	239.02	3.01	2.24	1.00	21.91
	1999	283.86	3.44	2.31	1.00	22.27
	2000	351.29	3.17	2.35	1.00	22.86
	2001	295.24	3.29	2.41	1.00	23.64

References

Agarwal, V., and N.Y. Naik, 2000, Multi-period persistence analysis of hedge funds. *Journal of Financial and Quantitative Analysis* **35**: 327–342

Ahearne, A. G., W. L. Griever, and F. E. Warnock, 2001, Information costs and home bias: An analysis of U.S. holdings of foreign equities. International finance discussion paper No 691, Board of Governors of the Federal Reserve System

Aleotti, A, 1990, *Borsa e Industria 1861–1989: Cento Anni di Rapporti Difficili.* Milan: Edizioni Comunita

Annaert, J., F. Buelens, J. de Ceuster, L. Cuyvers, G. Devos, M. Gemis, H. Houtman-deSmedt, and J. Paredaens, 1998, *Ontwerp van een Databank m.b.t. het Archief van de Beurs van Brussel.* TEW Working paper 98:11, Antwerpen: RUCA

Arnott, R.D., and P.L. Bernstein, 2001, What risk premium is "normal"? Working paper, First Quadrant

Arnott, R.D., and R. Ryan, 2001, The death of the risk premium: consequences of the 1990s. *Journal of Portfolio Management* **27**(3): 61–74

Ball, R., and J. Bowers, 1986, Shares, bonds, treasury notes, property trusts and inflation: historical returns and risks 1974–1985. *Australian Journal of Management* **11**: 117–137

Ball, R., P. Brown, F. J. Finn, and R. R. Officer, 1989, *Share Markets and Portfolio Theory*, second edition. St Lucia, Queensland: University of Queensland Press

Banz, R., 1981, The relationship between return and market value of common stocks. *Journal of Financial Econom*ics **9**: 3–18

Barclays Capital, 1999, *Equity-Gilt Study.* London: Barclays Capital

Barsky, J., and B. De Long, 1993, Why does the stock market fluctuate? *Quarterly Journal of Economics* **108**: 291–311

Basu, S., 1977, The investment performance of common stocks in relation to their price-earnings ratios a test of the efficient markets hypothesis. *Journal of Finance* **32**: 663–682

Bernstein, P.L., 1997, What rate of return can you reasonably expect...or what can the long run tell us about the short run? *Financial Analysts Journal* **53**(2): 20–28

Bianchi, B., 1979, Appendice statistica: il rendimento del consolidato dal 1862 al 1946, *in* Vicarelli, F. (Ed) *Capitale Industriale e Capitale Finanziaro: Il Caso Italiano.* Bologna: Il Mulino

Biscaini Cotula, A.M., and P. Ciocca, 1982, Italian financial structures: long-term quantitative aspects (1879–1970) *in* Federico, G., 1994, *The Economic Development of Italy Since 1870.* Aldershot: Elgar

Bittlingmayer, G., 1998, Output, stock volatility and political uncertainty in a natural experiment: Germany 1880–1940. *Journal of Finance* **53**: 2243–2257

Black, F., 1993, Beta and return. *Journal of Portfolio Management* **20**(1): 8–18

Bodie, Z., 1990, Inflation insurance. *Journal of Risk and Insurance* **57**: 634–645

Bodie, Z., 1995, On the risk of stocks in the long run. *Financial Analysts Journal* **51**(3):18–22

Bodie, Z., A. Kane, and A.J. Marcus, 1999, *Investments,* fourth edition. NY: McGraw Hill

Bond, T., and K. Adams, 2000, *Equity-Gilt Study 2000.* London: Barclays Capital

Boskin, M.J., E.R. Dulberger, R.J. Gordon, Z. Griliches, and D. Jorgenson ("The Boskin Commission"), 1996, *Final Report to the Senate Finance Committee from the Advisory Commission to Study the Consumer Price Index.* US Social Security Administration

Bouman, S., and B. Jacobsen, 2000, The Halloween indicator – "sell in May and go away": another puzzle. Working paper, Faculty of Economics and Econometrics, University of Amsterdam

Bowley, A.L., 1937, *Wages and Income in the United Kingdom Since 1860.* Cambridge: Cambridge University Press

Brav, A., and R. Lehavy, 2001, An empirical analysis of analysts' target prices: short-term informativeness and long-term dynamics. Working paper, Duke University

Brealey, R.A., R. Giammarino, E. Maynes, S.C. Myers, and A.J. Marcus, 1996, *Fundamentals of Corporate Finance,* first Canadian edition. NY: McGraw Hill

Brealey, R.A., and S.C. Myers, 2000, *Principles of Corporate Finance,* sixth edition. NY: McGraw Hill

Breeden, D., 1979, An intertemporal asset pricing model with stochastic consumption and investment opportunities. *Journal of Financial Economics* **7**: 265–96

Breen, W., 1968, Low price-earnings ratios and industry relatives. *Financial Analysts Journal* **24**(4): 125–127

Brennan, M.J., and E.S. Schwartz, 1985, On the geometric mean index: a note. *Journal of Financial and Quantitative Analysis* **20**: 119–122

Brown, R.H., and S.M. Schaefer, 1994, The term structure of real interest rates and the Cox, Ingersoll and Ross model. *Journal of Financial Economics* **35**: 3–42

Brown, S., W.N. Goetzmann, and J. Park, 2001, Careers and survival: competition and risk in the hedge fund and CTA industry, Working paper. NY: New York University

Brown, S., W.N. Goetzmann, and S. Ross, 1995, Survival. *Journal of Finance* **50**: 853–873

Bruner, R.F., K.M. Eades, R. Harris, and R.C. Higgins, 1998, Best practices in estimating the cost of capital: survey and synthesis. *Financial Practice and Education* **8**: 13–28

Buelens, F., 2001, De levenscyclus van de Beurs van Brussel 1801–2000. *Maandschrift Economie* **65**(2): 150–177

Campbell, J.Y., M. Lettau, B. Malkiel, and Y. Xu, 2001, Have individual stocks become more volatile? An empirical exploration of idiosyncratic risk. *Journal of Finance* **56**: 1–43

Campbell, J.Y., and R.J. Shiller, 1996, A scorecard for indexed government debt, *in* B Bernanke and J Rotemberg (Eds) *NBER Macroeconomic Manual.* Cambridge, Mass: MIT Press

Campbell, J.Y., and R.J. Shiller, 2001, Valuation ratios and the long-run stock market outlook: an update. Working paper No 8221. Cambridge MA: National Bureau of Economic Research

Capaul, C., I. Rowley, and W.F. Sharpe, 1993, International Value and Growth Stock Returns. *Financial Analysts Journal* **49**(1), 27–36

Carhart, M.M., J.N. Carpenter, A.W. Lynch, and D.K. Musto, 2001, Mutual fund survivorship, Working paper. NY: Goldman Sachs

Chan, L., Y. Hamao, and J. Lakonishok, 1991, Fundamentals and Stock Returns in Japan. *Journal of Finance* **46**: 1739–1764.

Christiansen, J., and B. Lystbaek, 1994, Afkast og risiko pa aktier og obligationer 1915–1993. *Finans Invest* **3**: 10–13

Claus, J., and J. Thomas, 2001, Equity premia as low as three percent? evidence from analysts' earnings forecast for domestic and international stock markets. *Journal of Finance* **56**: 1629–1666

Cooper, I., 1996, Arithmetic versus geometric mean estimators: setting discount rates for capital budgeting. *European Financial Management* **2**: 157–67.

Cooper, I., 2001, An open and shut case for portfolio diversification. *The Financial Times, Mastering Investment*: 6–7 (July 16)

Cooper, I., and E. Kaplanis, 1995, Home bias in equity portfolios and the cost of capital for multinational firms. *Journal of Applied Corporate Finance* **8**: 95–102

Conant, C.A., 1908, The world's wealth in negotiable securities. *Atlantic Monthly* **101**(1): 97–104

Cornell, B., 1999, *The Equity Risk Premium.* NY: Wiley

Cowles, A., and Associates, 1938, *Common Stock Indexes*, first edition. Bloomington, Indiana: Principia Press, Inc.

Credit Suisse First Boston, 1999, *The CSFB Equity-Gilt Study.* London: CSFB (Europe) Ltd

Das, S., and R. Uppal, 2001, Systemic risk and international portfolio choice. Working paper, London Business School

Davis, J., E.F. Fama and K.R. French, 2000, Characteristics, covariances, and average returns: 1929–1997. *Journal of Finance* **55**: 389–406

De Zoete & Gorton, 1955, *Equities and Fixed Interest Investment.* London: De Zoete & Gorton

Dimson, E., 1988, *Stock Market Anomalies.* Cambridge: Cambridge University Press

Dimson, E., and P.R. Marsh, 1983, The stability of UK risk measures and the problem of thin trading. *Journal of Finance* **38**: 753–783

Dimson, E., and P.R. Marsh, 1984, Hedging the Market: The Performance of the FTSE 100 Share Index. *Journal of the Institute of Actuaries* **111**: 403–30

Dimson, E., and P.R. Marsh, 1986, Event study methodologies and the size effect. *Journal of Financial Economics* **17**: 113–142

Dimson, E., and P.R. Marsh, 1987, *The Hoare Govett Smaller Companies Index for the UK.* London: Hoare Govett Limited (now ABN AMRO)

Dimson, E., and P.R. Marsh, 1999, Murphy's Law and market anomalies. *Journal of Portfolio Management* **25**(2): 53–69

Dimson, E., and P.R. Marsh, 2001, UK financial market returns 1955–2000. *Journal of Business* **74**: 1–31

Dimson, E., and P.R. Marsh, 2001a, *The Hoare Govett Smaller Companies Index 2000.* London: ABN AMRO

Dimson, E., and P.R. Marsh, 2001b, *Risk Measurement Service.* London: London Business School

Eatwell, J., 1982, *Whatever Happened to Britain.* London: Duckworth.

Eichholtz, P., K. Koedijk, and R. Otten, 2000 (January), De eeuw van het aandeel. *Economisch Statistische Berichten,* **85**(4238): 24–27

Elias, D., 2000, *Dow 40,000: Strategies for Profiting from the Greatest Bull Market in History.* NY: McGraw Hill

Elton, E.J., M.J. Gruber, and C.R. Blake, 1996, Survivorship bias and mutual fund performance, *Review of Financial Studies* **9**: 1097–1120

Fama, E.F., 1975, Short-term interest rates as predictors of inflation. *American Economic Review* **65**: 269–82

Fama, E.F., and K.R. French, 1992, The cross section of expected stock returns. *Journal of Finance* **47**: 427–66

Fama, E.F., and K.R. French, 1993, Common risk factors in the returns on stocks and bonds. *Journal of Financial Economics* **33**: 3–56

Fama, E.F., and K.R. French, 1995, Size and book-to-market factors in earnings and returns. *Journal of Finance* **50**: 131–184

Fama, E.F., and K.R. French, 1998, Value versus growth: the international evidence. *Journal of Finance* **53**: 1975–1999

Fama, E.F., and K.R. French, 2001, Disappearing dividends: changing firm characteristics or lower propensity to pay? *Journal of Financial Economics* **60**: 3–43

Fama, E.F., and K.R. French, 2002, The equity premium. *Journal of Finance,* forthcoming

Firer, C., and H. McLeod, 1999, Equities, bonds, cash and inflation: historical performance in South Africa 1925–1998. *The Investment Analysts Journal* **50**: 7–28

Fisher, I., 1930, *The Theory of Interest: As Determined by Impatience to Spend Income and Opportunity to Invest It.* NY: Augustus M Kelley

Fisher, L., and J.H. Lorie, 1964, Rates of return on investments in common stocks. *Journal of Business* **37**: 1–21

Fraser, P., 2001, How do US and Japanese investors process information and how do they form their expectations of the future? Evidence from quantitative survey based data, Working paper. Aberdeen: University of Aberdeen

Frennberg, P., and B. Hansson, 1992a, Computation of a monthly index for Swedish stock returns 1919–1989. *Scandinavian Economic History Review* **40**: 3–7

Frennberg, P., and B. Hansson, 1992b, Swedish stocks, bonds, bills and inflation (1919–1990). *Applied Financial Economics* **2**: 79–86

Frennberg, P., and B. Hansson, 2000, *Computation of a monthly index for Swedish stock returns 1919–1989—update to end-1999.* Unpublished note

Fujino, S., and R. Akiyama, 1977, *Security Prices and Interest Rates: 1874–1975.* The Documentation Center for Japanese Economic Statistics, Institute of Economic Research. Tokyo: Hitotsubashi University

Gallais-Hamonno, G., and P. Arbulu, 1995, La rentabilité reelle des actifs boursiers de 1950 à 1992. *Economie et Statistique* **280**: 3–30

Gielen, G., 1994, *Konnen Aktienkurse Noch Steigen? Langfristige Trendanalyse des Deutschen Aktienmarktes.* Wiesbaden: Gabler

Glassman, J.K., and K. Hassett, 1999, *Dow 36,000: The New Strategy for Profiting from the Coming Rise in the Stock Market.* NY: Times Books

Goetzmann, W.N., R.G. Ibbotson and L. Peng, 2001, A new historical database for the NYSE 1815 to 1925: performance and predictability. *Journal of Financial Markets* **4**: 1–32

Goetzmann, W.N., and P. Jorion, 1999, Re-emerging markets. *Journal of Financial and Quantitative Analysis* **34**: 1–32

Goetzmann, W.N., L. Li, and K.G. Rouwenhorst, 2001, Long-term global market correlations. Working paper, Yale School of Management

Gonzalez, A.S., and J.L. Suarez, 1994, Historical returns in the Spanish equity market. *Journal of Investing* **3**(1): 66–71

Gordon, M., 1962, *The Investment Financing and Valuation of the Corporation.* IL: Irwin

Goyal, A., and I. Welch, 1999, Predicting the equity risk premium. Working paper, Yale School of Management

Graham, B., and D. L. Dodd, 1934, *Security Analysis.* NY: McGraw Hill

Graham, J.R., and C.R. Harvey, 2001, The theory and practice of corporate finance: evidence from the field. *Journal of Financial Economics* **60**: 187–243

Graham, J.R., and C.R. Harvey, 2001a, Expectations of equity risk premia, volatility, and asymmetry from a corporate finance perspective. Working paper, Fuqua School of Business, Duke University

Grinold, R.C., and R.N. Kahn, 1999, *Active Portfolio Management,* second edition. NY: McGraw-Hill

Grullon, G., and D. Ikenberry, 2000, What do we know about share repurchases? *Journal of Applied Corporate Finance* **13**: 31–51

Grullon, G., and R. Michaely, 2000, Dividends, share repurchases and the substitution hypothesis. Working paper, Cornell University

Hamao, Y., 1991, A standard database for the analysis of Japanese security markets. *Journal of Business* **64**: 87–101

Hamao, Y., and R.G. Ibbotson, 1989, *Stocks, bonds and inflation 1989 Yearbook.* Chicago: Ibbotson Associates (Annual supplements, 1990–)

Hansen, K., 1976, Om afkastet af danske aktier i tiden 1900–1974. Optrykt i Nordisk Fjerfabriks jubilaeumsskrift. *Nordisk Fjerfabrik, aktieselskab,* 1901–1976

Harris, R.S., and F.C. Marston, 2001, The market risk premium: expectational estimates using analysts' forecasts, Working paper. University of Virginia

Haugen, R.A., 1999, *The New Finance: The Case Against Efficient Markets,* second edition. NJ: Prentice Hall

Hawawini, G., and D. B. Keim, 2000, The cross section of common stock returns: a review of the evidence and some new findings, *in* Keim, D.B., and W.T. Ziemba (Eds) *Security Market Imperfections in World Wide Equity Markets.* Cambridge: Cambridge University Press

Hirshleifer, D., 2001, Investor psychology and asset pricing. *Journal of Finance* **56**: 1533–1597

Houston, W.R., 1900–1914, *The Annual Financial Review (Canadian)*. Toronto: Houston's Standard Publications

Huber, G., 1985, Evidence sur la performance relative des marchés obligataire et des actions en Suisse 1960–83, Working paper. Geneva : Pictet & Cie

Ibbotson Associates, 1999, *International Equity Risk Premia*. Chicago: Ibbotson Associates

Ibbotson Associates, 1999, 2000, and 2001, *Stocks, Bonds, Bills and Inflation Yearbook*. Chicago: Ibbotson Associates

Ibbotson, R.G., and P. Chen, 2001, The supply of stock market returns. ICF Working paper No. 00–44, Yale School of Management

Ibbotson, R.G., and R. Sinquefield, 1976, Stocks, bonds, bills and inflation: year-by-year historical returns (1926–74). *Journal of Business* **49**: 11–43

Jagannathan, M., C.P. Stephens, and M.S. Weisbach, 2000, Financial flexibility and the choice between dividends and stock repurchases. *Journal of Financial Economics* **57**: 309–54

Jagannathan, R., E.R. McGrattan, and A. Scherbina, 2001, The declining US equity premium. Working paper 8172, National Bureau of Economic Research

Jog, V., and B. Li, 1995, Price related anomalies on the Toronto Stock Exchange. ASAC 1995 Conference Proceedings, Finance Division **16**(1): 47–59

Jorion, P., and W.N. Goetzmann, 1999, Global stock markets in the twentieth century. *Journal of Finance* **54**: 953–980

Kadlec, C.W., 1999, *Dow 100,000: Fact or Fiction*. NJ: Prentice Hall

Keim, D.B., 1983, Size-related anomalies and stock return seasonality: further empirical evidence. *Journal of Financial Economics* **12**: 473–90

Kocherlakota, N.R., 1996, The equity premium: it's still a puzzle. *Journal of Economic Literature* **34**: 42–71

Laforest, P., and P. Sallee, 1977, Le pouvoir d'achat des actions, des obligations et de l'or de 1914 à 1976. *Economie et Statistique* **86**: 61–67

Lakonishok, J., A. Shleifer, and R. Vishny, 1994, Contrarian investment, extrapolation, and risk. *Journal of Finance* **45**: 1541–1578

Lamberton, D. McL., 1958, *Share Price Indices in Australia.* Sydney: Law Book Company

Levy, H., and D. Gunthorpe, 1993, Optimal investment proportions in senior securities and equities under alternative holding periods. *Journal of Portfolio Management* **19**(4): 30–36

Li, H., and Y. Xu, 2000, Can survival bias explain the equity premium puzzle? Working paper, Cornell University Graduate School of Management

Litzenberger, R.H., and K. Ramaswamy, 1979, The effect of personal taxes and dividends on capital asset prices: Theory and empirical evidence. *Journal of Financial Economics* **7**: 163–95

Loeb, G.M., 1996 (originally published 1935), *The Battle for Investment Survival.* NY: Wiley Investment Classics

Longin, F., and B. Solnik, 1995, Is the correlation in international equity returns constant: 1960–1990? *Journal of International Money and Finance* **14** : 3–26

Lund, J., 1992, Rationelle bobler i de danske aktiekurser 1923–1991 — an empirisk analyse. *Nationalokonomisk Tidsskrift* **130**: 483–497

Maddison, A., 1995, *Monitoring the World Economy 1820–1992.* Paris: Organization for Economic Cooperation and Development

Maddison, A., 2001, *The World Economy: A Millennial Perspective.* Paris: Organization for Economic Cooperation and Development

Marquis, D.R.P., 1934, *Archy and Mehitabel.* London: Faber and Faber

McCulloch, J.H., 1980, The ban on indexed bonds, 1933–77. *American Economic Review* **70**: 1018–21

Meghen, P.J., 1970, *Statistics in Ireland.* Dublin: Institute of Public Administration

Mehra, R., and E. Prescott, 1986, The equity premium: a puzzle. *Journal of Monetary Economics* **15**: 145–61

Merrett, A., and A. Sykes, 1963, Return on equities and fixed interest securities 1919–1963. *District Bank Review* **155**(4): 17–34

Merrill Lynch, 2000, *Size and Structure of the World Bond Market: 2000.* Global Fixed Income Research Team, Merrill Lynch

Michie, R.C., 1992, Development of stock markets, *in* Newman, P., M. Milgate, and J. Eatwell, (Eds) *The New Palgrave Dictionary of Money and Finance* 1: 662–8. London: Macmillan Press

Miller, M.H., 1977, Debt and taxes. *Journal of Finances* 32: 261–276

Mitchell, B.R., 1998, *International Historical Statistics: Europe 1750–1993.* London: Macmillan Press

Modigliani, F., and M.H. Miller, 1958, The cost of capital, corporation finance and the theory of investment. *American Economic Review* 48: 261–297

Moller, B., 1962, *The Swedish Stock Market.* Gothenburg: AB Seelig & Co

Nagel, S., 2001, Accounting information free of selection bias: a new database for the UK 1955–2000, Working paper. London Business School

Nelson, C.R., and G.W. Schwert, 1977, Short-term interest rates as predictors of inflation: On testing the hypothesis that the real rate of interest is constant. *American Economic Review* 67: 478–86

Nielsen, S., and O. Risager, 1999, Macroeconomic perspectives on stock and bond investments in Denmark since the first world war *in* Andersen, T.M., O. Risager, and S.H.E. Jensen (Eds) *Macroeconomic Perspectives on the Danish Economy.* London: Macmillan Press

Nielsen, S., and O. Risager, 2000, Stock returns and bond yields in Denmark 1922–99. Working paper, Department of Economics, Copenhagen Business School

van Nieuwerburgh, S., and F. Buelens, 2000, Stock market development and economic growth in Belgium: 1300–2000, Working paper. Stanford University

Odean, T., and B. Barber, 2001, Boys will be boys: gender, overconfidence, and common stock investment. *Quarterly Journal of Economics* 116: 261–292

Odell, K.A., 1992, Regional stock markets, *in* Newman, P., M. Milgate and J. Eatwell, (Eds) *The New Palgrave Dictionary of Money and Finance* 3: 312–5. London: Macmillan Press

O'Shaughnessy, J., 1998, *How to Retire Rich.* NY: Broadway Books

Panetta, F., and R. Violi, 1999, Is there an equity premium puzzle in Italy? A look at asset returns, consumption and financial structure data over the last century. Temi di Discussione 353, Bank of Italy

Panjer, H.H., and K.P. Sharpe, 2001, *Report on Canadian Economic Statistics 1924–2000.* Ottawa: Canadian Institute of Actuaries

Parum, C., 1999a, Historisk afkast af aktier og obligationer i Danmark. *Finans Invest* **3**: 4–13

Parum, C., 1999b, Estimation af realkreditobligationsafkast i Danmark i perioden 1925–1998. *Finans Invest* **7**: 12–15

Parum, C., 2001, An equally weighted index of Copenhagen stock prices 1900–1914. Unpublished note

Pettit, J., Gulie I., and A. Park, 2001, The equity risk measurement handbook. NY: Stern Stewart *Evaluation* **3**(3): 1–12

Rajan, R. and L. Zingales, 2001, The great reversals : the politics of financial development in the 20th century. Working paper No 8178. Cambridge MA: National Bureau of Economic Research

Rätzer, E., 1983, *Die Pensionskasse aus Ökonomischer Sicht.* Berne: Paul Haupt

Rau, P.R., and T. Vermaelen, 2002, Regulation, taxes, and share repurchases in the U.K. *Journal of Business*, in press

Reinganum, M., 1981, Misspecification of capital asset pricing: empirical anomalies based on earnings yields and market values. *Journal of Financial Economics* **9**: 19–46

de Ridder, A., 1989, Aktiemarknadens risk-premie. *Ekonomisk Debatt,* **17**(1): 33–37

Roden, D., 1983, *Equity and fixed interest investment from 1918,* 28th annual edition. London: de Zoete & Bevan

Rosenberg, B., K. Reid, and R. Lanstein, 1985, Persuasive evidence of market inefficiency. *Journal of Portfolio Management* **11**(3): 9–17

Ross, S., R.W. Westerfield, and B. Jordan, 2000, *Essentials of Corporate Finance.* NY: McGraw Hill

Sandez, M., and F.G. Benavides, 2000, La Bolsa de Madrid entre 1919 y 1936. *Revista de la Bolsa de Madrid* **87**: 32–39

Schumann, C.G.W., and A.E. Scheurkogel, 1948, *Industrial and Commercial Share Price Indices in South Africa.* Bureau for Economic Research, Faculty of Commerce, University of Stellenbosch

Schwartz, D., 1997, *The Schwartz Stock Market Handbook,* third edition. Stroud, Gloucestershire: Burleigh Publishing

Schwartz, S.S., and W.T. Ziemba, 1991, The Japanese stock market 1949–1991 *in* Ziemba, W.T., W. Bailey and Y. Hamao, (Eds) *Japanese Financial Market Research.* Amsterdam: Elsevier Science

Schwert, G.W., 1990, Indexes of United States stock prices from 1802 to 1987. *Journal of Business* **63**: 399–426

Sharpe, W.F., 1964, Capital asset prices: A theory of market equilibrium under the condition of risk. *Journal of Finance* **19**: 425–42

Sharpe, W.F., 1994, The Sharpe ratio. *Journal of Portfolio Management* **21**(1): 49–58

Shiller, R.J., 1981, Do stock prices move too much to be justified by subsequent changes in dividends? *American Economic Review* **71**: 421–35

Shiller, R.J., 2000, *Irrational Exuberance.* NJ: Princeton University Press

Shleifer, A., 2000, *Inefficient Markets.* Oxford UK: Oxford University Press

Siegel, J.J., 1998, *Stocks for the Long Run*, second edition. NY: McGraw Hill

Siegel, J.J., 1999, The shrinking equity premium. *Journal of Portfolio Management* **26**(1): 10–17

Siegel, J.J., and R. Thaler, 1997, The equity premium puzzle. *Journal of Economic Perspectives* **11**: 191–200

Siegel, L.B., and Montgomery, D., 1995, Stocks, bonds, and bills after taxes and inflation. *Journal of Portfolio Management* **21**(2): 17–25

Smithers, A., and S. Wright, 2000, *Valuing Wall Street.* NY: McGraw Hill

Solnik, B., 1974, Why not diversify internationally rather than domestically? *Financial Analysts Journal* **30**: 48–54

Spoerer, M., and N. Foidl, 1999, Survival of German firms between 1936 and 1951 and the implications for the equity premium puzzle. Working paper, University of Hohenheim

Stattman, D., 1980, Book values and expected stock returns. Unpublished MBA Honours paper, University of Chicago

Stehle, R., 1997, Der size-effekt am deutschen aktienmarkt. *Zeitschrift für Bankrecht und Bankwirtschaft* **9**(3): 237–260

Stehle, R., R. Huber and J. Maier, 1996, Rückberechnung des DAX für die Jahre 1955 bis 1987. *Kredit und Kapital* **29**: 277–304

Stewart, G.B., 1991, *The Quest for Value.* NY: Harper Business

Stolper, G., K. Hauser, and K. Borchardt, 1967, *The German Economy: 1870 to the Present.* NY: Harcourt, Brace and World

Switzer, L., 2000, An equally weighted index of Montreal stock prices 1900–1914. Unpublished note

Taylor, A.M., 2001, A century of purchasing power parity. *Review of Economics and Statistics*, forthcoming

Thomas, W.A., 1986, *The Stock Exchanges of Ireland.* NH: Francis Cairns Publications

Timmermann, A., 1992, Udviklingen i de danske aktiekurser 1914–1990. *Nationalokonomisk Tidsskrift* **130**: 473–482

Treynor, J.L., 1994, The invisible costs of trading. *Journal of Portfolio Management* **21**(1): 71–78

Treynor, J.L., and F. Black, 1973, How to use security analysis to improve portfolio selection. *Journal of Business* **46**: 66–86

Urquhart, M.C., and K.A.H. Buckley, 1965, *Historical Statistics of Canada.* Toronto: Macmillan Company

Valbuena, S.F., 2000, Sources and methodology of Spanish Bolsa returns in the 20th century. Working paper. Madrid: Universidad Complutense

Vandellos, J.A., 1936 (reprinted 1974), *El Porvenir del Cambio de la Peseta.* Instituto de Investigaciones Economicas, Banca Mas Sarda

Weil, P., 1989, The equity premium puzzle and the risk-free rate puzzle. *Journal of Monetary Economics* **24**: 401–421

Welch, I., 2000, Views of financial economists on the equity premium and other issues. *Journal of Business* **73**: 501–37

Welch, I., 2001, The equity premium consensus forecast revisited. Working paper, Yale School of Management

Weston, F., S. Chung, and J.A. Sui, 1997, *Takeovers, Restructuring and Corporate Control*, second edition. NJ: Prentice-Hall

Whelan, S., 1999, *From Canals to Computers: The Friends First Guide to Long-Term Investment Returns in Ireland.* Dublin: Friends First Asset Management.

White, E.N., 1992, New York Stock Exchange, in Newman, P., M. Milgate and J. Eatwell (Eds) *The New Palgrave Dictionary of Money and Finance* **3**: 33–4. London: Macmillan Press

Williams, J.B., 1938, *The Theory of Investment Value.* Cambridge, Mass: Harvard University Press

Wilson, J.W., and C.P. Jones, 1987, A comparison of annual common stock returns: 1871–1925 with 1926–85. *Journal of Business* **60**: 239–258

Wilson, J.W., and C.P. Jones, 2002, An analysis of the S&P 500 Index and Cowles' extensions: price indexes and stock returns, 1870–1999. *Journal of Business*, in press

Woodward, G.T., 1990, The real thing: dynamic profile of the term structure of real interest rates and inflation expectations in the United Kingdom, 1982–89. *Journal of Business* **63**: 373–98

Wydler, D., 1989, Swiss stocks, bonds and inflation 1926–1987. *Journal of Portfolio Management* **15**(2): 27–32

Wydler, D., 2001, *The Performance of Shares and Bonds in Switzerland: An Empirical Study Covering the Years Since 1925.* Geneva: Pictet & Cie

Ziemba, W.T., and S.L. Schwartz, 1991, *Invest Japan: the Structure, Performance and Opportunities of Japan's Stock, Bond and Fund Markets.* Chicago: Probus Publishing Company

About the Authors

Elroy Dimson is Professor of Finance at London Business School, and is an elected Governor of the School. At London Business School, he has been Chair of the Finance area, Chair of the Accounting area, Dean of the MBA and Executive MBA programs, and Director of the Investment Management Program. He has held visiting positions at the Universities of Chicago and California, Berkeley, and at the Bank of England. Dr Dimson has been Chairman of a closed-end fund and director of several pension funds and financial institutions. He is a member of the Advisory Board of Edward Jones, a large US based stockbroker, and is currently President of the European Finance Association. He has published articles in *Journal of Business, Journal of Finance, Journal of Financial Economics, Journal of Portfolio Management, Financial Analysts Journal*, and many other journals. His books include *Stock Market Anomalies* and *Cases in Corporate Finance* (with Professor Marsh). Dr Dimson holds a BA and MCom from the Universities of Newcastle and Birmingham, and a PhD in Finance from London Business School.

Paul Marsh is Esmée Fairbairn Professor of Finance, and is academic director of the School's Masters in Finance and Corporate Finance evening programs. Within London Business School, he has been Chair of the Finance area, Deputy Principal, Faculty Dean and an elected Governor. He acts as a consultant to many leading companies and financial institutions and has advised on several public enquiries. He is a Director of Majedie Investments and, until recently, he served on the Board of M&G Group. He has published articles in *Journal of Business, Journal of Finance, Journal of Financial Economics, Journal of Portfolio Management, Harvard Business Review*, and many other journals. His books include *Cases in Corporate Finance* (with Professor Dimson) and *Short-termism on Trial*. With Professor Dimson, he co-designed the FTSE 100 Share Index and the Hoare Govett Smaller Companies Index, produced at London Business School. Dr Marsh holds a BSc (Econ) from London School of Economics, and a PhD in Finance from London Business School.

Mike Staunton is Director of the London Share Price Database, a research resource of London Business School. He produces the London Business School *Risk Measurement Service*, which is edited by Professors Dimson and Marsh. He has taught at universities in the United Kingdom and Switzerland. Dr Staunton is co-author with Mary Jackson of *Advanced Modelling in Finance Using Excel and VBA*, published in 2001 by Wiley, and co-author with Elroy Dimson and Paul Marsh of two editions of *The Millennium Book*, published by ABN AMRO and London Business School. He has had articles published in *Journal of Banking & Finance, Journal of the Operations Research Society*, and *Business Strategy Review*. Dr Staunton holds a BSc from Manchester University, and a MBA and PhD in Finance from London Business School.

Index